The Captains' Coup

Daniela F. Melo is a political scientist and lecturer in social sciences at Boston University (CGS). Her work is published in such academic journals as *Comparative European Politics*, *Social Movement Studies*, and *Foreign Policy Analysis*. She is co-editor, with Paul Manuel, of *After the Carnation Revolution: Social Movements in Portugal Since 25 April 1974* (Liverpool University Press, 2025). Melo held a Fulbright fellowship in Portugal, has served as a consultant to the US State Department regarding domestic politics in Portugal and Spain, and is a frequent contributor of political analysis to various Portuguese media outlets, commenting on US politics and foreign policy.

Timothy D. Walker is professor of history at the University of Massachusetts Dartmouth, where he serves on the executive board of the Center for Portuguese Studies and Culture, and is graduate faculty of the Department of Portuguese. Walker is also an affiliated researcher of the Centro de História d'Aquém e d'Além-Mar (CHAM), Universidade Nova de Lisboa, Portugal. From 1994 to 2003, he was a visiting professor at the Universidade Aberta (Open University) in Lisbon. He is the recipient of a Fulbright dissertation fellowship to Portugal, and fellowships from the Portuguese Camões Institute, the Luso-American Development Foundation and the Calouste Gulbenkian Foundation.

The Captains' Coup
From Dictatorship to Democracy in Portugal (1974–1976)

Wilfred Burchett

Edited by Daniela F. Melo and Timothy D. Walker

Afterword by Tariq Ali

VERSO
London • New York

This English-language edition first published by Verso 2025
First published as *Portugal depois da revolução dos capitães*
(Lisbon: Seara Nova Press, 1975) and *Portugal antes e depois
do 25 de Novembro* (Lisbon Seara Nova Press, 1976)
© Wilfred Burchett 1975, 1976
Preface © Timothy D. Walker 2025
Introduction © Daniela F. Melo 2025
Afterword © Tariq Ali 1978, 2025

Source repository of Wilfred Burchett's original manuscript: Wilfred Burchett, 'The Captains Coup' (typescript), Papers of Wilfred Burchett, 1953–1998, National Library of Australia Manuscripts Collection, MS Acc10.031.

'The Portuguese Laboratory' originally published in Tariq Ali, *1968 and After* (London: Blond & Briggs, 1978). Published here with the kind permission of Tariq Ali.

All rights reserved

The moral rights of the authors and editors have been asserted

1 3 5 7 9 10 8 6 4 2

Verso
UK: 6 Meard Street, London W1F 0EG
US: 207 East 32nd Street, New York, NY 10016
versobooks.com

Verso is the imprint of New Left Books

ISBN-13: 978-1-80429-836-7
ISBN-13: 978-1-80429-837-4 (UK EBK)
ISBN-13: 978-1-80429-838-1 (US EBK)

British Library Cataloguing in Publication Data
A catalogue record for this book is available from the British Library

Library of Congress Cataloging-in-Publication Data
A catalog record for this book is available from the Library of Congress

Typeset in Minion Pro by Hewer Text UK Ltd, Edinburgh
Printed and bound by CPI Group (UK) Ltd, Croydon CR0 4YY

Contents

Preface | Timothy D. Walker   vii

Acknowledgements   xiii

Introduction: Journalism from a 'Remarkable Outsider' | Daniela F. Melo   xvii

Book I (1975)
PORTUGAL AFTER THE CAPTAINS' COUP   1

1 The Backdrop   3
2 Daylight   15
3 Conspiracy   27
4 Motivations   41
5 Strategy   55
6 Militants   67
7 Counterattacks 1 and 2   81
8 Organisation   95
9 Counterattack 3   109
10 Monopolies   127

11	Multinationals	135
12	Alentejo	145
13	Trás-os-Montes	159
14	Reflections	171
15	Sardines	181
16	Decolonisation	191
17	Happy Birthday	209

Book II (1976)
PORTUGAL BEFORE AND AFTER THE 25TH OF NOVEMBER — 227

18	Turning the Wheel Back	229
19	Balance Sheet	239
20	The Future	249

Afterword | *Tariq Ali* — 263
Index — 311

Preface

Timothy D. Walker

Twelve years ago in Lisbon, Daniela Melo and I, while browsing in a venerable *alfarrabista* (antiquarian book shop), sadly now defunct, on Rua Nova da Trindade in the Bairro Alto, chanced upon a little-known yet fascinating publication: Wilfred Burchett's *Portugal Depois da Revolução dos Capitães* ('Portugal After the Captains' Revolution'). Published in Lisbon by Seara Nova Press in 1975, it examined and explained the Armed Forces Movement coup d'état of 25 April 1974, and the democratic revolutionary period in Portugal, up to May Day, 1975. We soon learned that there was a second, smaller volume, *Portugal Antes e Depois do 25 de Novembro* ('Portugal Before and After the 25th of November'), published as a sequel by the same press in 1976, with additional reporting from Burchett to explain subsequent events through November of 1975.

As scholars of Portuguese history and politics, we were, to put it mildly, intrigued. How had Burchett's works on the *25 de Abril* escaped our attention? To our astonishment, a thorough bibliographic search revealed the total absence of an English edition of these books. The first Portuguese volume had been immediately translated into Italian, Norwegian and Spanish (a Mexican edition), and published during 1975; a Japanese edition appeared the following year. Burchett's sequel volume appeared only in Portuguese. It struck us at the time, given the importance of these works – in terms of Burchett's experience, perspective and inimitable analysis, as well as for the unique contemporary interviews he conducted – that producing a version of the texts as originally written in English would be of obvious utility and benefit. This seemed especially so in 2012, as we approached the fortieth anniversary of the Portuguese Revolution, and of the books' initial publication.

To us, it was self-evident that these books, with their incisive political observations from Wilfred Burchett, a figure of unquestioned journalistic eminence, would be of use to anyone interested in the Portuguese transition to democracy, the dismantling of the Portuguese colonial empire, and the global wave of democratic revolutions initiated by the Portuguese Carnation Revolution. So, we resolved to see Burchett's volumes made available for a wider English-reading audience – as historical documents, exceptional for their vivid testimonies, and as iconic examples of 1970s activist political journalism. In the event, the project took far longer to complete than we had anticipated.

In Portugal, Wilfred Burchett followed his long-established method of seeking interviews with a range of key persons directly involved in historical events of global importance – from political and military leaders to the average working people who carried out such events, or whose lives were changed by them. (As Burchett spoke fluent French, he could converse directly with many Portuguese politicians and military officers, for whom French had been a required part of their Salazar-era education. To conduct interviews with most Portuguese labourers, however, he relied on interpreters.) Such singular content – often gathered in remote parts of the country where other journalists did not venture – and the unique window it provides into the Portuguese revolutionary *zeitgeist* of the mid-1970s, inspired us to bring this new edition of *The Captains' Coup* to print, as Burchett originally wrote it.

Further justifying a new edition is this: of the more than thirty books he published during his career, these two are the only ones that have never appeared in English. Consequently, Burchett's reporting on revolutionary-era Portugal is among his least-known work. In published retrospectives or collections that cover the great breadth of Burchett's activities as a journalist, his work on Portugal – because of the lack of an English-language edition – is always either glossed over in passing or left out entirely. In our view, such circumstances represented a severe gap in the historical record that needed to be corrected.

Of course, beyond the challenges of finding a publisher and arranging for the publication rights, the viability of this project hinged mainly on locating the original English-language manuscripts for these volumes. Burchett and Seara Nova Press had relied on translators Luís de Sttau Monteiro and Ana Clara Soares, respectively, to produce the two books in Portuguese. Reverse-engineering the texts back into English was a non-starter: it would involve too much guesswork, trying to replicate Burchett's phrasing, and the author's authentic voice would be too remote, impossible to recapture. So, it was imperative that we locate the original texts.

We searched in Portugal for Burchett's original (typed, we assumed) manuscripts, but we had no luck. The Portuguese translators' families did not have them. We made inquiries with the original publisher, Seara Nova. Upon visiting their offices in central Lisbon, though, we found that this small firm had moved location several times and maintained incomplete records from the 1970s. They had no files from their Burchett publications. Nor did the Portuguese Communist Party, when we inquired at their regional headquarters located on Avenida da Liberdade, one of Lisbon's most elegant thoroughfares. As a significant enduring force on Portugal's political landscape, and having supported Burchett's journalism half a century ago, we hoped that the PCP might have preserved examples of his work in their records, but we were disappointed.

Then, in the course of our inquiries we were provided an email address for Wilfred Burchett's son, George Burchett, an artist born in Vietnam and living in Hanoi. Naturally, we wrote to him to seek his advice and assistance. Might he be able to tell us if his father's papers had been preserved and, if so, where? Did he know if copies of the original manuscripts we sought had survived? Much to our relief and delight, he endorsed our project enthusiastically. While he did not know the answer to our second question, and did not recall ever seeing manuscripts for the Portuguese volumes, he assured us that Wilfred Burchett's personal papers had been archived with professional rigour. It was George who directed us to the National Library of Australia, in Canberra. He had deposited the world-renowned journalist's papers directly to the NLA for safekeeping following his father's death in 1983.

The NLA collection we required is called the Papers of Wilfred Burchett (officially, MS Acc10.031). These papers reside in fifty-five large archival boxes full of diverse materials that had been carefully preserved, but not catalogued in any detail, nor even fully organised.

Distance and expense prevented us from visiting Australia in person, so our investigation was conducted by email correspondence, assisted by the National Library of Australia reference staff. They provided us with a basic listing of the contents of Burchett's papers but, upon first reading this topline inventory, there was no indication of any material related to Burchett's specific publications about Portugal.

However, upon closer examination of the archival inventory, we found that the materials were preserved chronologically. So, based on their date, we narrowed our search to a handful of likely boxes and asked the NLA archivists to make a thorough search of their contents. After a few weeks of waiting, we received an excited email from Canberra: sure enough, the book manuscripts were there!

Wilfred Burchett generated more than 1,000 pages of material that have survived from his multiple trips to Portugal (notes, interview transcripts, dispatches, article drafts), archived in five separate boxes. We ordered digital copies of all of them. As it turned out, there were several versions of the books: marked-up drafts in states of increasing refinement. Among these were Burchett's final, edited, 'clean copy' manuscripts for each book, intended for his publisher and translators in Portugal. After years of searching, we finally had the key component required to proceed.

Finding a publisher willing to take on this project, however, proved surprisingly difficult. Perhaps we were naïve, but we thought the obvious merit and timing of this project, so near the approaching half-century anniversary of Portugal's 'Carnation Revolution', would make securing a book contract with a prominent university press a foregone conclusion. Not so. Our carefully argued proposals to academic presses were repeatedly turned down – usually without explanation or even, in some cases, without any response at all. Burchett's unjustly tarred political reputation endures, apparently, for editors in the Anglophone scholarly publishing world, despite the high esteem in which he was held by many distinguished journalists for the remarkable accuracy of his reporting. Pulitzer Prize–winning chronicler Studs Terkel provides just one example of the accolades that Burchett received from his colleagues:

> There are two journalists living today ... who are rocklike in their integrity and in their courage. One is ... Wilfred Burchett, the Australian journalist you might say is a universal journalist ... He's

Preface

been everywhere, . . . and often every side calls upon him because he is right there with his information that others lack, because the information is from his own experience and being there.

(Studs Terkel, interview with Wilfred Burchett, 24 October 1977)

In time, we changed our strategy. Sound advice from historian Marcus Rediker led us to approach Verso Books, a more appropriate home for Burchett's work, where the value of this project was quickly recognised. Ten years after our chance encounter with *The Captains' Coup* in a Lisbon bookshop, Verso accepted our proposal; we could not be happier with the result.

As we prepared this text, we corrected some obvious minor typographical errors, including the spelling of Portuguese words and names, with diacritical marks added according to current usage. Some Portuguese words have been italicised, when appropriate. In cases where Burchett inadvertently left out a word, we have inserted an appropriate word for clarification. Burchett's original typescript has been copyedited, with minor textual changes introduced for clarity, but no substantive changes in content or organisation were made. Regarding the footnotes: Burchett's original annotations are indicated by [AN] (Author's Note), while new footnotes, added to provide historical context, are marked [EN] (Editors' Note). Burchett's in-text parenthetical notes have been converted to author's footnotes, and his underlining for emphasis in the original typescript has been changed to italicised text.

Lisbon, Portugal
1 May 2024

Acknowledgements

This project has been a labour of professional dedication, but also one of many pleasures, resulting from the people with whom we have had occasion to meet and interact. First and foremost, we would like to thank George Burchett, son of Wilfred Burchett, for his gracious and enthusiastic support of our efforts to publish this volume of his father's work in English. He directed us to the collections of the National Library of Australia, where he had deposited his father's papers and photographs to be archived, and he provided suggestions that helped to guide our search through these materials.

Special thanks to the reference librarians of the National Library of Australia – Damian Cole, Margy Burn, Pip Manifold and Kate Boesen – who helped us to identify the specific boxes of materials within the large Burchett Papers collection where the original *Captains' Coup* manuscript was likely to be, and then who meticulously searched those boxes to locate the final edited draft copies that became Burchett's books about revolutionary Portugal. Because of their dedicated work, we were able to obtain digitised versions of these key documents. We wish to thank other members of the National Library of Australia staff, including reference librarian Bing Zheng for arranging the necessary permission to publish Burchett's text from the NLA manuscript collections, as well as Lisa Qin, Qin Qin, and the technicians of the Wilfred Burchett Photographic Archive, for helping us to access images Burchett made while reporting from Portugal between April 1974 and November 1975.

In Lisbon, we owe a debt of thanks to the Portuguese author and literature professor Rui Zink who, inspired by the story of Burchett's journalism across Portugal, kindly assisted us in our quest to locate an elusive copy of the original English-language manuscripts at various institutions in Lisbon. We are also grateful for the assistance of Levy Baptista and Rosa Macedo of the Seara Nova publishing house, who searched their records for information about Burchett's publications in Portuguese, and who supported our undertaking to publish these works in a new English edition.

For essential assistance with photographs of the revolutionary period in Portugal, we are grateful to Catarina Santos, archivist of the Fundação Mário Soares e Maria Barroso, and Florbela Janeiro of the Sociedade Portuguesa de Autores, who arranged for us to use images from those institutions' collections. Several living photographers and illustrators – eyewitnesses of the Portuguese revolutionary period – generously provided permission for the use of their images: we offer sincere thanks to Alfredo Cunha, Carlos Gil, Ignácio Ludgero, Paulo Barral, João Abel Manta, Eduardo Gageiro, and especially Fernando Ricardo and his son André Ricardo, for their invaluable contributions to this volume. Thanks go to Kenton Thatcher and Vasco Ferreira, as well, who kindly provided key assistance with personal contacts.

To Patrick Smith, a journalist and editor who had worked with Wilfred Burchett during the years following the '25 de Abril' coup in Portugal, shared some memories of his experiences with us, and enthusiastically supported this project, we offer our appreciation.

Our profound gratitude goes to Professor Marcus Rediker of the University of Pittsburgh, who facilitated our contact with Verso Books and endorsed our qualifications to undertake this scholarly objective.

We offer our sincere thanks to the Verso Books staff: Sebastian Budgen, Cian McCourt, Chris Doyle, Mark Martin, Jeanne Tao, Daniel Cheng and Melissa Weiss, for their support of this project, and their work in bringing Wilfred Burchett's perspective on the Portuguese Revolution to a much larger readership.

The preparation and editing of this volume manuscript was accomplished with the essential aid of a Publication Completion Support Grant from the Office of the Dean of the College of Arts and Sciences, University of Massachusetts Dartmouth, for which we are deeply grateful. Additionally, financial assistance provided by publication subvention

Acknowledgements

grants from the University of Massachusetts Dartmouth Department of History and the Office of the Dean of the College of Arts and Sciences helped to bring this volume to press. Profound thanks are due to Carol Hansen for her tenacious administrative support.

Photographs and images created by Alfredo Cunha (Figure 3.2), Carlos Gil (Figure 1.2), Inácio Ludgero (Figure 3.3), Carlos Alberto (Figure 2.1) Eduardo Gageiro (Figures 2.2, 3.1, 17.1), Paulo Barral (Figure 12.1) and João Abel Manta (Figure 4.1) are used by permission of each photographer or artist. Permission was granted through the Sociedad Portuguesa de Autores; images supplied by the Fundação Mário Soares e Maria Barroso.

Photographs by Fernando Ricardo (Figures 1.1, 6.1, 7.1, 7.2, 9.1, 12.2, 15.1, 16.1, 20.1, 20.2) are used by permission of the photographer. Images were supplied through his son, André Ricardo. The photograph of Wilfred Burchett (Figure 0.1) is provided by George Burchett from his personal collection and used by permission.

Figure 0.1. Wilfred Burchett working in his home office at Meudon, France, a suburb of Paris on the western outskirts, about halfway to Versailles. The Burchett family lived there from 1968 to 1982. This photo, taken in the mid-1970s (photographer unknown), is contemporary with Portugal's Carnation Revolution. Burchett composed and revised most of *The Captains' Coup* manuscript here, on an electric typewriter, using interview notes he had prepared in Portugal each evening on his portable typewriter (pictured). According to his son, George Burchett, 'My dad always filled notebooks with unreadable hand-scribbled notes, which he then typed at the end of the work day.' (Image courtesy of George Burchett, from his personal collection. 'It was one of my favourite sounds,' George wrote, remembering his adolescence in France. 'If I heard the typewriter early in the morning, it meant Dad was home!')

Introduction
Journalism from a 'Remarkable Outsider': Wilfred Burchett's Lens on the Portuguese Revolution

Daniela F. Melo

In the morning hours of 25 April 1974, a movement led by captains and servicemen in the Portuguese Armed Forces set in motion the manoeuvres that, within twenty-four hours, would bring down Europe's oldest conservative dictatorship and abruptly end more than five centuries of Portuguese colonialism.[1] The group, which came to be known as the Armed Forces Movement (MFA in the Portuguese acronym), planned to take over the management of state affairs until free elections could be held. However, as news of the coup d'état spread, ecstatic crowds took to the streets in support of the MFA – and soon enough, citizens began to make pressing political demands. Within a few days, it became transparently clear that what had started as a military coup had now evolved into a fully fledged revolutionary process.

In order to carry out the coup, the MFA secured media broadcast sites, closed the airports and all territorial borders. Three days later, when the airport reopened, the Australian journalist Wilfred Burchett – well known for his controversial coverage of the 'other side' (meaning non-Western forces) during conflicts in Korea and Vietnam – secured a ticket on the first flight from Paris to Lisbon. Like most journalists, he

---

1 John Pilger once described Burchett as a 'remarkable outsider' in his introduction to the interview he conducted with Burchett for his television programme *The Outsiders*. See Wilfred Burchett, interview by John Pilger, *The Outsiders*, 1983, vimeo.com.

claimed that he felt the need to be in the thick of history. He was eager to see for himself what might become of this strange situation: a military coup that promised democracy, development and decolonisation under civilian rule. In stark opposition to the trends of military coups in the 1970s – think Latin America – these Portuguese officers claimed to not want power after the transition. This uncharacteristic aspect intrigued Burchett from day one.

Burchett would go on to interview some of the main protagonists of the Portuguese Revolution, including MFA leaders like Vasco Gonçalves, Ernesto de Melo Antunes and Otelo Saraiva de Carvalho. He zigzagged across the country, venturing into the inland northern region of Trás-os-Montes, to fishing towns like Peniche, and into the heart of the Alentejo region, in the south. His narrative is colourful and rich in detail, discussing the Portuguese Revolution in its national and international dimensions with the skill that only an experienced international correspondent could achieve. After decades of reporting from hotspots like China, Korea, Vietnam and Cambodia, the journalist was well positioned to understand the magnitude of the Portuguese revolutionary process and the disintegration of empire in the global context of the Cold War.

In a style reminiscent of George Orwell's journalistic output in books like *Homage to Catalonia* or *The Road to Wigan Pier*, Burchett offers a mixture of reflection, analysis and intimate interviews with important historical protagonists of the revolutionary process in the capital, Lisbon, but also with average people in the provinces – farmers, fishermen, factory workers. As a result, he captured the *zeitgeist* of the revolution like few could. He unapologetically revealed his enthusiasm for the captains who led the coup and for the social mobilisations taking place in the streets, factories and farms around the country.

Burchett's journalistic output during the Cold War was often labelled by his detractors as communist propaganda against the West. But Burchett always vehemently denied being a member of a communist party. In an interview with John Pilger towards the end of his life, he answered the question about his purported Communist membership in a telling way:

> Pilger: Have you ever been a communist? Have you ever been a member of the Communist Party?

> Burchett: No, and I'm not saying this because I dislike or despise [inaudible]. It just simply hasn't occurred, probably because I have been travelling around all the time. By the time maybe that I started thinking about that, who are right? Which ones are right? The Yugoslavs?[2]

He was a self-avowed anti-colonialist, thus against imperialism and on the side of the liberation and self-determination of the so-called Third World. This positioning and the point of view in his reporting clearly aligned him with the communist world. Given his answer to Pilger, it is safe to assume that he did consider the idea of joining a communist party, but never acted on it. Purported evidence to the contrary remains a controversial aspect of his biography.[3]

When he arrived in Lisbon, as he recounts in the volumes printed here, his first connection with the dissident left of the Estado Novo was happenstance.[4] He cashed travellers' cheques at the bank where Vasco Martins worked. Martins had been the director of the publisher Seara Nova, which, during the Portuguese dictatorship, had published Burchett's books on Vietnam, and would later contract his volumes on Portugal. He went on to use connections with the Portuguese Communist Party to find his way around the country.

Throughout his travels in Portugal, Burchett offered remarkable eye-witness reportage and analysis, interspaced with verbatim interviews, and vivid descriptions of the settings. Burchett's two books on the transition to democracy in Portugal, reproduced here for the first time with minimal editing for clarity, in their original English versions, are neither to be taken as an academic exercise to narrate the history of the revolution nor as a distanced, dispassionate journalistic assessment of the events. No, Burchett has a clear point of view and political preferences. Yet, his interviews are so rich and the analysis so frequently insightful as to render these writings a valuable historical document in their own right.

---

2   Burchett, interview by Pilger, *The Outsiders*.

3   For a summary of this and other controversies surrounding Burchett's biography, see Jamie Miller, 'The Forgotten History War: Wilfred Burchett, Australia and the Cold War in the Asia Pacific', *Asia-Pacific Journal: Japan Focus* 6, no. 9 (2008).

4   The Estado Novo refers to the Portuguese dictatorship established by António de Oliveira Salazar in the late 1980s and deposed by the MFA in 1974.

Furthermore, it bears mentioning that, of all the titles in Burchett's opus, these books are the least known, often skipped in bibliographies of his work. Burchett was a prolific author, penning more than thirty books that frequently became bestsellers across the world. In his biography of Burchett, Tom Heenan refers to letters exchanged between Wilfred and his brother, Winston Burchett, in which he first revealed that not many presses appeared interested in his books on Portugal.[5] In fact, these works would never be published in their original rendering, until now.[6]

The Long Shadow of Burchett's Journalism

Wilfred Burchett requires little introduction for those who lived through the Cold War and can remember his reporting from some of the world's most hotly contested spots, as various US presidents and general secretaries of the USSR attempted to reshape the global order in their own image.

Famously, Burchett was the first journalist to report on the horrific effects of atomic radiation after the Hiroshima bombing. His first-hand account of the radiation sickness and devastation in Hiroshima was strenuously disputed by President Truman's administration but proved to be accurate. At a press conference in Tokyo held soon after Burchett's report, the US spokesperson accused Burchett of falling prey to Japanese propaganda. Days later, Burchett learned that General McArthur had withdrawn his press accreditation and that he was, therefore, required to leave Japan immediately.[7]

This episode proved to be the first of many in the following decades that pitted Burchett's journalistic mission against the foreign policy of the United States and his own native country, Australia. As the Cold War evolved and Burchett's coverage offered in-depth, sympathetic considerations of the communist side's motives, and the perspective of anti-colonial liberation movements, he became *persona non grata* with Western governments, including that of his homeland, the Australian

---

[5] Thomas Heenan, *From Traveller to Traitor: The Life of Wilfred Burchett* (Melbourne: Melbourne University Publishing, 2006), 306–7.

[6] Burchett quickly moved on to covering Angola's independence process and subsequent role as a proxy for Cold War conflicts.

[7] Wilfred Burchett, *The Shadows of Hiroshima* (London: Verso, 1983), 23.

government. In fact, citing his purported communist affiliation and active attempt to lower the Australian troops' morale during the Korean War, the Australian government refused to renew his passport – effectively an attempt to revoke his citizenship.[8] For years, Burchett travelled on a North Vietnamese *laissez-passer* and, later, a Cuban passport.

Burchett embraced his journalism with an activist point of view, while persistently rebutting Western accusations of printing propaganda for the other side. By his own attestation as well as objective accounts, his journalistic ethos was driven by a strong sense of social justice and a genuine desire for human equality. A product of his century and experiences, his journalism favoured the rights of the downtrodden and the aspirations of those seeking to wrest self-determination from the colonial powers that oppressed them.[9] In the same interview with John Pilger, Burchett summarised his approach with a simple image:

> You've got to be ready to live with yourself. You need to be able to look at your children in the eye and look at yourself in the eye when you shave in the morning and not be ashamed of anything you've done. And I'm not ashamed of anything I've done despite all the attacks . . . I'd call myself an independent radical . . . I'm not, in fact, a commie.[10]

In his introduction to the book *At the Barricades*, the *New York Times* journalist Harrison Salisbury illustrated how – despite his advocacy journalism – Burchett was able to earn the trust of his colleagues around the world. According to Salisbury,

> Burchett's conventional journalistic companions have found him a well-informed, useful source and a warm and decent friend. They

---

8   Gavan McCormack, foreword to Wilfred Burchett, *Rebel Journalism: The Writings of Wilfred Burchett*, ed. George Burchett and Nick Shimmin (Cambridge: Cambridge University Press, 2007), xvi–xvii.

9   Burchett was transparent and apparently comfortable in his role as an independent radical during a deeply charged historical period. In truth, he did not have much of a choice when it came to which conflicts to cover once the Australian government withheld his passport renewal. The *laissez-passer*, while constraining his movements, also provided a unique opportunity for him to report from the communist sphere. His status as *persona non grata* in the West opened doors that were not available to other Western journalists.

10   Burchett, 'The Outsiders'.

almost always could check out a report or a rumor with Burchett regardless of whether it fitted Communist ideology or party propaganda. On most occasions, they got a straightforward answer, one which was trustworthy, and which stood the test of time. In written reportage it might be a different story. Burchett was an advocate, and he wrote in support of the cause to which he adhered at a given moment.[11]

Burchett's sympathies for revolutionary government shifted across the years as the Cold War unfolded. He was close friends with Ho Chi Minh and Zhou Enlai and openly manifested his admiration for them. However, after periods of enthusiasm, he had changes of mind regarding the Soviet Union, China and Cambodia.[12] As his biographer Tom Heenan points out, by the late 1970s, Burchett considered that 'only Vietnam remained true to the revolutionary legacy'.[13]

A clear example of Burchett acting according to his ethic as an 'independent radical' is his role as an intermediary between the United States and Hanoi for the release of American prisoners of war. In a series of developments well documented in Heenan's study of Burchett's life, US Ambassador-at-large Averell Harriman aggressively sought to make contact with Burchett to enlist his help in the negotiations.[14] Burchett acquiesced, apparently keen to be of aid in a humanitarian mission. Heenan concluded that 'Harriman had found Burchett a reasonable man who could be entrusted with a confidence. As the need for dialogue between the two protagonists increased, so too did Burchett's influence.'[15]

In an interview for the 1980 documentary film *Wilfred Burchett: Public Enemy Number One*, directed by David Bradbury, Burchett commented further about his motives and journalistic moral compass:

> I've come to believe over the years that my duties as a journalist go beyond my responsibilities to an editor or to a publisher and that my duties as a citizen of the world go beyond my responsibilities only to

---

11 Harrison Salisbury, introduction to Wilfred Burchett, *At the Barricades* (New York: Times Books, 1981), vii.
12 Salisbury, introduction, vi–viii; see also Heenan, *From Traveller to Traitor*, 315–19.
13 Ibid., 319.
14 Ibid., 202–8.
15 Ibid., 208.

Introduction

my own country. In other words, I reject the 'my country right or wrong'.[16]

Interestingly, President Nixon's and Henry Kissinger's strategy of 'thawing' in the early 1970s not only opened the doors to China, but to Wilfred Burchett as well. The Nixon administration pursued a foreign policy strategy known as détente, the easing of tensions with the Soviets. A key aspect of this strategy involved Vietnam and China. In short, Nixon sought to use the rivalry between China and the USSR as leverage with both Hanoi and Moscow. Reaching out to Beijing and 'breaching' the Chinese wall, Nixon hoped, would aid negotiations with the Soviets on arms control, and strengthen Washington's position in the stalled negotiations with Hanoi for US withdrawal from Vietnam.

It was in this context that Wilfred Burchett once again got pulled in as a participant in backroom diplomacy. In 1971, Burchett received an invitation to visit Kissinger at the White House. Burchett was at the United Nations covering the debate about China; on 19 October, he made the trip to Washington, DC, for a private breakfast with the secretary of state and national security adviser to discuss North Vietnam and Ho Chi Minh's openness to negotiations. The contact between the two took place at the suggestion of Ross Terrill, an influential Harvard political scientist and expert on China, whose work informed the Nixon administration as it readied its approach to China. Terrill wrote that he 'had known from talks with Kissinger that he was rather interested in Burchett's writings, and that he regarded Burchett as a highly intelligent and well-informed man . . . Henry later rang me. He found his talk with W.B. highly interesting.'[17]

Soon after, Ross Terrill wrote a letter to the renowned Australian journalist Bruce Grant, telling him the details of Burchett's visit with Kissinger. While requesting anonymity, Terrill considered the story too 'piquant' to remain in obscurity.[18] In a subsequent article for the Australian publication *The Age*, Grant pondered why his government

---

16   David Bradbury, dir., *Public Enemy Number One: A Biography of Wilfred Burchett* (New York: Filmmakers' Library, 1981), available at Internet Archive, archive.org.
17   This letter from Terrill is cited in Bruce Grant, *Subtle Moments: Scenes on a Life's Journey* (Melbourne: Monash University Publishing, 2017), 193.
18   Ibid.

continued to ostracise and attack Wilfred Burchett when even the Americans recognised his value. 'Wilfred Burchett's reporting,' Grant wrote, 'has given him an international reputation as an intelligent and well-informed man, despite his political prejudices.'[19] He further argued that Burchett's 'value as an observer of politics in Hanoi, Peking and Moscow has now been put to the test by Kissinger', concluding that, at a juncture in which Australia needed its own sources of information, 'Burchett could be considered such a source, long neglected'.[20]

In fact, it is abundantly clear that the Americans paid close attention to Burchett's writings and statements and regarded him as a credible interpreter and interlocutor with the Vietnamese. Burchett made frequent appearances in the presidential daily briefings in the Johnson and Nixon administrations, as the CIA kept a close eye on all his journalistic production.[21] In 1972, when Nixon and Kissinger arrived for their groundbreaking meeting with Zhou Enlai, Burchett was in Beijing, finding himself once again present at a momentous juncture in history. Burchett and Nixon shook hands, reportedly.[22]

When the Portuguese Revolution erupted, the United States administration was embroiled in a national scandal – Watergate. Three months into the revolution, President Nixon announced his resignation and his vice-president, Gerald Ford, took the reins of government. Henry Kissinger was front and centre in formulating US foreign policy posture towards the Portuguese provisional governments throughout 1974. I could find no evidence that Kissinger was preoccupied with Burchett's travels and writings about the Portuguese revolutionary process. The converse is also true: in these books, Burchett does not expend much energy considering the role that the US government or the CIA may have been playing behind the scenes in the MFA's revolution as it developed.

This is particularly interesting when one considers the proliferation of conspiracy theories at the time regarding US Ambassador Frank Carlucci and a possible CIA operation in Portugal. Burchett briefly

---

19 Bruce Grant, 'Journalist Burchett Met with Kissinger', *The Age*, 28 December 1971, 4.

20 Ibid.

21 See, for example, Central Intelligence Agency, 'The President's Daily Brief', 14 December 1967, cia.gov; Central Intelligence Agency, 'Weekly Summary', 27 October 1967, cia.gov.

22 Heenan, *From Traveller to Traitor*, 277.

refers to this conspiracy theory in Chapter 20 of *The Captains' Coup* but does not develop the topic.[23] Either way, his analysis does not centre on the role of the United States in the Portuguese story, but does highlight the Portuguese MFA struggle within the context of the broader Cold War moment, as well as contemporary struggles for decolonisation, specifically in lusophone Africa. At the heart of it, though, Burchett appreciated how much of the revolutionary process was an internal Portuguese affair, playing out between old and new elites and political activists, all vying for relevance in the upcoming regime.

Contextualising Burchett's take on the Portuguese Revolution

Burchett was not a scholar, but, rather, an extremely well-informed observer with a knack for finding angles that mattered to his readers. It was that intuition that made him an important voice among dissident journalists. His telling of the first year of the Portuguese Revolution offers a powerful account of the early stages of the revolutionary process, as well as of the root causes that led to the coup of 25 April 1974.

The interviews he secured with multiple leaders within the MFA are long, detailed and provide unparalleled insight into their thinking during this time. They merit being added to the historical record. That said, he was not the only journalist to enjoy access and secure coveted interviews with the MFA leadership; as the Australian historian Michael Pearson noted, individuals like Otelo Saraiva de Carvalho and Vasco Gonçalves were hardly camera-shy, seizing every opportunity to speak with national and international journalists.[24] No, Burchett's most poignant interviews are not the ones with the officers or party leaders. The most arresting statements in his book come from his descriptions of the countryside, of common folk going about their lives as the revolution is unfolding. Equally fascinating are his interviews with illiterate peasants, which

---

23   Yet, in other writings for newspapers like *Le Monde*, Burchett clearly states that the CIA is carrying out a Chile-style operation in Portugal in late 1974. See Wilfred Burchett, 'L'Art de "dé-stabiliser" un gouvernement', *Le Monde diplomatique*, October 1974, monde-diplomatique.fr.

24   Michael N. Pearson, 'Carnations, Captains and Communists: Burchett on Portugal', in Ben Kiernan, ed., *Burchett: Reporting the Other Side of the World, 1939–1983* (London: Quartet Books, 1986), 279–87.

elevated the voices of these individuals in telling their own stories of political and especially economic repression at the hands of landlords and *patrões* (bosses), and their hopes for the future. The testimonies are powerful: the lack of access to education, to healthcare, to living wages, the ubiquity of child labour . . . it all conjures up an image that only older generations now remember of a Portugal that has completely vanished.

Even so, it is fair to say that Burchett's interpretation of the Portuguese Revolution is one that is, primarily, elite-centred. He places the Armed Forces Movement and the Portuguese Communist Party (PCP) on the foremost plane of action, and other key institutional actors – like the Socialist and the Social Democratic parties – on the secondary plane. This is not to claim that he was oblivious to other social actors in the revolution. As a seasoned political journalist who had covered many social and anti-colonial uprisings around the world, he was attuned to that dimension, as illustrated by his interviews and insights, which explained how average citizens engaged in the revolutionary process. A focus on the elites was to be expected, considering his target international audience for the book. That is, Burchett was seeking to contextualise the events of the Portuguese Revolution for an international audience that knew little about the country. Thus, he spent considerable time explaining the structures of power in Portuguese society and the macro socio-political variables that led mid-ranking military officers to stage a coup against the regime, as well as the emerging positionings of new actors during the revolutionary stage.

Like Burchett, the first wave of academics writing on the events of 1974–75 emphasised the elite-driven processes of the revolution.[25] Other

---

25 See Philippe C. Schmitter, *Portugal: Do autoritarismo à democracia* (Lisbon: Imprensa de Ciências Sociais, 1999); Thomas Bruneau, *Political Parties and Democracy in Portugal: Organizations, Elections, and Public Opinion* (Oxford: Westview Press, 1997); Lawrence Graham, 'Redefining the Portuguese Transition to Democracy', in J. Higly and R. Gunther, eds, *Elites and Democratic Consolidation in Latin America and Southern Europe* (Cambridge: Cambridge University Press, 1992), 282–99; Lawrence Graham, *The Portuguese Military and the State: Rethinking Transitions in Europe and Latin America* (Boulder, CO: Westview Press, 1993); Howard J. Wiarda, *The Transition to Democracy in Spain and Portugal* (Washington, DC: American Enterprise Institute Press, 1989); Guillermo O'Donnell, Philippe Schmitter and Lawrence Whitehead, eds, *Transitions from Authoritarian Rule: Southern Europe* (Baltimore, MD: Johns Hopkins University Press, 1986); and Kenneth Maxwell, *The Making of Portuguese Democracy* (Cambridge: Cambridge University Press, 1995).

scholars highlighted the role of the PCP and the influence of Marxism–Leninism throughout the period, often ignoring competing ideologies within the broad umbrella of socialism that were also a part of the revolutionary process (for example, the Maoists) and social movements that were not involved with labour (like radical feminists, or LGBT groups). A few studies, like Nancy Bermeo's well-known investigation of the land occupations in southern Portugal, expanded on the role of specific social movements in the revolution, often from a structural perspective.[26]

In more recent years, a new wave of scholarship has revisited this approach, focusing the spotlight on the social movements that converted a coup into a revolution.[27] Historians, sociologists and political scientists have been reassessing the revolutionary process from a bottom-up perspective, often influenced by social-movement theory. Doing so involves thinking about the Portuguese Revolution as a complex process that resulted from the interaction of institutional (e.g. parties) and extra-institutional (e.g. activists) actors, competing to shape the cycle of contention and seeking to influence the emerging new regime. Such social-movement organisations were key actors that are largely absent from Burchett's narrative, though he does cover the trade unions and the landless peasants' movement in the agricultural south.

A final critical note on this matter is that Burchett's treatment of institutional elites is uneven. As mentioned earlier, his journalism makes it clear that he is well disposed towards the MFA and its programme. In fact, he casts the Revolution as a struggle primarily between three main camps: the MFA, the Communists and the reactionary right. While mentioning other institutional actors, like the centre-left Socialist Party (PS), the centre-right Social Democratic Party (PPD-PSD) and other smaller parties on the far left, he often casts them as supporting actors in the struggle. Yet, the PS and the PSD played oversized roles after winning the Constituent Assembly

---

26 Nancy G. Bermeo, *The Revolution within the Revolution: Workers' Control in Rural Portugal* (Princeton, NJ: Princeton University Press, 1986).

27 See Diego P. Cerezales, *O poder caiu na rua: Crise de estado e acções colectivas na revolução portuguesa 1974–1975* (Lisbon: Instituto de Ciências Sociais, 2003); Pedro Ramos Pinto, *Lisbon Rising: Urban Social Movements in the Portuguese Revolution, 1974–1975* (Manchester: Manchester University Press, 2013); and Daniela F. Melo, 'Women's Mobilization in the Portuguese Revolution: Context and Framing Strategies', in *Social Movement Studies* 15, no. 4 (2016), 403–16.

elections of April 1975. Their leaders – especially Mário Soares and Francisco Sá Carneiro – were instrumental in bolstering the centrist, pro-Western-style democracy faction of the MFA, and in securing international financial and political support for the centrist forces in the provisional government.

In fact, as the revolution evolved into its most intense phase in 1975, Portugal went through a situation of dual power. Revolutionary legitimacy was heavily contested between the political parties that won the election to the Constituent Assembly – the centrist PS and PPD-PSD – and the parties to their left that lost the election but had strong pockets of support south of Lisbon, were well established in many of the trade unions, and claimed extra-institutional revolutionary legitimacy. That is, they asserted that they rightly wielded support from the social movements representing 'the people'. Concomitantly, the MFA was fracturing along three separate visions for the post-revolutionary regime, only one of which aligned with support for the PCP.[28]

Unfortunately, Burchett was not in Portugal during the period that came to be known as the *Verão Quente* ('Hot Summer'), when there was a credible threat of civil war, and episodes of violence were erupting across the country. At the end of his first book, he extolls the alliance between the MFA and 'the People' in almost romantic terms and seems hopeful – almost naively confident – that counter-revolutionary forces would not be able to shake that alliance.

In the second book (Chapters 18–20 in the present volume), his tone has completely changed. Written after the Hot Summer, he captures its tensions and tries to disentangle the complex and quickly changing dynamics between the institutional and extra-institutional actors, and their alliances, which were also in flux. As he does so, he tends to favour the PCP's narrative about the evolution of events between the Constituent Assembly elections of April 1975 and the events of 25 November 1975, when the 'centrist' MFA faction came out victorious over the far-left factions and set the country on the path towards a Western European model of social democracy.

---

28 The other two visions within the MFA are frequently described as one aligned with the far left and Otelo Saraiva de Carvalho, and the other aligned with the centrist parties and Melo Antunes.

Burchett's fascination with the MFA was understandable because the MFA was, in fact, a very unusual type of institution. The MFA was a pro-democracy, leftist military organisation. It led a coup d'état not just against the Estado Novo regime, but against the top echelons of the Portuguese Armed Forces. Despite its ideological fracturing throughout 1975, the MFA adhered to its basic promise of wanting to transition the country to democracy, development and decolonisation. In 1982, with the dissolution of the Revolutionary Council as an institution, the MFA quietly retreated from public life. Power had been ceded to elected officials and the military returned to their barracks.

Burchett's second book also captures the uncertainty and disillusionment that the Communists and far left felt about the revolution in its final weeks. Like the PCP and much of the far left, Burchett entertained the possibility that the 25 November actions were planned by counter-revolutionary forces within the MFA and the parties to the right of the PCP (perhaps even the CIA). He also considered the alternative: that these insurrections were not centrally organised in any way that could lead to a left-wing coup within the provisional institutions. In summary: the centrists and the far-left parties accused the PCP of seeking to mount a coup with the help of rebellious armed forces units; the PCP, in turn, blamed the far left for fomenting insurrection in some armed forces units, denied any PCP role in an attempted coup, and accused the centrists of being counter-revolutionaries; finally, the centrist parties (and the centrist MFA faction) defended their actions, maintaining that they were a response to a coup attempt, and that their consolidation of power was a path correction setting the revolution on the road to democracy (one of the primary original goals of the MFA in overthrowing the Estado Novo).

It is telling that, fifty years later, the memory of that day remains a matter of great dispute in Portugal. Two new parties on the right, Iniciativa Liberal and the far-right Chega, have politicised the memory of the revolution using events of 25 November 1975 to galvanise the electorate against the left. In 2024, Chega attempted to turn 25 November into a national holiday, claiming that it was the 'true day of freedom and democracy'.[29] All the parties on the right approved, instead, a motion to

---

29 'Chega propõe instituir feriado nacional no Dia 25 de Novembro', Partido Chega, 6 May 2024, partidochega.pt.

celebrate 25 November in parliament every year with a solemn session. The entire left voted en bloc against it.[30]

Burchett quite accurately predicted that the right would almost immediately reassert itself politically, and that opportunities for mobilisation would be severely curtailed after 1975. Furthermore, he warned that the gains made by the popular movements (of urban and rural squatters, agricultural and industrial workers), such as Reforma Agrária, would soon be retrenched. This retrenchment process occurred over many years, but it is fair to say that Burchett was correct on that point.

As the Portuguese Revolution turns fifty, Burchett's insightful books appear more relevant – and may prove more valuable – than ever. His experiences in Portugal are of interest to historians, political scientists and sociologists, but also a great starting point for a general public interested in this period, because his telling is so vivid and engaging. These books are also a must-read for those interested in the great debates about journalism, its value, ethics and power. Burchett was, after all, the ultimate dissident journalist during the Cold War. His unique style of merging interviews with storytelling and analysis transports the reader to the events and emotions of the most significant years in Portuguese contemporary history. And, as the past turbulent ten years of political developments in the country reveal, the Portuguese elites still need to come to terms with the legacy and memory of the MFA and the revolution. Rediscovering and reading Burchett's books about this unique 'captains' coup' is a good start.

---

30 Maria Lopes, 'Serviços do Parlamento propõem para o 25 de Novembro cerimónia igual à do 25 de Abril', *Público*, 13 September 2024, publico.pt.

BOOK I (1975)
Portugal After the Captains' Coup

[Editors' note: This text has been prepared using Wilfred Burchett's original clean corrected typescript manuscripts, which we found among his archived papers held in the National Library of Australia. Burchett's typescript has been copyedited, with minor textual changes introduced for clarity, but no substantive changes in content or organisation were made. The spelling of some Portuguese words and names has been corrected, and diacritical marks added according to current usage. Burchett's original footnotes are indicated by [AN] (Author's Note), while new footnotes, added to provide historical context, are marked [EN] (Editors' Note). Burchett's in-text parenthetical notes have been converted to author's footnotes, and his underlining for emphasis in the original typescript has been changed to italicised text.]

1

The Backdrop

The plane in which I flew from Paris to Lisbon on April 28, 1974, carried a strange assortment of passengers, virtually all Portuguese. A sprinkling of intellectuals, a few who could have been businesspeople or officials, the majority humble folk, many with strained, anxious faces. Exiles? Migrant workers? Draft-dodgers? A few hours earlier it had been announced that Lisbon airport was open again following a military coup three days previously, which had reportedly ended half a century of fascist rule. But had it? Had a military dictatorship merely replaced a fascist dictatorship? The country was now being run by a military junta, which sounded ominous. Was there any real change? Did the same security police control incoming passengers? The latter questions were put to me in an anxious voice, by a middle-aged Portuguese sitting next to me. He had guessed from the portable typewriter wedged between my legs that I was a journalist. I could only shrug my shoulders. It was my first-ever visit to Portugal and I was also worried about security checks and whether an entry visa was needed for an Australian passport. I had rushed to Orly airport to claim any available 'waiting list' seat on a flight that was booked out within minutes of the radio announcement that Lisbon was receiving planes again.[1]

---

1   [EN] Wilfred Burchett was living in Paris at the time of the 1974 coup d'état in Portugal.

I was still grappling with problems of lack of visa, lack of health card, lack of hotel reservation or any contact in Lisbon, when the 'Fasten Seat Belts... Stop Smoking' announcement told us we were coming down for landing. Tension built up among the passengers. Faces which had visibly paled during the final minutes were pressed against the portholes as we taxied to the reception area after bump-down, as if trying to see what lay ahead.

There was nothing to worry about. The atmosphere at passport control was that of the headquarters of a political party after victorious election results. No officials at all. Men and women in civilian clothes – the only time in nine of my subsequent arrivals and departures – gaily stamping passports and travel documents after a glance to see that the photographs bore some resemblance to the faces of the owners. Every time the stamps banged down, there was a flashing smile and a '*Vitória*' for the Portuguese or a '*Bem Vindo*' (Welcome) for myself and a handful of other foreigners.

Once beyond the minimal passport and customs controls, the pale, strained faces started to glow. Shouts, tears, frenzied embraces – children pushed forward towards unrecognised fathers and uncles. A high proportion of passengers were involved in emotional reunions after years of exile.

More '*Vitórias*' and '*Bem Vindos*' from a taxi-driver, who, once he spotted my typewriter, recommended the Tivoli Hotel. There, filling in the hotel form, a sudden slap on the back from an old colleague: 'You here? No problems getting in?' I described the atmosphere at the airport. 'Then things really have changed. But what brings you here?' he insisted. 'Isn't this a bit out of your orbit?' Our previous encounters had been connected with Asian problems, specifically those of Indochina.

It was a question to which I did not have a complete answer at that moment. I had acted impulsively and intuitively, as old war horses are supposed to do at the smell of gunpowder. But gunpowder as such does not interest me. I have smelt too much of it. News of the 25 April coup had taken the world – including all but a couple of hundred Portuguese – totally by surprise. Like most of my colleagues, I like to be on the spot when history is being made. The overthrow of Europe's oldest continuing fascist regime in itself would have justified professional interest. What had really jerked me into action, however, was that some points of the Programme of the Armed Forces Movement, which carried out the

The Backdrop

coup, had globe-shaking implications. That is, if they were to be implemented. A tremendous rock had been dropped on 25 April, the shock waves of which would radiate out far beyond the confines of Europe where repercussions from Spain to Greece were predictable – to shake the power pattern in the whole of southern Africa.

If the captains, who apparently formed the backbone of the Armed Forces Movement, meant what they said – that one of the key motives in toppling the fascist regime was to end the African wars – this was of staggering significance. Whether they realised it then or not, the wars could only be ended on the basis of total independence for Portugal's African colonies. A dramatic and totally unexpected new element would be introduced to the African scene. Where would this leave Rhodesia and South Africa and their few client states?

The major part of my journalistic career had been spent in covering anti-fascist wars, independence struggles and national liberation movements in Asia. It was inevitable, according to my experience, that the national liberation movements in Guinea-Bissau, Mozambique and Angola would also be victorious.[2] But when, and at the cost of how much blood? The captains' coup looked like a short cut. It was this aspect, even if not clearly formulated in my mind at the time, that pushed me to bid a hurried farewell to my astonished family and speed towards Orly airport with the faint hope of getting on the first plane into Lisbon after the coup. My mind was more occupied with the problem of getting to the spot than with what I would do once there!

Why a coup – and why by captains? Could the armed forces of any colonialist country really take an anti-colonialist position? Did the coup-makers really intend to put an end to the African wars on a realistic basis? These were the questions foremost in my mind. There were other tantalising side issues, such as the rare chance of an inquest into a fascist regime while the body was still warm. Could such a regime really be dismantled without bloodshed? Nazism in Germany; fascism in Italy and Japan, all had collapsed by pressure of force from outside, with foreign armies of occupation supervising the dismantling process. Were

---

2 [EN] Guinea-Bissau, Angola and Mozambique were colonial territories in sub-Saharan Africa claimed by the Portuguese since the fifteenth century. Beginning in the early 1960s, all three colonies became sites of ongoing armed liberation and independence struggles, to which the Portuguese government had responded by deploying military forces from the metropole to contest anti-colonial militant groups.

the Portuguese capable of doing it themselves? And how do people react to freedom when most of them do not know its smell or taste?

A stroll along Avenida da Liberdade, where the Hotel Tivoli is located, an hour after arrival gave a whiff of the atmosphere. Although it was a chilly evening – colder, I was told, than is normal for early spring in Lisbon – there were thousands of relaxed, gay fellow-strollers on the streets, waving carnations. Every now and again a group of a dozen or so soldiers, sailors, youths and girls, arms linked, hurried along shouting what had already become a theme slogan: 'A People United Can Never Be Defeated'.[3] Marine guards outside the Ministry of Information and Tourism, where Avenida da Liberdade leads into Praça dos Restauradores, had carnations stuffed into their rifle barrels and pinned to their tunics. They posed for portraits with whoever thrust their arms around their shoulders. Fraternisation was total – it was soon clear that rank-and-file troops were the heroes of the day.

The question of questions for every journalist in a totally unfamiliar situation is where to pick up the threads. The Tivoli Hotel, as the airport taxi-driver knew, was a sort of unofficial foreign correspondents' headquarters – especially the bar – a Stock Exchange of Rumours, as one colleague expressed it. But hardly the place to dig deep into what had happened and why; or what was to be the shape of things to come. For such questions, contacts with Portuguese were indispensable. But how?

It proved easier than expected. At the bank early on Monday morning when I presented my passport to cash a travellers' cheque, there were some hurried whispers, then someone was nudged forward to ask if I was the author of books on Vietnam. Hands were thrust out, autograph books produced for signatures when I acknowledged that I was. I had almost forgotten that, miraculously as it had seemed to me, a number of my books had been translated and published in Portugal. But that they should be so well known in a bank? It turned out that one of the directors of the publishing house, Seara Nova, was also an official of the bank![4]

---

3 [EN] The original phrase in Portuguese is 'O povo unido jamais será vencido!' It was likely adopted from Spanish-speaking political activists on the left in Colombia and Chile in the early 1970s.

4 [EN] Lisbon-based publishing house Seara Nova (New Harvest) was the press through which Wilfred Burchett subsequently published, in 1975 and 1976, the Portuguese-language versions of his two books about the Portuguese Revolution, which are combined into this English-language volume.

The Backdrop

Would I like to meet him? Within minutes I had established contact with Senhor Vasco dos Santos Martins, the dynamic and highly knowledgeable assistant director of Seara Nova, who reminded me that we had corresponded over matters concerning my books. He turned out to be an invaluable contact and contact-maker.

The fact that various of my books on Indochina had been published in Lisbon proved to be an 'Open Sesame' for doors the opening of which made possible the chapters that follow. Literally every political personality and member of the Armed Forces Movement whom I later met, from Prime Minister Vasco Gonçalves onwards, introduced themselves as readers of one or more of those books.[5] As they played such a role in facilitating my own introduction to Portugal it is perhaps appropriate to explain how books with such a strong bias in favour of national liberation movements in Asia could be published in a fascist Portugal that spent half its budget in trying to crush just such movements in its African territories. It was in subsequent meetings with Vasco Martins that I learned how this came about.

Book censorship (like many other repressive activities) operated in an original and subtle way in Portugal. Manuscripts did not have to be submitted in advance. Publishers could *print* what they liked. But before a finished work went out to the bookshops, three copies had to be submitted to censorship. If the work was found to be 'undesirable', copies would be seized by the political police from the printery or publishing house. To be destroyed, it was assumed. But, in fact, Vasco Martins told me that, after the 25 April coup, they found the seized books – including an almost entire edition of one of mine – neatly labelled and stored at the PIDE (political police) headquarters.[6] The publisher obviously took a considerable financial risk in publishing works that the censor might ban. But Seara Nova – and, presumably, other publishing houses – found a way of partially getting around this. They had a large list of

---

5 [EN] General Vasco dos Santos Gonçalves (1921–2005), graduate of the Portuguese military academy; served overseas in Goa, Angola, and Mozambique with the Engineering Corps. Joined the Armed Forces Movement in 1973. A planner of the 25 April coup d'état, he served as prime minister from 18 July 1974 to 19 September 1975.

6 [EN] PIDE: Polícia Internacional e de Defesa do Estado (International Police for the Defence of the State), the principal state security and surveillance agency in Portugal during the Estado Novo (New State) regime.

regular subscribers who paid for any books sent to them. There was no law against mailing books to individuals in advance of the censor's decision. Thus, a first edition, tailored to the number of subscribers, could always be distributed. This is what happened in the case of one of my early, but most widely published books on the Vietnam war, which appeared almost simultaneously in a dozen languages.[7]

A second edition was also cleared for distribution. The US Embassy protested, however, according to Vasco Martins; the clearance was withdrawn; the police moved in and seized the stocks at the publishing house. Under-the-counter sales continued for a long time because of stocks scattered all over Lisbon from which the bookshops were discreetly supplied. Among the copies which escaped seizure were several hundred ordered by the Portuguese Military Academy, where future captains were studying. It became a textbook for the study of Viet Cong tactics, in the highly probable event that they would be used by the national liberation movements in Portuguese Africa. 'Highly probable' because cadres from those movements were being trained in Vietnam, and among the first recipients of the Portuguese-language editions of this book were leaders of the national liberation movements in Guinea-Bissau, Mozambique and Angola! The effect on those studying at the Military Academy was the opposite to that intended.

Major Melo Antunes, one of the most prestigious leaders of the Armed Forces Movement and who is usually credited with having drafted its political programme, was one of those who read my books on Indochina.[8] He was later to tell me: 'It was a great shock for the young officers to note that it was impossible for the United States, despite fantastic military technology, to defeat the people of a small, underdeveloped country. The lessons of the Vietnamese struggle – described in your books – played a most important role in the political development of the younger officers. There were factors which even right-wing officers could not ignore.'

---

7 [AN] *Vietnam: Inside Story of the Guerilla War* (New York: International Publishers, 1965), published by Gallimard, Paris, also in 1965 under the title: *La Seconde Résistance – Vietnam 1965*.

8 [EN] Ernesto Augusto de Melo Antunes, Jr (1933–1999), Portuguese military officer, political theorist and early member of the Armed Forces Movement (MFA). His political programme's concepts, adopted by the MFA, included the 'three Ds': decolonisation, democratisation and development.

The Backdrop

An artillery captain, an activist in the 25 April coup and doing a refresher course at the Military Academy at the time when *Why the Vietcong Wins* was required reading, commented: 'What was clear to even the dumbest right-winger was that if a mighty country like the USA could not win against a small backward country like Vietnam, how could small, backward Portugal win in the African territories, that were twenty times as big as Portugal with twice its population?'[9]

If I have dwelt so long and with total lack of modesty on the door-opening effect of my Indochina books, this is because I was never allowed to lose sight of the almost obsessive interest of politically conscious Portuguese in the struggle of the Vietnamese people. From that first contact with the bank clerks, obviously on the Seara Nova subscription list, I became used to being hailed as the man who introduced the Vietnamese struggle to the Portuguese public. Some half-dozen books published by Seara Nova had even found their way into the cells of political prisoners!

To speed me on my way on that first Monday morning, Vasco Martins sent me to the editorial offices of the monthly review *Seara Nova*, associated with the publishing house. It was bringing out a special number to commemorate 25 April.

At the editorial offices there was a blurred vision of tired, bearded men – the same strained, anxious faces as those of many of the plane passengers – rushing from room to room, desk to desk, with limp proofs of news reports and editorials from the daily papers. Eyes red from lack of sleep, others were hammering away at typewriters, trying to recapitulate aspects of half a century of fascism to get their magazine on the streets as soon as possible after May Day – only two days distant by then. Explaining this, an exhausted editor took me aside, begging me to return at a calmer moment:

'You can't imagine,' he said, 'we are rushing to press for the first time without censorship; without anyone to say what we can and what we cannot publish. For the dailies it's easier. What is published today is forgotten tomorrow. But we are a responsible monthly.' (Censorship of

---

9 [EN] Burchett refers here to the original title of his book published in 1968 by Guardian Books (New York) as *Vietnam Will Win!* According to his son, George Burchett, the Guardian Books editors insisted on a more 'triumphalist' title for the volume, which then proved prophetic.

newspapers and periodicals had been on a different basis to that for books.)

Monday, April 29, was in fact a big day. Under banner headlines the evening papers carried a decree that May 1 in future was to be known as Workers' Day, and become a national holiday. There would be nationwide celebrations. In the Tivoli restaurant that evening, the head waiter interrupted the taking of my order to stare at the headlines of my evening paper on a vacant chair. He picked it up. Other waiters gathered round. For the benefit of those who were illiterate, he read out the May Day announcement. Then another headline: 'Riches should be in the hands of the working people and not the bankers and parasites.' It was an extract from an interview with socialist leader Mário Soares who had returned from exile the previous day.[10] The waiters seemed dumbfounded – but in an approving way. 'That such things can be printed, and the papers bought in the streets, is something beyond our experience,' explained the head waiter, as he resumed taking the order. I was joined by the back-slapping colleague of the previous day and told him what had happened.

He related in turn that, together with some ten thousand-odd other people, he had been at the railway station when Mário Soares arrived (a couple of hours before my plane got in). 'Incredible scenes,' he said. 'I asked a wildly cheering chap alongside me who he was. "Portuguese," he replied. "Yes," I said, "but any particular party?" He replied: "I'm a Communist."[11] The woman interpreter gasped: "That's the first time in my life I've heard anyone admitting he was a Communist," she said. It brings home to you what these people have been through, and how things have changed,' commented my colleague.

---

10 [EN] Mário Alberto Nobre Lopes Soares (1924–2017), anti-fascist student activist and academic, arrested and exiled for opposition to the Estado Novo; co-founder of the Portuguese Socialist Party. Soares returned to Portugal immediately following the 25 April 1974 coup and was named Minister for Overseas Negotiations, responsible for negotiating the independence of Portugal's colonial territories. Soares would play a fundamental role in Portugal's transition to democracy and serve as prime minister from 1976 to 1978 and 1983 to 1985.

11 [EN] The Portuguese Communist Party (Partido Comunista Português, or PCP), founded in 1921 by factions of the labour union movement, soon affiliated with the Comintern (1923). The PCP was outlawed in 1926, after a military coup ended the First Portuguese Republic. During the Estado Novo, the PCP had to operate in secrecy, enduring state persecution, until legalised in December 1974, following the 'Carnation Revolution'.

The Backdrop

The following day, this was even more apparent. Communist leader Álvaro Cunhal returned from fourteen years of exile – after eleven years of prison which ended with a dramatic escape.[12] The road to the airport was choked with carloads of welcomers. The main slogans scrawled on red banners and chanted by the several thousand people at the airport were, 'Cunhal in the Government', 'Long Live the PCP' and 'Long Live Unity Between Armed Forces and People'. Paratroopers in tiger-striped camouflage uniforms, also shouting these *Vivas* and giving the 'V' for victory sign, hoisted an exhausted and bewildered-looking Cunhal on top of an armoured personnel carrier, where he sat arm in arm with Mário Soares. The armoured car formed part of an enthusiastic procession of military vehicles which carried the two leaders through streets lined with cheering people, straight to the presidential palace for a meeting between Cunhal and the provisional president, General António Sebastião Ribeiro de Spínola.[13] (He had received Mário Soares immediately on arrival two days earlier.)

All this was but part of the backdrop for May Day, a tumultuous explosion of popular joy which, by its improvised, unrehearsed nature, could never be repeated. The broad Avenida da Liberdade became a throbbing artery along which pulsed people in their tens of thousands to join up in mid-afternoon, with tens of thousands of others converging on the Lisbon Stadium under a sea of hastily assembled banners. Carnations – exclusively red this time – were everywhere. They had already been adopted as the symbol of the revolution, spiking even the machine guns of armoured cars and tanks, the latter submerged in that human flood of hundreds of thousands that filled the stadium to capacity and blocked all the approaching avenues.

It was the great coming together of armed forces and people. The main theme on banners and shouted slogans was 'Unity between Armed

---

12 [EN] Álvaro Barreirinhas Cunhal (1913–2005), long-time political revolutionary and opponent of the Salazar regime. Arrested by the PIDE for political activism, imprisoned and exiled, Cunhal became secretary general of the Portuguese Communist Party from 1961 to 1992, and served as minister without portfolio in several provisional governments following the coup of 25 April 1974.

13 [EN] General António Sebastião Ribeiro de Spínola (1910–1996), a top military commander in Portuguese Guinea between 1968 and 1972. Spínola published *Portugal e o Futuro* ('Portugal and the Future') in March 1974, a book advocating ending the colonial wars. As a senior officer who supported the MFA's 25 April coup, Spínola was named the first president of Portugal following the dissolution of the Estado Novo regime.

Figure 1.1. Political demonstrators with party affiliation signs and revolutionary slogans fill one of Lisbon's principal thoroughfares, the Praça dos Restauradores (Restoration Square) and Avenida da Liberdade (Liberty Avenue), during Portugal's first legal International Workers' Day celebration, 1 May 1974, a week after the 25 April coup d'état. (Photo by Fernando Ricardo)

Forces and People', 'Long Live the Armed Forces', added to 'Victory' and 'A People United Can Never Be Defeated'. The police, still unpurged and long associated with the bloody repression of half a century's attempts to mark May Day in some form or another, had been taken off the streets by a decree the previous day, which made the armed forces responsible for maintaining law and order. The demonstration was, in part, a deliberate outpouring of gratitude towards the Armed Forces Movement which explains why the few army vehicles, including tanks and armoured cars, were piled with young people waving banners and shouting slogans, carnations sprouting out of machine-guns and bazooka barrels as a symbol that they would never be turned against the people.

The psychological effect of this outpouring of esteem and affection on rank-and-file soldiers would leave its mark for years to come. They had returned to their origins – become part of the people – after years in the wilderness of hostility, despised by some for repressing Africans in the colonies and the people at home, by others for their inability to win the wars in the colonies and contributing to lowered living standards at home. In any case, despised!

Among the slogans carried by the general public were more specialised ones carried by organised trade unionists, demanding a purge of stooge leaders imposed by the fascist regime, better wages and working conditions and an end to the colonial wars. As the marching crowds were swallowed up by the stadium and telescoped into the streets leading to it, endless lines of decorated cars honking the 'Victory' signal paraded up and down Avenida da Liberdade, the name of which finally seemed to be justified. The keynote speakers at the Stadium – both cheered to the skies – were Mário Soares and Álvaro Cunhal, appealing for unity between people and armed forces to consolidate the overthrow of fascism and guarantee its non-return.

Festivities continued long into the night and the small hours of next morning, demonstrators splitting up into groups for parties at family or organisation levels, or just thronging the streets, the car-owners honking their horns.

Asked by local journalists next day for my impressions, I could only compare it with the entry of the Vietnam People's Army into Hanoi in October 1954, when, block by block, as the VPA advanced and French troops withdrew, the city blossomed into a sea of red flags and banners. It was a valid comparison, except that the Hanoi residents twenty years earlier had been celebrating liberation from eighty years of foreign rule, and today's Lisbon residents the end of forty-eight years of Portuguese fascism. But gratitude for the liberating role of their respective armed forces was the same.

Figure 1.2. Álvaro Cunhal, left, leader of the Portuguese Communist Party (PCP), and Mário Soares, leader of the Portuguese Socialist Party (PS), onstage during a political demonstration held at Lisbon's main sports arena, the Estádio da FNAT (Fundação Nacional para a Alegria no Trabalho). This rally marked the culmination of May Day celebrations in Lisbon, 1 May 1974. (Photo by Carlos Gil)

2
Daylight

Elvira Nereu, a serene, Madonna-faced young woman – in charge of a pool of typists at Unilever Limited when I met her shortly after arriving in Lisbon – was awakened about 10:00 p.m. on the night of 25 April by a shouted message: 'Coup d'état! Courage.'[1] It had originated hours earlier from a car that had passed up and down a nearby road, honking it out in a special code – one hoot for A, two for B, three for C and so on. It had then been tapped from wall to wall and along the water piping that connected most of the cells in Caxias prison, a gloomy white stone building about twelve miles along the coast, west of Lisbon, where Elvira Nereu was held prisoner. As her cell was isolated from the rest, she was one of the last to get the message. A newcomer and unlikely to be familiar with prison 'Morse', the message was finally shouted to her from windows in the same block of cells.

'A coup?' she told me later. 'Left, or right?' There had been rumours of a right-wing coup by Kaúlza de Arriaga a few months previously.[2] Was this it? If so, we would be even worse off than before. If it were left-wing,

---

1   [EN] Maria Elvira Barreira Ferreira Nereu (1941[?]–), member of the Portuguese Communist Party and political prisoner who was being held in the Caxias jail on 25 April 1974. Nereu served as an officer of the PCP and as a consultant to the communist parliamentary group in the National Assembly.

2   [AN] General Kaúlza de Arriaga, known for his extreme right-wing views, was a former governor-general of Mozambique, later head of the Portuguese Air Force. [EN] Here Burchett made two misstatements. Kaúlza de Arriaga (1915–2004) served the Estado Novo as junior secretary of state for aeronautics from 1953 to 1955, and as commander in chief of Portuguese military forces in Mozambique from 1969 to 1974.

there would be retaliation against the prisoners. In any case, further sleep was impossible.

'Early next morning, Marine troops came to reinforce the usual GNR sentries.[3] That looked very suspicious. As they moved in, everybody started cursing them. "Sons of Bitches", "Assassins" and so on. But they took no notice.'

She had been arrested with forty-seven other people – parents, schoolteachers and pupils – a few weeks earlier. They had got together, ostensibly to work out rules for improving the administration of the school which her son Pedro attended. In fact, they were discussing how to organise at least some modest action to mark May First. Every year people risked their lives and liberty to make at least some May Day gesture. It was the season during which the PIDE (Political Police) were more than usually vigilant.[4] Someone had tipped them off, the area was cordoned off, the house surrounded, and all forty-eight were bundled into police vans and taken to the headquarters of the PSP (Public Security Police). Those over fifteen were handed over to the PIDE who transferred them to the Caxias prison. After preliminary investigation, those who paid a fine of 2,000 escudos admitting 'illegal association' were allowed to go.[5] Half a dozen, including Elvira Nereu as the only woman, refused such an admission of guilt. They were given the no-sleep torture treatment – of which more later – to try to extract the name of the organisation to which they were suspected of being linked.

'Why had the Marines come?' continued Elvira Nereu in her soft, shy voice. 'It could only be to reinforce the GNR. Perhaps there really had been a leftist coup, in which case, we were all to be wiped out. I decided to take a shower and at least be clean for whatever awaited me. There was a rattling of keys in locks and the noise of doors being opened. I was ordered to come out, and was sure something bad was about to happen. I replied that I would come when I was dressed. When I stepped out, the

---

3 [AN] National Republican Guard which, among other duties, provided guards for jails such as Caxias where mainly political prisoners were held.

4 [AN] By this time the name of PIDE (International Police for the Defence of the State), had been changed to DGS (Directorate General of Security), having had five other names since it was founded as the PE (Special Police) when the first military dictatorship was set up in 1926. The name PIDE is that most generally used in Portugal today.

5 [AN] The value of the escudo at that time was roughly twenty-five to one US dollar.

first thing that struck me, looking along the corridor, was that all the doors were opened for the first time. Then I could see people embracing each other in the courtyard, all tears and smiles. I saw faces of old friends, swallowed up by the prison years ago, who I knew were there but had never seen. A young officer who didn't belong to the GNR explained that there had been a coup, and we would soon be released. Then I nearly collapsed because my husband was there, dressed up as a medical orderly. [Later, he turned up again, having borrowed a camera to come in with a group of journalists!]

'Outside the prison walls, relatives and friends of the prisoners pressed around giving carnations to the Marine soldiers – the GNR guards outside had disappeared. Those of us who had saved up some sweets from the weekly visits of relatives, started handing these out to the soldiers also. It was obvious that something really big had happened.

'We saw some of the hated inspectors being led into the cells. Some of us started hurling threats and insults at them, but the veteran politicals said: "Stop it! Show them that we are different."

'The officer came back and explained that he was from the Armed Forces Movement, and it was they who had carried out the coup. "You have waited a long time," he said. "Be patient a little longer. Return to your cells because there are still some bureaucratic questions to settle. Not all prisoners can leave immediately." We asked that at least our cell doors be left open. He replied: "Impossible. I have no orders for that." So, we returned to our cells and the same guards locked us in again. It was then about 10:30 a.m. on the 26th. I started to think that it had been too good to be true. Useless to start packing – even though the officer had said we would be freed in "a couple of hours". But what if the coup had been crushed already?

'During this time soldiers had grouped around the walls under the windows and asked who we were. When we said we were political prisoners, they said: "What's that? Political prisoners. Never heard of such things." When we explained that Caxias was especially for political prisoners, one of them said: "Now I understand why you insulted us. Our unit came to take over what we thought was just one more strategic position and we had no idea why everyone started yelling at us."

'We very quickly had good relations with the Marines. But one of the vilest of the guards warned them: "Don't go near them" ' – meaning us. ' "They're capable of killing you. They even insult the national flag." To us, because we were throwing our food down to the soldiers who hadn't eaten all day, the same guard said: "Those soldiers are like Gypsies. They'll take everything you've got and ask for more!" The prison guards were a rotten lot to the last – trying to create ill feeling between us and the troops.

'We had really interesting discussions with the soldiers. They kept leaving their positions to come below the windows and talk with us, telling of their hard life in the services, their experiences in the colonial wars. Their officers ordered them back to their positions from time to time, but they kept wandering back to speak with us. Time dragged on. The "two hours" lasted all day. The warders acted as if nothing had changed, refusing the simplest requests. But it was clear they were a bit shaken. They had lost some of their arrogance. An Army officer – an old acquaintance – came in and greeted me. The guard outside probably thought it was my husband. "What goes on in here's not my fault," he said. "I'm really a market gardener outside Lisbon and got drafted into this job."

'In the latter part of the day we were allowed out of the cells again, women mixing with women in the courtyard at one level, men with men at the other. That in itself was a great moment which we celebrated by brewing some coffee.

'Messages started to arrive from the new authorities. The officer read them out. "Maybe not all of you can be freed," he said. "Some are considered common-law criminals – those who have taken part in bank robberies or have killed PIDE agents." There were violent discussions on our level. Some of the women were not very politically conscious and thought only of getting out – and home. But, finally, we got agreement that we were all political prisoners. "If the Army doesn't release all of us, none will go," we told the lawyers who had come into the prison by this time. "We will stay here and consider ourselves prisoners of the new regime." The lawyers relayed this to the Armed Forces Movement. The men took the same stand. One who had robbed a bank volunteered to remain behind.[6] Another also, who had bumped off a PIDE agent. But the others refused to leave without them. "All or none" was our slogan. By that time word had come in about what had been going on outside

---

6 [AN] Elvira Nereu was referring to Palma Inácio, the heroic head of LUAR (League of Union and Revolutionary Action), terribly tortured during repeated periods of imprisonment. A master of escape techniques, he had been rearrested in Lisbon in November 1973 and was serving a fifty-year sentence imposed *in absentia* for his part in a spectacular bank robbery.

– including the storming of the PIDE headquarters. "There are soldiers who killed PIDE agents today," we said. "Are they to be considered common-law criminals?" The representatives of the Armed Forces Movement appreciated this argument and by that time big pressure was building up outside the prison to get us released.

'Around midnight the officer came back and said: "Pack your bags quick and get moving. You must evacuate your cells immediately to make way for the PIDE agents who have been rounded up." That was the great moment. Everything was clear. We left the cells exactly as they were when we entered – just the bare walls. People who had been there for years packed their books – everything that visitors had brought them – wrapping their possessions in their own blankets. The only things left behind were slogans we scrawled on the walls to welcome the new inmates: "Down with PIDE" ... "Death to the PIDE Assassins" ... "Long Live the MDP" [Portuguese Democratic Movement] and others.

'As we came out with our bundles, the MFA officer said: "There are many people gathered outside – they are very excited. You know better than any how to behave in a situation like this. Things are still not entirely secure. We don't know who may be among the crowd. There are cars waiting. We advise you to leave directly with your own family members for home and not wait around."[7] Hundreds of people were waiting to escort us in triumph back to Lisbon, but the MFA people were frightened that PIDE agents still around might want to wreak some last-minute vengeance. As we came out to the embraces of relatives and friends, we could hear shots fired in the distance.'

'What was the first thing you did when you got home?' I asked.

'Telephone the fiancée of one of the Marines who had been at the prison all that day and night, and assure her that he was alright,' she replied.

Released in the small hours of a Saturday morning, she was back at her old job on the Monday, having spent the weekend with her husband and other friends working to ensure that May Day was the greatest celebration in living memory.

---

7   [EN] The MFA acronym stands for Movimento das Forças Armadas (Armed Forces Movement, or AFM), the group of mainly mid-level Portuguese Army officers who planned and conducted the coup d'état that overthrew the Estado Novo regime. Wilfred Burchett used both acronyms in his original texts for this volume. To avoid confusion, we have used the Portuguese 'MFA' where the acronym appears throughout this edition.

Figure 2.1. Pro-democracy activist José Tengarrinha, centre, and other political prisoners held by the Estado Novo regime at Caxias Prison in Oeiras, west of Lisbon, mingle freely prior to their release to waiting family members on 26–27 April 1974, while MFA marines and soldiers secure the prison grounds. (Photo by Carlos Alberto)

Another who emerged from Caxias at the same time was José Magro, after a total of twenty-one years in various prisons.[8] Awaiting him, amongst others, was his magnificent wife Aida. In thirty years of marriage, they had spent about one year together. When he was out of prison during those years, she was in, and vice versa. Or when they were out together, one or the other was engaged in clandestine work which meant they could never meet. A lean, wiry man of fifty-four with a beaming smile, optimistic face and great sense of humour, he told me later:

'As I came out, there were roars: "Death to you" . . . "Assassin, assassin!" That's a strange welcome, I thought. Then I understood the shouts were for a well-hated PIDE bigshot who was just being escorted in past me. The shouts changed to "*Viva, viva!*" and the next thing was my wife saving me from being strangled by over-enthusiastic comrades. Then she did some strangling herself.'

---

8 [EN] José Alves Tavares Magro (1920–1980), anti-fascist political activist and writer, member of the Portuguese Communist Party, for which he served as a representative in the Constitutional Assembly (1975) and, afterwards, the National Assembly of the Portuguese Republic.

'How did you learn there had been a coup and that you were to be released?' I asked.

'I was being held in the prison hospital and was kept well informed as to what was going on through a common-law prisoner, who had access to more information than we politicals. He informed me at 6:30 a.m. – reveille time – on the 25th that a coup was being carried out. This was confirmed later on by our clandestine radio. The hospital personnel said nothing, but there was a helicopter hovering overhead and a feeling of tenseness among the guards. I was comforted by their depressed looks. Behind that depression lay fear. The signs were sufficient to set up a defence disposition. PIDE might take advantage of the special situation to liquidate at least the main cadres.' [José Magro was himself a veteran member of the Central Committee of the Portuguese Communist Party.]

'My wife managed to establish contact with me during the morning and we agreed that it was desirable that military units occupy the prison as soon as possible. Until then, friends and supporters should gather outside.'

'What did setting up a defence disposition entail?' I asked.

'Establishing contact amongst ourselves and with outside. We took it in turns to stand on a chair under a window from where we could signal to friends and progressives who were maintaining a constant vigil outside – always twelve to eighteen carloads of them – to prevent PIDE reinforcements being sent in. We were determined that if we could not prevent the liquidation of prisoners, at least there would be witnesses.

'Early next morning, the Marines took over from the GNR and we breathed more freely. An officer came and said: "I've got champagne to celebrate your liberation. But I'm still awaiting the official order to release you." We replied: "Better open the champagne only when we're really to be freed." Finally, the officer came back at about 2:00 a.m. on the 27th with the order – and the champagne. He couldn't believe it when the others told him I'd covered my head with a blanket and gone to sleep. He asked to see for himself. The others asked him not to wake me. I knew there would be plenty of work ahead and I'd better get as much sleep as possible while I had the chance,' he said with a cheery smile.

António Dias Lourenço was another who surfaced that morning after a total of seventeen years in prison.[9] Twenty years earlier, he had made a most dramatic escape from the grim seventeenth-century fortress built by the Spaniards at Peniche, some sixty miles north of Lisbon and now the centre of the sardine-fishing industry. Lowering himself by knotted strips of sheets to a point where he could plunge from a great height into the icy waters of the Atlantic in mid-December 1954, he swam several kilometres out to sea and around a mole that formed part of the fishing fleet harbour. Protected by the fishermen and brought back to safety, he carried on several years of clandestine work before being arrested to spend his last stretch of twelve years in Caxias prison. Later, I visited the Peniche Fortress and, looking at the jagged outcrop of rocks through which he had plunged, and the distance he had to cover in the wintry seas to clear the moles, I could only marvel at the courage, determination and physical endurance of the man. Today he edits *Avante*, the official weekly organ of the Communist Party. An irrepressibly jovial man, he jumped up from his chair to embrace me when I walked into his office:

'Ah . . . Your books on Vietnam. I read them in prison, and they were a great source of comfort for us. We felt it was all part of one struggle and that we were winning.'

To my question, 'What was the first thing you did when you came out of Caxias?', he replied:

'I went almost straight to the headquarters of the Democratic Movement.[10] I had their address whereas I knew the Communist Party had not yet surfaced legally. I asked for something useful to do. "Go to the trade union headquarters," I was told. "You'll find plenty of old acquaintances there. Try to persuade them that May Day this time must be a great national event and not just a trade union affair. It should reflect unity and victory for the whole people." So, I went to the trade union headquarters and after six hours of very tough discussion, it was

---

9 [EN] António Dias Lourenço (1915–2010), Portuguese political activist, writer, journalist and prominent leader of the Portuguese Communist Party. Arrested multiple times and held as a political prisoner by the Salazar regime, he took part in two noteworthy escapes from the Peniche prison, in 1954 and 1960.

10 [AN] The Portuguese Democratic Movement (MDP) was the successor to the CDE (Democratic Electoral Commission) which was a legal opposition body formed to contest the general elections in 1969 and 1973. It provided a cover for communists, socialists and anti-fascist Catholics. Its origins are dealt with in greater detail in a subsequent chapter.

agreed that this year May Day should be a great people's celebration of the overthrow of fascism, the victory of anti-fascist forces, marking the unity between people and armed forces. It should be a mobilisation of people from all sectors of the population – a fitting event to mark a great historic victory.'

Rivalling Caxias in notoriety as a political prison was Peniche, through which virtually all political prisoners had passed at some time or another. The day of the coup found the Peniche sardine fishermen in the middle of one of their periodic fights for better conditions. There were always several elements in their long and complicated struggles. The men who did the fishing; the capitalists who owned the boats; the government-appointed port commander who was the final arbiter in all disputes, and the ever-present PIDE to take care of 'agitators' who became too active. By mid-March, a committee elected by the one thousand-odd sardine fishermen had drafted terms which the boat-owners seemed inclined to accept. The port commander, however, turned them down and put pressure on the owners to resist their fishermen's demands. A lock-out had thus started on 23 March. After three weeks, during which no boats put to sea, there was a meeting between port commander, owners and fishermen. 'Either you sign the contracts the way the owners want them, or you'll all be sacked,' said the port commander, according to Carlos Cordeiro, the thirty-one-year-old president of the fishermen's committee. Cordeiro went on:

'On April 25, five of the thirty-nine sardine boats were actually ready to put out to sea, but the crews were still hesitating and the boats were still in port. By mid-morning, troops started marching into the city. This looked like disaster. We were used to fighting the police, but the last time troops had been used against us was nearly forty years earlier. Then, our fathers had been forced to capitulate. They could stand up to the police but not the army! We lined the streets together with our wives, backed by port workers, shopkeepers – everybody – hurling the worst sort of insults at the troops as they came marching down the main street. They took no notice of us and swung off towards the fortress.

'Soon afterwards, to our stupefaction and great joy, the political prisoners started coming out. By that time some of us had picked up news over the radio from Lisbon. All of a sudden, it was the great fête. Barrels of wine were rolled out, tables were set up in the streets, fish were soon being grilled everywhere, the troops and prisoners hugged by everyone and plied with food and wine. The whole town went wild. The troops, including their officers, were the heroes. And, of course, the prisoners. By nightfall, everyone was drunk. Officers who mildly tried to get their troops together were persuaded to "have another drink" instead. It was the greatest day anyone could remember in Peniche. The response to every fresh communiqué from Lisbon was renewed shouts of "Long live the Armed Forces Movement" and more barrels of wine rolled out into the streets.'

There is no question but that the release of the political prisoners, starting within a few hours of the coup, and the fact that the cells they vacated were immediately filled by the detested PIDE thugs, was the single most dramatic symbol for ordinary people that things had already changed. Virtually no element of the active population had escaped the attention of PIDE, whose all-pervasive presence was felt in every factory, every office and enterprise, every educational establishment, every village – wherever there was any organised economic, social or political activity. This included inside the various branches of the armed forces, as the leaders of the Armed Forces Movement knew only too well.

According to Rogério de Carvalho, now directing research into PIDE activities among the files at Caxias prison – and who himself spent fifteen years in fascist prisons – PIDE employed some 3,000 regular police agents and 4,000 to 5,000 investigators, plus many scores of thousands of informers.[11] Files on over one million people were found in the Caxias archives, and those transferred there from the Lisbon headquarters of PIDE. This represented one in three of the active part of the population. Informers included priests who sold, at standard rates, information received in the sacred privacy of the church confession boxes.

Any act which brought a person in contact with officialdom – apart from the more obvious case of denunciation by an informer – was sufficient for PIDE to open a file. An application for a passport, or for a job in some branch of the administration, meant automatically opening a file and surveillance at some degree of intensity. Under such a system,

---

11 [EN] Rogério de Carvalho (1920–1999), notable Communist militant, member of the PCP Central Committee (1963–88), and anti-Estado Novo leader. Arrested and tortured by the PIDE, he participated in a collective escape from the Peniche prison in 1960.

Figure 2.2. An officer of the Armed Forces Movement removes a portrait of Estado Novo dictator António Salazar from an office wall in the PIDE (state security police) headquarters at Rua António Maria Cardoso, no. 22, following the coup d'état and surrender of the building on 26 April 1974. (Photo by Eduardo Gageiro)

virtually everyone lived and worked under the omnipresent shadow of the PIDE. The fact that the only blood shed during the 25 April coup was in a shoot-out with PIDE diehards at their Lisbon headquarters was symptomatic.

It was also significant, in the light of what transpired later, that freeing the political prisoners at Caxias was delayed by over twenty-four hours because of dissension within the Military Junta as to what categories were to be released. One faction, which can be assumed to have been backed by Spínola, wanted a selective release – to exclude those involved in revolutionary violence. The struggle which started within the Junta leadership, and within the Caxias prison, within hours of the coup over 'all or none', set the shape for things to come. That the captains came down on the side of 'all' at that point, and on that issue, was symbolic for what followed later. Probably many of the captains were almost as puzzled as the Marines under Elvira Nereu's cell window at the number and the quality of the political prisoners. But, faced with that situation, just as in diverse situations later, they instinctively took, or backed, the right decisions.

As to why the Armed Forces Movement did what they did; why it was the captains who took the lead; why in the various crises which followed the coup it was they, and not the generals, who dictated the solutions – thereby hangs a tale which probably most of the captains could not even guess at. The truth is that there were parallel currents at work. Most of those moving in one current did not know of the existence of the other. Probably no single person knew until a very late date that 25 April 1974 was the point at which the currents would converge to produce an explosion, the historic importance of which it is still difficult to measure.

3
Conspiracy

When the first secret meeting of the captains took place in the outskirts of the lovely old town of Évora on 12 September 1973, the main subject of discussion was not PIDE, political prisoners, or a possible coup d'état. It was called because of professional discontent over what seemed to be a short-sighted and easily corrected decree by premier Caetano. 'There was a shortage of officers', explained an artillery captain, who must remain anonymous, but played a leading role in the events that followed. 'The Military Academy was no longer stuffed with the sons of the rich upper classes but was glad to accept the sons of the lower middle class. Once the national liberation struggles started in Africa, soldiering became a dirty and dangerous business – a low-prestige profession. Because of battlefield losses and draft-dodging, there was a real shortage of officers. Because social standards were lowered, there developed a big class difference between those at the levels of captains, even majors, and the colonels and generals. To fill the gaps, in July 1973, Caetano offered anyone with university graduation a six months' militia-type training at home, followed by commissions – with active service privileges and pay equal to, and even above, those of captains with long service records in Africa.

'The 12 September meeting was to protest against the idea of youngsters with six months' home training being promoted over the heads of those with four and more years of training and overseas service. Apart from anything else, this would have a terrible effect on the battlefield. About 140 to 150 officers took part, mostly captains but with three majors and a few lieutenants also. We mainly discussed the injustice of the new decree – but also the deterioration of the military situation in Africa. We elected a committee representing the different branches of the armed forces to bring pressure on the government to withdraw the decree.

'At that time, we had no thought of making a coup. There was no unified political viewpoint. We were naïve. We thought it was enough to point out the injustice, and the government would correct it. We wanted the law repealed and the prestige of career officers safeguarded. The committee was elected to work for this.

'Our strength was that the government needed us, but we also recognised the dangers. PIDE was bound to be informed. But, with the wars going badly, we felt that, if our movement was strong and united enough, the government would not dare arrest us. We were definitely "not expendable", and we took a calculated risk based on this analysis.

'We continued to meet secretly, always in a different place. At the beginning, we did not know each other's viewpoints. Because of built-in loyalties, there were those who reported back to the Ministry of Defence everything that was discussed. It was impossible to keep secrets. The minister became worried at the way things were shaping up and started some shadowboxing. A document was circulated setting forth all the government had done to improve the lot of the armed forces. We were all supposed to sign this document, but refused. This was the first open act of defiance.

'As members were posted overseas, the Movement was exported with them, to Guinea-Bissau, where Captain Otelo Saraiva de Carvalho was very active; to Mozambique and Angola. Discussion groups started there at the same level. It was the captains – as company commanders in the field – who were taking the greatest losses in Africa, so it was natural they should be the most active in discussing and clarifying the situation.

'We quickly found that there was plenty of solidarity and unity of viewpoint, but due to the harsh realities of war, coordination of effort was difficult with brother officers on active service, because of the vast distances involved. It quickly became clear that the only place where action could take place was in Lisbon itself. We could only communicate with the territories when someone was posted on active duty abroad, or brother officers came home on leave. At a later stage, we took advantage of holidays to send trusted officers on special contact missions to Africa.

'The defence minister at the time was General Horácio Viana Rebelo, and most of us were naïve enough to think that if we could exert enough pressure

Conspiracy

to get him changed, the July decree would be repealed, and our troubles would be over.[1] We were after a changed attitude towards us. At all costs, we wanted to avoid any division within the armed forces, because we feared this would lead to civil war. We absolutely wanted to avoid anything like a Spanish-type civil war. Or a Chile, or any other Latin American–type coup. We were against any type of putsch that could lead to a military dictatorship.

'In December 1973, we thought we had won out when the Defence Ministry was split up. A civilian, Dr Joaquim Moreira da Silva Cunha, was appointed minister of defence, and General Alberto de Andrade e Silva was made minister for the Army.[2] But it was a typical Caetano move to change names and not policies. Andrade e Silva was quite aware of the discontent that had prompted our discussions. He thought the only problem was economic. So, he gave a pay rise to the lower officers and NCOs. This may have impressed some of the sergeants, but it was too late to have any effect on the captains. The discussions had gone far beyond the repeal of the July decree by this time. The whole question of the African wars had been posed and, in the light of that, the nature of the regime at home. Beyond that, we had discussed the war in Vietnam, the role of the United States in global politics – the whole world situation. We were getting more ideologically motivated. In these discussions and analyses, those with the most logical answers were those most listened to.'

In other words, parallel currents had started to converge. Those who started coming up with the most 'logical answers', as the artillery captain expressed it, had long been waiting and working for just such a conjunction of circumstances, as will be seen in a subsequent chapter. There was nothing accidental about this, except the actual timing. Caetano's attempt to ward off trouble by 'changing names and not policies' was very typical of what some critics refer to as the 'immobilism' of this regime. The National Union Party

---

1 [EN] Horácio José de Sá Viana Rebelo (1910–1995; in the original, Burchett erroneously gave his first name as Alberto) was a long-serving Portuguese military officer, politician and colonial administrator (Governor-General of Angola, 1956–59). He served the Estado Novo as minister of defence from 1968 to 1973.

2 [EN] Dr Joaquim Moreira da Silva Cunha (1920–2014) was a professor in the Faculty of Law at the University of Lisbon. He served as the overseas colonial minister (Ministro do Ultramar) for the Estado Novo from 1965 to 1973, and as minister of defence from 1973 to 1974. Alberto de Andrade e Silva (1906–1990) was an army engineering officer who served as commander in chief of Portuguese Armed Forces operations in Angola (1963–65), chief of the army general staff, and the Estado Novo's last minister of the army prior to the 25 April coup.

of Salazar became the People's National Action Party, but the fascist content remained exactly the same: PIDE (International Police for State Security) became the DGS (Directorate of General Security), but its functions remained the same. Andrade e Silva, as new minister for the Army, applied the same policies as his predecessor.

'As a reserve officer,' continued the artillery captain, 'he knew what the captains were up to, and also that the discussions had taken on a specific political character. He was not the only senior officer who knew of this. On 20 December, the Spanish prime minister, Admiral Carrero Blanco, was assassinated, and Caetano went to Madrid for the funeral.[3] A right-wing general, Kaúlza de Arriaga, a former military commander in Mozambique who knew about our discussions, approached us and offered his services to lead a coup while Caetano was in Madrid. We refused. Not only that, but one of our officers stood up in the military academy and denounced Kaúlza de Arriaga's move.[4]

'A rightist military putsch was the last thing we wanted. But, by January 1974, we were unanimous that the fascist regime itself had to be changed and, given the nature of the regime, this could only be done by a military coup. The Caetano–Tomás[5] dictatorship had to go. And this would have to be done by military force.

---

3   [EN] Luis Carrero Blanco (1904–1973), a Spanish Navy officer, politician, prominent supporter and close confidant of fascist dictator Francisco Franco. Named prime minister in June 1973, he was assassinated six months later in a Madrid bombing by members of the Basque separatist group ETA (Euskadi Ta Askatasuna).

4   [AN] General Kaúlza de Arriaga was among a number of high-ranking officers arrested in September 1974, for their implication in what was intended to be a Chile-type coup against the provisional government.

5   [AN] Admiral Américo Tomás had been president since June 1958, elected then for a seven-year term, renewed in 1965 and 1972. His opponent in 1958 was General Humberto Delgado who, in the first contested elections since the military dictatorship was set up in 1926, got 22 per cent of the vote. After severely attacking the conditions in which the elections were held, General Delgado sought political asylum in the Brazilian Embassy in Lisbon and finally set up an opposition headquarters in Algiers. He was murdered by PIDE agents on the Spanish–Portuguese frontier in 1965 (February). Marcelo Caetano became prime minister in September 1968, ten days after dictator Salazar – in power for thirty-six years – fell from a deck chair at his villa in the luxury resort of Estoril and suffered a head injury from which he remained in a coma until he died in July 1970. [EN] Here Burchett repeated the contemporary public story. In fact, Salazar didn't seek hospital treatment until nearly three weeks after his accident. Following surgery, he lapsed into a month-long coma. Upon regaining consciousness and lucidity, he lived for another twenty-three months but was never told that he had been removed from power.

'We came to this decision reluctantly. In 1969, when Caetano became prime minister, we had some hopes that he would change things. Before he took office, he had proposed that the problems of the African territories should be solved within the framework of a confederation. This was at least a step forward. Salazar had rejected the idea, but a lot of us thought this was not Caetano's fault. We felt that he should be given the benefit of the doubt and that, if the officers showed their strength, this would encourage Caetano in his previous ideas. There were grounds for thinking this. In April 1962, he had quit his post as rector of Lisbon University because police were sent in during student unrest. But, by January 1974, there was virtual unanimity that Caetano had turned into a jellyfish and would have to be overthrown.

'A much smaller committee was elected to replace the original ad hoc one. The new committee was entrusted specifically with the task of organising a coup. It was entrusted with full powers to plan whatever action it considered most effective. By that time, we knew that all telephone conversations between members of what had already become the Armed Forces Movement were tapped. Communications from then on were direct, personal contacts, the wives of members often acting as couriers. Although the committee was smaller, it was more representative in terms of military units, and covered all of Portugal.

'Another incident, meanwhile, had revived the same sort of indignation as at the time of the July decree, which had set the slow fuse sputtering towards the powder keg. There had been student troubles at Coimbra University. As punishment, the most militant students were drafted into the military academy. While many of us welcomed them as radical and ideologically motivated reinforcements, we also resented the idea that the Armed Forces were regarded by the government as a penal institution. It was the final straw which persuaded a few waverers that direct action was the only option left.

'The new committee was divided into two parts. A political sub-committee to draw up a programme; a military sub-committee to coordinate military action between the various branches of the armed forces. Strictest secrecy was imposed from this moment.'

(The artillery captain did not say so, but it is fairly certain that Major Melo Antunes was in charge of the political sub-committee. We know from the then captain Otelo Saraiva de Carvalho that he was in charge of the military sub-committee.)

'After the setting up of the new committee, PIDE activities against the Armed Forces Movement were intensified. Activists among the officers were shadowed. It was impossible to use telephones. The government was petrified with fear, but, as usual, unable to take decisive action. Caetano did make one move, however. At one of our secret meetings – on 8 March – it was revealed that Army Minister Andrade e Silva was going to try to break up our organisation by transferring four of our leaders out of Lisbon. One to Bragança in the remote northeast of Portugal, another to the Azores islands, a third to Madeira, and a fourth to Guinea. We decided to "kidnap" them to prevent their removal. There was a kind of a showdown. The committee decided to present the four officers together with one member of the Armed Forces Movement to protest to the Army minister. All five were arrested.

'This was a catalyst. The government imposed a state of alert. We contacted the commanders of the units to which the officers belonged and asked for their support. It must be understood that many of the military units were commanded by captains only; there were others, where there were fifteen to twenty captains and a few majors, which were commanded by lieutenant-colonels or colonels who, in general, opposed the MFA. However, by the time the second committee was formed, six lieutenant-colonels and one full colonel were supporting us. The arrest of the five officers brought us still more support.'

In the meantime, the publication of Spínola's book, *Portugal and the Future*, had exploded like a bombshell in Lisbon.[6] Considered one of Portugal's most illustrious soldiers – solidly right-wing; the most 'successful' military commander in Guinea-Bissau – General António de Spínola shocked the Caetano–Tomás dictatorship by proclaiming that there was no possible military solution to the African wars. 'To win a subversive war by military methods means defeat from the outset,' he wrote, 'unless one possesses unlimited resources to enable the war to continue for an unlimited period and to make an institution of it.'

---

6 [EN] Publication of the book *Portugal e o futuro* in February 1974 by General António Ribeiro de Spínola helped to galvanise the group of Portuguese military officers who, two months later as the Armed Forces Movement, would topple the Estado Novo regime. Spínola argued authoritatively that Portugal's colonial wars in Africa could not be settled by force of arms and advocated a policy of negotiated autonomy for the 'overseas provinces'.

Spínola was consciously – or unconsciously – paraphrasing Henry Kissinger in one of his more astute analyses regarding America's war in Vietnam:

> We fought a military war; our opponents fought a political one. We sought physical attrition; our opponents aimed for psychological exhaustion. In the process, we lost sight of one of the cardinal maxims of guerrilla war: the guerrilla wins if he does not lose; the conventional army loses if it does not win.

Then came an image which every Portuguese (not to mention every Spaniard) would appreciate. 'The North Vietnamese used their main forces the way a bullfighter uses his cape – to keep us lunging into areas of marginal political importance.'[7]

The main point made by Spínola was that, as a military solution was impossible, only a political solution could be envisaged. In fact, he had taken over the idea of Caetano – before the latter became prime minister – of a confederation of Portugal and the African territories in which Lisbon would be responsible for foreign affairs, defence, central finance and 'coordination'. It was not much of a solution, but a shock for the ordinary Portuguese citizen to realise that the blood of his sons and the treasure from his bank account – if he had one – were wasted in a hopeless cause.

Shortly after the Spínola book appeared, the Armed Forces Movement circulated a clandestine 'manifesto' which pointed out, among other things, that 'members of the military who know the facts know that the solution to the overseas problem is political and not military', and that the effort demanded to continue in Africa had become 'humanly unbearable'. The Movement was now concerned with greater issues than pay increases. The government was urged 'to avoid sowing discord among the different branches of the armed services'.

To what extent was Spínola working together with the MFA? And to what extent was General Francisco da Costa Gomes, chief of staff of the Armed Forces and Spínola's immediate boss, informed as to what was going on? It was widely rumoured that it was Costa Gomes who had encouraged Spínola to write his book, promising to protect him from the consequences. These were questions I put to the artillery captain,

---

7   [AN] Henry Kissinger, *American Foreign Policy: Three Essays* (New York: W. W. Norton & Company Inc., 1969), 104.

whose account of the events was far more complete than I had from any other of the participants.

'Spínola had already started to write his book while he was in Guinea,' he replied. 'It was a result of his contacts with members of the Armed Forces Movement. Among his merits were his close contacts with junior officers, and even rank-and-file soldiers, and his physical and moral courage. He liked to discuss, and dared to oppose, the official line. There was also contact between the MFA and Costa Gomes.[8] When the latter decided to appoint Spínola his number two, we agreed. We had contact with Spínola through a major on his staff, but we didn't want to compromise the position and prestige of either Spínola or Costa Gomes in case our action failed. So, their names were kept in the background.

'Things moved quickly after the arrest of the five officers. On 14 March, Caetano called in the top generals to swear an oath of loyalty to the government. Costa Gomes and Spínola refused. Caetano sacked them both. On the following night, the 5th Infantry Regiment, stationed at Caldas da Rainha, about fifty miles north of Lisbon, mutinied. The rank-and-file and the junior officers arrested the senior officers, including the commander and his deputy, who had refused to join them – and started to move towards Lisbon.'

The mutineers, who set out in a column of armoured cars, were turned back about eight miles from Lisbon by police and troops loyal to the Caetano government – thirty-three of their officers being arrested, according to an official communiqué from the Defence Ministry on 19 March. Various versions have been published as to what actually happened. One, widely accepted in the Western press, is that, following the dismissal of Costa Gomes and Spínola, the committees charged with organising the coup met in the Military Academy on the evening of 15 March and decided on action in the small hours of 16 March. The agreed code signal was given but Caetano was informed, and GNR units surrounded the Academy. The MFA coup committee then sent another signal cancelling the action, but the Caldas da Rainha unit did not get it and started out at the agreed time. The artillery captain insisted that it was, in fact, a planned sortie, a dress

---

8 [AN] General Francisco da Costa Gomes, a mathematician by education, had taken part in one of the early attempts to overthrow the Salazar dictatorship. Reinstated as chief of staff of the Armed Forces after the 25 April coup, he replaced Spínola as provisional president, after the governmental crisis of September 1974.

Conspiracy

rehearsal to test the reactions of various branches of the armed service and units whose loyalty to the MFA were still in doubt. MFA communications were tested out – also their ability to use ultra-sophisticated techniques to jam all radio communications other than their own.

That a meeting had taken place in the Military Academy on the night of 15 March, and that the National Republican Guard had been called out, was confirmed. (Also, that the commander of the Academy, General Amaro Romão, was replaced three days later.[9])

The period between 16 March and 25 April was used by the MFA to win over units which had shown signs of wavering during the 16 March 'march on Lisbon', and to put the finishing touches to the plan of action scheduled to go into effect half an hour after midnight on the morning of 25 April.

Figure 3.1. Soldiers of the Armed Forces Movement (MFA) celebrate following a tense standoff with tanks loyal to the Estado Novo regime (visible in the distance) near Lisbon's main waterfront square, the Praça do Comércio, and adjacent government ministry buildings. Early on 25 April 1974, loyalist forces refused orders to fire and joined the MFA coup d'état, avoiding bloodshed. In the foreground are MFA leaders Captain Salgueiro Maia, with rifle (left), and Colonel Carlos Maia Loureiro, flashing a peace sign (centre). (Photo by Eduardo Gageiro)

---

9 [EN] General António Amaro Romão served as commandant of the Portuguese Military Academy in Amadora, Lisbon, from 18 November 1968 until 19 March 1974.

At that hour precisely, Rádio Renascença, with which the Armed Forces Movement had forged good contacts, broadcast the first few lines of 'Grândola Vila Morena', a popular protest song, banned until then. This was the signal for certain unit commanders all over the country to move into action. By 3:00 a.m. the Lisbon airport had been seized and closed to traffic. All bridges and strategic approaches to the capital were also secured; radio and TV stations were occupied. Tank forces were installed in the Town Hall Square – all without a shot fired.[10] What was incredible for this type of action was that the rank-and-file troops taking part had no idea that they were involved in a revolution. As ever, they obeyed the orders of their unit commanders – the captains. A few learned of what they had done, like any other citizens who happened to be listening to Rádio Clube Português, at 4:20 a.m., when the MFA broadcast its first communiqué advising people to stay indoors and ordering all military units (not engaged in the action) not to intervene, in order to avoid unnecessary bloodshed. At 4:45 a.m., the same radio broadcast renewed warnings to the rest of the armed forces. Two hours later, this was repeated but with the added warning that it would be considered a 'grave crime' to offer any opposition. By the time the general public tuned in to their ordinary 7:30 a.m. news bulletin, they heard a communiqué explaining that the aims of the MFA were to liberate the country from decades of oppression, and that the military garrisons of Lisbon and Porto had rallied to their movement. By midday, Carmo, where Caetano had his headquarters, and the PIDE centre at Rua António Maria Cardoso, were surrounded.[11] President Tomás had taken refuge in the headquarters of a Lancers regiment considered loyal to the regime – but which was also surrounded. Caetano and his cabinet were given until 5:00 p.m. to surrender.

---

10 [EN] Burchett refers here to the Praça do Município, a small but strategically located urban square in the Baixa neighbourhood, or lower city. It is the site of Lisbon's city government headquarters, from which movement can be controlled to or from various government ministry buildings, the Navy high command offices and the capital's main waterfront square, the Praça do Comércio.

11 [EN] The Largo do Carmo is a small public square in central Lisbon's Bairro Alto neighbourhood. There, Marcelo Caetano, head of the Estado Novo, took refuge in the headquarters and barracks of the National Republican Guard (GNR), a formidable military police force loyal to the regime. On 25 April 1974, Armed Forces Movement troops with armoured vehicles surrounded the GNR HQ, forced a capitulation, and arrested Caetano.

Conspiracy

Figure 3.2. Entrance to the headquarters of the Republican National Guard (GNR), Largo do Carmo, 25 April 1974. GNR Major Fernando Bélico Velasco (with dark glasses) discusses their surrender to MFA troops commanded by Captain Salgueiro Maia. Inside the barracks, Estado Novo leader Marcelo Caetano negotiates with General António de Spínola, 'so that power does not fall to the man in the street'. (Photo by Alfredo Cunha)

A huge crowd had gathered in the meantime at Carmo, where, as the 5:00 p.m. deadline approached, Caetano was showing signs of bowing to the inevitable. The question was, to whom should he surrender? This is where Spínola came into the picture. Caetano said that, to prevent 'the man in the street' from taking over, he was ready to transfer his powers to General Spínola. While prepared to play a role, Spínola disclaimed any connection with the Armed Forces Movement, demanding from them, however, that his position be formalised before he accepted a transfer of powers from Caetano. This hastened the setting up of a seven-member Junta of National Salvation, to be presided over by Spínola. By 5:00 p.m. Carmo had surrendered, and, within an hour, the protocol transfer of powers was completed.[12]

---

12 [EN] The Junta of National Salvation (Junta de Salvação Nacional) was a committee of seven Armed Forces Movement officers, led by General António de Spínola, designated to maintain, and exercise the executive functions of, the Portuguese government following the overthrow of the Estado Novo regime (the 'Captains' Coup'). During the 'Carnation Revolution' (April 1974–April 1975), the Junta of National Salvation was the *de jure* governing body of the Portuguese state.

At 9:00 p.m. there was firing from the PIDE headquarters into the huge crowd that had gathered outside. Four civilians were killed and about a dozen wounded, a fifth dying in hospital some hours later. These represented about half the total casualties in the Lisbon area. Troop reinforcements were brought in, fire from the PIDE headquarters was returned, and it surrendered some twelve hours later. At 8:00 a.m., Caetano, Tomás and the ministers of defence and the interior were flown in an Air Force plane to Madeira, apparently as part of a 'gentleman's agreement' between Spínola and Caetano. The Portuguese are said to be proud of the fact that – unlike the case in Spain – the bull is not killed in the ring! But plenty of Portuguese were furious that the fascist leaders had been flown into such luxurious exile – and, later on, permitted to leave Madeira for Brazil.

It seems that Spínola used the protocol question posed by Caetano as the condition for the surrender of himself and his cabinet, to force a decision on his nomination as head of the seven-member Military Junta, and thus his confirmation as the provisional president. As broadcast in the small hours of 26 April, the proclamation of the Armed Forces Movement stated: 'Within a maximum delay of three weeks after the seizure of power, the Junta of National Salvation will elect from among its members, one who will carry out the functions of president of the Portuguese Republic, who will exercise powers similar to those laid out in the present constitution. The remaining members of the Junta of National Salvation will assume the functions of chief of staff of the Armed Forces; chief of staff of the Navy; chief of staff of the Army; chief of staff of the Air Force, and will form part of the State Council.'

In any case, by the morning of the 26th, the captains had handed over the attributes of state power to a military junta headed by General Spínola; the press was received by the Junta at 9:30 a.m. of the 26th and given the programme of the Armed Forces, which had been drawn up almost three months earlier. Essentially, it provided for the dismantling of the fascist state; the immediate destitution of the president, the prime minister and cabinet; the dissolution of the National Assembly, State Council and the official Acção Nacional Popular party;[13] the destitution

---

13 [EN] The Acção Nacional Popular (Popular National Action or ANP) was a Portuguese political organisation founded in February 1970 by Marcelo Caetano as the single ruling party of the Estado Novo regime. The ANP was essentially a rebranding of the União Nacional (National Union) state mono-party founded by António Salazar in 1932. Following the 25 April coup, the Armed Forces Movement issued decrees that dissolved the ANP.

Figure 3.3. First press conference of the Junta de Salvação Nacional (JSN) at the 1st Engineering Regiment Headquarters, Pontinha, on the night of 25–26 April 1974. General António de Spínola, JSN president, delivers statements to journalists. He is flanked on his left by Colonel Galvão de Melo, Navy Captain Pinheiro de Azevedo, General Costa Gomes and, to his right, Brigadier Jaime Silvério Marques. MFA Captain Otelo Saraiva de Carvalho is in the rear row. (Photo by Ignácio Ludgero)

of civil governors of the various continental districts, as well as those in the overseas territories; the abolition of the PIDE, the Portuguese Legion – another paramilitary organisation, the functions of which included ensuring the security of leaders of the fascist state – the Youth Corps and other fascist organisations;[14] an amnesty for political prisoners, the end of censorship, and a purge of the Armed Forces and paramilitary organisations.

The programme also stipulated: 'Recognition of the principle that the solution to the wars overseas is political and not military; the creation of conditions for a frank and open debate at the national level of all the overseas problems aimed at a new overseas policy that will lead to peace.' It provided for the setting up of a provisional government within three weeks and the creation of conditions for the election of a national

---

14 [EN] The Mocidade Portuguesa (Portuguese Youth), a fascist organisation for children founded in 1936 under Salazar's Estado Novo regime. Membership was compulsory between the ages of seven and fourteen, but voluntary thereafter until age twenty-five. It was dissolved in April 1974, after the Carnation Revolution.

constituent assembly within twelve months, 'elected by universal, direct and secret ballot, according to an electoral law worked out by the future provisional government'. Regarding the economic and social front, the programme called for a new economic policy 'placed at the service of the Portuguese people, in particular the least-favoured sections of the population, with urgent attention to the fight against inflation and the excessive level of living costs which will necessarily imply an anti-monopolist strategy'.

The programme, though vaguely worded on some issues, was one which progressive forces could endorse, and around which mass support could be generated. It was a document that the members of the Armed Forces Movement were fiercely determined to defend against all detractors – from left, right or centre. Anyone at any level who did not grasp this – including President Spínola – was heading for trouble. That the programme was holy writ was made plain to me by some of the captains during my first days in Lisbon, and I became ever more aware that this was really so as events unfolded. Another fact of life of which one quickly became aware was that it was the captains who held the real power – not the generals. Editors in faraway places – like some of the generals on the spot – had difficulty in grasping this. But that is the way it was. The troops moved when their unit commanders – the captains – told them to move.

4
Motivations

Major Melo Antunes emerged from the start as one of the extremely interesting personalities of the Armed Forces Movement. A plump man with the calm, reflective face of an intellectual, shrewd eyes twinkling behind his spectacles, it was difficult to picture him in uniform. In a university lecturer's chair, yes. Yet he was one of the key planners of the coup and perhaps the chief architect of the Movement's political programme. He headed the Armed Forces Movement's coordinating committee, the precise functions of which were not publicly defined in the period immediately following 25 April. In any case, he had his office in the São Bento palace, the government headquarters, so it was a fair assumption that the committee he headed had at least a watchdog function from the beginning to ensure that government decrees were strictly within the framework of the programme. Later, when the first civilian-led government foundered on the tasks allotted to it, Melo Antunes was to play a leading role in dismantling Portugal's African empire.

Coming from a well-to-do family, there seemed no objective reason for him to throw in his lot with the conspirators in what was, after all, a very risky enterprise. Still less to him having played the leading role he did. When we met, after a preliminary conversation about Vietnam, I asked bluntly if there was any special reason for his acting as he did in the preparation and execution of the coup.

'My development,' he said, 'was perhaps not typical for others. As a student, I was somewhat autodidactic, researching into things beyond the requirements of my formal studies. Although I was attached to the literary faculty, I became very interested in social and political problems. I went into the Army only because this was a family tradition. But the fact of becoming a soldier did not stop me from thinking, or exercising the critical faculty that I had developed towards things in general.

'When a student, I was convinced that literature would be my vocation. As things turned out, I have written nothing. But, for twenty-odd years, I resisted fascism in some way or another. As a student, it was possible to have some activity. But, during my fifteen years in the Army, I found it impossible to express any criticism of the Army or the regime. I maintained contact with my left-wing friends, however, and was active whenever possible. I read everything I could lay my hands on, and I acted in a political way when this was feasible.'

I asked if there was anything special in his military career that had pushed him to play an active anti-fascist role.

'My three terms of service in Angola – two years each,' he replied, 'made the strongest contribution to my real understanding of the colonial question. Those experiences defined my attitude to colonialism and to the fascist regime. Reality comes from practice. Practice in the Army – as in other fields – taught me reality. And in all those years of active service, I never lost my critical attitude. How to apply it was another matter.'

'Was there any specific episode which had a decisive influence?' I asked.

'In the elections of 1969, I wanted to stand as a candidate of the CDE opposition,' he replied.[1] 'After all, there were officers in the National Assembly for the fascist União Nacional party – why not officers for the legal opposition movement? I was a captain at that time. But the government ordered me to withdraw my candidature. I was subject to military discipline and had to stand down. Systematic persecution followed, continual transfers and other punishments. This proved decisively that other means had to be found to change the regime.'

'Now that you have found the means and changed the regime, can you consolidate; hang on to power and end the wars in Africa on a realistic basis?' I asked. 'Are you optimistic, in other words?'

---

1 [EN] CDE stands for Comissão Democrática Eleitoral (Democratic Electoral Commission), founded as a coalition of opposition parties to the authoritarian Estado Novo regime in Portugal, initially to dispute the legislative elections of 1969.

'I'm a measured optimist, not a triumphalist,' he replied, his eyes twinkling behind his glasses. 'We are all clear about the difficulties ahead. We are starting from a very low level – the lowest living standards in Europe. The grave economic situation is one of our big difficulties. My brother officers and I realise that one of the specific causes is the colonial problem which is difficult to solve – even with goodwill on both sides. We can solve the problem of Guinea quickly.[2] Mozambique will be a little more difficult because of white, racist extremists. But we are not going to let them stand in the way of a settlement. It is still not clear what role South Africa and Rhodesia intend to play in bolstering up our white extremists in Mozambique, but that cannot be decisive. Angola is more complicated, because the national liberation movements there still have no common negotiating position. The aim of the previous regime was to keep them at each other's throats. It is not ours. Within the Armed Forces Movement, we are absolutely sincere in wanting to end the African wars on the basis of the total independence of these countries.'

I asked whether the sort of political discussions which prepared the way for the 25 April coup still continued.

'It is very natural that we continue to discuss and analyse the developing situation,' he replied. 'The main factor for us is the task in hand. Political consciousness develops from practice. We are not theoreticians; we are men of action. We deal with realities. Solving the day-to-day tasks confronting us had a continuing effect on our political consciousness. This develops as we face up to new problems – a normal and natural development. The fact that there has been a change in the social composition of the officers' corps at the level of captains and majors facilitates this. The aristocratic character of the officers' corps lost its importance in recent years, and this had a positive effect on political consciousness.'

As to what were the main problems of the moment, Melo Antunes ticked them off on his fingers: 'Democratisation, decolonialisation, economic progress. Of the three, decolonialisation must have priority. Unless we solve that, we cannot go ahead with economic restructuration. Without progress on the economic front, there will be difficulties

---

2 [AN] Our conversation took place a few days before the announcement that Portugal recognised Guinea-Bissau as a fully independent country and would sponsor her membership in the United Nations.

with democratisation.[3] I have great confidence in our people,' he said in conclusion. 'We can build up a modern progressive society – without copying other systems. Maybe we can provide a model for some other countries – Spain, for instance. But we should be original – not fitting into any established models. We should build up a new society adapted to the concrete conditions of Portuguese realities, based on authentic social justice and the sovereign will of the people. Although we come from different social backgrounds, this is an aspiration shared by most members of the Armed Forces Movement.'

Prime Minister Vasco Gonçalves, who I had been warned was an aloof, austere person who shunned publicity, I found warm and sensitive, and an attentive listener. He never missed a point but was frugal with his responses, as befitted his position, and the complex situation at the time.

When I asked why he had associated himself with the Armed Forces Movement, he replied: 'First of all, I must make it clear that some of your colleagues were incorrect when they described me as a leader of the Armed Forces Movement. The leadership was collective. Later on, when we have all the data, there will be an official history of the Movement. Until then, we are limiting what is published. As far as the reason for my involvement is concerned, from the time I was a young officer at the Military Academy, I was known as an anti-fascist. Later, when the Movement had developed to a certain point, the captains wanted some higher officers to know what was going to happen. I was one of them.'

When I pressed as to what he thought was the main compelling motive of the captains, Colonel (by then Brigadier) Gonçalves replied:

'Their firsthand experience in the wars in Africa was absolutely decisive.'

As the agreement to recognise the independence of Guinea-Bissau had been signed a few days previously, I congratulated the prime minister for the speed with which things had moved on that front since he had assumed office. His rather sombre face lit up in a smile. 'I can assure

---

3 [AN] It was interesting that in a discussion at about the same time with Álvaro Cunhal, he put the priority on democratisation – in practice, that meant clearing the fascists out of the infrastructure without which, he felt, it would be impossible to push ahead with decolonisation or to tackle the main economic problems.

you that we are very touched by that sort of remark,' he said. 'Not everyone understands how complex and difficult these problems are. We have made great efforts which few people can appreciate. There are objective difficulties.'

I put to him the same question that I had put to Melo Antunes, as to whether there was any development of political consciousness within the Armed Forces Movement?

'It developed very rapidly,' he replied. 'It started with the study of strictly professional matters, but the captains soon found these were linked with much broader political questions. They, in turn, could not be considered in isolation from problems of still broader importance – the nature of the regime. The captains were led step by step to see that only by the overthrow of the regime itself could even the smallest of other problems be solved. Since then, there has been an accelerated development of political consciousness. It is practice that teaches. In the seven months that elapsed from their first meeting to the 25 April coup, the young officers learned more about politics than in ten or more years previously. It was a case of condensation in time, and the process has continued at an accelerated pace since then.'

Changing the subject, I asked whether the prime minister felt that the country's economic problems could be solved within the framework of the MFA's programme.

'We have the heritage of half a century of fascism, compounded by the problem of colonialism, and even by the international situation – rising prices for raw materials, especially fuel – and recession. Our people are not very political yet. Many hoped that the fall of fascism would be like the salvo of the *Aurora* in the Soviet revolution: ushering in a new era that would solve all the country's problems, including their own personal problems.[4] After all they had suffered under half a century of fascism, this is understandable. It is normal that they should press on with claims for better conditions. We have to understand this, and at least ensure that an inevitable regime of austerity and sacrifices shall be shared equally by all social classes. The key to everything is to

---

4 [EN] The Russian warship *Aurora*, a cruiser completed in 1903, reportedly played a crucial role at the beginning of the Bolshevik Revolution of 1917, firing the initial salvo that signalled the attack on the Winter Palace, the Romanov Tsar's imperial residence in Saint Petersburg.

maintain national unity, and that also means unity between the people and the armed forces.'

One thing that emerged from my discussions with personalities of the quality of Vasco Gonçalves, Melo Antunes, the anonymous artillery captain and others, was that the Armed Forces Movement had to be considered as an independent political movement of considerable weight. No matter how much tradition dictated that the armed forces remain aloof from politics, the MFA was deeply involved in the political, social, and economic life of the nation within three months of toppling the fascist regime.

The extent to which military service in Africa had created an anti-war, anti-colonialist psychology within the Armed Forces Movement – as stressed by Melo Antunes and Vasco Gonçalves – was astonishing, but it was confirmed whenever one spoke with the junior officers. Coupled with this was bitterness, born of experience, towards white racists and any local jingoists who tried to whip up enthusiasm for continuing the struggle. On the other hand, there was a lot of concern about the lack of prestige of the armed forces and the role of the MFA in restoring that prestige. It was a tribute to the leadership of the MFA that, from the beginning, they equated the restoration of that prestige with the ending of the wars in Africa. The pattern of military service for officers was a rotation of one year at home and two years in Africa, where many of the captains had served four tours. The rank-and-file conscripts were called up for three years, of which two were in Africa.

'We caught it from both ends,' the artillery captain said. 'We had to stand up to reproaches from the man-in-the-street at home, who thought we were living off the fat of the land overseas and were responsible for the economic difficulties at home. We were despised by the white racists for not massacring the Africans fast enough, and thus ensuring security for the settlers. The masses despised us because they thought we had become officers for the privileges it brought, and that overseas duty was especially profitable. In the old days, this was why the aristocracy always sent at least one son into the Army. In Africa, we were made to feel the contempt of the racists; at home on leave we had to put up with the contempt of the higher-ups because we were not winning, and that of the masses because we were in uniform. Officering at the captains' level was a dangerous, unpleasant business with about an even chance of death from an enemy bullet, or from malaria or dysentery.

Motivations

From the time of the Goa defeat, the armed forces – especially the officer corps – were in disgrace.[5] Those of us serving in Africa felt there was a Goa at the end of every road. A Goa in Guinea, a Goa in Mozambique, and another in Angola. We were made the scapegoats for the failures of impossible policies in Africa. We were the scapegoats in Africa itself and at home, because of the inflation and lowered living standards which were the results of the continuing wars, and failure to win those wars.

'We couldn't do anything right. There were terrible massacres in African villages, for which most professional officers in the field were ashamed. Such things made us hated and despised by the Africans and the decent Portuguese settlers who lived on good terms of racial equality with the Africans. It lowered the prestige of Portugal, and the armed forces, abroad. The only ones to glory in such atrocities were the dyed-in-the-wool fascists from home, and local racists. This only deepened the hatred of fascism and racism among the younger officers. Service in Africa really opened their eyes. There were numerous occasions when the Army intervened to prevent racist brutalities. Then, we were jeered at for not being "tough" enough. "Go home and leave us your guns. We'll finish the job ourselves." This was a typical slogan of the ultra-racists. It contributed to the mutual feelings of contempt, which exploded in the demonstrations against the armed forces in Beira in Mozambique in January 1974, and which were a great eye-opener for many of us.' (Among those who were deeply shocked was another artillery captain, born and reared in Mozambique, Otelo Saraivo de Carvalho, who had been a school classmate of Samora Machel, by then leader of FRELIMO, the national liberation movement of Mozambique.[6])

---

5 [EN] Goa is a diminutive territory on the west coast of India, held as a Portuguese colony for over 450 years, beginning in November 1510. Following Indian independence from the United Kingdom in 1947, the Estado Novo steadfastly refused to consider relinquishing control of Portugal's 'overseas provinces' in South Asia. On 17–19 December 1961, Indian military units invaded Goa, along with Damão and Diu, quickly overwhelmed the small Portuguese garrisons, and incorporated these territories into the Indian Union by force. This humiliating debacle frustrated the Portuguese officer corps and demonstrated Portugal's military vulnerability, providing encouragement to popular independence movements in their remaining colonies across Africa.

6 [EN] FRELIMO: Frente de Libertação de Moçambique (Liberation Front of Mozambique), founded in 1962 by anti-colonial activists Eduardo Mondlane and Samora Machel as a nationalist movement fighting for the independence of Mozambique from Portuguese colonial rule.

A number of officers cited what had happened in Portugal's Indian colony of Goa as the start of demoralisation within the armed forces. Several even claimed that this marked the beginning of the 'Long March' which led to 25 April. What was it all about? On December 18, 1961, after months of fruitless negotiations, some 30,000 Indian troops invaded the Goa enclave by air, sea and land. Within twenty-four hours, resistance by the Portuguese garrison of 3,000 men had ceased. Goa was reincorporated into Indian territory after 463 years of Portuguese overlordship – an injection of self-esteem for the India of Prime Minister Nehru.[7] He had felt the need to undertake this action in view of the fast-developing crisis with China on India's northern frontier.

José Francisco Nereu (husband of Elvira, mentioned in an earlier chapter as one of those liberated from Caxias prison), an intelligent, energetic and resourceful person who was to become my valued friend, guide, reserve-driver and interpreter – of Portugal as well as its language – was serving as a young medical orderly in Goa at the time of the Indian invasion. He was an obvious person to ask why there was such bitterness among Army professionals.

'As soon as the attack came,' he replied, 'Salazar sent a message to General Vassalo e Silva, the governor-general, ordering the garrison "to resist to the death of the last man". Leaflets had earlier been distributed to the effect that, should India attack, there would be São Francisco de Xavier – the patron saint of Goa – and 10,000 archangels with flaming swords by our side to smite the enemy. General Silva also sought the opinions of the unit commanders, which was most unusual.

'When the attack came at midnight on 17 December, we saw plenty of Indians, and there were plenty of bombs and shells – but no sign of São Francisco de Xavier and his archangels! Nor did we have a single anti-aircraft gun to fire at the Indian planes. The artillery units were the first to run up the white flag. Our only naval unit, the 1,700-ton frigate, *Alfonso de Albuquerque*, put up a stiff fight against three much bigger Indian warships – including a cruiser – before she was badly damaged and ran aground, with the captain gravely wounded.

---

7 [EN] Jawaharlal Nehru (1889–1964), the anti-colonialist and independence activist who became a leader of the Indian nationalist movement and served as India's first prime minister from 1947 until his death.

'General Vassalo e Silva and the garrison with him at the Vasco da Gama fort fought back for a bit, but surrendered on the afternoon of the 18th.[8] From the governor-general on down, we were all in disgrace – especially the officers – for not being dead. Salazar, in fact, treated us as if we *were* dead. He didn't want anything to do with us. It got to be very embarrassing. The Indians weren't interested in feeding or looking after us. They wanted to send us home, but Salazar wouldn't have us. After about six months, and very strong Indian insistence, we were sent back – smuggled in the dead of night – no relatives to welcome us. The officers were punished, being at least kicked out of the service. For them and their comrades in the officer's corps, it was a very depressing and traumatic experience. For me, after being held for a few weeks, it was a great chance to get out of the Army, having served my time.

'If the officers afterwards talked of "a Goa" at the end of the road in Guinea or elsewhere, they meant disgrace, humiliation and dishonour. This feeling was not limited to just those who had served in Goa.

'It was very typical of Salazar – of Caetano too, later on – to issue ridiculous orders that no one intended obeying,' continued José Francisco. 'By the time we returned home, the national liberation struggles were underway in Africa, and it was natural for the officers – especially those who commanded in the field – to wonder if the Goa formula was to be applied in Africa. Die or be jailed! The official disgrace of the Goa officers, decreed by Salazar, started a decline in the prestige of the officers' corps from which it only recovered after 25 April.'

In evaluating the strength and cohesion of the Armed Forces Movement, and the influence of the MFA on the armed forces as a whole, an understanding of the state of mind that existed on the eve of 25 April 1974 is of crucial importance. It explains not only why the younger officers did what they did, but also the impact of the psycho-political action – not as spontaneous as it first appeared – in making the armed forces the heroes of the hour.

---

8   [EN] General Manuel António Vassalo e Silva (1899–1985) was the last governor-general of the Estado da Índia, the Portuguese colonial outposts in India (Goa, Damão and Diu). Attacked by an overwhelming Indian military force, on 19 December 1961 he surrendered the Portuguese colonies, which were then subsumed into the nation of India. Here Burchett mistakenly identifies a Portuguese military base in Goa, called Alparqueiros, as a 'fort'. More accurately, this installation was a base located near Goa's main port facilities at the town of Vasco da Gama.

Figure 4.1. Political poster asserting the unity of purpose between the Portuguese people and the Armed Forces Movement: MFA, Povo/Povo, MFA (Armed Forces Movement, People/People, Armed Forces Movement). Cultural Dynamisation Campaign; Imprensa Nacional – Casa da Moeda (National Printing House and Mint), 1975. (Poster by João Abel Manta)

No longer were they an object of contempt from the masses, but brothers! Heroes! Liberators! Barriers between armed forces and people, between officers and rank-and-file, were swept away by popular acclaim. The prestige of the armed forces was restored overnight, and was of a quality hitherto unknown. The programme contributed greatly to consolidating the historic act of overthrowing the fascist regime. It proved that what had happened was not some impetuous putsch, but a well-thought-out action.

'There had been several attempts at coups in the past,' the artillery captain explained. 'But in the past, it was always a leader in search of a movement or mass support. Now, for the first time, there was a collective which organised, worked out its programme, and later chose its titular leaders.[9] It is a much more solid affair to have the will of many, instead of the ideas of one.'

That the MFA was a collective movement and was adopted by the masses from the moment it surfaced, was of capital importance in the various crises which exploded during the months that followed the coup. My first question to Prime Minister Vasco Gonçalves had been one that was in the minds of many people who wished the new provisional government well: 'Is there not the risk of a Chile-type countercoup?'

'I do not think there are the conditions to have a Chile in Portugal,' he replied, speaking very deliberately. 'The decisive factor is that the members of the Armed Forces Movement are absolutely united around their programme.'

By all one could learn, the determination of the MFA leadership to defend the programme was strengthened as time went on. In this context, there was a very significant passage in the speech by Vasco Gonçalves at the Belém presidential palace on 18 July 1974, during the ceremony to confirm him as prime minister. To fully appreciate his remarks, it is necessary to know that Vasco Gonçalves had been imposed as prime minister by the Armed Forces Movement, in defiance of another choice by President Spínola. This followed a serious crisis caused by the previous prime minister's attempt to abandon key aspects of the MFA programme.

---

9 [AN] He was referring to the MFA having offered titular power to the Junta of National Salvation, under General Spínola.

In a pointed reference to the fact that the captains had imposed their will on the generals, the new premier said: 'Mr President of the Republic: these are the words of a soldier who places the interests of his country above all else; one whom the courage and patriotism of your young officers have led you, sir, to appoint to the post of prime minister.' Then, to everyone's astonishment, he turned towards Spínola and continued: 'My last remarks are for you, sir. You also collaborated in drawing up our programme, as did General Costa Gomes. You, like us, pledged yourself to support and carry out the programme of the Movement of the Armed Forces. For all these reasons, you may be sure, sir, that I shall make every effort to carry out the noble task you have entrusted to me, which can be summed up by the integral fulfilment of the programme of the Movement of the Armed Forces.'

This was the first revelation that Generals Spínola and Costa Gomes had taken part in drafting the Armed Forces programme; secondly, it was an implied rebuke to Spínola that he had permitted the previous government to attempt to sabotage the programme; thirdly, it was a warning that no such attempts would be tolerated in the future.

As far as the Armed Forces Movement was concerned, the programme was more than just the blueprint for all essential activities for the twelve months' transitional period after the coup. It was a document around which maximum support could be rallied within the armed forces. And the newly restored prestige, to which the officers attached such importance, was reliant upon the implementation of the programme. It had also become the programme of the provisional government, accepted by all parties and personalities participating in that government. It thus had been accepted as a precious bridge between armed forces and people, reinforcing those links established in the first hours after the coup.

Discussing this latter aspect, Pedro Soares, a silver-haired veteran of the Communist Party's Central Committee, insisted that what had happened on 25 April should not be regarded as a coup, nor as an isolated development.[10]

---

10 [AN] A revolutionary from his student days at the Faculty of Literature at Lisbon University, Pedro Soares had spent eleven-and-a-half years in prison, including two terms in the dreaded Tarrafal concentration camp in the Cape Verde Islands, where over forty revolutionaries, including the secretary of the Communist Party, Bento Gonçalves, died of ill-treatment and disease. Pedro Soares returned from exile in Italy after April 25.

'We consider that the disintegration of the fascist regime was due to the struggle of the democratic forces that the Armed Forces were well able to interpret and exploit. The regime was overthrown at the high point of its decadence. What is very important is the political development of the armed forces since the coup. Our people, who were considered abroad as non-political, immediately seized on the importance of what the armed forces did. The days that followed 25 April were not only given over to fraternisation – to celebrating the joy of a great victory – but people were also employing new aspects of revolutionary tactics. They mingled with the armed forces, explaining the significance of what they had done; the tasks of the future for the democratisation of life. All democratic forces consciously worked in this way to reinforce the links between the people's movements and the armed forces.

'Old-fashioned concepts of the role of the armed forces have to be ditched in this sort of situation,' continued Pedro Soares. 'That is why we fight against the position of ultra-leftists who misinterpret the situation and see the armed forces as the chief support of the neo-capitalist forces in this country. It is a grave error to think that the role of the armed forces is to maintain the present economic set-up of foreign monopolies, local monopolies and bankers.

'When the full history of this period is written, 25 April will be seen as the culmination of a very long and complex struggle – a scientific, dialectical process – the successful outcome of which was foreseen by our party,' he concluded, urging me to read the programme adopted at the Communist Party's sixth congress in 1965. I did read it, and found it a remarkable and revealing document, which explained much about the essential ingredients of the 25 April action and the likely course of events to come.

5
Strategy

In an introduction to the third, and first legal, edition of the Portuguese Communist Party's 1965 programme, publisher António Dias Lourenço noted that: 'Many points in the programme of the Portuguese Communist Party concerning this phase of the national, democratic revolution have already been realised, or are on the way to being realised. The implementation of various other points can be envisaged within the present process of democratisation.'[1] This was due, he said, to the 'close alliance between the essentially patriotic and democratic Armed Forces Movement and the united people's movement'.

The eight-point 1965 programme, which remained valid for the whole period up to and immediately after the 25 April coup, consisted of:

(1) Destroy the fascist state and set up a democratic regime.
(2) Liquidate the power of the monopolies and promote general economic development.
(3) Carry out land reform, handing out the land to those who work it.
(4) Improve the living standards of the working class and the people in general.

---

1 [AN] Mentioned in Chapter 2, as the editor of *Avante*, official organ of the Portuguese Communist Party, which published the third edition in May 1974.

(5) Introduce democracy into education and culture.
(6) Free Portugal from imperialism.
(7) Recognise and ensure to the peoples of the Portuguese colonies the right to immediate independence.
(8) Pursue a policy of peace and friendship towards all peoples.

What is very interesting is the long-range strategy outlined nine years earlier as to how to achieve the vital point one, namely:

Destroy the fascist state and set up a democratic regime . . . It was, and still is, the fascist government which by its very nature blocked, and still blocks the road to a peaceful solution of Portugal's political problems, and obliges the revolutionary forces to deploy violence to destroy fascist violence.[2]

The only way of overthrowing the fascist dictatorship and setting up a provisional government is by a national uprising and a popular armed insurrection which, due to the militarist nature of the state, implies the participation and neutralisation of an important part of the armed forces.[3]

The victorious people's insurrection can take place only in a revolutionary situation in which the Democratic Movement, by its organisation, and by the disposition and determination of the masses taking part, creates the conditions for launching an armed assault against the government.[4]

Only mass struggle by the people can lead to a victorious people's insurrection. Organisation and struggle by our young people, and by the women, *as well as the maintenance of a strong revolutionary organisation within the armed forces*, are the essential aspects of the development of the people's struggle against the fascist dictatorship.[5]

---

2 [AN] Programme of the Portuguese Communist Party, third edition, Edições Avante, May 1974, 72.
3 [AN] Ibid.
4 [AN] Ibid., 73.
5 [AN] Programme of the Portuguese Communist Party, third edition, 74. My italics, W. B.

The unity of anti-fascist forces, the organisation of revolutionary forces, the intensification and generalisation of the mass struggle – all these create the conditions for a victorious national uprising, a people's armed insurrection, which will overthrow the fascist dictatorship.[6]

Through the struggle for the overthrow of the fascist dictatorship and the setting up of a provisional government, the Portuguese Communist Party will establish with other democratic and patriotic forces a common political programme. The Portuguese Communist Party will not pose as a condition of its participation in a provisional government the adoption of the party programme. It will participate in a provisional government as long as this fulfils its fundamental task of establishing democratic freedoms, and that of carrying out free elections to a constituent assembly, which will determine the organisation and form of a future democratic regime.[7]

Nine years later, the fascist regime was overthrown by the Armed Forces Movement on the basis of a political programme which the Communists and other anti-fascist organisations could support. A provisional government was set up in which communists and other anti-fascists could participate. It was pledged to create conditions for democratic elections to a constituent assembly. With seemingly nothing in their hands to start with, the Communist Party was in a position to take immediate advantage of developments which the leadership had foreseen with considerable accuracy. Leadership and members had obviously worked hard and efficiently to be in a position to take full advantage of the sort of situation created by the 25 April coup.

When I asked a senior communist cadre about the similarity of a number of points in the programme of the MFA and that of the Communist Party programme, he replied: 'The party much earlier, and the MFA much later, had separately made great efforts to discover the real aspirations of the people. As their starting point was the same – patriotism and determination to overthrow the fascist regime – it was natural that they arrived at the same sort of conclusions and that their respective programmes reflect this.'

---

6   [AN] Ibid., 75.
7   [AN] Ibid.

It is logical to assume that there were underground communist cadres, and others with anti-fascist convictions, who often came up with the 'most logical answers', as the artillery captain expressed it, when discussions started among the officers as to the nature of the war; in whose interests were they fighting in Africa. And related subjects. Even if there was no direct participation of the masses in the military side of the 25 April action, their immediate psycho-political support – such as massing outside the PIDE headquarters and the Caxias prison – represented elements of a people's uprising. That the PIDE recognised this is shown by the fact that they fired on the crowd milling around in front of their headquarters. Playing a conscious role in the monster May Day demonstration, with all the spontaneous outpouring of popular enthusiasm that went with it, were also political activists at work launching the idea of a People/MFA alliance. Among them, and probably in the forefront, were Communist Party militants, some released from prison only a few days earlier, others surfacing after years of clandestine existence. The PIDE and other repressive agencies of the dictatorship had never been able to uproot the disciplined Communist Party underground organisations.

Returning to the Tivoli Hotel, while the celebrators still flooded the streets on May Day, I had been surprised when a well-informed American correspondent, a specialist on Portugal, said: 'All this confirms what I have always suspected – that the Communist Party is by far the best-organised political force in this country.' Hard-working and perceptive as he was, he could have had no idea how correct he was.

From the 1930s onwards, the Communist Party had maintained organisations within the armed forces, separately at rank-and-file, non-commissioned officer, and officer level, in all three services, Army, Navy and Air Force. Sometimes, these were discovered and decapitated – but never uprooted.

One of the earliest organisations was in the Navy, traditionally considered the most radical of the three services. A veteran in pioneering this work was Manuel Guedes – sixty-four years old at the time of the April coup. A more typical 'sea dog' of any country would be difficult to find. Massive head, barrel-like chest, muscled, ruddy-faced, tough as any that sailed with Vasco da Gama and the other great Portuguese navigators three centuries earlier. Plus, twenty years in fascist prisons.

'I joined the Navy when I was seventeen – in 1927,' he explained. 'My mother died when I was five, so I was brought up in an orphanage, where at least I learned to read and write. You had to be literate to get into the Navy – not so with the Army. In the period of the Republic [1910–1926], the Navy had democratic traditions, progressive even. Navy personnel were always the most applauded at armed forces parades, so I felt proud to have been accepted.

'In 1931, something happened which upset a lot of us. There had been several uprisings in the armed forces against the military dictatorship, which took over in May 1926. A number of officers and men had been deported to Madeira, the Azores and Guinea. In mid-1931, these deportees in Madeira, together with the local garrison, staged an uprising. I was on the *Vasco da Gama*, the flagship of the fleet at that time. Forty-eight hours before the uprising, we had been anchored off Funchal [the port-capital of Madeira], and our officers had been contacted by the rebel leaders seeking support. But the rank-and-file sailors had not been contacted. We were suspicious as to what was going on. No sooner had we returned to Lisbon than we had to set out to Madeira again – this time to help quell the revolt.

'The sailors were unhappy about this. But the officers had told us nothing. We had a meeting and decided it was not our affair – we would just obey orders. The Navy helped put down the revolt. When we got back to Lisbon, the ordinary people judged us as reactionaries who had taken part in repression against our compatriots and comrades-in-arms. The rank-and-file felt very bad about this. Most of us had progressive ideas, but no organisation, no ideology. We were deeply hurt that people treated us as outcasts.' (This sensitivity of the Portuguese armed forces to public opinion is perhaps something special to a small country – with only two main ports and leave centres, Lisbon and Porto – where soldiers and sailors back on leave cannot avoid, even if they wanted to, contact with the broad public. The importance of the public attitude is something that emerges in any discussion with members of the armed forces. It lends added importance to the mass action after 25 April, which made the servicemen feel that they had won overwhelming public approbation.)

'In August 1931,' Manuel Guedes continued, 'while I was on shore leave, I was approached by the youth section of the Communist Party. "Were conditions not ripe to set up a Party organisation in the Navy?" I was asked. I said I thought they were. "Would I take on the job of starting it off?" By the time I rejoined my ship, I had agreed, and within a month, I had forty readers of *Avante* and a small, organised group. As the *Vasco da Gama* only held a crew of 200, this was a good start. The field was fertile, the seeds sprouted rapidly. According to naval regulations, sailors changed ships after three years, so the members of our first group were soon dispersed. At the beginning of 1932, my job was to link them all together so as not to lose any, and to get each of them to organise groups on their own ships.'

The organisation started by Manuel Guedes in the Portuguese Navy – almost certainly the first within the armed forces as a whole – has persisted to this day, despite lots of ups and downs. In February 1932, for instance, the entire leadership of the Communist Party's youth section ashore, which directed the activities of Guedes, was arrested. Contact was lost, and re-established only after six months.

I asked, 'What was the main point your organisation was trying to make at that time, and how?'

'There were three main opposition groups in those days,' he explained. 'Republicans,[8] Anarchists[9] and Communists. The point that united them was opposition to the fascist regime. Our organisation published a manifesto: "End Dictatorship", which appealed for unity of political action. The Anarchists and some of the Republicans were imbued with *golpismo* – the idea of a military putsch. Our line was that only by mass action could the dictatorship be overthrown, and a democratic regime set up. Salazar had taken over in July 1932, and we stepped up our propaganda for united front activity. The main thing was to organise and push a correct line.

'By this time, I was editor of *O Marinheiro Vermelho* [The Red Sailor], which became the biggest underground Party paper. By the time I was

---

8 [EN] The Portuguese Republican Party (Partido Republicano Português, or PRP), founded in 1876, operated as the principal political opposition during the final years of the Portuguese constitutional monarchy. The PRP advocated for the replacement of the monarchy with a republic. Following the assassination of King Carlos I and his heir, Prince Luís Filipe, in February 1908, a revolutionary coup d'état on 5 October 1910 established the Portuguese First Republic (1910–1926), a period marked by political fluctuation and instability.

9 [EN] Anarchism in Portugal dates back to the mid-1880s, with the emergence of the international organised labour movement and revolutionary unionism. Anarcho-syndicalism had an enduring influence on the Portuguese General Confederation of Labour (Confederação Geral do Trabalho, or CGT), founded in 1919. Anarchist political groups faced state suppression after 1896; the Estado Novo outlawed all anarchist activity after 1926, forcing the movement underground, limiting it to clandestine activities until the 'Captains' Coup' in April 1974.

first arrested in May 1933, we had 300 party members in the Navy and 700 regular readers of the paper. I published 1,000 copies, 300 for shore distribution and 700 among the fleet. The fleet fluctuated between twenty to thirty-five ships with 4,000 to 5,000 sailors, so over 10 per cent were taking our literature, which meant that many more were reading it. Whenever new ships were added, we managed to get some of our people transferred, so there was always a nucleus to set up a new organisation.'

I asked how he came to be arrested and what happened immediately after.

'It was an accident,' he replied. 'Above the restaurant where I ate when I was ashore, there was a printing shop. It was a legal, commercial shop – but it also printed our paper. While I was having a meal, I learned that a typesetter, a Party man, had been arrested at his home. I went upstairs to warn the others. The PIDE were already there. One of them had spotted me in the restaurant. "What are you doing here? First in the restaurant – now here." He demanded my identity card. "A sailor, eh? And this is where *The Red Sailor* is printed. Come along!" I said that I just happened to know the family of the young chap arrested and had dropped in to tell the others that he wouldn't be at work. "Come along!" I was arrested with some of the printers. These typographers were just honest people – ready to lend a hand where they could, but not politically organised. One of them broke down under torture and said that I was the *Marinheiro Vermelho* editor. So, they started to work on me.'

Pressed for details, he said: 'A PIDE torturer sums you up like a tailor. He looks at the size and shape of your body and knows how to cut the cloth. If you are larger, the torture is appropriately stronger. The death penalty was abolished at the end of the last century, so PIDE cannot legally kill you. A doctor is on hand with a stethoscope – not to protect the victim, but to tell the torturers that "he can take some more." The no-sleep torture had just been introduced when I was taken. After having been beaten up the whole of the first night, I was given the "statue treatment". You stand against a wall for hours, for days and nights on end.

'You lose count of time. A dropsy-type condition develops, all the body liquids descend into the extremities. Your stomach drops, your feet and hands swell up and become very painful. Every now and again, questions were put to me. I told them nothing.

'Then the no-sleep torture was applied. Two chairs in a room – usually no table. A microphone suspended from the ceiling between the two chairs. This is to record the victim's reactions. Guards are instructed to keep you awake but forbidden to speak to the prisoner. The microphone is also to monitor them. An inspector comes from time to time and sits on the chair opposite to put questions. If you start to doze off, a guard thumps you in the ribs, or stamps on your foot. If you fall to the floor, they march you round, punch you or lash you with steel-tipped whips.

'After about the third or fourth night without sleep, you start having hallucinations. Afterwards, it's difficult to separate what actually took place from the hallucinations.

'Once the guards put a small table between the chairs. One of them spun a coin on the table. After several days and nights of complete silence, the noise of that coin seemed deafening. When the spinning started to slow down, the walls seemed to be closing in on me. When it started to wobble, I felt on the edge of collapse. As it fell on its side, I did collapse. I was ordered to get up and walk. I tried but my legs failed me. The guards hauled me up and, with their arms under my armpits, they walked me round and round. Then the inspector came in with more questions.

'In my case, they really wanted information – they wanted me to admit that I was the editor of *Red Sailor*. In other cases, they already had the information they wanted. But the torture and questions continued. The aim was to destroy you politically and psychologically. They wanted to break you; to make you talk, because they knew that no one could be trusted again in the revolutionary movement once he had "talked". The law forbade physical execution of prisoners, but political execution was just as effective. That is why we communists steeled ourselves never to speak.

'When Álvaro Cunhal was arrested for the first time, in 1936, he had a key in his pocket. As they knew he was living clandestinely, the PIDE used every imaginable means to force him to disclose what house the key belonged to. He refused. When they finally gave up, Álvaro Cunhal said: "Now that you have finished, I can tell you the key is to my father's house. I could have told you at the beginning, but I wanted to prove to you that communists don't yield to torture." ' (The PIDE files, available after 25 April, were almost eulogies regarding Álvaro Cunhal's stoicism under the severest forms of torture.)

'After three months of interrogation, I was handed back to the Navy for trial. But, as I had admitted nothing, and the only evidence against me was that extracted from the typographer under torture, the Navy sentenced me to eighteen months. This was served out in the "brig" with other Navy men, so it was easy to re-establish contact and direct our party organisations from there.

'When I was released, I was placed in charge of all Party work in the Navy, including links between shore installations and the fleet. But I had to be based ashore. On the eve of May Day, 1935, I was arrested again, and this time we were dealt a very serious blow. A meeting had been set up between representatives of the Navy and some Republicans, to have a broad-based action to mark May Day. I was there to represent the Communist Party. But there had been a leak. The police swooped on us, and we were all arrested. The Navy representative broke under torture, and all the leading cadres at the headquarters of our front (the ORA or Revolutionary Navy Organisation[10]) and in the Party organisation were arrested. This led to the arrest of over 200 sailors from shore-based installations and a Navy training ship. Thirty of them were tried and sentenced. The Party comrade charged with Army affairs was also arrested. Although ours had been decapitated, cells in other fleet units were not affected and continued to function. Nor were the cells of officers and non-commissioned officers in the shore installations and training ship broken up. The Navy organisation continued to function, and *Red Sailor* continued to appear.'

I asked if he was subjected to the same type of interrogation under torture as the first time.

'No,' he replied. 'The no-sleep technique was dropped between 1935 and 1938, in favour of more direct forms of torture introduced by Gestapo instructors. But PIDE found the no-sleep torture more effective, and introduced it again in 1938. Also, from 1935 onwards, the educational level of PIDE agents was raised. Most of them had been almost illiterate, but as of 1935 the leadership started recruiting university dropouts, also Army personnel at the level of sergeants.

'When the interrogation started, I said: "You know me already. I know a lot of things but I'm not going to reveal them. I must warn you that if you start torturing me this time, you'll have to go through to the

---

10   [EN] In Portuguese, *Organização Revolucionária* da *Armada*.

end. I will resist and that means you'll have to kill me. But it won't do you any good, because you know I won't talk." The chief PIDE inspector pretended he knew everything about me anyway. I had been caught with a copy of *Red Sailor* in my pocket. But they did not torture me as before. There was a change in tactics.

'For forty-five days, I was held in complete isolation. Every time my family located the prison where I was held, I was transferred. It was as if I had been kidnapped – spirited away. No visits, no food parcels, no change of clothes. For my family, it was as if I were dead. It was made clear to me that the cat-and-mouse game would stop if I talked. Towards the end of that forty-five days, I was held in the Lisbon Aljube central prison, in what was known as a "drawer" – a cell about four feet wide and just six inches longer than my body, with a very low ceiling. No possibility of standing up or exercise. Through scratchings on the wall, I learned that there was a student in a neighbouring drawer who had been there for six months.

'Eventually, I was tried and sentenced to four years as a "member of an illegal organisation". Again, there was nothing firm against me, except for the copy of *Red Sailor* in my pocket.

'After being sentenced, in December 1935, I was put in a big cell at the Peniche fortress, together with the thirty other sailors. There was just room for the beds. We started editing another paper, *The Potemkin*. Using a dry sort of dough made from bits of bread, we rolled it smooth and then wrote on it by hand, to get an impression. We then inked over the bed and pressed the paper down on it. At the start we could only get seven or eight copies from one bedding, but gradually we worked up to twenty. We produced it monthly, writing about prison conditions and interrogation methods, so that comrades outside would know how to face up to the PIDE with honour.

'After a few months, I was handed over to the Navy for another trial – charged with plotting together with the Republicans. One of the latter had talked under torture and said that the reason I was with them when the arrests were made was that the Republicans were planning a putsch and wanted Communist Party support. I was delegated by the CP to discuss the matter. This was only partly true, as I was there to dissuade any putschist attempts. In any case, I was hauled up before a special military tribunal.

'At the first four sessions of the court, the lawyers argued that, since there had been a big amnesty for political prisoners to mark the tenth anniversary of the military dictatorship, the trial should be abandoned, and the prisoners freed. The fifth session was to be on the actual anniversary date, 28 May 1936. The fourteen of us were delivered to the court building as usual in police vans, which drove off after we got out. But the session had been cancelled because of the holiday. There were no guards outside. Relatives and friends who always gathered to get a glimpse of us going into court crowded around and said: "Now's the time. Beat it." So, instead of going up the steps into the court, we were completely enveloped by the crowd, scattering in small groups in all directions.

'We made a complete getaway. The Party sent me and another comrade off into Spain, where we arrived with a pistol each, but no identity documents. We were soon picked up and jailed for lack of identification and for carrying "lethal weapons".'

Before moving on to the next part of the Manuel Guedes saga – so typical of the life that many militants lived – there were some points to be clarified about the organisation of Communist Party cells within the armed forces.

'Was your work in the Navy typical of what went on in the other services?' I asked.

'Yes, but because of the progressive traditions in the Navy, Communist Party influence was stronger than in the other services.'

'Is it correct to speak of strong Communist Party infiltration into the armed services?'

'No,' he replied. 'Infiltration is definitely not the correct term. The Party never trained people especially for such work. Nor did it send cadres to penetrate the armed forces. But it also did not put obstacles in the way of Party members who chose the armed forces as their career. Among the naval officers, for instance, there were former students who were communists before they became officers. They remained communists and were linked up with an appropriate organisation. At whatever level they functioned, they continued their Party work. The same was true in the Army and the Air Force. Others joined the Party while on active service. But it was never a question of "planting" people inside the armed forces.

'Similarly in the Army. When young people were called up to serve their stretch of military service, those who were communists were put in touch with the Party organisation in the units to which they were assigned. They remained and worked as communists, just as they would at any other place of work to which they had been transferred. This was true for over forty years, until the conditions ripened for April 25. At various times, however, an important aspect of Party work was to insist on a mass line and to discourage the putschists plans of various individuals, which could only have ended in disaster.'

The fact that Communist Party strategy was based on the certainty that fascism could only be overthrown by violent means, and that this was only conceivable if there were participation in this overthrow by one part of the armed forces, and the neutralisation of another part, shows that their leadership and that of the Armed Forces Movement were thinking along parallel lines in the six months or so that preceded 25 April. Rank-and-file CP members could immediately recognise that what happened on that day was what they had been taught to expect would eventually happen, and for which they had presumably worked. The conclusions that the CP leadership had reached through Marxist analysis, the MFA leadership had reached through the hard school of practical experience and the gradual elimination of all other possible courses of action. It was this that made possible immediate and total communist support for the MFA.

That the MFA immediately produced a short-term programme which the CP could unreservedly support explains much of the identity of views between MFA and CP leaders during the various crises that followed the setting up of the first provisional government, all of which involved, in some degree or another, deviations from the programme. The CP recognised that the latter was one around which maximum anti-fascist unity could be built, at the same time laying down realistic ground rules on which the African wars could be ended, on the basis of decolonialisation and independence for the former colonies and territories.

If the People–MFA alliance could be cemented, then the MFA would have a substitute for a solid class base – even though it was a graft – the lack of which would otherwise be its greatest weakness.

6
Militants

Few who observed events in Portugal after the 25 April coup would dispute the vigour with which the Communist Party surfaced or the influence which it exerted over large sections of the population. Obviously, opinions differed as to whether this was good or bad. The Party was passionately denounced by some on the left as 'revisionist', 'bourgeois reformist', 'transitionalist', and other specifically Portuguese terms of ideological denigration. The Right kept quiet for a time – having no publishing outlet for its views. But the strength and vitality of the Communist Party was astonishing and undeniable – surprising even some of its leaders returning from exile. It was quickly established that, for better or for worse, the Communist Party had to be considered one of the constants of Portugal's political life, irrespective of how things evolved after the coup. Its capacity for survival had even been reluctantly admitted by a PIDE demoralised and frustrated by the failure of its efforts to track down and exterminate the party's underground leadership and infrastructure.

It was difficult, after long and deep discussions with people like José Magro, Pedro Soares, António Dias Lourenço, Manuel Guedes, and many others, not to be infected by their optimism that, having survived half a century of highly efficient and ruthless repression, the Communist Party could stand up to whatever might be thrown against it in the future. This confidence is partly born of the fact that those who came out of the prisons, who surfaced from years of clandestine work and exile, constitute a party of cadres tempered by survival and work under seemingly impossible conditions which demanded a rare capacity for sacrifice.

In listening to the experiences of some typical militants who survived and found time to talk to me, what was impressive was the human qualities needed to face up to a medieval type of ideological Inquisition, backed by a modern Gestapo–CIA ruthlessness and computerised efficiency. Those who fell into the clutches of the PIDE were up against a Torquemada equipped with more sophisticated methods of torture and instantly available files on the activities and thoughts of the physically and intellectually active part of the population.[1] To stand up to this required a more-than-ordinary quality of courage. But it is those who did stand up to it who now constitute a barrier against any forces which try to sweep back the tide set in motion on 25 April. The experiences of such people are of universal interest.

While Manuel Guedes, in Republican Spain, was claiming the status of a political refugee, Franco launched his counter-revolutionary coup. 'The place where we were being held quickly fell under Francoist control,' he explained. 'My comrade and I were sentenced to twenty-eight months in jail for "no means of identification and illegal possession of firearms". This sentence, in fact, saved our lives. The local fascists wanted to shoot us, and we were actually taken out and tied up to execution posts. But the prison director intervened, because our sentence was for imprisonment only. There were nearly thirty Spanish anti-fascists in the same jail. They were arrested because they had started carrying out land reform on their own initiative. The local fascists wanted summary trials and executions; the prison director was for proper bureaucratic legal procedures. The main reasoning of the fascists was that, if you were in jail, you must be a communist. All communists had to be shot. The courts were in permanent session. Spaniards were being taken out all the time. If someone came back with a thirty-year jail sentence, everyone congratulated him. Because, if he was freed and went back to an area under fascist control, he was shot just for having been in prison. Our prison turned out to be a sanctuary for over two years.

---

1 [EN] Burchett's allusion is to the infamous Dominican friar Tomás de Torquemada (1420–1498), the first Grand Inquisitor of the Spanish Inquisition, known for his brutal and fanatical religious persecutions.

'Later, the fascists demanded a new trial to prove that we had been carrying on political work on Spanish territory. But the Spanish political police had no evidence of this. They contacted PIDE, who sent an agent who recognised us. So, we were back where we started. PIDE wanted us in their custody, so they demanded extradition, and we were sent back. Eventually, we were handed over to the Navy again, because the Navy insisted that, unless PIDE had proof of the political activity of any of their personnel who had been arrested, they had to be returned to the Navy for trial. It was because of this that we had been taken before the previous military court from which we had escaped. This time we were lucky again, because our case came up before Rosa Coutinho, who gave us only eighteen months.[2] This was November 1938, so we were released in June 1940.

'In 1941, there was a reorganisation of the party which was of capital importance. It was a tough period, with the fascists advancing on all fronts. Franco had won in Spain. The Nazis had occupied most of Europe and were advancing on Stalingrad. Salazar felt strong enough to proclaim an amnesty. Quite a few good comrades were released. Despite the depressing news from all fronts, there was a hard core within the Party who believed in final victory. In that period when fascism was at its peak, the decision was taken to create a nucleus of professional revolutionaries, who would go underground to coordinate clandestine work among the masses. When I say "clandestine", it is to make the distinction from "illegal" work. All party work was obviously "illegal". But clandestine work meant a complete break with your normal life; it meant cutting off from your family, from your work, from the place where you lived. You became a full-time revolutionary with a tiny wage provided by the Party to take care of bare necessities. You might have to wear a disguise, to live with some trusted party member or sympathiser who would not know your real name – and would never ask questions.

'People who came into the ranks at that time, and volunteered for

---

2   [AN] António Alva Rosa Coutinho was later known as the 'Red Admiral' and became one of the seven original members of the Military Junta of National Salvation immediately after 25 April. He was one of the three members to be retained after the resignation of Spínola during the crisis of September 1974. Appointed to head a temporary military junta in Mozambique, he played a key role in negotiating that country's independence. [EN] Burchett was in error here; Rosa Coutinho negotiated the independence of Angola, not Mozambique.

such work, were those who truly believed in the victory over fascism, despite everything. For me, this came at the end of a long period during which I had been able to contribute nothing, so I concentrated all my energies on this new phase. It was a period during which our Party was isolated in every way. We had been expelled from the Comintern because of rightist deviations.[3] All the reorganisation was done by ourselves, without any contact with the outside. Through a nucleus of clandestine workers, we were able to direct mass activities, such as strike actions for better conditions, utilising the legal organisations permitted under fascism. It was because of this that our influence continued to grow, not only among the workers and peasants, but among the lower middle class, among intellectuals – and within the armed forces. We had doctors, engineers, economists, university professors, journalists and writers within our ranks, and through these we were able to exert considerable influence on the intellectuals.

'The leadership since 1941 has been logical, consistent and unwavering – unity has been maintained with surprisingly few ups and downs. We are now a party of experienced cadres who can be daunted by nothing.'

Manuel Guedes did not enter into the details of his work during the following ten years, apart from making it clear that he continued with his speciality of organising within the armed forces, and that, during that period, he was a member of the Communist Party's ruling secretariat. He was arrested again in May 1952, and sentenced to four years of imprisonment the following March as 'a leading member of the Communist Party'. Although he was due to be released in 1956 – the term of the prison sentence dating from the time of arrest – his period of detention was constantly prolonged as a 'measure of state security'.[4]

---

3   [EN] 'Comintern' refers to the Communist International, also known as the Third International, an organisation founded by Vladimir Lenin in 1919 to advocate and advance communism throughout the world. Led and controlled by the Communist Party of the Soviet Union, the Comintern organised seven World Congresses in Moscow between 1919 and 1935.

4   [AN] Under a decree adopted in 1949, by the simple recommendation of PIDE, imprisonment could be repeatedly extended, each time for a period from six months to three years. This was another way of getting around the fact that the Constitution did not provide for the death penalty. The sentences of leading revolutionaries were invariably prolonged under this measure and in many cases amounted, in fact, to life imprisonment. Salazar thus considered they were dead politically, if not physically. He was

He remained in prison until 1965, thus completing a total of twenty years.

How do people stand it and come out smiling? When I asked Manuel Guedes as a final question: 'How do you see things now?' he puffed out his powerful chest and said:

'The perspectives have never been better. There'll be rough sailing ahead – but considering the storms we've already battled through . . .' He smiled and left it at that. I had the feeling that this is probably the reply he would have given at almost any point in his forty-three years as an active militant.

While waiting in an anteroom for an interview with Álvaro Cunhal, I chatted with his secretary, Joaquim Fernando Duarte, a tall, lean young man who had learned of the 25 April coup via the tapped-out message along the water piping at Caxias prison. He recalled that, after his first arrest, while he was mournfully pondering his fate at the Peniche fortress, someone touched him on the shoulder. It was José Magro with his habitual smile: ' "Cheer up," he told me. "Don't be depressed. It's not so bad here. You'll get used to it after a while. You can have plenty of rest, and there's time to read and study. It's only the first few years that are tough." ' Duarte, who had also retained his sense of humour, recalled that when the journalists entered the Caxias prison on the 25th, a radio reporter thrust his microphone under the nose of one of the inmates: 'What's your name?' he asked. 'What,' roared the prisoner, 'you think you can get my name with such tricks?' It was a veteran revolutionary, José Carlos, arrested only a short time before, and tortured even up to the night of 25 April to get him to reveal his identity. Weakened by days and nights of no-sleep treatment, he thought the radio journalist was another PIDE inspector with a new tactic. Broadcast later over Lisbon radio, the exchange made a big impression. Later, it was incorporated into a gramophone record that recaptured the atmosphere of those historic days.

José Magro, regarding whom almost every political prisoner I talked to had some anecdote, as they all had been in one or another of the prisons in which he was held, is an unforgettable personality. I suspected

---

mistaken because, as the example of Guedes proved, the militants continued to operate from prison and when the wheel of history took an unexpected turn they surfaced as the best and most experienced political activists.

that the reason his mouth is fixed in an optimistic upturn at the corners is that, during his years of prison, he adopted this expression to confound his torturers and to cheer up newcomers like Duarte.

At our first meeting, I recalled how North Vietnam's prime minister, Pham Van Dong, had told me that, despite the terrible conditions on the 'Hell Island' of Poulo Condor – where he had spent six years – the prisoners had transformed it into what Pham Van Dong described as a 'higher school of political education'. Some of the finest cadres of the Vietnamese Revolution had passed through the 'school'. 'Was anything similar possible in the various prisons in which you were held?' I asked.

'Certainly,' he replied. 'But not only in formal political studies. In behaviour. In standing up to your enemies. The first serious test is when you are arrested. Although I was confident I would betray no secrets, I was curious to know if I could stand up to what lay ahead after my arrest. But I found it relatively easy to resist. When you have decided to do what is necessary – you can resist. The greatest form of torture – physical and mental – was the no-sleep form. I was beaten frequently right at the beginning, but I realised this was only the softening-up part. As I had been doing clandestine work, their main aim was to find out where I had lived. They failed.

'The next thing was to force me to name my comrades – and of what organisation I was a member. After several days of "no-sleep", the inspector thought the time was ripe to break me. "Tell me something worthwhile and you can go and sleep," he said. "Just tell me the house where you lived." I always remember my reply, because I had such a good feeling after I had said it. I must apologise to your wife [who had accompanied me for the interview] for repeating the exact words. "If there is one thing I cannot stand," I replied, "it is a shit. And I regard you as a shit." He ordered me back into the "no-sleep" room. I refused to move. I wanted a confrontation with the inspector there and then. But he called for the guards to drag me away – back into the no-sleep room.'

'How can one endure twenty-one years in prison and come out normal?'

'The frontiers of human endurance are greater than it first appears,' he said. 'And the possibilities that are there at the beginning increase day by day as part of the adaptability of the human organism. What seemed impossible yesterday can be achieved today without difficulties. Gradually you give yourself more time to surmount successive obstacles. This is part of a "logic of struggle" for which you develop certain laws. Consciousness strengthens day by day and brings into play all its potentialities and those of the body and mind.

'Of course, when I was arrested the first time, I could not foresee that I would spend altogether twenty-one years in prison. But, later on, at the end of ten or fifteen years, with all that I had stored up and understood in between ... It is not a question of becoming "hardened", as is often said. On the contrary. Year by year, I felt increasingly more sensitive to the sufferings of others than to my own. But a growing understanding of reality, of its relativity and dialectics, enabled me to overcome, one by one, the various problems that emerged.

'The first test was the interrogation. The second was the whole period of imprisonment. There were serious problems – family problems, sentimental problems, political problems. But I found that you can always go further today than you could yesterday. Twenty-one years in prison would have been impossible to contemplate at the beginning. At the end of fifteen years, it was possible.

'I was thirty years old when I was arrested the first time. I had a companion from whom I was separated for twenty-three years, with the exception of three days. Sometimes she was in prison while I was out. Or, either she or I was doing clandestine work, and we couldn't meet. Despite all this, she represented a great source of strength for me during all those years. And I for her. Now,' he said with a smile that was especially rich, 'we are enjoying our second honeymoon.'

I asked what he considered was the worst moment during all those years of prison and clandestine work. 'Did you never feel that you had sacrificed the best years of both your lives in vain?'

'I never lost hope,' he replied. 'But the worst moment was shortly before my second arrest. My wife had been arrested, and it was important for us that I should help her at the police station. But I couldn't. My sister, who was also a clandestine party worker, died at that time. Then my younger brother had a terrible accident – and was actually dying at the very moment my wife was arrested. My mother showed great fortitude – but it was too much. I was obliged to be alone with our youngest daughter. And it was then that the question was raised of my going into clandestinity.

'Of course, I didn't hesitate. But I had to abandon my family at that critical time. That was the most difficult moment of my life – although I was not in prison at that time.'

Our discussion was taking place in the offices of the Communist Party's central committee. At one moment, Aida Magro came in to remind José of an appointment later in the day. A proud, beautiful woman, with flashing black eyes and a fine carriage, it was easy to visualise the scorn with which she faced her captors and interrogators. They had been sweethearts from childhood and had shared the same political ideas, the same dangerous life of revolutionaries. José had joined the Communist Party in 1940, she two years later. One of her first political acts had been collecting cigarettes for sending to imprisoned militants. Another had been organising the 'Feminist Movement', which originally consisted of three persons: herself, her sister and the sister of José, working under the latter's guidance. They began by creating a small private lending library in Lisbon, which specialised at first in romance novels – which 'were eagerly devoured in those days'. In time, they began to introduce more political books into circulation, and extended their activities to Porto and other provincial cities.

First arrested in 1957, the year her husband was released after six years and a half. They managed to meet for three days before she was arrested – she served a three-year sentence at Caxias prison but continued to be held under the 'measures of state security' formula. She was still there when her husband was brought in again after his first thirty months of liberty.

'We then spent two and a half years in the same prison,' she recalled. 'He on the lower floor, I on the upper. But those sadists so arranged things that husband and wife could never meet. It was a struggle even to correspond. In the meantime, my husband and some other comrades were preparing to escape in Salazar's armoured car. Before the day came, he managed for the first time in two and a half years to visit me – it was a farewell visit, in fact.'

Seeing them together even for a moment, smiling at each other like young lovers, caused a particular tug at the heartstrings in reflecting on the sacrifices this magnificent couple had made for the cause in which they believed.

I asked José Magro about what is known as the 'armoured car escape'.

'It was the chauffeur who was the real hero,' he said. 'He was a political prisoner, too. We had an absolute rule to refuse to do any work or collaborate in any way with the prison authorities. But this comrade, who was a good mechanic and driver, showed great interest in the one armoured car that was kept in the prison courtyard.' (It was rumoured that this had been a personal gift from Hitler to Salazar, but José Magro was not sure it was the same vehicle.)

'He was always tinkering with the engine, paying no attention to the abuse and curses from the other prisoners. Gradually, he won the confidence of the prison authorities and became a driver. He received even worse abuse as a traitor and collaborator, and was held in complete contempt by everyone. This went on for about a year. Then, one day, when a group of us were in the courtyard, he was bent over the engine as we approached to curse him, as usual. He whispered: "Now! Jump aboard!" We had a quick look around. There were no guards. Within seconds we were aboard, he in the driver's seat charging for the main gate, which gave way – and there we were, speeding towards Lisbon. We were well away before the guards could react. We abandoned the vehicle in the outskirts and dispersed. That was in December 1961, and I immediately started clandestine work again in the Lisbon area.'

'My first time arrested I had served six and a half years, then out for two and a half years, and in again for two and a half years. I began to think there was perhaps some law of averages that decreed I should spend two and a half years in and two and a half years out. But the third time, I'd been out for only six months and was in for the following twelve years – until 25 April!'

I asked whether hopes for escape receded as the years went by, if one became reconciled to the permanency of prison life.

'The possibility of escape was always in the centre of our thoughts,' he replied. 'Either to escape ourselves, or to facilitate the escape of others. One of my most ambitious projects was to get out of the Peniche fortress. The cell in which I and some other comrades were placed was relatively close to the outer wall – or so it seemed in the brief glimpse we had before we were locked in. We calculated that a tunnel of about four or five metres should bring us to the wall. So, we started work. But even after five or six metres, we still had not reached the wall. Air became a problem as we continued, especially as we were using a kerosene lantern which ate up the oxygen. We decided to wire our tunnel for electricity. Wire was smuggled in, and we linked it up with the prison lighting system. When we switched it on the first time, the whole system blew out. If only we had been sufficiently advanced for an escape that night!

'The miracle was that the guards never did find out why the whole fortress had so suddenly blacked out. We managed to get the wiring right and could dispense with the kerosene lantern. The question of air remained a problem, however. We tried fanning by hand. That was no good. An ordinary fire-bellows was smuggled in. Still no good. At great risk of being discovered, a length of nylon tubing was smuggled in, wrapped around a visitor's waist. This led from the cell floor to where the digging was going on. It was great to get our nostrils on to the end of that tube.

'We continued on to about ten or eleven metres, but by that time – as we discovered later – we had a solid fourteen metres of earth and stone above us – not to mention a guard and his sentry-box atop that! We started to get earth fall-ins. Our tunnel would have to be lined. Half the valises and boxes in which the prisoners kept their belongings in the cells disappeared – the guards still suspecting nothing. They went into props and linings for our tunnel. Eventually we reached the outer wall and widened our tunnel there into the size of a small room – with a little shelf for a lamp. We had a silent celebration – and breathed more freely. All we had to do now was to make a hole through the wall. One more night's work and we would be out.

'We had a warning system – a string attached to the leg of whoever was digging. Two tugs of that cord and your heart started beating faster. You had to crawl backwards as fast as arms and legs could carry you to the cell, throw yourself on the bunk and pretend to be fast asleep when the guard appeared.

'On the night before our intended assault on the wall, the lookout man was spotted. It was my night off, but I was awakened and informed. I immediately tried to fob off the prison guard by telling him that a comrade was sick and one of us had been trying to attract his attention. But nobody came to check on the "sick" comrade, which was ominous. Next morning, nothing happened, so I went to see the chief guard with the same story – in reality, to smell out the situation. It was clear our cell was under observation. Impossible to continue the work. The following day, we were ordered out of the cell. The chief "anti-escape specialist" had arrived. Half an hour later, we saw the nylon tubing, the electric wiring, the remnants of cases and valises – the fruit of just one month's work – being removed. No good being downhearted. It had almost worked. The experience served for other, successful escapes – even if not for us,' he concluded with his fantastic smile.

The most dramatic and important escape from the Peniche fortress was that of Álvaro Cunhal, Pedro Soares, José Carlos and six others – communist leaders who had already served a total of seventy-seven years in Salazar's jails. Held in individual cells, each with heavy steel doors with complicated automatic locking mechanisms in a specially built maximum security annexe of Peniche, they were entrusted to guards chosen for their ferocity. The only possibility for communication with each other was during the closely watched recreation period. 'But in all the prisons we had developed methods of micro-communications,' explained Manuel Guedes, 'even by tapping one's teeth with the fingernails.' On the night of 3 January 1960, together with one of their guards, they all escaped.[5] Through patient political work, one of the guards was won over. On the escape night, the chief guard was chloroformed, 'the dose carefully calculated not to kill', as one of those who helped plan the escape related, adding: 'We even got José Alves – the friendly guard – to cover him with an overcoat after he passed out. It was very cold.'

Guard Alves wore an outsize overcoat himself that night, in order to escort each prisoner separately – concealed under the coat – on what sentries would have assumed was his ordinary, measured beat from the prison walls to a watchtower at a corner of the massive perimeter walls of the fortress. Here, each escapee in turn shinned down a knotted rope to a lower level, then raced across to a much lower outer wall where friendly hands awaited to help him down into the street – and away.

'After everyone had been escorted to the main wall,' continued my informant, 'José Alves went back and stacked his rifle in the rack before joining up with the others. A few passers-by in the small hours of the morning were agape with astonishment when they saw what was going on. But nobody tipped off the guards. For the ordinary people, political prisoners were heroes who had sacrificed their liberty to try to rid the country of fascism. This feeling was especially widespread among the Peniche fishermen. The action was 100 per cent successful.' (José Alves later wrote an open letter to his National Republican Guards unit,

---

5 [AN] This feat is reminiscent of the escape of Prince Souphanouvong and fifteen other leaders of the Pathet Lao, together with ten of their guards – all dressed in MP uniforms – from a closely guarded Vientiane prison in Laos, the same year – 23 May 1960, to be exact. It was described in detail by the author in *This Furtive War* (New York: International Publishers, 1963).

urging his former colleagues to take similar action when the opportunity arose!)

The escape of the secretary-general and eight of the most feared leaders of the Communist Party obviously threw the Salazar regime into a panic. The head of PIDE (Captain Neves Graça) was sacked, for a start. The whole repressive machinery was mobilised as never before. A vast manhunt was launched throughout the country with house-to-house searches, roadblocks, and unprecedented controls at frontier-crossing points, seaports and airports. But the outside planning had been as meticulous as that on the inside. It was a clean getaway. For some, like Álvaro Cunhal and Pedro Soares, it was the beginning of fourteen years of exile; for others, a return to clandestine activity to lead the struggle from inside the country. It is impossible to imagine that at least some of the escapees would not have been recaptured within the first few days or weeks, had it not been for popular sympathy with the fugitives. The rewards for betrayal were high; the penalty for concealing knowledge of the whereabouts of the escapees, also – but still higher was the hatred for the regime, and the esteem for those who ran such risks, and paid such prices to oppose it. At least, that was the explanation from one of those who helped organise the escape.

The life of the militant was total devotion to the cause; total sacrifice of everything that life meant – home, family, vocation – everything except the cause itself. The rewards were torture, prison, clandestine existence, ruined health, being on the run between the 'in' and the 'out' periods. But always fighting, organising, not only looking for chinks in the enemy's armour, but creating them – parrying and thrusting at an enemy enormously superior in all the material means of combat. It also meant cheering up the demoralised, even when their own situation was at its blackest.

One of my discussions with Álvaro Cunhal took place the day after PIDE agents in Lisbon's Aljube prison had staged a demonstration – in the name of 'human rights' – for better conditions, and their speedy release. The day before that demonstration, I had watched sleek, suntanned – and very arrogant – ex-PIDE agents playing volleyball in a courtyard of the Peniche fortress, receiving unsupervised visits and non-controlled parcels from their families. I asked Álvaro Cunhal what he thought of all this. He is an impressive, alert person with a lean, intelligent face, dominated by bushy dark eyebrows crowned with a shock of white hair. His deep-set eyes have the same burning quality that first impressed me with Vietnam's Pham Van Dong. Also, the same sudden flash of a smile that completely transforms an otherwise sombre face.

Figure 6.1. Álvaro Cunhal, leader of the Portuguese Communist Party (PCP) with PCP Banner, speaking at a political rally in Lisbon, May 1974. (Photo by Fernando Ricardo)

He laughed at my question. 'I spent eight years in the Aljube prison, seven of them in total isolation. During the first one and a half years, I had no books, no ink or paper, no visits, no facilities whatsoever. Later, I was able to have a few books and writing materials, and my lawyer father could visit me for a few minutes each week. [It was during this latter period that Cunhal wrote a classic work on the agrarian question in Portugal which was later smuggled out and published in Brazil.[6]] The arrogance of the PIDE agents and their privileged treatment is only because they have protection from high up in the government.'[7]

---

6 [EN] Álvaro Cunhal, *A questão agrária em Portugal* (Rio de Janeiro: Civilização Brasileira, 1968). In Cunhal's portrait of anachronistic property holding, wealth distribution and unfair labour practices in rural Portugal, he describes what can be done to eliminate persistent poverty.

7 [AN] This was during the period when Spínola was still president, and a counter-revolutionary coup was being prepared.

'What do you count the worst moment in your own imprisonment?' I asked.

He laughed again. 'I never counted the worst moments. I think ... No. I can't recall anything that could be considered a "worst moment". I never, ever lost hope in our cause. The question of personal life – remaining alive – is not important. When you are engaged in a fight, in struggle and action, you expect victory for your cause. It's that which counts; I always knew we would win.'

'Was there any possibility of political work inside the various prisons?'

'It depended on the time and place. There were places where we were forty or fifty together. Then we could do something – but always clandestinely. We used general education courses to cover political courses. We tried the whole time to educate cadres. The great triumph of our party over fascism is that, even under the very worst conditions, we were able to find ways and means of maintaining our contacts with the masses, and to lead them in the various aspects of the anti-fascist struggle. We never ceased fighting alongside the masses. Continuous struggle was the very life of the Party. We lived by breathing in the aspirations of the masses. We had a corps of militants completely devoted to the masses and to the Party, who never shrank from any sacrifice.'

7
Counterattacks 1 and 2

In the October 1973 elections, the Acção Nacional Popular (Popular National Action) party won all 150 seats, just as its predecessor the União Nacional (National Union) party had won all 130 seats in the 1969 elections. It was not surprising, in view of the fact that all 150 candidates in the 1973 elections were unopposed, while electoral opposition in 1969 had proved a farce. In 1969, the legal opposition was grouped in two factions, the CDE (Democratic Electoral Commission), headed by a progressive Catholic economist, Professor Pereira de Moura,[1] and the CEUD (United Democratic Electoral Commission) headed by Dr Mário Soares.[2] Dr Soares had returned from imprisonment on the island of São Tomé the previous year, having been in and out of jail about a dozen times from May 1961 onwards, when he had signed a manifesto protesting the terms under which elections were to

---

1 [EN] Francisco José da Cruz Pereira de Moura (1925–1998), a respected economist and university professor who opposed the authoritarian Estado Novo regime. In 1969 he co-founded the Comissão Democrática Eleitoral (CDE) to dispute election results, which gave rise to the Movimento Democrático Português (MDP), one of the most important opposition organisations in Portugal prior to 25 April 1974.

2 [EN] The CEUD (Comissão Eleitoral de Unidade Democrática) might best be translated as 'Democratic Unity Electoral Commission'. A democratic, socialist, political-opposition organisation founded in 1969, it sought to dispute candidates of the Estado Novo regime in National Assembly elections. Mário Soares was a candidate in the CEUD lists. Persecuted by the state security police (PIDE), the CEUD was dissolved in 1970, and Soares went into exile in France.

be held in November of that year. The 1969 programme of the CEUD was considered somewhat more conservative than that of the CDE.

Violence was used against both the CDE and the CEUD in the 1969 campaign, to the point that a delegation from the Socialist International was expelled from Portugal for having referred to 'intolerable interference' in the electoral campaign by fascist strong-arm groups. Both groupings were ordered to disband following the elections. Instead, they fused into a single grouping, the CDE, this having polled three times as many votes as the CEUD in the few places where the counting of votes was more or less controlled.[3]

In the 1973 elections, the CDE stood as a single opposition body with the support of communists, socialists, progressive Catholics and other anti-fascist forces. There were no illusions about making any inroads into the monopoly of the Acção Nacional Popular party, but electioneering provided a legal tribune to put an opposition viewpoint.

More importantly, as things turned out, it provided a cover for setting up organisations in even the remotest corners of the country – not to mention solid bastions in the urban centres. A tiny flag of opposition was planted, more or less legally, everywhere. The CDE became a symbol of resistance. Due to the arrest of candidates and police brutality in breaking up their meetings – even press conferences – the sixty-six CDE candidates announced their withdrawal just three days before election day. They had had their say, which was what counted. Theoretically, withdrawal at such a late date was 'illegal'; the CDE was again ordered to disband and dismantle its headquarters, bases and offices. The ban was defied, and the organisations were still functioning on 25 April 1974! About that time, however, the name was changed to MDP (Portuguese Democratic Movement), a name which had spontaneously developed in some of the urban centres during the latter part of the 1973 election campaign. (In many of the rural areas, for months after the coup, one found a hyphenated version, CDE-MDP, to stress the respectable parentage of the latter half.)

The right could afford to regard with derision the CDE in 1969 and 1973 – but not after 25 April 1974. For almost half a century, the

---

3   [EN] Burchett's original sentence was confusing, so in the published Portuguese text the passage was altered to clarify that, while both the CDE and the CEUD were ordered to disband, the CDE did not comply. See page 126 in the 1975 Seara Nova Portuguese edition.

establishment party never felt the necessity, still less the urge, to go to the country, explain its policies, fight for votes, or indulge in any of the demagogic acrobatics that right-wing parties are obliged to perform in non-fascist countries. It never felt the need to have a popular base, popular support. The União Nacional and later the Acção Nacional Popular had the repressive machinery of the state behind them. The PIDE, the Portuguese Legion, the GNR and other paramilitary organisations were at their beck and call. If they wanted to smash up opposition political meetings in that later period, when an opposition movement was officially tolerated, there was the youth organisation (the Mocidade Portuguesa) modelled on the Hitler Jugend to provide the truncheon gangs. The dissolution of the Acção Nacional Popular brought the moment of truth – the former establishment was politically naked. And, what with the dissolution of the PIDE, the Portuguese Legion and the fascist youth organisations, and the 'treachery' of the armed forces, it was disarmed, as well. At least as far as immediate muscle-power was concerned. The CDE-MDP suddenly appeared very big indeed. To survive, it had had to win popular support and institutionalise that support.

'The ruling class is now all belly – no head, arms or legs,' was how one trade union militant expressed it, as we stood together and watched the May Day legions march by. 'We've got them on the run, and they can't even run,' he added, recalling the old days, when people like him were clubbed over the head for the slightest attempt at remembering that May Day even existed. It was an understandable oversimplification. While the props had been knocked out from under the political and repressive half of the fascist regime – without even a press left to defend it – the economic half remained intact. That half immediately launched a counterattack, proving that a head was also still there.

Literally within twenty-four hours of the 25 April coup, the CUF (Companhia União Fabril – United Manufacturing Company), the greatest single monopoly, not only in Portugal but on the Iberian Peninsula, without any strikes or threats of strikes, proposed wage increases which the management had refused even to discuss in January. CUF owns shipbuilding and repair yards, shipping lines, and steel, chemical, cement and textile plants. One of the main pillars of this industrial and trading giant is the Totta and Azores Bank, which it entirely owns. Starting over a century ago by manufacturing soap from coconut oils from the African colonies, then processing tobacco, CUF built up its economic empire from the profits of colonial enterprises, consolidating and expanding under the protection of the fascist regime. It had steadily collected about 80 per cent of the government's export promotion fund.

CUF's offer of a significant pay hike started a pattern of 'solicitude' by other big monopolies – including the multinationals. ITT, for instance, notorious for its role in Chile, having earlier refused to honour a work contract providing for a pay rise from 2,800 to 4,000 escudos per month, offered a minimum wage of 10,000 escudos a few days after 25 April![4]

That higher wages were long overdue was obvious, but the sudden change of heart by the big monopolies and multinationals was suspect. The events of 25 April had, in fact, caught Portugal in a wave of strike actions for higher wages. That of the Peniche sardine-fishermen, mentioned earlier, was only one of many. The Communist Party had also published a resolution on 26 April, calling for demonstrations and strikes to secure wage increases and better working conditions.

Within a week or two, there were three types of action on the wages front. First, offers of big pay increases by some of the monopolies, backed by new-born 'agitators' known by veteran militants to be company stooges. Second, classic strikes, with or without trade union leadership, backing up the moderate demand for doubling the basic minimum wage. Third, anarchic-type strikes demanding very big wage increases, and the take-over of any enterprises which refused. Parallel with these actions was a reorganisation of the trade union movement, which included a purge of PIDE agents and company stooges, and a complete restructuration.

Those engaged in the restructuration process did not have the benefit of a US Congressional report pinpointing the CIA as organising and financing the wave of strikes that preceded the anti-Allende coup in

---

4 [EN] The official monetary unit of Portugal throughout most of the twentieth century was the escudo (in English, escutcheon, or shield), recognised internationally as a strong and stable currency during most of the Estado Novo period. During the 1960s and early 1970s, journeyman labourers earned very low wages, as little as sixty escudos per day (less than US$2.50) for adult male agricultural workers. Women and children performing similar work typically earned much less.

Chile.[5] But, in a discussion I had with Canais Rocha,[6] a veteran workers' leader, repeatedly arrested and ferociously tortured under the old regime, and two of his main aides, Álvaro Rana and Costa Pereira, at the newly constituted Southern Trade Union Federation headquarters,[7] they made the point that it was a race between the unions to bring the situation under control and the monopolies to create the sort of economic chaos which provided the climate for the coup in Chile. Many honest and militant workers, and some of their trusted leaders, were involved in the strike wave.

The monopolies had nothing to lose. Enormously strong financially, and with still stronger foreign backing, but weak politically, economic sabotage was their only immediately available weapon. By suddenly spearheading the drive for higher wages, they would force the small and medium enterprises out of business and accelerate the ever-greater concentration of power in the hands of the few big concerns. The whole development of CUF and the second biggest monopoly – Champalimaud – had been a process of weakening, then absorbing, their smaller competitors. By offering wages three to four times higher than those they previously paid, they sought to set off a chain reaction that would create economic and social conditions favourable for a countercoup – which seems to have been envisaged at a very early stage. (Throughout Portuguese modern history, all political changes have been by coups and countercoups.) By appearing as the champion of high wages, the monopolies would also discredit the Communist Party, which had accepted to lead the Ministry of Labour in the provisional government. It was a "heads I win, tails you lose" situation, as far as the monopolies were concerned.

After presenting that general framework, Canais Rocha said: 'Corrupt elements among the workers are also being used as provocateurs

---

5   [EN] On 11 September 1973, Chilean General Augusto Pinochet rose to power in an anti-Marxist military coup d'état supported by the United States Central Intelligence Agency, which overthrew the democratically elected 'Popular Unity' government of President Salvador Allende, a democratic socialist politician.

6   [EN] Francisco Canais Rocha (1930–2014), carpenter, historian and anti-Salazar labour union organiser in the Santarém region. Twice arrested by the PIDE, first in 1952, and imprisoned from 1968 to 1973. After 25 April 1974 he became the first general secretary and national coordinator of the Confederação Geral dos Trabalhadores Portugueses (General Confederation of Portuguese Workers), the largest trade union federation in Portugal.

7   [AN] There was also a Northern Trade Union Federation.

– trying to divert workers from urgent organisational tasks to start a generalised wave of wage claims, which would cause mass unemployment in the small and medium enterprises where conditions at this time do not permit the payment of such wages. Objectively, this accelerates the process of the monopolies taking them over. The result would be mass unemployment, and the monopolies would again have big reserves of cheap labour available. They would then cut wages back to a lower level than when we started. We have to watch the strategy of the monopolies very closely and consolidate our own gains so as to go faster later on.'

The Ministry of Labour at the time was pushing for a minimum monthly wage of 3,300 escudos. 'Is that not a bit low?' I asked.

'It will double the wages of more than half the workers,' said Álvaro Rana, 'and it will mean equal pay for women workers who have been the most exploited till now. It will apply especially to that half of the working class employed in industry and the service branches. When the ultra-leftists called for a minimum wage of 6,000 escudos, the big monopolies got their agents to take up the cry. They could afford to pay such wages for a time, smash the small and medium enterprises, and then really turn on the workers.' (Later, many of the multinational enterprises, with those owned by the United States in the lead, were to close down and throw their workers onto the streets, on the pretext that having to pay the minimum wage of 3,300 escudos had made their businesses 'non-competitive'. Cheaper labour was available in such places as South Korea, Taiwan, Singapore, *et cetera*.)

Strikes had broken out in the transport system, in the bakeries, and in other areas which could easiest provoke mass discontent, by hitting the people in their stomachs and legs.

'These were unusual types of strikes,' said Canais Rocha. 'We consider strike action is resorted to only after other methods of obtaining satisfaction are exhausted; only after having taken into account the short-term, medium and long-term interests of the workers, within the framework of the general political situation. And only after careful preparation. That includes the preparation of public opinion. But many of these strikes were taking place without even claims being staked in advance, let alone negotiations or preparation of public opinion.'

Although the trade union leaders did not labour the point, it was clear that when they spoke of taking into account the 'framework of the general political situation' in considering strike action, they meant that the role of the politically conscious section of the working class and that of the monopolies had suddenly been reversed. From their underground command posts in the past, the Communist Party had waged 'multiple warhead' offensives against the fascist regime. They constantly attacked on the economic and social fronts to satisfy real and pressing demands of the working class in the towns, of the agricultural labourers, and of the small peasants in the countryside. Operating through such legal structures as existed within the 'corporative state', through semi-legal activities or illegal strike actions, the total amounted to a political assault against the regime itself. But, with that regime overthrown and with the Communist Party in the new government, even heading the key Ministry of Labour, strategy and tactics obviously had to be changed. Basic economic demands of the workers had to be satisfied, but not at the risk of endangering the political advantage of being part of the regime. It was this switch of strategy and tactics that the ultra-left was unable to accept. Advantage, they reasoned, should have been taken of the overthrow of the regime to launch an assault against Portuguese capitalist society in general. Any means to achieve this were justifiable, including – indeed especially – economic chaos.[8]

Just as the main hope of the anti-fascist forces – excluding the ultra-left – was to maintain and consolidate their alliance with the armed forces, so the main hope of the rightist, pro-fascist forces was to smash that alliance at all costs. The fears of the veteran trade union militants, even if not precisely formulated in our discussion, was that provocateurs, and even misled enthusiasts, would push the strike situation to a point at which the armed forces would intervene 'to restore law and order', with disastrous consequences for the People–Armed Forces Movement alliance. Two well-known former PIDE spies within the labour movement had been picked up for distributing super-militant

---

8 [EN] In his typescript final draft, Burchett provided a footnote number on this page but no footnote text, apparently to alert his translator and publisher. There is a difference here between the formatting of the original English version, where quoted interview passages are woven into the text between Burchett's questions, and the Portuguese version, where the same interview material is given in an unbroken passage – seemingly a verbatim transcription of a conversation with Canais Rocha. The text here has been reproduced as Burchett originally wrote it; he alludes to the themes in that interview but articulated the topics in his own words. There is no substantive difference between the two versions.

appeals to continue the strike of Metro workers, that had been launched without any prior claims or negotiations.[9]

It was in these circumstances that the trade unions – obviously supported by the Communist Party – called a most unusual type of workers' demonstration on 1 June. The main theme was: 'Down with Strikes for Strikes' Sake'. Called at a few hours' notice, about 10,000 workers, marching under the banners of their freshly purged trade unions, turned out for a rally which ended at the Ministry of Labour. About halfway along the two-mile route, they were joined by groups of soldiers and Marines. Interspersed with Communist Party banners and national flags were slogans such as 'Watch Out for Class Enemies', 'Railway Workers Condemn Provocateurs and Irresponsible Adventurers', 'Fascism Overthrown but Capitalism Still with Us'.

In a speech in front of the Labour Ministry, where the marchers were joined by several thousand more demonstrators, Canais Rocha claimed that the workers 'repudiated the nefarious activities of enemies of the working class and intended to neutralise or strangle at birth such manoeuvres. The workers were unequivocally demonstrating their alliance with the Armed Forces Movement.' The communist minister of labour, Avelino Gonçalves, congratulated the trade unions for having 'traced with exemplary maturity a realistic line of trade union action, repudiating opportunism and adventurism, which would lead to economic chaos and divisions among the democratic forces'.

To what extent the demonstrators reflected real feeling among the organised workers was very difficult for an outsider to know. But the 1 June demonstration did mark the end of that first phase of economic counter-offensive. The more dangerous type of strike action – that capable of producing armed clashes – faded away. The Metro and bread strikes represented a turning point, because most workers seem to have recognised in these the truth of what some of their most tried and trusted leaders had been saying – that is, that the strike weapon had been taken over by their class enemies and transformed into the first major counter-offensive against the new regime.

'Managers who, a few months ago, would have called in the PIDE or the gendarmes at the mere threat of a strike,' said Pedro Soares, summing

---

9   [EN] Burchett refers here to the Lisbon public transport subway train system, the Metropolitano.

up the Communist Party viewpoint at that time, 'were all of a sudden offering big pay hikes through their agents. The working class saw through this very quickly, showing great political maturity. They warned the trade unions and action was taken in time.'[10] (While we were talking, a secretary brought in a note that had just arrived from a worker in one of the CUF companies, reporting another unsolicited offer to treble the minimum wage announced by the government a few days earlier.)

'The aim is very clear,' Soares commented. 'The monopolies, which were the origin, the foundation, and main pillar of the fascist regime, want to continue their domination. They will continue to try to disrupt the economy and the political and social life of our country to preserve their economic positions and return to political power, so as to slow down the process of democratisation. We remain very vigilant. We think that the policy of the provisional government should be to enable the truly democratic forces to assert themselves and to reinforce their political activity. This includes democratisation of the administration and respect for the programme of the Armed Forces Movement. We think also that the provisional government must adopt a law to protect the small and medium interests in industry, commerce and agriculture – to give them financial help to prevent their elimination by the monopolies.

'As long as the monopolies exist, especially so long as they are dominated by foreign capital, the danger of counter-revolution will exist. We have overcome the first counterattack, but we must prepare for a second and a third, and still more.'

The second counterattack was not long delayed. To understand how it came about, one has to understand also that the members of the Armed Forces Movement correctly considered themselves as politically immature, inexperienced in government and administration. Having done their main job of overthrowing the fascist regime, they felt they should hand over power to a civilian government of national unity, supervised from on top by the military Junta of National Salvation, where their interests would also be represented. They were conscious of

---

10 [EN] As above in footnote 8, here Burchett provided a footnote number but no text. It is possible that he intended to comment about Pedro Soares (1915–1975), a political activist since 1931, imprisoned for twelve years by the Estado Novo, and a member of the Portuguese Communist Party's Central Committee.

the need to retain a watchdog role. As stipulated in their programme, a civilian provisional government was set up within three weeks. Heading it was sixty-nine-year-old Professor Palma Carlos, a liberal lawyer who had been active in defending certain categories of political prisoners, but who was no friend of the left. Representing the unity of the anti-fascist former opposition were three ministers without portfolio: Francisco Pereira de Moura (Portuguese Democratic Movement); Francisco de Sá Carneiro (Popular Democratic Movement, founded after 25 April); and Álvaro Cunhal.[11] The Socialist Party was represented at the top by Dr Mário Soares as foreign minister.

Cabinet decisions had to be approved by a twenty-one-member state council, comprised of the seven-member Military Junta, seven members of the Armed Forces Movement, and seven civilians 'of recognised merit' acceptable to the MFA, Junta and government. Apart from their representation in the state council, the captains also had their people in many other positions – especially as secretaries to ministers – where they could best perform their role of 'watchdogs'. In general, however, it looked as if the leaders of the Armed Forces Movement were quite content to see the civilians take over.

Within a few weeks of the installation of the provisional government, it was an open secret that there were dissensions over economic policies and, above all, over the pace and nature of decolonisation. The captains got somewhat of a shock on 7 June, when Spínola made a speech in Lisbon which sounded suspiciously like an obituary to their Armed Forces Movement. It was like one of those post-war 'gallant ally' speeches by certain Western leaders, telling the Soviet Union that, now the war was over, they could pack up and go home from Germany and elsewhere.

'It is impossible to exaggerate the debt of gratitude the country owes to those valiant workers in the movement of 25 April,' said Spínola, continuing: 'Now when its task is ended, let me express the appreciation of the nation to all those who acted, beyond pressures or conformism, in

---

11 [EN] Francisco Manuel Lumbrales de Sá Carneiro (1934–1980), an attorney and politician, was elected to the Portuguese National Assembly in 1969. In early May 1974, he co-founded and became the first leader of the Partido Popular Democrático (Popular Democratic Party, soon thereafter known as the centre-right Social Democratic Party, or PSD). During 1974, he was named a minister without portfolio in two provisional governments. Later, in 1980, he would serve eleven months as prime minister of Portugal, until his death in a plane crash.

the higher interests of the community.' The captains were far from feeling that their 'task was ended', and this explains the rather blunt words – reported in an earlier chapter – that the newly chosen prime minister addressed directly to Spínola on the following 18 July.

Figure 7.1. Mário Soares, leader of the Portuguese Socialist Party (PS) with PS flags and banner, speaking at a political rally in Lisbon, May 1974. (Photo by Fernando Ricardo)

On 5 July, Premier Palma Carlos had issued an ultimatum to the state council.[12] Either he must be granted far wider powers, or he would resign. The 'wider powers' included authority to hold presidential elections within three months, to confirm Spínola as the head of a presidential-type regime; postponement of the elections scheduled by 31 March 1975, to November 1976; authority for the prime minister to choose his cabinet without reference to the president. At an all-night session of the State Council on 8–9 July, only three of the twenty-one members supported Palma Carlos. The only point ceded was that, in future, a prime minister could name his cabinet without presidential veto. Palma Carlos was allowed to resign. Three of his supporters within the cabinet also resigned, including a Spínola protégé, Lieutenant Colonel Firmino Miguel, the defence minister.

On 11 July, most of Lisbon's morning and evening papers announced that the president had chosen Firmino Miguel as premier. There were photographs, interviews and biographical sketches of the prime minister-elect. But, on 12 July, it was announced that the new prime minister was the fifty-three-year-old Colonel Vasco dos Santos Gonçalves. It was then learned that Firmino Miguel – reappointed as defence minister in the new cabinet – had not been associated with the Armed Forces Movement, whereas Colonel Gonçalves had lent it his full support from the moment he was informed of its existence and aims. Rather striking evidence that the Armed Forces Movement by no means regarded its 'task as ended'! Moreover, the captains, obviously having decided that the civilians had let them down, strongly reinforced their position within the government. Majors Melo Antunes and Vítor Alves, both known for their progressive views, became ministers without portfolio. Lieutenant Colonel Manuel da Costa Braz became minister of the interior, Captain José da Costa Martins became minister of labour, and Major José Sanches Osório, minister of social communications (information minister). Seven cabinet posts out of the seventeen were held by officers – not all of them, however, members of the Armed Forces Movement. Contrary to many predictions of foreign correspondents, Álvaro Cunhal remained a minister without portfolio.

---

12 [EN] Adelino da Palma Carlos (1905–1992), an attorney, politician and prominent long-time opponent of the Estado Novo. He was chief officer of the Portuguese Bar Association from 1951 to 1956.

The Armed Forces Movement reinforced its position in a much more decisive way than by the increase of military officers in the cabinet. At the same time as their nominee – Vasco Gonçalves – was named prime minister, the formation of a new 'Continental Operational Command' (COPCON) was announced, charged with 'coordinating security operations in metropolitan Portugal' and – among other things – with guaranteeing the execution of the programme of the Armed Forces Movement.[13] The head of COPCON was General Costa Gomes and its deputy was Otelo Saraiva de Carvalho, promoted to brigadier general for the occasion. A 'captain' who masterminded the military side of the 25 April coup, he was also and concurrently named military governor of the Lisbon area. COPCON was in fact an 'anti-coup' command, the captains having reacted very seriously and realistically to the attempt of the first provisional government to tamper with their programme.

Symptomatic of the atmosphere were some sharp words exchanged in front of the TV cameras when the former military governor of Lisbon, Brigadier Jaime Silvério Marques, in handing over his command, made some condescending remarks about the rapid promotion of younger officers.[14] The riposte of Otelo de Carvalho, straight from the shoulder as is his custom, was that he did not notice too many older officers around when the younger ones staked their lives and careers on 25 April. This prompted Brigadier Marques to break protocol by making a second speech, in which he explained that he had always been an anti-fascist!

Speaking to journalists after the ceremony, Brigadier Otelo de Carvalho made it very clear that COPCON was a command 'of operational control at the national level, and at the same time a command of intervention ready to employ force if necessary to ensure the fulfilment

---

13 [EN] COPCON, the acronym for Comando Operacional do Continente (Operational Command of the Continent), the military central command for continental Portugal created on 8 July 1974 by president António de Spínola and the Armed Forces Movement. Its chief purpose was to maintain domestic political order and protect the democratic process initiated by the Carnation Revolution. Led by Otelo Saraiva de Carvalho until September 1975, COPCON was dissolved following the events of 25 November 1975.

14 [EN] Jaime Silvério Marques (1915–1986), brigadier general and colonial administrator who, as governor of Macau (1959–62), developed the territory as a gambling centre. Four days after the 25 April coup, he was appointed to the Armed Forces Movement's Junta of National Salvation, a post he held until 30 September 1974.

of the MFA programme'. He compared COPCON's functions in the military operational field with that of the MFA's coordinating committee in the political field.

The second, political, counterattack thus resulted in a considerable strengthening of the Armed Forces Movement, and this was to prove decisive in the third, and much more serious, counterattack some two months later.

Figure 7.2. Brigadier General Otelo de Carvalho (right), head of COPCON and principal architect of the tactical plan for the MFA 25 April coup d'état, with Navy Admiral António Rosa Coutinho (left), speaking at a meeting of the Junta de Salvação Nacional, 1974. (Photo by Fernando Ricardo)

8
Organisation

One of the reasons advanced by Palma Carlos for demanding postponement of the elections was that the 'Communists' had gained ground too quickly in the rural areas and that more time was needed for the Centrist parties to get organised. In fact, this was a reflection of the total absence of any grassroots organisation of the Right – the neo-fascists – except for some regions in the north, where the Catholic Church was strong and acted for the Right by proxy in continuing the old litany about the 'red menace'. Not only did the ultra-reactionary forces have no open organisation, but they had no leaders who were not hopelessly compromised with the old regime. The July crisis was, in part at least, a crisis of finding the formula for a fascist succession in a more acceptable garb. Not that there was any lack of political parties operating under more 'respectable' labels.

The liberal-conservative weekly, *Expresso*, in its issue of 1 June 1974, published a prophetic analysis on the options of the Right, under the title: 'The "New" Strategy of the Right in Portugal'. Drawing attention to the obvious embarrassment of the 'guilt by association' stigma attached to most of those who would like to promote a rightist revival, the author commented:

> It is possible to distinguish two likely tactics within rightist strategy; one legitimate – 'democratic' – the other clandestine, counter-revolutionary. The second would give somewhat slower results,

demanding a hard core of militants that would take some time to assemble. Even with support from abroad, they could not count on any benevolent attitude on the part of the Armed Forces Movement, and would presumably only try this after other persuasive or legitimate means had been exhausted, or when there had been a substantial worsening of the economic situation.

If well played, the legitimate game would presuppose the following conditions:

1) That the Right achieves unity.
2) That it can be assured of support from important economic groups.
3) That it can guarantee its discreet support for personalities of the old regime.
4) That it presents a demagogic 'sophisticated' facade.
5) That key positions are not held by those who are compromised with the old regime.
6) That in promoting the creation of a party of the extreme right an alibi of 'moderation' is established.
7) That contacts are strengthened with the most conservative right-wing forces in Europe.
8) That, for reasons of organisational efficiency, it exploits the files of adherents of the old regime, or the administrative files to which the latter have access.

After listing the advantages that the rightists could expect to gain from such tactics, the author continues: 'If these efforts were frustrated then the more radical way would be open, as in Chile, to attain the same objectives by other methods.' Pointing out that the Right was far from being united, however, and had spawned a proliferation of parties, the author notes that one of the first of these to surface was the MFP (Portuguese Federalist Movement) and that, while its policy on colonial affairs was clearly 'federalist', little was known about its views on national politics.[1] (Another that surfaced early was the PDC [Christian

---

1 [AN] The MFP was active in contacting foreign journalists, leaving their glossy literature in hotel mailboxes or slipped under the doors of hotel bedrooms, with telephone numbers to call if the recipients were interested in 'personal contacts'.

Democratic Party], which modestly stated that it was a party 'without leaders', but immodestly announced that it could be considered to represent 'about 40 per cent of the electorate'. The PDC was the first to employ that unfortunate Nixonian term of the 'silent majority', which Spínola was later to adopt with devastating results for his own career! There was also the Liberal Party, the Independent Republicans, and others.)

The author of the *Expresso* article commented:

> More and more parties 'without leaders', without representation in the provisional government, or even participation in the various meetings and round-table discussions in which those parties considered as more representative take part, have been trying to enlarge their bases but have run into difficulties for lack of regional and local support.

Therein lay the real rub that produced the ultimatum of Palma Carlos. Potential power for the Right was eroded because of past contempt for the people, or even for seeking public support. PIDE loyalty was simpler! Palma Carlos, in fact, should have been the last to complain about what had been going on in the rural areas. As prime minister, he had presided over the cabinet meeting which drafted the programme of the provisional government, published on 16 May. The first of its eight articles, 'Organisation of the State' (paragraph g), provided for 'step-by-step abolition of the corporative system and its replacement by an administrative machinery adapted to the new political, economic and social realities', and (paragraph i) for 'the strengthening of local autonomy, with a view to the active participation of the people in the political sphere of the respective organs', while paragraph j referred to the need for 'rapid reform of the administrative institutions'.

All this was in strict conformity to the letter and spirit of the MFA programme. It was part of the process of dismantling the fascist infrastructure. The people went at it with great gusto, encouraged it must be said by the local organisations of the CDE-MDP. If the MFP, PDC, Liberals, Independent Republicans and other faceless, leaderless 'Johnnies-come-lately' had no such organisations in the rural areas – so much the worse for them!

I attended a number of mass meetings in the rural areas where the local people, gathered together in a mass assembly, voted out of office the old fascist administration, and elected by popular acclamation a new one comprised of people they trusted. It was one of those rich moments of history – like the start of land reform in Vietnam in early 1954, when the peasants made bonfires of their title deeds and records of debts. A moment that could never be repeated. Gnarled hands were clasped around hats or tugging at shawls as peasant men and women waited for the meetings to start. They were to take part for the first time in their lives in what it has become fashionable to term a 'decision-making process'. What they did would be irreversible. Control was being wrested from the hands of those who had dominated the countryside for centuries – and never more completely than in the last half century of fascism. There was nothing that Palma Carlos and the various rightist parties that had mushroomed into existence in Lisbon could do about it.

The first such meeting I attended was with Lopes Cardoso, who headed the Socialist Party's technical committee on agriculture. He was a gaunt-faced, bearded, intense man, marked – like so many left-wing activists – by the attentions of the PIDE torture squads. The meeting was at Azambuja, about twenty-five miles northeast of Lisbon, an area famous for its fighting bulls. Black and slightly humped, there were herds of them browsing placidly enough in the fields through which the road led to Azambuja. There, the main street was lined with solidly bedded posts, with iron sockets into which planks could be thrust to stop any bulls erring from the straight and narrow as they were rushed to the local arena. Windows were also closely barred against an impetuous toss of the horns.

In a big, whitewashed hall was a platform supported by bags of wheat. Slogans around the walls translated as: 'Ensure Fascism Does Not Return', 'MDP Is the People's Strength', 'CDE-MDP for Strength and Freedom', 'End the Colonial Wars', and the ever-present 'A People United Can Never Be Defeated'. Local artists had contributed with sketches to illustrate titles such as: 'A Hoe Doesn't Mean Slavery. We Give Our Labour – We Want Our Bread', 'Right to Struggle – Right to Strike'.

It was interesting to watch the stocky, determined-looking women surge forward to the front of the platform as soon as the speakers took their places. After Lopes Cardoso, on behalf of the MDP, had spoken of the importance of such actions going on all over the country, an agricultural labourer from a neighbouring district reported on how the people in his area had set up a new council. A tractor driver from a local absentee landlord's estate spoke of the struggle there by the agricultural labourers before 25 April. One of the red-faced, muscled women made a loudly applauded, eloquent appeal for equal pay for equal work in the fields and at a tomato-processing plant, where many of the women present worked. The wife of Lopes Cardoso, Fernanda, who came from the Azambuja region, made a simple, moving speech – also much applauded – supporting the previous speaker. A local labourer summed things up when he said: 'We will set up a council, so that those who work will decide how things are run. We must have proper contracts and regular days off. The owners must pay for our holidays.'

The chairman then read out the names of those who had been nominated for the new administrative council of Azambuja and Vila Nova da Rainha (a neighbouring town). There was applause for each name, renewed as its owner stepped up to the platform – usually with an embarrassed grin. There were cheers for one grey-haired man with a deeply lined face, who, my interpreter whispered, had been a much-persecuted organiser of the agricultural labourers.

The names of those elected were sent to the minister of the interior, together with the minutes of the meeting, and it was expected that the new council would be confirmed within one or two weeks. In the early stages of this grassroots, democratic procedure, members of the former 'corporative' body were outraged and sent the police – as they had been used to doing for decades. But the MDP would alert the nearest garrison, and a representative of the Armed Forces Movement would arrive to observe that democratic procedures were strictly respected. If necessary, he would send a report to this effect to the Military Junta.

I asked Lopes Cardoso whether the new council members were progressive people. 'It so happens,' he said, 'that this area has a solid socialist tradition. The main thing is not that those elected are progressive, but that they have the confidence of the local people. The people tend to elect those who stood up for their rights in the past – despite the risks and sacrifices.'

Of one burly, ruddy-faced man with a stubble of beard, who had applauded extra heartily as each name was read out, I asked: 'What are your main problems?'

'I used to have ten hectares of land here,' replied Jerónimo Nunes Mascata. 'I've a wife and seven children. In one bad season I had to raise a loan from the bank, which I couldn't pay off. I had to sell four hectares to keep the bank quiet. But from the other six hectares I can't make enough to pay off the loan, so I work as a stonemason, which means I can't work the land as I should. I used to grow wheat before; now it's no longer profitable. The big owners have all the irrigation, so they can produce more cheaply. Our market's gone. Another big problem is marketing. I get six escudos a litre for our wine, but the consumer has to pay ten to twelve escudos. It isn't fair for either of us. The middleman pockets the difference, just for sitting on his behind.'

'Will things be better, now that you have your own council?'

'Of course! These are all people we know. And this is only a start. Now we have a council without the big proprietors and absentee landowners, we'll turn the *Casa de Povo* into a real peasants' association.[2] The next thing will be to set up a marketing cooperative. We can decide things in our own interests now, and not have them decided over our heads by the big proprietors, and only in their interests.'

Another stocky, brick-faced man, Manuel Abreu, introduced himself as an agricultural labourer.

'The trouble is we have no contracts – we hope that will now be corrected. We work as many days a week as the owner decides. We get 120 escudos a day and we want 200 – plus contracts. There are lots of days when the boss decides there's no work – it's not our fault – but then we get no pay, and we've all got wives and kids to keep. We need an organisation to look after our rights – the new council's a good start. Seventy per cent of the land here's in the hands of absentee landlords. They don't even know our names, let alone care what happens to us. Plenty of labourers around here have killed themselves after they got too old to work. We need pensions. How can you eat if there's no more work and no pay? I'm fifty-three [he looked nearer seventy] and I've worked for the same landowner since I was seven, but I'll be chucked out the moment his manager says I'm not fit for a full day's work.'

'Of course I've never been to school,' he replied with a bitter laugh to my question. 'The great majority of labourers and peasants in this region are illiterate like me.'

---

2   [AN] The *Casa de Povo* (People's Centre) in village and district centres, like the *Casa dos Pescadores* (Fishermen's Centres) in the coastal areas, was a typical institution of the 'corporative' state. Supposed to eliminate class conflict by bringing owners and those who served them under one roof, they were entirely dominated by the propertied class and held in contempt by the people.

A circle had quickly formed around us, once it was explained that I was a foreign journalist. Everyone wanted to add something. One of the sturdy women with bulging arm muscles, Maria Teresa Covas, blushing furiously, was pushed forward by other women – who could have been her twin sisters – to say a few words on their behalf. 'We work ten hours a day, five days a week. The boss lines us up on Monday morning and tells us what he's going to pay for the week's work. Is that fair? He decides, and we have to take it! We need contracts. I'm thirty-four and I've worked since I was eleven – the same with most of us here. Now that we've got our own organisation, we're going to change things.'

Whether the hopes of Jerónimo Mascata, Manuel Abreu, Maria Covas and the others would be realised was impossible to know, but what was certain was that councils such as these were being set up all over the country, and the peasants and agricultural labourers were at least making their voices heard for the first time.

'A purge of municipal councils associated with the ousted dictatorship is giving the Portuguese Communist Party one of its best opportunities yet to establish a local power base,' is how Henry Giniger of the *New York Times* reported what was going on, in a despatch from Lisbon on 23 June 1974. 'The purge,' he continued,

> is under the direction of Joaquim Magalhães Mota, the anti-Marxist minister of the interior, who said last week that the country's political future was at stake at the local level, and that Portugal's first election since the coup would probably be held in about three months – for new local councils. Meanwhile, administrative committees are being organised to fill in. The communists want to gain control of these, and of 400 smaller, district units.

After giving some background on the Communist Party and its growing influence in the trade unions and within the MDP, Giniger quoted Interior Minister Mota, one of the founders of the PPD (Popular Democratic Party), affiliated with the MDP, as saying that the latter now 'had no plausible reason to exist, and that it was in reality a "cover for the Communists" . . . Shortly after the coup,' the despatch continued,

> the Movement (MDP) began to provoke popular demonstrations in front of the town halls. In summary elections, the old councils were

thrown out and new ones seated. Mr. Mota said that he had approved ninety-eight such substitutions but acknowledged that the Movement – and consequently the communists – dominated most of them. Applications are pending for the approval of ninety-four others proposed by the Movement.

Both the socialists and centre-left groups acknowledge that the communists have a head start.

Although Giniger, a good and careful correspondent, exaggerated – according to my own observations – the influence of the Communists and their role in setting up the local councils, there is no doubt that they were reaping the fruits of not only having been the only ones to do any real research into rural problems but, as Giniger pointed out, of having maintained 'for almost fifty years some cohesive structure, mostly because it was the only group willing to take the risk, and the only one endowed with sufficient discipline, according to experts here.'[3]

The MDP activists, by no means a majority of them communists, were also reaping the fruits of having nailed their anti-fascist banner to the mast a good five years earlier, and of having planted that mast, no matter how precariously, in every corner of the country. In the poverty-stricken Trás-os-Montes (Behind the Mountains) in the northeast, for instance, the Communist Party has never had any bases. But the CDE maintained bases there from 1969 onwards, and the CDE-MDP now enjoys great prestige, as I observed in a visit there in the summer of 1974. The sort of people being elected to the local councils, as far as an outsider could tell, were the same as those in areas adjoining Lisbon and Porto, where the influence of the Communist Party was traditionally strong (as it was also in the Alentejo region of absentee landlords in the south). Members of the new councils were being elected for the same reasons everywhere: the local people were confident that they would defend their interests. It was also a reaction against the generalised contempt for the former 'corporative' councils, dominated by local big shots – held responsible for the shocking state of the rural economy, which had provoked the emigration that had emptied half of the villages.

---

3 [AN] Apart from Álvaro Cunhal's major work on the agrarian question, there was the *Estruturas Agrárias em Portugal Continental* (Agrarian Structures in Continental Portugal) – written, like Cunhal's work, in prison – by Júlio Silva Martins.

One of those most active in promoting the new councils – and whom I accompanied on visits to the Alentejo and Trás-os-Montes regions – was Professor Pereira de Moura, founder-president of the CDE and who continued to be president of the MDP. He was tremendously applauded whenever he spoke, not only because of his concise, factual speeches, but as a tribute to his courage as an anti-fascist Catholic leader who not only stood up to be counted when this involved great personal risk but was in the forefront of those who did likewise.

It was not, in fact, the idea that the Communists were 'gaining ground' that so much worried Palma Carlos, and others far to the right of him for whom he spoke, but the fact that people were taking things into their own hands all over the country, and it would be awfully difficult ever to prise those hands loose again. That was one inescapable impression from observing things on the spot. Another was the very close relations between the local MDP committees and the representatives of the MFA, who were everywhere – quiet, discreet, efficient watchdogs. On one memorable occasion, in an area where agents of the absentee landlord had set fire to crops in the fields, I was present when the local MFA representative said to the head of the local MDP committee: 'If things get really tough, come to the garrison headquarters and I'll give you as many weapons as you need.'

José Tengarrinha, the dynamic, deputy leader of the MDP, a fiery and popular orator, with whom I also attended council-electing meetings in the rural areas, explained the popularity of the Movement as follows:[4]

'It has a lot of prestige as the follow-up to the CDE in the elections of 1969 and 1973. The CDE was the anti-fascist movement par excellence. At first, it was an umbrella organisation for socialists, social democrats, communists, anti-fascist Catholics and others. But since the 25 April coup, many people who did not want to be affiliated to political parties joined the MDP. We provided an outlet for their activities – young, dynamic people who want to play a role in building up a new democratic structure, but who don't want to have a specific political label

---

4 [EN] José Manuel Marques do Carmo Mendes Tengarrinha (1932–2018) was a journalist, historian and political prisoner of the Estado Novo regime. He played a key role in the Portuguese transition to democracy in 1974–75 as a deputy to the Constitutional Assembly and a founder of the MDP/CDE political party: Movimento Democrático Português (Portuguese Democratic Movement)/Comissão Democrática Eleitoral (Democratic Electoral Commission).

pinned on them. Membership has increased very rapidly due to the general politicisation that has taken place since 25 April, and because of the prestige the Movement acquired from 1969 onwards. The MDP will certainly play a major role in the pre-electoral period, and perhaps a still more important one after that.

'The MDP is the most developed movement throughout the country and with the broadest base. For most people, it is the organisation they know best. People know that we came forward to help get rid of fascism, even within the limited framework that existed before the 25 April coup. That is why we have such broad support. Without that, it would have been impossible for us to bring about the changes in local administration. The Lisbon municipal council was changed by us. In Porto also, as well as the rural councils. For strictly political parties, this would be impossible. You could not have achieved a radicalisation of local power without the MDP leading the change. It is not only that our central organisation has great prestige, but the MDP people, right down to the parish level, all have great prestige in their communities.' Having visited twenty to thirty parish, shire, and district MDP centres, I can testify that this was correct.

During the summer of 1974 – the period when the universities were closed – the MDP organised a vast literacy campaign, with thousands of students and teachers going into the countryside to bring the rudiments of reading and writing to the peasantry. José Tengarrinha, who helped direct the campaign, explained that the method being used was that of Paulo Freire, a Brazilian 'who developed a method of combining courses in reading and writing with social and political content that corresponds to the problems of the people. They learn to read and write, and to speak out about their problems at the same time.[5] We want to tackle this on a step-by-step basis to get rid of obscurantism and give the rural people a minimum of political consciousness; not only the ABCs of reading and writing, but also of the situation in our society, and the role the people can play in this.'

The simple truth was that, had the elections for local councils been held 'within three months', as the *New York Times* quoted Interior

---

5 [AN] Twenty years earlier, I had recorded for future students of the English language in Hanoi a series of texts devised by the late President Ho Chi Minh for learning spoken English, based on a similar combination of language with political and social content.

Minister Mota as advocating, the overwhelming majority of peasants would have had no vote. It was because of the high rate of illiteracy that the new councils were elected by a show of hands. The average rate of illiteracy among the peasantry is around 50 per cent; in the Trás-os-Montes area, up to 70 to 80 per cent. It was typical that, before the literacy campaign started, the priests in the most backward regions of the north were urging the peasants not to cooperate – warning them of a 'red invasion' by 'godless, immoral' people who would 'live in common, in tents, like gypsies'.

I visited the newly elected head of the administrative council of Montalegre, considered impossibly backward even as compared with the rest of the Trás-os-Montes area. Dr Cruz, the new mayor, was in bed recovering from tonsilitis, but insisted on receiving the rare visitors from afar. A florid man with deep, piercing eyes – joyful despite his ailment – he explained that the *concelho* (shire) of Montalegre, together with neighbouring Chaves, comprised the district of Vila Real.[6]

'In general, people in this area ignored politics completely,' he said. 'Even more so than in other parts. For forty-eight years, one single family – the Canedos – governed the Montalegre region. Now democratic councils have been elected in all fourteen *freguesias* [parishes]. Only two have been confirmed so far, but we expect the other twelve will soon be confirmed as well. People here have known nothing but fascism, and what they think depends mainly on what they hear from the priests.'

I asked, 'What was the main form of opposition from those who were once fascists – members of the Canedo family, for instance?'

'They don't openly preach a return to fascism,' he said. 'That would be too unpopular. They pretend they are democrats and always have been! They use their professions and the social standing their wealth gives them to say: "The new regime doesn't seem to be working too well. Perhaps they are trying to do too much . . . moving too fast." They try to exploit people's fears – saying that their land is going to be taken away, for instance. The same with the Church, that has always exerted a lot of influence. In the past, it always defended fascism. Now the priests claim they are all for "democracy" – it is a great word these days – and always

---

6 [EN] A *concelho* is a traditional Portuguese territorial unit dating to medieval times, a regional government subdivision of a larger province or district. Administratively, a *concelho* is similar in concept and function to a county or municipality.

have been. But they say that our democratic movement is the wrong kind; that we favour burning down the churches. Of course, we respect religious beliefs and practices, but we won't tolerate direct sabotage – the burning of crops, for instance.'

'What do the people expect of the newly elected councils?'

'They are only just beginning to see their needs, and to realise they have the right to ask for them to be met. They need help with credits, marketing and guaranteed prices. If they know they have solid outlets, they can increase production – even with their backward, traditional methods. What depresses them and sends them off the land is to find that what they produce is not wanted; that whatever they suggest is turned down. Until 25 April, any initiative by the peasantry was something to be suppressed. Now, they expect us to transmit their needs and ideas, and the government to respond. If that doesn't happen, they'll turn back to the priests, who'll say: "What did we tell you? This democratic movement is no good. The provisional government is no good."

'Agricultural methods have not changed here for centuries,' he continued. 'There are two types of activity: cultivating maize and potatoes, and cattle-breeding. The methods for both are extremely primitive. People take their cows to the mountains in summer and bring them back when they have calves. Each village collectively owns a couple of bulls up in the mountains, which are expected to serve only the cows of the village that owns them. Cultivation is on a similarly haphazard basis. No seed selection, no improvement of strains. "Picturesque" is the word Salazar used to justify the stagnation of rural life. Nothing should be changed. But people are now ready for change. The great thing is that they are no longer afraid to open their mouths and say what they think. This really worries the priests and the local fascists.'

It was a tribute to the common sense of the people of Montalegre that they had chosen someone of the calibre of Dr Cruz to head their local council. A doctor of medicine who took no fees from his poorer clients and was known for his devotion to duty, he had been a CDE candidate in the 1969 and 1973 elections. It was easy to believe that he was seen as the champion of enlightenment against the forces of obscurantism, and that the latter regarded him as the devil incarnate.

A man typical of the new winds blowing 'behind the mountains' in the Trás-os-Montes and across the Alentejo plains in the south – creating much worry in certain circles in Lisbon – Dr Cruz symbolised what seemed an irreversible current in Portugal. It was encouraging to find his counterpart in many other small towns and villages, where militants had brought into local leadership the men they trusted.

One of the points of dissension that arose between the Socialist Party on the one hand, and the CP and MFA on the other, after the big Socialist vote in the Constituent Assembly elections, was the demand by Mário Soares to dismantle the local councils and elect new ones. In fact, these councils came into being through a revolutionary process in which the Socialists were conspicuous by their absence in many of the most politically difficult areas of the country. The new councils were set up when the pro-fascist forces were still half paralysed and incapable of reacting. But the authority of the priests and pro-fascist notables was still intact in many rural regions. A ballot box–type of election, as demanded by Mário Soares, would have restored to office those who had been thrown out. Under the banner of 'democracy', the deposed notables would soon be back in power, either directly or through their stooges and vassals.

In today's Portugal, a clear distinction must be made between voting strength and organisational strength. When it comes to manning barricades to control arms, or to expropriate the untilled fields of absentee landlords, the activists of the CDE-MDP are in the forefront – even though they won less than 5 per cent of the vote in the Constituent Assembly elections – but only a tiny percentage of those who voted Socialist, and none at all of those who voted for the Popular Democrats! Few are in a better position to appreciate the difference between electoral strength and organisational strength than the leaders of the Armed Forces Movement.

9
Counterattack 3

In a speech on 10 September 1974, to proclaim Portugal's recognition of Guinea-Bissau's independence, President Spínola called for a 'silent majority' to assert itself against 'totalitarian extremists working in the shadows'. Whether he intended it or not, this was the first shot fired in an attempted counter-revolutionary coup. It was no coincidence that the appeal was made on that occasion. Spínola was against ending the African wars on the basis of independence. He was for clinging on to the colonies under the formula of confederation. But, as president, he had to bow to the decisions of the Armed Forces Movement and the second provisional government under Premier Gonçalves. Shortly after the formation of that government – on 27 July – he had made the following historic pronouncement:

'Portugal is ready from now on to initiate the process of transfer of powers to the peoples of the overseas territories . . . We are now open to all initiatives to start planning and executing the process of decolonisation in Africa, with the immediate acceptance of the right to *political independence* to be proclaimed in terms and by dates to be agreed on.'[1] Terms had virtually been agreed upon by then for the independence also of Mozambique; but Spínola and the economic and financial interests that he represented, or at least that supported him, were above all opposed to independence for Angola – next on the list – with its rich reserves of raw materials.

---

1   [AN] My italics, W. B.

Immediately after the 10 September speech, glossy, expensively produced posters began to appear all over Portugal showing a man's face, lips stitched together, and a text appealing for 'Silent Majority' support for Spínola and a 'No to Extremists'. At the same time, other posters – issued in the name of the 'Progress Party' – appeared, illustrating the theme of 'Communism – Worse Than Fascism!'

The word went out that there would be a monster rally of the 'Silent Majority' in the Lisbon bullring on 28 September.[2] Foreign journalists who followed up the leaflets slipped under their hotel room doors, with invitations to contact the MFP (Portuguese Federalist Movement), received free tickets for a bullfight to take place in the Lisbon arena on 26 September. Tickets were accompanied by a nod and a wink to expect something sensational. Ostensibly to raise funds for the Returned Soldiers Association, it was virtually an official occasion. It turned out that large blocks of seats had been reserved for organised groups. President Spínola was greeted with unusually enthusiastic applause and shouts of '*Viva!*' The first 'sensation', however, was when Prime Minister Gonçalves arrived, to be greeted with boos, accompanied by derogatory shouts against the Armed Forces Movement. This was very much out of line with any demonstration until then.

The voices of those who cheered for the prime minister and the Armed Forces Movement were drowned out by opposition cries. Some of the more fervent supporters of the prime minister were physically assaulted. Then came shouts of 'Long Live the Overseas Territories' in several variants, which produced feverish applause. This was the first organised and public demonstration against the 25 April coup.

Foreign journalists were obviously not the only ones in that very select audience to have been offered free tickets, as several Lisbon newspapers later noted.

While the bullfight continued, with most people's attention focused on an energetic conversation between Spínola and an obviously angry Gonçalves, word was passed around that, after it was over, there would be an attack on the Communist Party headquarters only a few hundred yards away. By the time people streamed out of the arena, however, the

---

2 [EN] The capital city's main bullfighting arena, an ornate late-nineteenth-century Moorish-style brick building in the Praça de Touros at Campo Pequeno, a large public square in Lisbon.

way to the CP headquarters was blocked by hastily mobilised party militants. Members of some of the organised groups from the bullring suddenly appeared wearing helmets, with clubs – and even knives and pistols – in their hands. The clubs were used against the heads of the defenders, other weapons were brandished with shouted threats that they would be used 'later'. The attackers were easily beaten off, but the incident was a foretaste of things to come.

The 26 September incident was a full-dress rehearsal for what was planned two days later – a 'silent majority' rally in the same arena on the evening of 28 September, to support the themes of the glossy posters! From the time this rally was announced, there were energetic protests from the Democratic Movement, the Communist and Socialist Parties, and others. These were supported by the civil governor of Lisbon, who pointed out that, in any case, such a rally was 'unauthorised'. Spínola insisted, in the interests of 'freedom of expression', that it be held. The Armed Forces Movement at first maintained a neutral position. Leaders of the Democratic Movement, in the meantime, had been informing the MFA about arms entering Portugal from Spain and being smuggled towards Lisbon, and of plans to infiltrate commando groups into the capital as 'participants' in the rally. The MFA leadership began to take these reports very seriously after the bullring incident.

Because they had taken the precaution of infiltrating the most active of the right-wing organisations, the Democratic Movement was better informed even than the MFA regarding preparations for an attempted counter-revolutionary coup.

Despite almost unanimous demands by the Lisbon press on 27 September to ban the rally, Spínola stuck to his position. Later, he preferred to ban the press rather than the rally! The Democratic Movement, supported by other left-wing parties and organisations, then issued an appeal to halt or control all traffic moving towards Lisbon. Throughout Friday the 27th, barricades and checkpoints were set up all over the country – especially at the approaches to Lisbon.

The trade unions responded to the appeal: train-drivers halted the trains, bus-drivers the buses, that were to transport tens of thousands of people – mostly from the politically backward areas of the country – who had been given free tickets and encouraged to converge on the Lisbon bullring.

Activists from the Democratic Movement, and the Communist and Socialist Parties, went to the barricades and checkpoints to direct the work, joined later by local units of the armed forces, on instructions from the MFA. Patient explanations were given as to why people were being turned back and why cars and trucks were being searched for arms. That such vigilance was justified was shown by the search of a hearse in the outskirts of Lisbon. Despite the indignant protests of the driver and his companion, the men and women at the barricades demanded that the coffin itself be opened. It was found to contain machine-guns and bazookas!

In a rare display of unity, members of the 'ultra-left' presented themselves to the headquarters of the Democratic Movement, and especially the Communist Party, asking to be sent wherever their services could be used. 'They turned out to be among the most energetic and disciplined workers,' a veteran of the Party's central committee told me later, adding, 'That didn't inhibit them from attacking us as reformists, revisionists, social fascists, *et cetera*, in the next issues of their press.' There was, in fact, a veritable 'mobilisation of the masses' – a term with which I had become familiar in Vietnam – to prevent an intended pro-fascist coup.

Arms confiscated by the civilian controllers were turned over to the local MFA representatives, who usually passed them back to the local Democratic Movement representative – in case things got really hot. By the 27th, the coordinating committee of the MFA had also demanded that the rally be banned – but Spínola still refused.

Detailed plans for a military coup, involving several pro-fascist military leaders – General Kaúlza de Arriaga amongst them – were among the booty confiscated at the checkpoints.

A cabinet meeting, which began at the São Bento governmental palace late on the evening of the 27th, and at which a majority demanded the banning of the rally, was moved to the Belém presidential palace, with Spínola, instead of Gonçalves, presiding. Later, Brigadier Otelo Saraiva de Carvalho, military governor of Lisbon and deputy-chief of the anti-coup COPCON command, was convoked to the presidential palace. His immediate chief, as commander of COPCON and head of the country's armed forces, General Costa Gomes, was already there. The atmosphere was described by Brigadier de Carvalho as follows:[3]

---

3 [AN] When I asked Otelo de Carvalho, during my sixth visit to Portugal in January 1975, exactly what had happened in the small hours of 28 September, he handed me a small book, *Cinco Meses Mudaram Portugal* (Five months that changed Portugal), in which he had set forth in great detail exactly what happened, authorising me to quote

Counterattack 3

Around 2:00 a.m. on the morning of the 28th, I was summoned to Belém Palace, to find everyone in a state of great tension, in an atmosphere you could cut with a knife. Virtually all those most closely linked with the president of the republic were there – the chief of staff of the armed forces and the chief of staff of the Army. I was aware that the grave problem of the moment was that of the barricades being set up, and how to dismantle them as soon as possible. The fact was that, after tremendous discussions, no one had come up with a solution. I was called in to the council chamber, where I found General Spínola deeply shaken and in a state of great agitation. I also met the prime minister, Vasco Gonçalves, and I later learned that he had already been attacked and insulted by those members of the Junta of National Salvation who were later purged, which fully explained his ill-concealed state of depression and revolt. I also learned later that, when they started to insult him, he wanted to leave the palace, reacting violently against an order to resign – to quit his post. With that character which we all know, he energetically replied: 'I am not here for myself, but for something which is much stronger than all of you here – I am here only by a decision of the movement which has placed its confidence in me. I will absolutely not resign.'

When I told General Spínola that Radio Clube Português continued to call for the erection of barricades, he immediately ordered the closing down of Radio Clube Português, Radio Renascença, *et cetera*, keeping on the air only the Emissora Nacional – by order of the president.[4] He also ordered that the radio and TV stations be occupied by forces of the Republican Guards (GNR) and the Police. I had already placed military forces to occupy these positions, from 6:00 p.m. on the 27th, because I was concerned about the 'silent majority' demonstration; so I informed him of this, and I think he took it as evidence of preparations for a possible coup d'état on my part.

The truth is that, since his attitude towards me for months past had been one of total intolerance, because he believed the rumours with which he was bombarded, to the effect that I was a Marxist and

---

directly from that. In order to save the time of one of the busiest men in Portugal – and my interview took place at the height of the fourth crisis – I gladly accepted. It had come off the press a few days earlier, published by Portugália Editora, Lisbon, January 1975. The portions quoted run from pp. 23 to 31.

4   [AN] Emissora Nacional: National Broadcasting.

traitor, when my only intention was 'to take the ship to a safe port' in all circumstances, I did not oppose his orders for replacing the troops. I did not want to add to the problems or aggravate the situation.

At a certain point, the fact of my being retained at Belém Palace started to worry my comrades in those units which were in a state of alert. I had told COPCON that I was going to the presidency, but that I would not stay for more than forty-five minutes, because I thought it was only to find a solution to the problem of the barricades, and that this would be dealt with quickly. But an hour went by – a second hour – and then, every minute, telephone calls started to pour into the Belém Palace, all of them asking for me. So I started to centralise there my command post for those units that were getting nervous. Anxiety grew like a snowball. Calls poured in from all over the country. From Porto, from Coimbra, Caldas da Rainha, from the Navy, from the Air Force – calls that took on an ever more alarmist tone – asking what was going on, whether I had been arrested or, if not, when would I be leaving and returning to COPCON?

Some units wanted to march on Belém, even against my orders, because they noticed that I wasn't speaking freely on the telephone and was obviously under surveillance. In fact, whenever I was called to the telephone, there was always a comrade from the presidency alongside to overhear what I said. I spoke in monosyllables – yes, no, okay, I'm alright, no problems, everything's fine, we're here to discuss a problem – the sort of words one can use in such circumstances. But the comrades sensed that this was not my language, not the language of someone entirely at ease.

Tension was building up in such a way that, at one point, the situation looked extremely dire and I began to fear that these comrades, convinced that I was arrested with a gun in my back, were poised to march on the Belém Palace. I lied, saying that nothing serious was happening, that I was only solving the problem of the barricades – but I must say, at that point I did fear that some units would lose their heads and come racing to the rescue.

Regarding the rumours that Spínola tried to replace the palace guards with units absolutely loyal to himself, Otelo de Carvalho explained that there was in fact no replacement, although there were many orders and counter-orders, great confusion, and plentiful rumours. For instance:

News reached the palace, via the radio of a mobile detachment of the Republican National Guards, that two artillery units from the 1st Light Artillery Regiment were moving towards Belém. There was then a counter-order from the Palace to reinforce its defences with a squadron from the 7th Cavalry Regiment. But this order to the 7th Cavalry was not issued by me, even though it is one of the units under the command of COPCON and the military governor of Lisbon. The commander of the 7th Cavalry Regiment did not doubt the validity of the order. He was summoned to the presidency, where he saw me, along with General Silvério Marques, who had given the order, so obviously he executed it.

All these events led me at one point to turn to General Costa Gomes and say, 'General, things are in such a state that I'm afraid my comrades will start to believe that I really have been arrested. The best thing would be for me to return straight away to COPCON, while you stay here commanding the forces. You set up your headquarters here; I will send you a senior officer to maintain liaison with COPCON, while I return to COPCON to quieten down our people there.' I said this because, when I met General Spínola at Belém, he said: 'Now look here! General Costa Gomes from now on assumes command of the armed forces, and you therefore cease to be their direct commander.' I replied: 'General, I have always known that General Costa Gomes is in charge of the armed forces, that he is also the commander of COPCON, and that I am his deputy. I came here to give any help needed, but it is General Costa Gomes who commands. I have never doubted this in any way.'

After I had spoken to General Costa Gomes, he agreed that I should leave for COPCON, as I was not doing anything where I was. (Or was I doing too much?) But, as I started to leave the palace, someone from the president's staff stopped me and pleaded with me not to go, as I was maintaining some sort of balance. If I went away, he didn't know what might happen. Appreciating the validity of this argument, I decided to stay a little longer.

In the meantime, tension had built up to such a level in some units that I again insisted on leaving. But when I tried to leave the second

Figure 9.1. Armoured vehicle of the 7th Cavalry Regiment guarding the Presidential Palace in Belém against the perceived threat of a potential putsch against President Spínola from COPCON and MFA forces, 28 September 1974. (Photo by Fernando Ricardo)

time, I was stopped by Lieutenant Colonel Firmino Miguel, who came over and said:[5] 'Look here, Otelo, you'd better be patient. [First, Miguel behaves extremely honestly.] I'll tell you what no one else has yet had the guts to say. You were summoned to the presidency by General Spínola in order to detain you. You cannot leave the palace.' For the first time, someone had found the courage to tell me why I'd been summoned! I replied to Firmino Miguel: 'Very well – so I'll stay, *senhor*.[6] But I am fed up with all this, and I regret that our General Spínola has so much lost confidence in me that he brings me here in order to detain me. If I am forced to stay here, I will, but I cannot be responsible for the consequences. My prolonged presence at Belém

---

5 [EN] Mário Firmino Miguel (1932–1991), a military officer and politician who played a key role in the Armed Forces Movement during the Portuguese transition to democracy. In July 1976, in the first constitutional government led by Prime Minister Mário Soares of the Socialist Party, he was named minister of National Defence; he kept this post in two subsequent governments (1976–78).

6 [EN] In Portuguese, *senhor* literally means 'lord' or, in this context, 'sir'. Burchett maintained the use of the Portuguese word in his English-language text, possibly to emphasise the military nature of this exchange.

has already so alarmed the country that a point will be reached when it will be impossible to restrain the troops any longer, and they will march – against the palace itself. So, watch out! I'm detained here, and will be unable to solve this problem.'

In the end it was decided that, faced with such a situation, it would really be better if I left for COPCON, accompanied by General Spínola and members of his entourage, by General Costa Gomes and his staff, by General Silvério Marques, *et cetera*. I said: 'Alright, *senhor*! Let's all go to COPCON.' As there were so many people, however, I warned: 'I must remind you that COPCON is an operational command. There are no beds. It is very cramped, there aren't even any chairs for you to sit on.'

When we were already in the cars and waiting for the gates to be opened, I was called back into the presidency, where General Spínola told me that he wouldn't come with me after all; but I should return to COPCON to prove that I had not been arrested and that we were all working together. We had complete confidence in each other, and I must calm down my comrades. Accordingly, I telephoned to COPCON, where my chief of staff was at the other end of the line. General Spínola spoke first, stating that I had not been arrested. "Otelo is right beside me. He has not been arrested. We are working in close cooperation. He is perfectly alright." Then Costa Gomes spoke, and I followed him: "Everything is fine, I'll be there in five minutes. Tell the comrades not to do anything rash, to remain calm and I'll be coming over at top speed." This call did not reassure them, and made my own personnel at COPCON more suspicious than ever. But, in fact, within ten minutes I left Belém, accompanied by some trusted officers of General Spínola – charged I suppose with supervising my activities at COPCON, seeing what I was going to do or not do. As soon as I arrived, I replaced the police and Republican Guards with our own armed forces and continued to replace them at the people's barricades. From then on, what happened is public knowledge.

It is clear from Otelo de Carvalho's account that a flash point was averted by the narrowest of margins. One false move, and Portugal would have been plunged into a Spanish-type civil war – something the captains wanted to avoid at all costs.

At the presidential palace, Spínola had launched into a violent attack on the Communist Party – and the Lisbon press – for the vigour with which they opposed the 'silent majority' rally. The erection of the barricades and checkpoints was 'proof' of a communist 'plot' to seize power. Communiqués were broadcast in the small hours of the 28th from the Emissora Nacional, in the name of the minister of social communications, announcing that the rally would take place and ordering the barricades to be dismantled so that free movement towards Lisbon could be restored. Spínola was said to be counting above all on the Air Force, which controlled the paratrooper units, and which had been the most reticent in its support of the 25 April coup. The commander and deputy commander of the Air Force were two of the seven members of the Military Junta.

Spínola, however, badly miscalculated. Instead of news of the movement of units loyal – so he thought – to himself, his headquarters was bombarded with calls from units wanting to rush to the rescue of Otelo de Carvalho, who personified the Armed Forces Movement. The true relation of forces in the country was revealed by those telephone calls early on the morning of the 28th. It seems that this moment of truth finally dawned on Spínola just as he was about to set out for the COPCON headquarters. His own telephone conversation was the signal of defeat.

At the barricades, it was a political confrontation. Spokesmen for the Armed Forces Movement got down from their vehicles and explained what the whole thing was about, persuading the Republican National Guards to return to their barracks without a shot fired.

By the time the Voice of America was announcing in its early morning transmissions on Saturday, 28 September, that 300,000 people from 'all over Portugal' were expected to take part in the 'silent majority' rally that evening, the military situation had been brought under control and some of the key plotters had already been arrested. The Lisbon public awoke that morning to a confused situation. Those who had heard contradictory radio communiqués were waiting to learn the real state of affairs from the morning papers. But Spínola had taken the extraordinary step of banning all newspapers. Activists from the Democratic Movement set up information centres at key sites, explaining what had happened and distributing hastily Roneoed communiqués.[7] At midday,

---

7 [EN] A rapid reproduction printing process similar to mimeograph machine technology.

a communiqué was issued in Spínola's name announcing the cancellation of the rally. By mid-afternoon, the Democratic Movement issued a communiqué with the first list of those who had been arrested. Apart from Kaúlza de Arriaga, there were two other well-known fascist generals, Pereira de Castro and Barbieri Cardoso, plus a dozen lower-ranking officers. Civilians included a son of Marcelo Caetano and a member of the Champalimaud family – the country's second biggest monopoly grouping. The following day, it was announced that nineteen members of the Espírito Santo family – the third biggest monopoly grouping – had fled to Madrid.

The captains were not taking any chances. In the small hours of Saturday morning, a COPCON unit had raided the headquarters of the Portuguese Action Movement (MAP), one of the innumerable parties operating under the 'centrist' label. In a room on the first floor, they found and arrested seven men, one with a telescopic sight fitted to his rifle. He was identified as a sharpshooter. A small pane in a window overlooking the residence of Prime Minister Gonçalves had been broken sufficiently to give a clear view of the prime minister's movements around his home, which was well within range of the rifle. Along with the arms, there were copies of a MAP 'manifesto' which, after warning of the threat to 'Portuguese permanent values and traditions' posed by the present situation, continued:

'Aware of all the difficulties and, despite the limited means at its disposal, the MAP wishes above all to awaken the conscience of all those Portuguese who are disturbed by recent events.'

Since the 'limited means' included a rifle with a telescopic sight intended to put a bullet in the prime minister's head, the discovery obviously served to 'awaken the conscience' of any MFA members who had any doubts as to what was afoot. Ironically enough, it was almost certainly Spínola's action, in putting Vasco Gonçalves under virtual arrest at a time when his movements would normally have brought him within range of what the press called the 'Dallas model' rifle, that saved his life. The raid on the MAP headquarters took place at 4:00 a.m., half an hour before the crisis at the Belém palace ended and the prime minister returned home. The tip-off had come from a vigilant local police unit.

Arriving in Lisbon from Paris on the afternoon of Sunday the 29th, I found the entrance to the Tivoli Hotel blocked by an excited crowd. A reception clerk who knew me – and my Vietnam books – from previous visits, elbowed his way down the steps to escort me through a hostile crowd into the foyer where grim-faced Marines, rifles at the ready, gave me dirty looks which changed into smiles after a few whispered words from the clerk. They had been searching for a CIA agent of Chilean origin, known to have registered at the hotel a few days earlier. The crowd had been mobilised by activists as a back-up action, to ensure that no one escaped. In fact, I was told at the reception desk that the Chilean had left precipitately for Madrid the night before, leaving some of his baggage behind in his haste. Similar searches were going on at the nearby Sheraton Hotel, where some Portuguese, suspected for their CIA connections, had held a premature celebration on the Friday evening.

At 11:30 on the following Monday morning, Spínola appeared on TV to announce his resignation in a tough, defiant speech aimed at further encouragement of the 'silent majority'. One of the captains, at my side during the TV address, commented: 'He was never really with us. He only joined the Armed Forces Movement to cancel us out. When 25 April was done, he wanted to send us back to barracks. His idea was to liberalise the regime – to make it more acceptable to his cronies in NATO – but not to permit real democracy.

'He wanted real power to remain in the hands of the same old social forces. Once the coup succeeded, he wanted to slow up the decolonialisation process – to play for time while a neo-colonialist outfit could be set up in the colonies. He favoured a more liberal regime there, too, because he was realist enough to know that the old system was finished. As a military technician, he knew we couldn't win. But he couldn't bring himself to accept decolonialisation on the only possible basis – total independence. What happened was a real confrontation between those who wanted to push on with the process of democratisation and decolonialisation, and those who opposed it. Spínola was with the latter.'[8]

---

8 [AN] Later, Brigadier Otelo de Carvalho was to accuse Spínola of having threatened to invite foreign troops into Mozambique to prevent FRELIMO taking over. After the United States refused this role, Spínola was accused of having asked South Africa – which already had troops in Mozambique – to intervene. South Africa also refused, having enough troubles, and potential troubles, at home. De Carvalho's charges were repeated in an interview with the Lisbon weekly, *Expresso*, on 4 January 1975, and again at a press conference on 29 April 1975 at which, in front of 500 foreign journalists, he added that Foreign Minister Soares was also a witness of the incident but, rather than confirm it, Mário Soares preferred to take refuge in 'diplomatic evasions'.

At the end of his resignation speech, Spínola announced that he would be succeeded as interim president by General Costa Gomes. It had been an open secret that the two had drawn ever further apart from the time of the July crisis. (Although they continued to have weekly lunches, even after the September events!) One of the first actions of Costa Gomes was to confirm Vasco Gonçalves as prime minister. On that night of 30 September, I watched a crowd of about 30,000 people, most of them marching under the banners of their trade unions, converge on the Belém palace to demonstrate their support for the new tenant. It was a miniature of the great May Day demonstration, huge considering that it was organised at a few hours' notice. In addition to the May Day–type slogans were those such as: 'Fascism Shall Not Pass' and 'Down With the CIA'.

There was tremendous applause when Costa Gomes appeared, with Gonçalves, Melo Antunes, and other members of the government and MFA leadership at his side. A woman standing nearby entered into a passionate conversation with a woman member of our little group:

'We can do anything,' she said. 'The people have chucked out the president and stopped the fascists. I was at the barricades with women from our factory searching the cars. The people can do anything – even the women – if we stick together.' It was an observation that had deeper significance than at first appeared. It reflected the confidence in their own strength, born of actual participation in practical action, of scores of thousands of ordinary people all over the country. They had acted shoulder-to-shoulder with the armed forces – and it was good for both of them. It was the May Day–type of fraternisation moved up to a higher level. Another psycho-political action born of urgent necessity which none of those taking part would forget. And, for everyone taking part in that action, there would be five or ten available in a future emergency, according to those who initiated the popular movement. Few with whom I spoke doubted that there would be future confrontations. But the role of the people had deep implications which politically conscious people recognised.

'It was not only thanks to our military intelligence services,' said Prime Minister Gonçalves later, explaining how the attempted coup was thwarted, 'but owing to great assistance from the press and the most vigilant sections of the population; from the Democratic Movement and the political parties.'

Just how serious that attempt had been was made apparent when COPCON forces raided the headquarters of the Federalist Movement/Progress Party on 2 October.[9] Situated in the very heart of Lisbon, on Avenida Infante Santo, this turned out to be a conspiratorial military-political command headquarters and arsenal. Apart from a quantity of arms seized on the spot, there was an inventory of others ordered from abroad – some presumed to be stored away in secret caches – which included fifty mortars (sixty millimetre) and 5,000 mortar shells; fifty bazookas with incendiary, armour-piercing and explosive rockets; 200 light automatic rifles with 100,000 rounds of ammunition; 900 hand grenades of various types; 100 Mauser and other types of pistol; cartridge belts and magazines to equip 2,000 men; 200 Molotov cocktails with equipment and chemicals – on the spot – for thousands more.

The headquarters section included sophisticated ITT[10] equipment for intercepting telephone and radio communications; maps of strategic nerve-centres of Lisbon and other cities; Roneoed extracts from a book detailing the step-by-step preparations for, and execution of, the coup in Chile; lists of those to be summarily executed, and others to be arrested and concentrated in the Lisbon stadium and bullring, *à la* Chile!

There were also lists of members, potential members, and financial contributors; coded communications – even model slogans to be used according to the occasion; iron bars, clubs and helmets of the type used outside the bullring on 26 September; and a huge stock of shirts stamped with what was obviously intended to be the local version of the swastika – three hunting horns arranged in a circle, presumably to emphasise the agrarian origins of Portuguese fascism.

From other documents, seized during the traffic controls on the 27th, the trail led also to the Liberal Party, and arrest warrants were issued for its leader, José de Almeida Araújo, and secretary, Lieutenant Colonel António Figueiredo. It was rumoured that they had fled to Switzerland.

---

9 [AN] The Federalist Movement changed its name to Progress Party just prior to the September events.

10 [EN] ITT Corporation, founded in 1920 as International Telephone & Telegraph Company, is a multinational manufacturing and engineering business based in Stamford, Connecticut.

A terse armed forces communiqué early on the Sunday afternoon announced:

> A meeting is currently under way between the coordinating committee of the Armed Forces Movement and the president of the republic. The logical political consequences are being drawn. The MFA continues to be vigilant with respect to all reactionary manoeuvres, whatever their origin. No one should have any doubts – least of all the Armed Forces Movement – that the only enemy of democracy and the spirit of 25 April is reaction and its agents.

The settling of accounts which that meeting with the president represented was undoubtedly a stormy affair. The result was that three members of the Military Junta – all of them right-wing Spínola men – had to go: the Army chief, General Silvério Marques; the head of the Air Force, General Diogo Neto; and his deputy, General Galvão de Melo.[11] With Spínola's resignation the following day, this left, of the original seven-member Junta, only General Costa Gomes; Vice-Admiral Pinheiro Azevedo, head of the Navy; and his deputy, the 'Red' vice-admiral, Rosa Coutinho.[12] Replacements were to be democratically elected by the Army and the Air Force officers, respectively. Spínola officers in the provisional government also had to go, including the defence minister, Firmino Miguel, and the social communications minister, Sanches Osório.

---

11 [EN] Manuel Diogo Neto (1924–1995), a decorated pilot and officer who, after the 25 April coup, was named a member of the Junta of National Salvation and commander-in-chief of the Portuguese Air Force. Carlos Galvão de Melo (1921–2008) was an officer of the Portuguese Air Force who, after serving in the colonial conflicts of the 1960s, left active duty for the reserves because he did not agree with the Estado Novo's policies in Africa. In 1974 he served briefly as a member of the Junta of National Salvation.

12 [EN] António Alva Rosa Coutinho (1926–2010), an officer of the Portuguese Navy and participant in the MFA coup. After 25 April, he was a member of the Junta of National Salvation, tasked with dismantling the PIDE and the paramilitary Portuguese Legion. From July 1974 to January 1975, he played a key role in negotiating Angolan independence as president of the Council of Governors and High Commissioner of Angola. He served on the Revolutionary Council but was removed following the attempted left-wing coup d'état on 25 November 1975.

The third counterattack, in other words, resulted in a considerable shift to the left at the top. Nothing, in fact, could be quite the same again. A Chile-type coup had been attempted – and defeated, for two major reasons. Politically, because the unity between people and armed forces had been consolidated and stood the test of concrete action. Militarily, because of the maturity and farsightedness of the Armed Forces Movement in setting up COPCON in the wake of the July crisis. Without COPCON, there would certainly have been civil war, and civil war under the circumstances would have invited foreign intervention. Within the leadership of the Armed Forces Movement, the fact that the names of some were on the list for summary execution, and others earmarked for the arena or stadium concentration camps, obviously made an impression. For the general public, the revelation of what the so-called centrist parties were up to – and the extent to which the leading monopolies were involved – was something that would be remembered on election day.

A spokesman of the Democratic Movement summed up the September events as 'a major victory. New conditions have been created for further struggle,' he said. 'It was a remarkable example for us of what can be done through mobilisation of the masses. In all serenity, the anti-fascist forces now see that we have enough strength to confront the dangers ahead. At the height of the crisis there was no panic, no nervousness – everyone went calmly about their tasks. This, once again, proved the difference between our situation and that of Chile. Here we have unity between the main progressive forces on the one hand, and unity between the people and the armed forces on the other. The extreme rightists exposed their hands, fuelling pressures to push ahead and clip the wings of the monopolies.'

The September crisis did indeed clear the obviously right-wing elements out of the government and the Junta of National Salvation. General Kaúlza de Arriaga, who was to have replaced Spínola as president had the plot succeeded, was put out of harm's way for a while, at least. The next crisis however, towards the end of January 1975, was to occur within the remaining political parties in the coalition government, with the Communist Party and the leadership of the Armed Forces Movement taking one side, the Socialist and Popular Democratic parties the other. Each side had its supporters within parties and movements outside the government. And, presumably, within the Armed Forces Movement.

The prophecy that the September crisis would clear the decks for tougher action against the monopolies was seen to be fully justified when the long-awaited and much-debated Economic Law was finally adopted.[13]

---

13 [EN] In the original typescript, at the end of Chapter 9, Burchett placed a note to his editors stating that 'additional material, summarising the most important provisions' of the Economic Law would 'be added to the following chapter', because 'details of the Economic Law were not available at the time of the dispatch of these chapters'. However, no such information appears in Chapter 10 of the 1975 Portuguese edition; the only other mention of the Economic Law is brief, at the beginning of Chapter 17, the final chapter of Burchett's first volume on the Portuguese Revolution. The present text is reproduced as Burchett originally wrote it.

10
Monopolies

At the height of the economic counter-offensive (May–June), about 1,000 company directors were sacked. They had been engaged in economic sabotage too blatant for even the then prime minister Palma Carlos to condone. Most of them were appointees of the Salazar or Caetano regimes – not for any competence in business affairs, but because this was a customary way for the fascist regime to compensate ministers or state secretaries for 'service rendered' after they left office. They could draw fat salaries from enterprises in which the state nominally had some direct or indirect interest. It was part of the fascist 'old-boy network' and helped maintain continuity. In the pre–25 April days, most of them attended an occasional managerial board meeting to justify their salaries. They only became really active after 25 April. One thing they had in common was that they were all faithful career fascists. This was only one aspect of the interlocking between the monopolies and the fascist administration, which complicated that part of the MFA programme which called for the dismantling of the fascist infrastructure.

The big Portuguese monopolies were not created through the ordinary process of capitalist competition in efficiency and good management. They were created almost ready-made, when Salazar decided after World War II that some industrialisation must be permitted. Until then he had been against industry, because he feared that this would create an industrial proletariat which would raise the spectre of communism. Portugal should remain an agricultural country – at most, processing tobacco and cotton from the colonies – producing wine at home, and cork to plug the bottles. But during World War II, when several of the belligerents found it convenient to establish industries in ostensibly 'neutral' Portugal, a lot of foreign currency was earned by exporting various products, from tin and wolfram to olive oil and canned sardines, to the same belligerents – not to mention the interest on hard currency placed in the 'safe haven' of non-belligerent Portugal's banks. Also because of wartime conditions, as it became difficult to obtain spare parts for imported machinery, these had to be made locally. By the end of the war, there was a lot of accumulated capital and an appetite on the part of the bankers for profitable investments – including in industry. But Salazar continued to be very prudent – haunted by that constant spectre of an emerging industrial proletariat. Whatever happened had to be a carefully controlled process, with industrial development entrusted to the hands of half a dozen or so big financial-industrial groups which had constituted the origin and pillar of the regime.

'Salazar was supposed to be a financial wizard,' explained one of Portugal's top economists, engaged by the provisional government to try to repair some of the economic wreckage inherited from fascism. 'That was the image he succeeded in creating abroad. In fact, he had no real grasp of economics or finance. All he cared about – and in this he was a model fascist – was political power exerted through the apparatus of repression. With plenty of capital accumulated during World War II, the bankers started putting on the squeeze to move into industry in a big way. [Those already well established in industry applied pressures to move into banking.] So, in the 1950s, Salazar was obliged to build some of the infrastructure needed by industry. Of course, this was financed by the taxpayers, not the bankers. Roads, some hydro-electric projects – often at the expense of the peasants whose lands were flooded – technical schools to train specialised workers; and a modest expansion of general education to provide foundation training for recruits for the technical schools.

'It was not only new for Salazar, but also for the bankers, to move into industry. Banking had its origins in the absentee landlords who lived in Lisbon and Porto, and the luxury resorts of the Algarve. They looked for investment outlets for the revenues extorted from the peasantry. Some of the banking firms grew out of those that controlled the processing industries based on raw materials from the colonies, especially cotton and tobacco. The *latifundia* and tobacco interests, married together in banking, were the decisive elements behind the military coup of 1926.[1] They were the ruling class and demanded that "order" be established and maintained. It was the alliance, and, in many cases, the identity, between the *latifundia* and the bankers that kept Salazar in power. So, when the bankers demanded industry, and industrialists sought to strengthen their power by demanding banks, Salazar could not refuse. Had he done so, his power base would have collapsed under him.'

To ensure a smooth transition from an almost exclusively rural economy to a partially industrialised one, areas of production were farmed out between the half-dozen established banking or trading enterprises under such conditions as ensured their dominance, either in specific branches of production, or in geographic regions in Portugal or the African colonies. CUF, which directly owns 10 per cent of all manufacturing, trading and banking concerns in Portugal, and partially owns a far higher percentage, was allotted chemical and metallurgical industries, petrol refining, mining, maritime transport, shipbuilding and ship-repair yards, the cellulose and tobacco industries, real estate, banking (the Totta and Azores bank), insurance, and export–import and internal trade.[2]

Champalimaud started with a virtual monopoly of cement production, investing the resulting super-profits in steelmaking so successfully that, by 1971, Champalimaud accounted for two-thirds of all sales of iron and steel in Portugal, although there were forty-seven other producers. Champalimaud, however, is the only one with blast furnaces and modern steelmaking capacity, and accounted in the same year for half the sales in all basic metallurgical products, although there were 128 other companies competing.[3] The same company also owns the Pinto and Sotto-Mayor bank, and three major insurance companies.

The Espírito Santo group is an example of a firm starting as an ordinary commercial bank in Lisbon, then financing exploitation in Angola

---

1 [EN] *Latifundia*, plural form of the Latin term *latifundium*, a large agricultural estate owned by an aristocratic family of ancient Rome and worked by peasants or slaves. In pre-revolutionary Portugal, the term was adopted to refer to the large estates in the southern Alentejo region, owned by socio-economic elites who typically supported the Estado Novo. Portuguese *latifundia* relied on landless, impoverished day labourers for their workforce.

2 [AN] CUF, Companhia União Fabril (United Manufacturing Company) is referred to earlier as Portugal's biggest single monopoly.

3 [AN] From *Sociedades e Grupos em Portugal* by Maria Belmira Martins, an authoritative woman economist. [EN] Published in Lisbon by Editorial Estampa, Colecção Polémica (Nova Série) No. 8, 1975; this edition went through two printings.

and Mozambique, specialising at first in coffee and sugar plantations, and gradually building up a whole industrial empire. Two-fifths of the capital of Espírito Santo is still invested in the African territories. Its specialties include rubber and tyre production; cellulose and paper; a new cement company in Portugal (CINORTE in Coimbra); breweries in Portugal and the African territories; banking and insurance; the hotel and tourist business – with important links with the Rockefeller and other American banking interests. It is associated with the First National City Bank of New York, the Banco Inter-Unido of Angola, and with the ITT Corporation in Lisbon's Sheraton Hotel.

Of 40,051 companies listed as operating in Portugal at the end of December 1972, 168 of them accounted for 53 per cent of total capital involved. Many of the 168 were polarised into single groupings, the whole economy being dominated by seven major groups, whose most typical feature is the merger of financial and industrial capital. Either banks branched out into industry and trade, or industrial groups founded their own banks. All own considerable investments in the African territories. These seven groups, especially the 'Big Four' among them, represented the economic base of fascism. (The fourth 'Big' is the Banco Português do Atlântico, which has a virtual monopoly on the production of cellulose, synthetic resins and glass, and owns hydroelectric power stations, cotton mills and textile plants, not forgetting chains of cinemas, advertising companies and parking lots.)

'When they started moving from processing raw materials from the colonies into developing local industry,' explained my economist informant, 'they were protected from the start by the state. To start a factory, you needed permission from the government. The big groups had no problems in getting approval to have a virtual monopoly position in the line they wanted. One would take steel, another cement, a third chemicals.

'The four biggest of them owned banks and non-competitive industries. They did not need to be efficient; they didn't need to modernise. Local markets were protected by customs barriers; prices were set by the government – which was themselves. A minister would go directly from the ministry, where he had set the price for cement – or allotted a ten-million-dollar contract – to the board of directors meeting, where he would announce the new price or the government contract. Government and monopolies were linked at all levels. PIDE or its predecessors ensured that there would be no labour troubles – so the monopolies were protected from all sides. No competition between themselves; no competition from abroad; no problems of industrial unrest. That is why our industry today remains very inefficient and non-competitive, in terms of international prices and quality. In its present state, it is incapable of serving the needs of a modern, developing economy.

'Another protection for the monopolies was their virtual exemption from taxation, the laws regarding which were legalistic marvels, designed to pamper the biggest and richest enterprises. When Salazar finally agreed to industrialise, he reasoned that the big existing groups must be accorded all sorts of tax rebates and exemptions to finance their expansion. A code of protection was worked out, ensuring that even the most exorbitant profits were not taxed as long as – on paper, at least – they were reinvested in expansion. Such exemptions applied only to the handful of big monopolies. As state revenues had to be maintained to finance the wars in Africa, in order to protect the interests of the monopolies there, the burden of increased taxation fell on the small and medium enterprises.

'Because of the integration of big finance with big industry, the banks were not interested in supporting the small and medium enterprises. On the contrary. They were interested in driving them bankrupt to accelerate their absorption by the monopolies. The only form of state support for small and medium enterprises was to ensure the same cheap labour power as for the monopolies, with no agitation for improved working conditions.'

This particular economist spoke with not only expertise but some passion on this subject, because he worked on a special committee, established after the setting up of the second provisional government, to help the survival of small and medium enterprises.

'When we speak today of the "economic heritage" of fascism,' he continued, 'it is not an empty phrase. As the only "aid" the small and medium enterprises enjoyed was cheap labour, and as they got no credits to invest in equipment, production was based on antiquated methods, employing much labour-power and with low productivity. They were always at a disadvantage. If any big enterprises started up, the state immediately built roads and power lines to support them. The big banks obviously reserved their credits for them also. For small and medium enterprises, the lack of infrastructure, especially roads and power lines, was always a major handicap. Neither the state nor the banks would help, and they rarely had the financial reserves to handle such problems.

'When the monopolies were forced to modernise in some sectors, they called in foreign capital. Officially, 51 per cent of capital in any enterprise had to be Portuguese, to ensure nominal control; but as the foreign companies controlled the market, they could dominate the activities, whatever percentage of the capital they held. The petrochemical industry, for instance, was built up with a minority investment of foreign capital, but it is controlled by British-based Imperial Chemical Industries through their monopoly of the markets. Many foreign enterprises wanted to put a foot into Portugal itself, in order to have a foot in the door of the African colonies. This was a major reason for investing in otherwise uninteresting projects here. They are interested in long-term planning. One group wanted to set up shipbuilding yards in South Angola. The Caetano government agreed, but some of our more realistic technocrats warned the group that they had better contact the MPLA, to see if they were interested or not in such a project.[4] The point is that this group used a small investment here to gain a foothold in Africa.

'Cheap labour here and the repressive machinery to keep it cheap was obviously an attraction for many foreign investors, once the doors began to open.'

Regarding the repressive aspect of fascism in the field of labour relations, it was instructive to talk with Carlos Carvalhas, secretary of state at the Ministry of Labour, a vital, energetic young person, typical of the new blood transfused into some of the ministries after 25 April.[5]

'We are now engaged in reforming the whole structure of this ministry,' he said. 'Before, it was known as the Ministry of Corporations and Social Assistance. In fact, it was more like a branch of the police. A large number of employees were doing exclusively police work, meaning the surveillance of "agitators"; of workers suspected of being behind strikes or demands for higher wages; those publishing leaflets, or even writing articles in the official trade union journals that the fascists feared could incite "unrest".

---

4 [AN] Popular Movement for the Liberation of Angola, which was generally regarded at that time as the broadest based of the three Angolan national liberation movements.

5 [EN] Carlos Alberto do Vale Gomes Carvalhas (1941–), politician and economist, joined the Portuguese Communist Party in 1969, having supported the anti-Salazar movement as a student. After the 25 April coup, he served as minister of labour and as an elected delegate of the National Assembly. Carvalhas succeeded Álvaro Cunhal as secretary general of the PCP, 1993–2004.

'Although the previous occupants used the period between 25 April and the establishment of the first provisional government to remove or burn many of the records, enough files were left for us to have a picture of how they worked. A key function of the ministry was to put the finger on militants for PIDE investigators to follow up, or to investigate cases reported to them by the PIDE and send the dossiers over to the Ministry of the Interior. The PIDE sent regular reports to this ministry – analyses of literature, legal and clandestine – of discussions among workers. The Portuguese Legion had a special branch for monitoring telephone conversations of suspected militants, the transcripts of which were sent here.

'There was a special "social action" department, for which the yearly expenditure of 120 million escudos did not appear in the ministry's budget but was a secret fund to finance propaganda. TV films, articles placed in the press about the ministry's "social work", special propaganda during election years – all these were financed from this fund. Furthermore, there was a scandalous and typically fascist trick whereby money deducted from workers' wages – ostensibly for a social assistance fund – was in fact diverted, either directly to the monopolies to finance their expansion, or indirectly via the banks they owned, or which owned them, for the same purpose.

'Every town had representatives of the ministry, some of whom did the same sort of police work as those in Lisbon, each branch connected with the centre by telex. Apart from urgent reports on any suspected "agitation" from the ministry's own agents, or those of the PIDE, the latter submitted overall reports every two weeks, with copies of literature and pamphlets, and the PIDE analysis of what was meant "between the lines".

Among a sheaf of such reports that Carlos Carvalhas had in his desk was one referring to his own activities as an expert consultant for the Metallurgical Workers' Union, falsely accusing him of having organised a meeting at COMETNA (the National Metallurgical Company, which belongs to the Champalimaud group), scheduled for 27 April, according to the PIDE report, to agitate for a strike. In the period just preceding 25 April, there were some 18,000 workers on strike in various industries, according to the PIDE reports, and its agents were being especially active, as was always the case, I was told, in the weeks preceding 1 May. Another report named a woman as having organised a strike at the US-owned firm Applied Magnetics, with a footnote saying that she had been sacked and her file sent to the Ministry of the Interior for 'appropriate action'.

'Typical of how the "corporative" system worked,' continued Carlos Carvalhas, 'is the fact that, although the ministry had the same juridical authority over the owners as over the workers, we have not come across a single case of surveillance of an owner or manager.'

An obvious question was, how was it possible to carry on any legal trade union activity within such a spy-ridden system?

'The trade unions had a legal existence within the corporative system,' explained Carlos Carvalhas, 'and the workers understood that, even under fascism, and imperfect and limited as the trade unions were, they could still be used as a weapon of struggle to improve conditions and embarrass the regime. The government tried to restrict trade union activities to a minimum. In theory, members could elect their own leaders; in practice, the PIDE checked the lists of nominees and struck out any suspected of communist leanings. This was done within the framework of the anti-communist laws. Anyone on the PIDE blacklist was ineligible for leadership. Despite that, it was often possible to elect leaders who had the confidence of the workers. Over the years, much experience was gathered on how to carry on the struggle for better conditions, even within the framework of the corporative system.'

Our conversation took place on 7 August, and there was a festive atmosphere in the secretary of state's office, as visitors kept popping in to exchange a few words and wring his hand. Earlier in the day, it was announced that a decree had been signed officially dissolving the corporations, which meant, among other things, that ordinary class forces would come into play, and the trade unions would have a life of their own.

With an entire Ministry of Labour's spies at their disposal, backed by a couple of networks of secret police, the big monopolies must have felt they were invulnerable for all time – the envy of the multinational concerns which later came to exploit the benefits of the same system. All that was changed by 25 April. With the organs of repression removed from their grasp, their ties with the ministries gone, the future of their African territories threatened, the trade unions getting organised – and widespread calls for action to curb their stranglehold on the country's economy – such circumstances explain why some of the monopolies were directly involved in the desperate counter-revolutionary coup attempt at the end of September. And in the still more desperate venture of 11 March 1975. In so doing, they dug their own graves!

11
Multinationals

As the approaching world economic depression cast its long shadows towards the end of 1974, the role of the 'multinationals' – enterprises wholly or substantially owned by foreign capital operating on someone else's territory – became increasingly often an object of public discussion. Portugal's experience in this field after 25 April contributes to an understanding of how the 'multinationals' operated. Until that time, for reasons explained in the previous chapter, Portugal seemed an ideal place to establish industries which needed a cheap and rigidly disciplined labour force. All types of finicky assembly work, from electronic parts to watches, but including automobiles; any industry where – if the wages were right and could be guaranteed to stay that way – it was cheaper to replace machines by men. Portugal was virtually the only European country which could compete with certain Asian countries – South Korea, Taiwan, Singapore, *et cetera* – when it came to cheap labour.

By almost every index used to measure living standards – consumption of essential foods, education, public health and per capita income – Portugal was at the bottom of the list of European countries, with Greece and Spain competing for second-to-last place. Thus, per capita income in US dollars for 1970 was set at $2,698 and $2,606 respectively for West Germany and France, $891 for Greece, $889 for Spain and only $610 for Portugal – slightly lower than the $632 for Mexico and $629 for

Panama.[1] Whatever statistics one studied, they justified the thesis of Portugal's new leaders that, economically, she belonged to the Third World of developing nations.

It was just this backwardness that made Portugal so attractive to the 'multinationals'. Another of the country's top economists, now employed by the government in studying, among other questions, the question of the multinationals, said: 'The watch-making firm Timex, for instance, deliberated over whether to set up business here or in South Korea. Eighty per cent of the production goes to Japan, so South Korea presented obvious advantages. The owners decided on Portugal, apparently because the long continuity of fascism was a guarantee of greater political stability. But our country gets no benefit whatsoever. On the contrary. The raw materials, technology and management come from outside; the production goes abroad. Some parts are made in Scotland, others in Besançon [France], but the assembly is done here under atrocious conditions. To set foot inside Timex, you have to get permission from the general manager. I, a Portuguese economist on an official mission, had to wait months to get that permission.

'When I did succeed, I found it like a prison. It reminded me of Charlie Chaplin's *Modern Times* – but this was real, and wholly tragic. Lines of girls bent over twitching assembly lines, making automatic hand movements, ruining their eyes, forbidden to speak to each other. After a year or two, they must start wearing glasses, and that marks the first step towards losing their efficiency and being thrown onto the street a year or two later. Taken on at fifteen or sixteen, they are chucked out at eighteen or nineteen, with ruined eyesight. This is only one aspect but, from a human viewpoint, one of the worst.

'There are Swedish and Finnish ready-made clothing firms which did not even bring in capital. They got loans from Portuguese banks to exploit our cheap labour and export the finished products to Western Europe.

'Once the door had been opened to the multinationals, Salazar and Caetano tried to project Portugal at home as a "technically advanced" country with "modern, sophisticated" industries. "We may not yet have

---

1 [AN] UN Statistical Yearbook, 1971. [EN] Full citation: United Nations Department of Economic and Social Affairs, *United Nations Statistical Yearbook (Series S), 1971 (Twenty-third issue)* (Lake Success, New York: January 1973).

colour TV," Caetano once said, "but we are already manufacturing colour TV sets." Nonsense! We were assembling parts brought in by Grundig and ITT, and the finished products were being shipped out to the world markets. If Grundig, ITT and the others pulled out, Portugal could not continue producing TV sets and other electronic equipment. The industrial secrets remain in the hands of the multinationals. There is no training of Portuguese workers in modern technology. Technique and management remain in foreign hands. If Timex pulled out, for instance, all that would be left for us would be the social problem of looking after girls with ruined eyesight. The government pretended that the invasion by the multinationals was a great contribution to national development. They would introduce new techniques; help to train a new generation of workers and management! The only real contribution they have made is to alert us to this new form of exploitation. Just as we exploit cheap African labour in the colonies, so the multinationals exploit cheap Portuguese labour on our own territory.'

His predictions as to what would happen if the multinationals – at least a certain category of them – pulled out proved to be correct. The case of the American company Applied Magnetics will remain classic in this respect. When the minimum basic wage for male and female workers was set at 3,300 escudos per month, Applied Magnetics lost interest in Portugal. It was involved in Timex-type operations; in this case, the assembly of magnetic heads to be incorporated into computers, the final assembly of which was done in the United States. It turned out that the 3,300 escudos per month was more than double the wages Applied Magnetics had been paying. As mentioned earlier, a woman suspected of agitating for better conditions was sacked forthwith, and the dossier on her 'case' handed over to the Ministry of the Interior. That was the sort of protection the multinationals appreciated in Portugal!

The first response by Applied Magnetics to the new minimum wage was to fire 116 workers and, by speed-up methods, to try to get the remaining workers – almost 600 – to maintain normal production. Instead, they agitated for the reinstatement of those fired! The next response of the management – apparently a reflex from the 'good old days' – was to ask the Ministry of Finance for a loan of five million escudos to cover the wage hikes. Carlos Carvalhas, at the Ministry of Labour, assured me that Allied Magnetics, in two years of operations, had pocketed eleven times the amount of capital originally invested. (The Lisbon press claimed that the magnetic heads were delivered to the parent company in the USA for $165 apiece, whereas the international market price was $5,000 dollars. The difference went into the profits on the completed computers.)

The monthly pay day fell on 23 July, but no wages were paid, on the pretext that the Ministry of Finance had turned down the request for a loan. Secretary of State Carvalhas called in Mr Cecil Fraser, the American manager, and asked him to pay the wages. Fraser promised this would be done, but instead he flew out of the country and, from the Hotel Sheraton in London, sent a telex to the effect that the factory could henceforth be considered closed. The Portuguese authorities were free to sell off the machinery and pay the back wages from the proceeds. In fact, Fraser had left a wages bill that far exceeded even his own inventory value of the machinery.

'The machinery was so much scrap iron,' Carlos Carvalhas told me, with Fraser's telex in his hand. 'It was designed to make a particular part for a particular computer and cannot be adapted for anything else. Such enterprises contribute absolutely nothing to our economy. No technology, no production for developing our own economy, or even for our markets.' The trade unions had to launch an appeal for funds to keep the unemployed Applied Magnetics workers going until other jobs were found for them. Within a couple of weeks, another US electronics plant, the Signetics Corporation, informed the Ministry of Labour that it was laying off 1,000 workers. A few days later, a third such plant, General Data Electronics, announced that it was closing down.

To what extent the reasons were purely economic – rising labour costs – and to what extent they were political were matters of conjecture. It was significant, in any case, that the close-downs came after the provisional government had moved to the left, following the resignation of Palma Carlos. Cecil Fraser listed the reason for the closure of Applied Magnetics as 'social and political problems with the Portuguese workers', and blandly stated that AMC (USA), the parent company, could not be responsible for the debts of AMP (Applied Magnetics Portugal), which was a 'Portuguese enterprise'. Faced with this example of multinationals' morality, Portuguese workers were understandably impressed. So were the representatives of the MFA attached to the Ministry of Labour!

When the crisis at Applied Magnetics was reaching its climax, the Lisbon evening paper, *Diário de Lisboa*, published an article by the economist Eugénio Rosa, which touched on other aspects of the role of the multinationals:[2]

> Fascism transformed Portugal into a colonised country as well as a colonial one. Portugal had, and still has, colonies, but it has also become a colony of foreign capitalists.
>
> Fundamental sectors of our economy have fallen into the hands of foreigners, or else they end up being exploited by big Portuguese capitalists linked with foreign imperialism.
>
> The examples are so many that it is impossible to present them all in this article. Suffice it to present a few cases to prove our point, starting with wholly foreign enterprises now installed in Portugal.
>
> In this group, which is enormous, we could start with Standard Electric's Oliva plant, which belongs to ITT (USA); Ford Lusitânia, which is the property of American Ford; Automática Portuguêsa, which belongs to the English Plessey Company; the Sociedade de Productos Lácteos belonging to Nestlé of Switzerland; General Motors of Portugal, which is American; Lever Portuguêsa, which belongs to Unilever of Britain; Mobil Oil Portuguêsa and Chrysler Portuguêsa, which are American; Robbialac Portuguêsa; Hoechst Portuguêsa, Bayer Portugal, AEG-Telefunken, Robert Bosch (Portugal), Siemens – all of them West German enterprises, *et cetera*; the complete list being too long to abuse the patience of our readers.
>
> Still longer is the list of enterprises in which big Portuguese capital is associated with foreign capital in the exploitation of Portuguese workers.
>
> To give a few examples, it is interesting to recall that Lisnave and Sacor, two of the country's biggest enterprises, belong, the first to CUF and Swedish capitalists, the second to local and American nationals.[3]

---

2 [EN] Eugénio Óscar Garcia da Rosa (1941–), an influential economist and politician; member of the Portuguese Communist Party (PCP).

3 [AN] Lisnave, mentioned earlier, owns the country's biggest shipbuilding and ship-repairing yards, with Dutch and Danish, as well as Swedish capital associated with CUF. In Sacor, which handles petrol refining and distribution, Mobil Oil (USA) is associated with the Espírito Santo bank and the Banco Português do Atlântico.

Rosa lists a dozen leading enterprises in which foreign capital is strongly represented, and continues: 'To sum up, the Portuguese economy is dominated by a network of big enterprises belonging either entirely to foreign capital or to foreign capital linked with big Portuguese capital.'[4] The author points out that Salazar opened the door to foreign capital in 1961, when the national liberation struggle started in Angola. The aim was to raise enough money to crush that movement, and the others which were soon to break out in Mozambique and Guinea-Bissau. Attractive terms were offered, such as the total transfer of profits and extremely low taxation – not to mention the fact that strikes were prohibited and labour agitation repressed with utmost severity. Foreign investments rose from 1.7 billion escudos in 1961 to eight billion by 1968. One of the results of the generous policy in export of profits was that a positive balance of payments of 3.8 billion escudos in 1962 was, by 1972, transformed into a negative balance of 2.7 billion. As for the Salazar–Caetano claim that the influx of foreign capital would create new enterprises that would open up vast new perspectives for employment in industry, Eugénio Rosa commented:

> One can truthfully say that foreign capital investment did not so much create new jobs in Portugal, as it created new employment in other countries with the surplus values created by Portuguese workers for the foreign investors.
>
> It is also undeniable that the influx of foreign capital into Portugal was not only used for setting up new companies, but, more often, for buying up existing Portuguese enterprises with capital easily obtainable for foreign investors from the national banks.
>
> The domination of the Portuguese economy and the economies of the colonies by foreign capital constitutes today one of the main obstacles to consolidating democracy in Portugal; to solving the grave economic problems which confront us, and to ending the colonial wars.

The extent and tempo of foreign capital penetration, as set forth in a rare study of this aspect of the Portuguese economy,[5] demonstrate that in

---

4 [AN] *Diário de Lisboa*, 12 July 1974.

5 [AN] *Investimentos estrangeiros em Portugal*, by Luís Salgado de Matos; Seara Nova Publishing House, Lisbon, December 1973, 99.

the period 1961–67, foreign investments totalled 20 billion escudos, whereas in the previous seven years (1953–60) they totalled 2 billion. The tempo continued to increase, according to the author, who writes, based on such meagre official statistics as were available, that: 'In 1971, private foreign capital investments reached between three to four times that of the 1953–60 period.'

It was also in 1971 that Portugal, for the first time in thirty years, started seeking foreign loans to finance the colonial wars. In the period 1969–71, foreign capital accounted for 66.9 per cent of all capital invested in new enterprises, or in buying into or expanding those already established. During that period, foreign capital participation in all branches of economic activity, from agriculture and forestry, through petrol refining and steel production, down to the service trades – hotels, tourism and others – amounted to 33.1 per cent.[6]

By 1970–71, the number of enterprises in which foreign capital was involved amounted to 21 per cent, but it was particularly heavy in what could be considered the strategic industries, as the following table shows:

Percentage of Portuguese firms receiving foreign capital investment, by industry[7]

Petroleum refining	100
Electrical machinery	81
Rubber products	72
Transport equipment	62
Chemical industry	48
Paper and paper pulp	43
Treatment of non-ferrous metals	43
Metallurgical and machine-building	38
Extraction industry	32
Transformation industry	30

These figures represent the proportion of enterprises in various branches of the economy in which foreign capital was involved, not the

---

6 [AN] Ibid., 134. The author bases his figures on 1971 reports of the Banco de Portugal.
7 [AN] Ibid., 135–6.

proportion of foreign investment in each branch. The author, with due objectivity, notes that even a majority holding of the capital in any enterprise did not automatically ensure obedience to decisions made outside the country. The state had the right to impose its own decisions. But he also noted that cases in which, with 'a minimum of foreign capital, enterprises were entirely dependent on decisions taken abroad, were much more frequent, because of the necessities of credit financing, the techniques employed, and through control of the markets on which the enterprises depended'.

If one accepts the official figure of 40,491 enterprises registered in Portugal in 1970, of which 990 were foreign-owned, then the latter amounted to only 2.4 per cent of the total. But if one takes the proportion of capital invested in these industries, it comes to almost 30 per cent. The average investment of Portuguese capital per enterprise is listed at 1,725 million escudos, that of foreign capital at 14,945 million – an average of over eight times as much, in the same branches of industry. These figures do not reflect foreign investment in nominally Portuguese-owned enterprises. But they obviously indicate that the amount of capital available for the modernisation, and thus the increased competitivity, of the foreign-owned enterprises was many times superior to that available to their local small and medium counterparts.

This was another of the attractions for the multinationals. For those interested in producing for the internal market, with more modern technology and the same cheap labour, they could undercut their Portuguese competitors and eventually drive them out of business.

Although for historical reasons, England still remains the biggest single foreign investor in Portugal, the USA, followed by West Germany and Britain, has been the biggest investor in recent years, providing 23.8 per cent of total investments in the 1969–71 period, compared to the Common Market countries' – mainly West Germany – 28.9 per cent, and Britain's 13.3 per cent.[8]

US investments in Portugal itself are mainly in car assembly, electric and electronic products, pharmaceutics, petrol distribution; the tourist,

---

8 [AN] According to the Bank of Portugal figures. [EN] Britain did not join the European Common Market (the EEC) until 1 January 1973; this is why Burchett referred to Britain's investment separately, as a non-European Common Market country for the period 1969–71.

hotel, food (Knorr and Heinz), wine importing – especially a rosé wine that seems to suit the American palate – and canning industries. British interests are mainly in trade, especially the export of timber, port wine and corks; the chemical (ICI) and electrical industries, insurance and tourism, ready-made clothing, and petrol distribution. West German investments are mainly in the electronic and chemical branches, with I.G. Farben and its affiliates strongly represented. These three countries, together with Belgium – with a much smaller participation – account for 75 per cent of all foreign investments in Portugal.

What are the attractions for the multinationals, especially the big industrial giants? Luís Salgado de Matos points out that there are two determining factors for foreign investors: the certitude of higher profits than is possible in his country of origin; and guarantees against losses, due either to political factors (nationalisation) or economic factors (inability to transfer profits). The decision to invest in Portugal should be placed within this general framework. Matos notes that, as far as American investors are concerned, an agreement was signed between the two countries guaranteeing against expropriation of any US enterprises; further, in the event of an investor liquidating his business interests, there would be full convertibility for the transfer of funds realised therefrom. The main factors guaranteeing high profits are indicated by Matos as cheap manpower and 'political stability'.

> In the case of clothing and tailoring, printing, electric and electronic material, and ceramics, it is the low wage levels that attract the foreign enterprises. Wages in Portuguese industry are, on average, one-third of those in Austria, one-sixth of those in Norway, one-fifth of those in England, one-seventh of those in Sweden. If we consider a Portuguese industry in which labour costs amount to 30 per cent of the total production costs – which is about what it is in furniture manufactures, electric machine-building, transport and printing – and if we suppose that all other costs of production are equal in Portugal with other countries whose wages are five times higher than in Portugal, then we see that the products of industry in countries which pay better salaries will be more than double those produced in Portugal.[9]

---

9   [AN] Ibid., 218.

According to International Labour Organisation figures for 1971, quoted by Eugénio Rosa in a second article, the average daily wage of a textile worker was 400 escudos in West Germany, 220 in France, 180 in Italy, and only sixty escudos in Portugal.[10] It was obviously these types of statistics that were decisive in influencing the multinationals in choosing between Italy, Spain or Portugal for setting up industries where wages made up a high proportion of production costs.

The biggest single foreign investor in Portugal is ITT, with the Standard Electric, Facel and Rabor plants engaged in the manufacture and assembly of electric and electronic instruments, the Oliva plant for sewing machines and other domestic appliances, the Imprimarte printing works, Avis Hire Cars, and the huge Sheraton Hotel in Lisbon. ITT's annual sales of over one billion escudos place it among the first ten money earners among manufacturing and trading enterprises in Portugal.

It is obvious that groups such as ITT had the same vested interests in maintaining the fascist regime in Portugal as in bringing to power the fascist Pinochet regime in Chile. And, inversely, the same vested interest in overthrowing the Gonçalves government as they had in overthrowing the Allende government.

It is predictable that any elected government will take a long, hard look at the conditions under which the multinationals operate in Portugal and, for a start, will at least plug the holes of tax evasion, cheap credits, unlimited transfer of profits, and other virtually supra-national privileges accorded them by the fascist regime.

---

10   [AN] *Diário de Lisboa*, 20 July 1974.

12
Alentejo

Among the many remarkable persons encountered in Portugal was a forty-nine-year-old agricultural labourer, Manuel João Passão, a short, slight man with a brown, wrinkled face and sharp twinkling eyes – stone deaf in one ear from a bashing-up by PIDE agents. He received me in his 'cottage', rented from the local absentee landlord. No windows or chimney, no piped water or sewerage, no lighting except that which streamed through the gaps in the roof where tiles were broken. Depressions in the packed-earth floor marked where rain had pelted down through those same gaps a few days earlier. A few rabbits were huddled in a hutch outside, some turkeys scrabbled in the garden. His 'cottage' was typical of others I visited in this area – a dozen or so kilometres from Montemor-o-Novo, a charming small town and marketplace, dominated by the ruins of a walled medieval city on a nearby hill, the ramparts of which dated back to Roman times. We were in the heart of the Upper Alentejo, one of the country's richest agricultural regions.[1]

We had met by chance over a midnight beer a week earlier, after a meeting to elect a new municipal council at Montemor-o-Novo, and he had invited me to come back and see how the agricultural labourers of the region lived and worked.

---

1 [AN] The Alentejo (other side of the Tejo or Tagus River) is divided into the Alto (Upper) and Baixo (Lower) districts.

'A labourer in these parts,' he said in reply to my first question about general conditions, 'is a thing, an object – something to be used like a hoe or an ox, but not to be considered as a human being. There are no laws to define our status. We are absolutely dependent on the whims of the *latifundia* – the absentee landlords. There is no protection whatsoever – no bargaining power as far as the law is concerned. The boss hires and fires and sets the daily wage. If he has no use for someone, he chucks him out regardless of his length of service. There is no defence against this, and no financial aid for unemployment.

'Under the best conditions, there is work for nine months of the year in this area – but that is the maximum. For the other months there is no income. That is why tens of thousands have emigrated from here during the past few years. Emigration was mainly from the North until seven or eight years ago, when it started here. The departure of thousands annually slightly improved the situation of those who stayed – a few extra days of work each season. But unemployment for three or four months every year remains constant.

'The greatest problem here is not even the wages – miserable as they are. It is chronic malnutrition. Because we live dispersed and far from shopping centres and markets, we get no meat or fish, no milk or fruit, even when we have the money to pay the prices. We live off a few vegetables planted around our hovels – off bread and olives, with an occasional bit of rabbit.'

To get to his house we had driven from Montemor-o-Novo along the main road to Lisbon, turning off along a dirt track leading through dense oak forests interspersed with olive groves and forests of holm-oaks, the bark of which has the mysterious properties which constitute cork.[2] It was the stripping season, and the trunks of the trees that had been operated on were blood-red in the afternoon sun. With twisted arms raised imploringly towards the sky and their freshly naked, smooth bodies, one had a strange impression of Christian martyrs nailed to crosses. We passed stubby tractors hauling trailers piled high with canoe-shaped sheets of cork bark, to be unloaded and stacked like

---

2 [EN] Burchett misidentified the forests of trees which provide cork. They are called 'cork oaks' in English (*sobreiros* in Portuguese), a mistake which was corrected to *montados de sobro* in the Portuguese translation.

sheaves of wheat at points where trucks picked them up for transport to the railhead.

At one point, Manuel stopped the car and drew my attention to placards behind a barbed wire–topped netting fence, which read 'No Hunting or Fishing', quoting an ancient law which provided for dire penalties in case of violations.

'A new form of thievery invented by Caetano,' he explained. 'These are the so-called *coutadas de caça* – hunting preserves – formed simply by netting off what were common lands before. The state put up 30 per cent of the cost for fencing them off – officially to protect them from wandering cattle. In fact, to lease them out to the big estate-owners as hunting grounds, which they could sublet to their wealthy cronies. Anyone had the right to go into the woods before, to hunt some rabbits, a partridge – or wild boar if you had a gun – to help solve the family food problem. Now, the big proprietors have built hunting lodges, which they lease out for hunting parties for their city friends. Any number of fields, of several hundred hectares in a single lot, good for wheat and other food crops, have also been enclosed and leased out for nominal rents.

'A decree by Caetano in 1971 permitted the big estate-owners to add to their existing holdings by up to another 70 per cent from the common lands in such enclosures, known as *herdades*. They rent these out for the hunting season, or for weekend carousing by the bankers and big company directors. The owners live in Lisbon and the luxury tourist centres. They usually have half a dozen sumptuously furnished villas and move from one to another according to their whims. Of course, they have a big house on the estate, with servants always on hand in case they decide to come for the weekend. They have absolutely no contact with the labourers who make their money for them. This is a triple crime. Tens of thousands of hectares of land are taken out of production. Hunting used to be an important supplement to the labourers' food supplies. Often it was the only way to get a bit of meat. The small animals that live behind the protection of the "No Trespass" notices come out at night and devour the grain and vegetables grown by the labourers around their cottages.'

An intriguing question was how Manuel, despite his obviously humble background, was so articulate – there were also well-thumbed books on some rough planks.

Figure 12.1. Self-adhesive political placard advocating the defence of agrarian reform and land re-distribution favouring landless agricultural day labourers; Alentejo district, southern Portugal, autumn 1974. (Drawing by Paulo Barral)

'Most people around here have had no schooling,' he replied to my discreet question about his education. 'Primary schools are often seven to eight kilometres away from living quarters. There is rarely any public transport. In the winter months, this meant slogging it out on foot against rain and snow. Even if there was a school close to home – who had money for tuition fees or to buy books? Or to buy clothes and footwear? Children with bare feet and ragged trousers or skirts were not welcomed. Schooling in general was out of the question. On the other hand, the fascist bureaucracy forbade "child labour". This meant in effect that they could work in the fields, because that was the only way for their parents to have them under supervision, but they were not paid. They were exclusively consumers – not allowed to be educated or to contribute anything to the family budget.

'I was lucky. The nearest school was seven kilometres away, and to get there meant crossing a river. My parents forbade me to go, although I wanted to. My grandmother, who adored me, took me into her home close to the school. So, I got one year's schooling, which gave me a taste for learning. I passed with a "very good" for admittance into the second year, but the number of places were limited. Only the children of the rich and well-dressed got those places. So, I started work as a cowherd at the age of seven – of course, without any pay.

'When I was fourteen, a lad two years older than me taught me to read. I quickly got to the point where I could read alone; in fact, I progressed so well that my "tutor" got somewhat jealous that I had left him behind. But I remained grateful to him for having opened up an entirely new world. One of the first complete books I read was an anticlerical novel, *De Profundis*, by an Italian writer whose name I've forgotten.[3] It made a deep impression. I developed a taste for factual, realistic novels like that which dealt with problems close to our lives. Abstract, metaphysical books did not appeal to me. Later I developed a taste for our own neo-realist school of writers, the works of Carlos de Oliveira, Fernando Namora, Alves Redol, and others who presented our lives as they were.'[4]

The earthen floor, the light from gaps in the roof, the tunnel-like arches that joined up the rooms, disappeared as Manuel João Passão

---

3 [EN] Manuel João Passão may have been referring here to *De Profundis*, published in 1948 by Italian author Salvatore Satta, or possibly to Oscar Wilde's work of the same title, the only pre-1974 Portuguese-language edition of which was published in Brazil in 1933 (São Paulo: Edições e Publicações Brasil).

4 [EN] Carlos Alberto Serra de Oliveira (1921–1981), Fernando Gonçalves Namora (1919–1989) and António Alves Redol (1911–1969) were all popular, critically acclaimed Portuguese authors associated with neo-realism, a literary movement of the mid-twentieth century that was influenced by the artistic, cultural and political concepts of socialist realism.

revealed how a taste for literature led him step by step along the path of social agitation.

'I was lucky because of my grandmother's insistence on at least that one year of schooling,' he continued. 'Without it, the cultural backwardness of the agricultural labourers is hard to imagine. The great majority have never had the chance to learn to read or write. They have no access to books or newspapers. The only contact with the outside world is through radio, and now, gradually, TV – a set installed in some public place. But we are so dispersed that TV hardly counts. It is mainly the spoken word that counts. Until 25 April, we were not supposed even to attend public meetings. But you saw how enthusiastic people were at the meeting a week ago. They were mostly agricultural labourers, drinking in every word – and every word a revelation.

'There are no vacations, so no chance to travel. Better expressed – vacation means no employment and no money. "Holiday" means a day without work or pay. I am one of the very few labourers here who have ever been to Lisbon – twice – for medical treatment for my ear.

'I have travelled far more than anyone else in this region, but I haven't visited even 5 per cent of my own country.[5] The only relaxation for most of us is the bistro. We arrive there after a hard day's work, half dead with fatigue, to drink a glass or two of wine with our friends. Because we are weak from lack of decent food, it only takes a glass or two and we get drunk. Then, money that should be kept for food goes into more drink, and this hits our wives and children. But the bistros are the only outlet for a bit of relaxation. They also belong to the bosses, and many of us think their main purpose is to demoralise, to impress the labourers with the hopelessness of life, lower their capacity for struggle, keep them in ignorance. In this way, the same boss exploits us through our work, by low wages, and wine.'

It would have been easy to write all this off as the justifiable outpourings of a malcontent – but it was a sober analysis of the social conditions against which Manuel Passão had fought and organised for most of his

---

5 [AN] This remark made a special impression because the previous day I had lunched with a Portuguese couple whose acquaintanceship I had made by chance, who had not one tenth of the knowledge of their country that Manuel had, but who spoke with great expertise about most of the well-known European tourist resorts. They knew of Graham Greene and Solzhenitsyn, but were unable to recommend a single Portuguese writer.

life. This became clear when we delved somewhat deeper into the general conditions in his part of the Upper Alentejo and found that everything he had to say was confirmed by specialists on that area, and by others who specialised on the overall situation of Portuguese agriculture.

Administratively, Montemor-o-Novo belongs to Évora, one of Portugal's eighteen administrative districts. Évora itself, a beautiful harmonious ensemble of white stone buildings and cobbled streets, dates to Roman times, and is the capital of the district which bears its name. Together with Portalegre district, it comprises the Upper Alentejo. From a hill in the centre of Évora city, the site of a second-century Roman temple to Diana, with wonderfully well-preserved fluted Corinthian columns, the rich plains of the Alentejo unfold as far as the eye can see – fields of ripening wheat interspersed with olive groves and forests.

Driving through the Alentejo, one was reminded of the Hungarian Hortobágy – vast plains dotted with ponds and lakes from which flights of wild duck took to the air at the sound of a gun.[6] And, like Hungary thirty years before, it was the domain of aristocratic absentee landlords, more at home in the gambling casinos than with those who managed their estates, let alone those who worked them!

Évora is the district where the smallest number of proprietors own the greatest amount of land, and where the number of agricultural labourers per estate is the highest. Within Évora district, Montemor-o-Novo is the *concelho* where this phenomenon is the most exaggerated.[7] According to title deeds, revealed by local officials, but which were secret until 25 April, 94 per cent of those who worked the land in Évora district had no property of their own. Of the remaining 6 per cent, 1 per cent were very big landowners; the last 5 per cent were very small proprietors who worked part-time on their own land and part-time for the big landowners.

'The small owners,' explained Manuel Passão, 'are caught in a squeeze between the state and the big landowners. There were state subsidies for wheat, for instance. But this went only to the big owners, who took the

---

6 [EN] Hortobágy National Park, a nature reserve and the oldest national park in eastern Hungary, designated a World Heritage Site.

7 [AN] Évora consisted of fourteen *concelhos*, Portalegre of fifteen, and Beja, as the centre of the Lower Alentejo, consisted of sixteen *concelhos*, or shires.

subsidies but rarely bothered about producing the wheat. They pocketed the subsidy money and invested it in something they considered more profitable. The small owners who really wanted to produce wheat were denied the credits they needed to modernise production. The money had all gone to the big owners. So, despite the state subsidies, paid for by the taxpayers, nothing was done to either modernise or promote grain production.

'The main source of income for many of the absentee landlords is cork. The trees have been there for centuries. The owners invested nothing in them originally, and almost nothing in their upkeep. They need a few hours pruning each year, plus the cost of removing the bark every nine years – that is, one ninth of the forest is stripped each year. For about 300 escudos per tree, the labourer removes bark for which the owner gets around 4,000 escudos – minus transportation costs. If the estate-owners can live comfortably off cork, for which there is an unlimited export market, why bother about producing food for our own people? That is the way they look at it. Pocket the subsidies for wheat and pocket the profits from cork without any investment. They grabbed the cork forests a few centuries ago, just as they grabbed the common lands a few years ago.'

Manuel then talked about the great strike movement that swept the Alentejo area from the end of 1961, culminating on 1 May 1962. Several of those with whom I have discussed this movement name José Magro as the main animator. Questioned about this, he replied with his usual cheery smile that he always worked in the Lisbon area. However, the period between December 1961 and June 1962 corresponds precisely with his six months of liberty following the armoured car escape!

'We had decided to launch a movement for an eight-hour working day,' recalled Manuel Passão. 'Till then, we had no fixed hours – we just worked from dawn to dusk. It was a movement throughout the Alentejo, but especially strong in Évora, Grândola, Montemor, Couço and Alcácer do Sal . . . There had been elections in November 1961, which gave us a chance for preliminary agitation work. Around that time some militants escaped from prison, so the left was considerably reinforced. We launched the slogan: "An Eight-Hour Day after May First". Where the workers were well organised, the estate-owners quickly gave in. After victories were won in Alcácer do Sal, Couço and Grândola, the labourers sent groups to other areas to step up the fight.

'Altogether, over 200,000 took part in the struggle! In some places it was complicated because of the *ranchos*, or seasonal workers. They are taken in trucks, twenty to twenty-five in a group – like cattle – wherever extra manpower is needed temporarily for cork-cutting, rice-planting, harvesting, and so on. They get less pay and work longer hours than the regular workers. The latter argued with them: "You can work here – but only eight hours a day and no more; otherwise, we'll chase you out." They usually agreed, not wanting to play the role of strike-breakers for the owners.

'At Águas de Moura, there's an estate of over 8,000 hectares owned by Mário d'Oliveira, where everything from rice planting to weeding and harvesting was done by hand. Once, when Mário d'Oliveira happened to be there, the labourers marched to his house – women in front, men behind. They demanded an eight-hour working day. He listened for a while, then stalked off. Next day, everybody marched back again. This time he made a polite speech, agreeing to the eight-hour day, but suggesting that it would be "easier" for the labourers to work in early and late shifts, and take a five-hour break at midday. But, as living quarters were far from the work sites, this would mean spending the five hours in the fields. They refused, and eventually he gave in. Some other owners sent for the PIDE or the Republican Guards; some of the leaders were arrested and beaten up. But the movement was too strong. The whole Alentejo was ablaze, and the fires couldn't be stamped out one by one. The owners needed the manpower, so they had to concede and accept the eight-hour day.'

The 1962 wave of strikes in the Alentejo almost assumed the dimensions of a classical peasants' uprising, and shook the Salazar regime to its core. In the opinion of some specialists, however, the end result was a deliberate downgrading of agriculture and an upgrading of forestry, to avoid large concentrations of potentially rebellious manpower. In the Montemor-o-Novo region, where there were fourteen estates of over 1,000 hectares and forty-one over 500 hectares, the number of agricultural labourers fell, according to Manuel Passão, from over 10,000 in 1962 to about 4,000 in 1974. These figures matched with others for the whole region, available in Lisbon.

'Emigration follows a regular pattern,' he said. 'The first step is for the labourer to look for work in Lisbon. Usually there is none, but through friends and contacts, he finds a way of getting out to France or West

Germany, where the demand for unskilled workers is much greater than here.'

On a dilapidated chest of drawers was a framed photograph of a young man in uniform. 'My son,' explained Manuel. 'He was called up when he came of age and sent "to defend the mother country overseas", as it is called. In the conditions under which we live, it is difficult to educate our children politically. My son knew of my ideas, but not of my activities. He stayed on in the Army after serving his time. Young people never return to their villages once they've been in the armed forces. We call this a second form of emigration. They get a taste for urban life, with its cheap attractions – cinema, pornography. Either they remain in the Army, or they migrate. Our society transforms the young – even if they don't have any money – into a sort of bourgeoisie, as far as tastes are concerned.' (It was not difficult to understand that young people like his son would accept almost any alternative to life in the type of hovel in which he had been reared, and which was standard for the labourers of the Alentejo!)

We visited some abandoned fields and barracks-type living quarters – the alternative to Manuel's hovel. Long, windowless sheds, where married couples managed as best as they could without any separating walls between families. A forestry guard had installed himself in an abandoned cattle shed, better than either Manuel Passão's 'cottage' or the barracks. We passed a fenced-in orchard where oranges were rotting on the trees – and looked at a modern piggery where a couple of hundred porkers, of a good breed but with their ribs showing, greeted us with expectant grunts. 'It was set up by the Torralta tourist company to supply their hotel chains,' explained Manuel, 'but when wages went up, they sacked the workers and left the pigs to starve. The forestry guard is feeding them until someone decides what to do with them.'

Alongside a large pond where a couple of dozen wild ducks were floating, smoke was rising from little fires around which women bent over cooking pots. Lengths of cork bark slung between trees served as hammocks for sleeping babies. It looked like a gypsy encampment. 'Families of cork-strippers,' explained Manuel. Pointing to a young man fishing in the pond, he added: 'He could be thrown into jail if the forestry guard reported him. Officially, he's poaching.'

I asked whether anything had changed since 25 April. 'Of course,' he replied. 'The fascists have been chucked out of the local councils. The

Democratic Movement helped set up an agricultural labourers' association. As a result, we have won important wage increases. Until 25 April, male workers averaged about eighty escudos per day, women only thirty-five escudos. There was a three-day conference at Évora to which labourers from the whole district sent delegates. We claimed 190 escudos per day for tractor-drivers, and for workers, 170 for men and 120 for women. Also, a forty-four-hour week, with 50 per cent overtime pay beyond the forty-four hours – the new conditions to go into effect by the end of August. The proprietors were also invited to send delegates. They turned up for the first two days, but didn't like what they heard. They refused the demands and boycotted the final session. So, we decided to strike. It was our own decision – no political parties involved. A few months earlier, the owners would have sent for the PIDE or the Republican Guards – now they couldn't. That's an enormous, revolutionary change, as far as we are concerned. After two weeks of strike, the owners were ready to talk. We didn't get everything we asked for, nor did we expect to. But we got the forty-four-hour working week, with 160 escudos a day for the tractor drivers, 140 for male field workers and 100 for women. This was our biggest victory since 1962.'

'What happens if a proprietor doesn't pay the new rates, or tries to squeeze out extra hours of work?' I asked.

'The first step is for someone from our association to take up the complaint with the *manajeiro* or *feitor* – the overseer who allots the daily work and manages the estate. If he refuses to settle, then we contact the Democratic Movement. That usually takes care of the matter. If not, we can take it up with the local representative of the Armed Forces Movement, or go on strike. But we use that only as a last resort, because too many strikes simply help the fascists who want to bring down the government.'

'Do the estate-owners take this sudden change in their status lying down?' I asked.

'Not all of them,' replied Manuel. 'There was a case recently in which a big field of wheat, just ready for harvesting, went up in flames. A sixteen-year-old shepherd boy had set fire to it. He was arrested and under police questioning explained that the estate owner, Joaquim Maia, had ordered him to do it to avoid paying the higher wages to the harvesters. The local people wanted to lynch Maia and he had to be rescued by the police. There were several such cases. The fascists spread word through their agents that this was the work of the "communists", but the people know better. Our association has no established vigilance brigades to guard against such sabotage. The owners have nothing to lose from such fires. The value of the crops is assessed in March, by which time the yield can be predicted. The owners insure it accordingly. So, Joaquim Maia was confident he would collect his insurance money. Instead, he's in jail for economic sabotage. You ask if things have changed!!! The estate-owners don't care about the loss of bread or wages, but the new government does. There are other owners who let their olives rot on the trees, or who are refusing to have the cork cut this year, on the pretext that this is no longer profitable because of the increased wages.'

'How can you fight against this sort of thing?'

'Take over the estates and work them ourselves,' Manuel Passão replied promptly. 'Turn them into big cooperatives or state farms, so they can be worked efficiently and become big centres of food production.'

Figure 12.2. Agricultural labourers taking their lunch at the Herdade do Outeiro, the first large estate to have been seized from the absentee landowner by landless workers and transformed into a cooperative farm. Alentejo region, southern Portugal, autumn 1974. (Photo by Fernando Ricardo)

'Our absentee landlords are total parasites. They've been used to living with the subsidies they got for wheat, which half of them never even planted; from cork and wood supplied to the paper mills. The cork and eucalyptus trees never even belonged to them in the first place. They take from the land but never put anything back in. They do nothing to promote employment. On the contrary, they keep thinking up new ways to get money without paying anything out in wages. They invest their profits from cork and timber in banks and insurance companies in the cities. There are tens of thousands of hectares of land which could be cultivated for food. The Alentejo could also be a great cattle-raising area, but if things go on like this, more and more people will emigrate. Today you can find whole streets of abandoned houses in the villages; tomorrow you will find entire villages abandoned – unless the land comes into the hands of those who are ready and able to farm it.'

Driving back to Lisbon over the rolling plains of the Alentejo, it was difficult not to agree with Manuel João Passão that vast areas of land suitable for food crops were lying idle under grass and bushes – fine for privileged hunters of hares, grouse and partridges – but disastrously wasteful for a country which imported even fodder for its cattle.

That Portugal was ripe for a sweeping land reform was evident, based on the situation in the Alentejo. In general, the situation was similar, as far as absentee landlords' estates were concerned, in all of southern Portugal, where the most fertile lands are located.

13
Trás-os-Montes

If the southern part of Portugal was reminiscent of Hungary before land reform, with its huge estates and absentee landlords, the northern part, with its smallholdings divided into dispersed, handkerchief-sized strips and plots, was reminiscent of Bulgaria. Holdings of a couple of acres were split up because of marriage and inheritance into a dozen or more tiny plots, with even trees divided between two or more families. Nowhere is this more common than in the Trás-os-Montes area. If fertile plains and a gentle Mediterranean climate are typical of the south, it is the mountains and harsh climate with vineyards clinging to stony slopes and occasional stretches of forest that are more typical of the north, especially the northwest. The contrast between the great tracts of the landed estates with few labourers in the south, and the lack of arable land in proportion to the villages in the north, was inescapable.

In his book, *Rumo à Vitória*, Álvaro Cunhal noted that, of 801,162 land holdings in continental Portugal, almost exactly half were of less than one hectare, while 3,546 were over 100 hectares, and 0.4 per cent of landholders owned 45 per cent of the land.[1] Of these, 848 absentee

---

1 [EN] Álvaro Cunhal, *Rumo à vitória: As tarefas do partido na revolução democrática e nacional* (Lisbon: Edições Avante, 1964). The title in English is 'Towards victory: The tasks of the party in the democratic and national revolution'. Cunhal presented his manuscript of this influential volume to the Central Committee of the Portuguese Communist Party in April 1964. Published and circulated clandestinely, it became a basic component and expression of the PCP's political programme.

landlords held 25 per cent of the total, 500 of the biggest of these holding more land than 500,000 smallholders. 'What does such a situation indicate?' he asks:

> It indicates the urgent necessity for a land reform that will distribute the land now in the hands of a small number of absentee landlords to the agricultural labourers and poor peasants. Such a reform would affect a very small number of parasitical families and would benefit many hundreds of thousands of peasant families.
>
> In practical terms, the problem is without doubt complex. We cannot remove the land from the south to the north, nor is it easy to move thousands of small proprietors from north to south. Given the great regional differentiation in the distribution of land holdings, one is tempted to say that in Portugal there must be not one, but two Agrarian Reforms. One for the zone of the big estates, the other for the zone of the smallholdings, taking into account the special features of each region.
>
> If the land of the 3,500 major holdings was distributed among the 400,000 of the smallest holdings, each of the latter would have ten times as much land as he has at present. If the estates of only the 500 biggest proprietors were expropriated and distributed to half a million smallholders, the latter's holdings would be doubled.[2]

Although the conditions and statistics referred to by Cunhal related to ten to twenty years earlier, the only change since had been that the small holdings grew smaller and more numerous, while the bigger properties grew bigger and fewer, as small and medium farms were swallowed up by the big landowners, exactly as small and medium enterprises were swallowed up by the big monopoly groups. Cunhal also pointed out that, of the 400,000 farms of less than one hectare, over 300,000 had no draught animals.

In the south, the agricultural labourers were quitting the villages because there was no work; in the north, they were doing so because of population pressure on the available land and lack of markets for even what was produced. It is difficult to get exact figures of how many have emigrated over the past ten to fifteen years – estimates run from 1.2 to 2

---

2 [AN] *Rumo à vitória*, 41.

million. When it began to assume large proportions in the early 1960s, emigration was strictly illegal. And not only for economic reasons. Young men were fleeing the draft – especially once the wars started in Africa. But, as the years went by, the money sent back by migrant workers in France and West Germany – where most of them went – started to make an appreciable contribution to the foreign currency reserves at a time when Portugal's balance of payments was starting to show a deficit. From 1969, emigration was legalised and remittances began to be Portugal's major source of hard currency – the main reason why the escudo remained stable in comparison with other Western European currencies. The fact that, as emigration went up, agricultural production declined, does not seem to have troubled the regime. Paris became known as Portugal's second largest city, and it was estimated by 1973 that there were 800,000 Portuguese in France, most of them in the capital, while entire villages in the Trás-os-Montes were abandoned.

Those one saw working the fields were mainly old people and women. Between the draft and emigration, the able-bodied males had gone. When migrants got stable jobs, they sent for their wives – who could work as domestics – but continued to send money back to support their children and the relatives who looked after them. Some families later returned to build modern cottages on the outskirts of the tumbledown villages.

The Trás-os-Montes covers some 10,000 square kilometres, with a population of a little over 400,000. Proportionately, it is the area which provides the greatest number of emigrants. Per capita production is the lowest in the country, 76 per cent of the population being engaged in agriculture, producing mainly for their own consumption.

At the headquarters of the Democratic Movement in Mirandela, in the very heart of the Trás-os-Montes, João Vicente, a specialist on the economic-social situation in the region, explained some of the reasons that pushed people into emigration.

'The first step is almost always Lisbon or Porto in search of work and a better life. In Lisbon, there is one doctor for every 400 inhabitants – in the Trás-os-Montes, one for every 3,000. In Lisbon, 90 per cent of houses have bathrooms and kitchens, 70 per cent have running water. Here the proportion is less than 10 per cent for bathrooms, kitchens and running water. In Lisbon, the average per capita consumption of electricity is 800 kilowatts – here, it is 60 kilowatts. Most of the tiny farms are split up into six or more parcels of land, impossible to cultivate by modern methods, even if credits were available to buy draught animals and implements. Around Mirandela, 80 to 90 per cent of people are illiterate. Even those who know the alphabet cannot usually read. Farming methods are two to three centuries behind the times. Because of emigration, 80 per cent of those who work in the fields are old people and children. There are no markets for what people produce, and where there are markets, there is no transport to get the produce to them.'

With José Francisco Nereu as guide, friend, and reserve driver, we toured the Trás-os-Montes area for ten days.[3] One of our early stops was at the small, somnolent town of Lebução, on the road from Mirandela to Montalegre, far from the ordinary tourist routes.[4] A small boy guided us to what he insisted was the only functioning restaurant. It was, in fact, the living room of two black-gowned elderly spinsters, Cândida and Clotilde. José quickly established that they could provide us with a meal. At the single dining table were two men, one solidly built and ruddy-faced with sleeves rolled up to the elbow and 'Mobiloil' stamped across his red shirt, the other slighter and smaller, also in his shirtsleeves. They introduced themselves as Macedo and Sebastião, respectively. Macedo asked if we were French, as that was the common language of our group, and when we replied that we were Bulgarian and Australian respectively, he roared and slapped his thighs: 'Clotilde, Cândida, quick, hide in the kitchen! PCP . . . PCP . . . There's a real live communist arrived! The sort your priest tells you eats babies for breakfast.' To us, he explained: 'I'm the imperialist agent of Mobiloil at Mirandela, and Sebastião drives the petrol truck outside.'

The two were obviously frequent visitors and on good terms with the sisters, one of whom came in holding a panting fawn-and-white rabbit by its ears for our inspection, as in some fish restaurants a flapping trout is brought in for approval before it goes into the frying pan.

'Bulgaria – I've read about it,' continued Macedo: 'It was under the heel of fascists like ours, twenty-five or so years ago. It was the country

---

3 [AN] On this, my fourth visit to Portugal since 25 April, I was accompanied by my wife Vessa Ossikovska, a Bulgarian journalist and art critic. José Francisco is mentioned in Chapter 2.

4 [EN] Here Burchett made a transcription error, calling the village he visited 'Lubação'. It was almost certainly Lebução, nowadays a parish of the town Valpaços in the Trás-os-Montes region, northern Portugal.

of Dimitrov. I read all about the Leipzig trial.[5] Go on.' With a broad wink to us, he said to Clotilde: 'Run and tell the priest that the communists have come to take over.' Turning to us, he said: 'They're typical fruits of fascism, these two. Priest-ridden as you can find.' He apparently added something which José Francisco deemed better not to translate, because Clotilde, who was preparing our end of the table, reddened and said solemnly: 'Our priest has been here for thirty-five years. He's a good man, never chases after women, and he has never talked about communists eating babies for breakfast. He is only interested in Church affairs.'

We asked Clotilde what she thought about the changes since 25 April. By her stammering reaction, it was obvious that she was not used to having her opinion asked about anything. 'Tell them what the priest told you last Sunday,' roared Macedo. After a pause, she said: 'All we hope is that things won't change too quickly.' We asked if she thought that ending the wars in Africa would be a good thing. Cândida, who arrived from the kitchen at that moment, said: 'It would be good if our men didn't get killed anymore. But . . .' and she hastened back into the kitchen, red-faced. José explained later that she probably thought she had uttered a heresy by suggesting that anything good could come from such a regime.

'My wife gave birth on 26 April,' said Macedo, 'and when the priest came for the christening, I said: "Good that he was born on this day. He'll grow up under democracy." The priest replied: "This godless regime won't last long." That's what they're like, those priests.'

By the time we had dealt with the rabbit, which Cândida had converted into edibility with great speed and expertise – and shared a bottle of the local *vinho verde* (literally 'green wine', a young, slightly sparkling wine which abounds in the northern part of the country) – we were a friendly company, despite Macedo's running and often ribald commentaries on the priests. We were accorded what we were told is a

---

5 [EN] Macedo refers here to Georgi Dimitrov Mihaylov, also known as Georgiy Mihaylovich Dimitrov (1882–1949), Bulgarian activist and politician, leader of the Bulgarian Communist Party, and first prime minister of the People's Republic of Bulgaria. The 'Leipzig trial' refers to the prosecution of Dimitrov and other communist activists (Marinus van der Lubbe, Ernst Torgler, Blagoi Popov and Vasil Tanev), on charges of setting the Reichstag fire in Berlin on 27 February 1933 and attempting to overthrow the German government. Judges of the German Supreme Court (*Reichsgericht*) conducted the trial from September to December 1933. All of the accused were acquitted, except for van der Lubbe, who was sentenced to death and executed.

rare intimacy in the Trás-os-Montes, of being invited, with Macedo and Sebastião, into the kitchen. The two sisters offered us all some liqueur and brought a piece of pottery as a gift to my wife, who replied with a short toast, saying: 'You are Catholics. I come from a communist country. What is important is that you receive people hospitably and make them happy – including Macedo and Sebastião. That is the way we can all be friends.' With that there were embraces all round, Clotilde and Cândida even coping with the drooping moustache of the handsome José Francisco.

Many such chance encounters fleshed out the picture of the area, impossible to get from statistics and the various briefings and formal interviews, valuable as the latter were. On another occasion, we had gone to look at a semi-deserted village – Cova da Lua – of solid, well-built houses clinging to the slopes of a well-grassed hillside. As we approached, some old men with brooms were moving out to sweep the roadway, as they explained, for a religious procession to the village the following day. A woman throwing feed to some caged turkeys invited us to have a *copo de vinho* – a glass of wine – an invitation which we had quickly discovered was almost a standard greeting in the Trás-os-Montes, where wine is more plentiful than anything else on the dietary scale. (In one village we were told of a famous occasion when a house caught fire and, as water was short, wine was used to extinguish the flames!)

We went into a basement manger where a couple of oxen were chewing their cuds, and from there into a smoke-stained storehouse. Suspended from iron hooks on solid beams, in between a couple of long-handled scythes, were the best part of two half pigs, smoked into *presunto*, a kind of bacon which, eaten with bread, is almost the staple diet of those who have it, in the Portuguese countryside. There were two big barrels of wine, a smaller barrel of *aguardente* (literally 'fire water'), distilled like Italian *grappa* from the residue of grapes after the wine juices have been extracted, huge round loaves of wheaten bread – baked once a week, our hostess explained – and a basket of turkey eggs.

While we were taking all this in and our hostess was filling a jug with wine, a charming, city-dressed young woman appeared like a fairy among the oxen. Alice, daughter of our hostess, had just returned home from her secretarial job in Porto to celebrate the religious fête with her lonely, widowed mother.

'Everything you see here is grown on the farm,' explained Alice, reading our thoughts. We asked how much land they owned to produce so many things? Neither could say. 'It's all scattered around. A bit here, a bit there.' How many plots – six, ten? They laughed. 'More. Ours is one of the biggest farms here. But we have a wheatfield in one place, a vineyard in another. A patch for vegetables somewhere else, odd olive trees scattered around. Some peach trees, pigeon lofts – all on different plots.' Alice gave up counting. 'It's all due to the inheritance system and it makes farming difficult. That's why so many young people have left. Farming has become impossible.'

'My husband,' sighed her mother, 'always dreamed of the day when the plots could be put together again, and the village could buy a tractor so that the land could be worked properly. Our neighbours felt the same way. If a village can own a bull together – why not a tractor?'

Wine was poured, *aguardente* also, although it was hardly midmorning. Slices of most appetising wholemeal bread were handed round with generous portions of *presunto*. We asked what they thought of the changes. Alice was very cautious: 'We must wait and see,' she said. Not so her mother.

'It's good,' she said forthrightly. 'One of the best things is that the wars will be finished, and the young men won't be taken away to kill and be killed any more. There are no young people left around here at all. They're either in the Army – some of them dead – or they've migrated, many because they didn't want to be sent off to the wars. The girls, like Alice, have gone off to get jobs, and if they're lucky to find husbands, in the cities. Others have followed their husbands into migration.

'Who would want to come back here? You see how backward and primitive everything is. In the 1959 elections, our village voted for Delgado.[6] We've been discriminated against ever since. The same with all the other villages that voted for Delgado. For instance, there was once a scheme for putting in public laundering facilities in the villages. But not here – we had to be punished for voting for Delgado.'

---

6 [EN] Humberto da Silva Delgado (1906–1965), Air Force general, diplomat, politician and founder of the Portuguese national airline, TAP (Transportes Aéreos Portugueses). Delgado dared to run as an opposition candidate to the Estado Novo's candidate, Américo Tomás, in the 1958 presidential election. Due to his popularity and outspoken criticism of Salazar, Delgado was driven into exile. He was eventually murdered in Spain on 13 February 1965 by officers of the PIDE.

Mother and daughter agreed that only cooperative farming could solve the problems of Cova da Lua and other such villages, with their tiny, scattered fields. But they were pessimistic as to the chances of those who had left ever coming back. A white-bearded man, who turned out to be eighty-three – sunning himself on a stone bench – was the only person in sight as we left. He symbolised a dying village which, to judge by the quality of the houses, was by no means a poor one.

At another village at the extreme limits of both the Trás-os-Montes and of Portugal – Rio de Onor, named after the stream that runs through it – we went a few yards into Spain by mistake. Just two squat kilometre stones on either side of a narrow footpath, with 'E' on one side and 'P' on the other – as we noted later – marked the frontier. No signs of frontier guards, passport or customs controls. We would have continued had not a woman, of whom José asked the way to Rio de Onor, replied:

'You've just walked through it. You're in Spain now.' Turning back, we encountered a tall blue-eyed man with a sleeping child slung across his shoulders. The child had fair hair – a reminder, like the blue eyes, of Celtic influence, which persists in parts of northern Portugal. He confirmed that we were in Rio de Onor and, after we explained who we were, introduced himself as António Dionísio Fernandes; Dionísio for short. He suggested that we repair to the local shop-bistro for a *copo de vinho*. To our surprise, it was a bright new place with electric fittings. But no electricity.

'It's been that way for three years,' said the bistro owner, pointing to the poles and power lines outside. 'This is the area that produces the most electric power in the country, but there's none for the local villages. Promises, but no power.'

A native of the village, Dionísio had returned from Angola after 25 April. 'I was uncertain how things would turn out,' he said. 'The white racists were threatening to make trouble. I had good relations with my African neighbours, so the racists considered me a traitor. There were all sorts of threats. So, I decided to leave. Anyway, now that things have changed at home, I'd like to be useful.'

'In what way?' we asked.

'I've got my truck, coming by sea. There's very rich land here – it'll grow anything. We could truck vegetables to Bragança [the nearest big town, about thirty kilometres distant], where they're badly supplied with vegetables. That is, if the local junta will let me. They oppose any change. I wanted to put a small generator in the stream here that would produce enough electricity for the whole village, now that it's wired for it anyway. But they wouldn't let me.'

'That band of fascists have to be kicked out,' said the bistro keeper, 'before anything can be changed around here.' It turned out that the parish to which Rio de Onor belonged had not yet elected its new council, and José Francisco, a stalwart supporter of the Democratic Movement, was shocked to learn that no representatives had yet visited Rio de Onor. It had been rumoured in Lisbon that some remnants of primitive communism were still surviving in this little frontier village, but it proved to be the romantic product of someone's imagination. Dionísio and the bistro-keeper laughed when we asked about this.

'There is a water-powered grain mill,' explained Dionísio, 'near where I would like to stick my electric generator. It's been there as long as anyone remembers, and people bring their grain to be ground into flour. It belongs to the whole village, but that's all.' The bistro keeper added: 'Like a lot of other places, we used to have a bull that was owned by the village, to service the local cows, but the junta took that away a couple of years ago. We also built a tiny school by ourselves.'

We asked about emigration. 'Of thirty-five families, fifteen have gone,' replied Dionísio. 'Others are waiting, like myself, to see if things are really going to change. If not – they'll go, and so will I.' He spoke with bitterness about the lands enclosed for hunting preserves, through which we had driven from Bragança – flat plains covered mostly with gorse and other shrubs and grass.

'There are thousands of hectares where maize, wheat and vegetables could be grown. But everything is fenced off. Nothing is allowed to change. As soon as I returned, I asked permission to build a house, because I intended to stay. I submitted a plan to the local junta, and it was approved. I made the cement blocks myself but, when I had it half-finished, the junta stepped in and said, if I built it, it must be in rough, undressed stone like the rest. It's very typical. My house would have been a symbol of change, but the fascists are enemies of change of any sort. So, it remains half finished.'

We pointed out that things were being changed and that, only a couple of days previously, the government had decided to give credits to small and medium enterprises.

'We don't even want money from the state,' he said. 'We'll earn money and give it to the state; but first, let's get our hands on the land. Cooperatives – that's the solution here. Open up the hunting reserves to cultivation. Use some of the electricity to raise the waterline. We'll put in irrigation ourselves and grow anything the country needs.'

While we were talking and sampling the local wine – the bistro-keeper nodding his head at everything Dionísio said – two sad-faced, Chinese-looking girls came in to buy some canned sardines. The elder one, who spoke English, explained that their mother was Chinese from Macau, their father was from Rio de Onor, but had been killed in Africa. They attended the local school with five other children. The nearest other school was at Bragança.

'Why did you emigrate?' we asked Dionísio. 'What are the specific reasons that make people leave their villages?'

'My case was a bit special,' he said with a smile. 'I had served three-and-a-half years in prison for helping some people across the frontier, and life here would have been impossible for me after that. So, I went first to France, where I picked up some notions of construction and electrical engineering, and later to Angola, where at least I would be among people speaking my own language. But most people leave out of hopelessness. There is no possibility of doing anything but living off what we grow. We can grow plenty of stuff here but, because of the total lack of transport, there are no markets. Every generation wants to live a bit better, but it's impossible if you are stuck in a village like this. My generation, in fact, lives worse than our parents, and our children will live worse than us if things continue like this. The fascists never lifted a finger to help the villages.

'The word started to drift back from those who had emigrated that life was better in other countries if you worked hard. And we Portuguese are a hard-working people. Usually, once people have discovered the outside world, they never want to return to the old, hopeless life here. There are a few like myself who feel that, if we can do some good for our country and ourselves, then we'll come back and pull our weight.'

An aspect of emigration that impressed us after conversations with people of the calibre of Dionísio was that, when they returned – even for brief visits – they brought fresh ideas with them. Not only new skills, which they'd had to acquire in order to subsist abroad, but new political ideas – from having lived in societies where at least they were free to organise in trade unions, free to discuss and exchange ideas, and where they had access to other views of society than the old obscurantist ideas imposed by fascism and clericalism. By the deference with which the customers treated Dionísio – those who dropped into the little shop for a drink, or to buy something and then stayed to listen – he was obviously someone who carried great weight in the community. On the other hand, some who returned after years of hard work – scraping and saving to build one of those bright, new cottages – were ready prey for the priests' propaganda that the Communists would come and take it all away.

On the way back to Bragança, we took a wrong turning on a road that got steadily worse, until it led us into a poverty-stricken village of tumbledown stone houses, half of them obviously abandoned. We stopped to ask one of a group of black-clad women the way back to the Bragança road. She was sewing some old grain sacks together to make what looked like a blanket, and seemed astonished to hear José Francisco speak to us in a language other than Portuguese. She insisted that we step in for a *copo de vinho*. Like other houses in the area, it was built for cattle below and people above – the heating in winter provided by the radiation of warmth from the cow or ox below. An old, chipped jug was produced, a neighbour came running up with glasses, and we sat on the steps to share a jug of thin, harsh wine.

It turned out that the son of our hostess had emigrated to Switzerland. What was he doing there? 'Ah,' she said proudly, 'that boy can do anything. He's learned to be a bricklayer. He came back and even built an English fireplace for me.' She took us up some rickety steps to show us the fireplace – her most prized possession. It was the only house in the village, as far as we could see, that had a chimney. Where exactly in Switzerland was her son? She didn't know but fumbled among some papers and produced a letter. The envelope bore a Geneva postmark. She asked José Francisco to read her the few lines – it was obvious that she knew the contents by heart but could not read herself – assuring that all was well and that he was thinking of getting married to a Swiss girl. 'He's a good boy,' she sighed. 'He sends me money every month.'

We asked if many other young men had gone away. She was surprised at the question. 'Of course. They've all gone. Why would they want to stay here?' Back on the steps for another jug of wine, one of the other women explained that, although she was from the village, she was married to a Spaniard and lived on the other side of the frontier. 'Things are a bit better over there,' she said. 'At least there's work for everyone.' Our hostess showed us a faded photo of her son – a square-jawed, solemn young man. 'There's talk of building an airfield near here,' she said. 'That should bring work and money to the village. Perhaps my son and others will come back if there's building to be done.' And she glanced around for confirmation from her neighbours. They were silent and looked at the ground. As we drove through the village to turn the car and get back on to the Bragança road, we did not see a single man.

14
Reflections

What seemed typical everywhere in the countryside was the total neglect by the state of any measures to improve the lot of the peasantry. Where there were decent roads, there was no public transport. Where there were schools, the only way of getting there was to walk. The same with the clinics, plus fees so high that no peasant could afford to set foot in them. We rarely saw even a draught animal working in the fields. Hoes and sickles were the universal implements of cultivation and harvest. Sometimes, lumbering through the villages were primitive carts with wooden disks for wheels, drawn by a couple of emaciated, panting oxen.

Back at Mirandela, exchanging our impressions with João Vicente, he explained that, formerly, most peasants owned an ox, or a cow or two, sharing the lower part of every cottage. 'But, with the enclosure of the common lands, where for centuries the peasants had grazed their cattle, few could still afford to keep them. In its latter years, the fascist government had a deliberate policy of discouraging agriculture, of taking land out of cultivation. Thousands of hectares where people grew wheat and maize for their own consumption were simply taken from them and planted with forests. Other fertile areas were flooded to create reservoirs for irrigation projects, which benefited only the big landowners. The rents they charged went up ten-fold for irrigation projects financed by the state through taxes. All this was a form of expropriation of the small peasants.

'There was an attempt to overcome the uneconomic pattern of the tiny, dispersed plots by joining them together into single fields, but this was also done in such a way that only the big owners benefited from it. The peasants who had at least owned their strips suddenly found they had become tenants of new landowners. The peasants were not against change. But whenever a new law or decree affecting their lives was introduced, it was bad for them. Any change in their lives as a result of government action was for the worse. Thus, many of them are now afraid of change – and the priests exploit this.' He went on to say that, although the condition of the peasantry was bad enough – they still had bits of land from which they could feed themselves, albeit on a very low subsistence level.

'There are tin mines in this area where people are worse off still,' he said. 'No local people would work under such slave-labour conditions, so the owners employ Cape Verde islanders, recruited from the Lisbon unemployed. Some of these mines are nothing but concentration camps.' When we suggested a visit, he shook his head. 'They are barricaded off and no visitors are permitted. After long delays, I was able to enter the Argozelo mine as a "medical worker" a week ago. Of eighty miners, seventy were suffering from silicosis, of whom ten were TB cases.[1] I visited a workers' canteen in the Ribeira tin mines.[2] The staple fare was stinking fish, *presunto* yellow with age which no peasant would touch, and worm-filled potatoes. The wine was chocolate in colour and so dense that you could not see the other side of the glass. But even for such poisonous meals, workers found they were in debt to the canteen when they went to collect their monthly wages. There were no safety precautions, not even helmets. Of course – no trade union. The manager warned me that any member of a trade union or the Democratic Movement who came there would be "shot on sight". So, we invited the workers to send a delegation to the Democratic Movement headquarters at Bragança. The manager warned that anyone who went would immediately be sacked. That's the way they'd been used to running things. The only difference was

---

1 [EN] Silicosis is a type of lung disease (pulmonary fibrosis) caused by breathing in tiny pieces of silica, a mineral commonly found in sand, quartz and other types of rock. Silicosis mainly affects mining and construction labourers exposed to silica dust while working.

2 [EN] The remote Argozela and Ribeira de Pena mining fields, located near the border with Spain in the far northern Bragança and Vila Real districts, respectively, both historically part of the Trás-os-Montes province.

that they couldn't say: "You'll immediately be arrested", as they would have done before 25 April.

'As soon as the minimum wage of 3,300 escudos for all personnel was announced, the women workers were sacked. They were mainly employed in transport work. All shift foremen are illiterate – there are no technicians. After 25 April, there was a three-day strike calling for regular medical inspections, and a school, so their children would not grow up like animals. Everything was rejected. Obviously, we are not letting matters rest there, but that sort of inhuman management mentality is typical of what fascism spawned. Gradually, we are changing these things.'

A few days later at Cachão, thirteen kilometres south of Mirandela, there was a vivid example of how change was being brought about. It was also an example of why, in the past, the farming community feared any changes instigated by the state. The government had invested some 700 million escudos in a huge transformation project for agricultural products.[3] This had been lauded as the final answer to all the peasants' marketing problems. They could bring to a single centre everything from fruit and vegetables, grain and grapes to milk and pigs, and everything would be canned, transformed into flour, wine, butter, cheese or bacon, to everybody's advantage. The place was big enough to handle all marketable production from the entire Trás-os-Montes area. And, sure enough, the complex swallowed up a high proportion of marketable produce. The only flaw was that the peasants never got paid – or, if they were, it was at prices far lower than those for which they were customarily fleeced. After months went by without payments, they obviously stopped sending their produce; the abattoirs, with a capacity of transforming 300 pigs per day into *presunto* and pork sausages, were lucky if they received 20 or 30.

The manager had been a well-known fascist stalwart, Camilo de Mendonça, the 'strong man of Mirandela'. He was now to be replaced by a Captain Bento of the Armed Forces Movement. The secretary of state for agriculture, Dr Alfredo Estêves Belo, had come to preside over the changeover. It was a festive occasion. In the board of directors' room, workers and peasants had gathered with banners: 'Cachão: Centre of Fascism in the North', '25 April Has Finally Come to Cachão', 'We Are

---

3   [EN] About €1.3 million, or nearly US$1.5 million in 2024.

with the MFA'. The secretary of state and the local garrison commander – Major Albuquerque, in uniform, while Captain Bento wore civilian clothes – took their seats at the head of the boardroom table. Suddenly there was a scuffle, and fifty or sixty diminutive women in pink overalls burst in, elbowing their way to the front.

José Francisco, who never missed anything that was going on and had a great eye for detail, joined our conversation to explain that they were cannery workers whose foreman had told them to remain at their machines, until an aide of Captain Bento quietly ordered that they be allowed to attend the ceremony. The atmosphere, as usual, was far more important than the official words. Secretary of State Belo, however, accused the former administrators of 'inefficiency in commercial management' and denounced the scandal of the 'non-payment for their produce that had caused hardship to innumerable farmers in the region'. The appointment of Captain Bento was 'a guarantee that the activities of the complex would be exercised from now on in such a way as to benefit the people, and ensure the application of the programme of the Armed Forces Movement'.

The names of men chosen for a four-member management committee were read out, three of whom had resigned from the old management before 25 April in protest at the way things were being run; the fourth, judging by the way his name was applauded, was obviously a popular local figure. The speech of Secretary of State Belo was punctuated by roars of approval from the peasants and workers.

We spoke with some of the women workers. Most were young, and of an extraordinarily uniform small size. (I was reminded of the especially low-framed textile machinery in Shanghai, exported from England after child labour was banned there, but continued in Shanghai for the same manufacturers.) Obviously, I did not have a tape measure, but noted that they only came up to my shoulder, which I later checked as just two inches short of five feet (145 centimetres). Whether they had been selected to suit standard short-legged machines, we could not discover. Certainly, people in the countryside were on average several inches shorter than their compatriots in the cities, and in the Trás-os-Montes, shorter than the average for the rest of the countryside – but this uniformity of size was impressive, to say the least.

'What will these changes mean for you?' I asked one of them. 'We have to wait and see. We can only hope. Nothing could be worse than now,' she replied. Another said: 'We work only to warm our bodies', and a third: 'We live in utter misery. We women all get 33.20 escudos per day, regardless of age or length of service. If we miss one day, our pay is stopped for three days. Men get 72 escudos per day for the same work. We all need a minimum of 100 escudos per day. Some of us have eight or ten children to feed.' A burly male worker interrupted to say: 'At least I can sleep peacefully tonight, for the first time since I came here ten years ago. The fascists have been knocked off from the top.' A greyhaired woman, the same size as the others, was pushed forward and introduced as 'Mama'.

'I think the new management will do a good job,' she said. 'We know some of them, and the young captain looks like a good sort. Till now we have only known exploitation. I've also worked here for ten years – from the time the complex was opened. We have no facilities of any kind. The mothers need nurseries and crèches, and we will push our demands for these.[4] Also, we need a school near where we live.' It turned out that they lived in company housing, about seven kilometres distant, and were brought to the complex 'like cattle' in open trucks. The nearest school to their village was thirteen kilometres away. A good housing complex alongside the plant was reserved for members of the administration, plant engineers, and a Mirandela priest who, as the women workers hastened to point out, 'had a perfectly good house in Mirandela'.

Amongst other charges against Mendonça was that he included 30,000 escudos a month for 'official lunches' in the expenses for running the plant. The plant itself was very modern, most of the equipment being from Italy, but it was obvious that much of it had never even been used. It was a monument to inefficiency and corruption. Which of these twin evils had swallowed up the greater portion of the peasants' unpaid produce was something for Captain Bento's management to discover.

Before leaving Lisbon for the Trás-os-Montes, we had been warned by our friends, including the most politically sophisticated among them, that apart from this being the most economically backward part of the country – which it was – the inhabitants were completely apolitical or reactionary, totally hostile to new ideas and those who espoused them

---

4   [EN] 'Crèche' is a term of French derivation used in British English and in continental Portuguese to mean a nursery where babies and young children are cared for during the working day.

– which we found they were not. The few encounters described above, samples of dozens of others, proved this. Apart from spontaneous hospitality, insistence on sharing a *copo de vinho* and a bit of bread and *presunto* with the visitors from afar, we found people everywhere eager to discuss their problems, and their hopes for a new deal. Certainly, it was 25 April which had loosened their tongues and their inhibitions. The PIDE had disappeared, and the Republican Guards concentrated on traffic problems instead of bullying peasants who were too outspoken. But we found that ordinary people needed no textbook explanations as to why their lives were so miserable.

Opinions might differ as to the remedy, but not over the fact that the fascist regime had been their mortal enemy. Every measure that clipped the wings of the former fascist big-shots – such as the action at Cachão – was a cause for public rejoicing. The untying of tongues and the airing of grievances at meetings to elect new councils, or to set up peasants' associations, were powerful factors in the awakening of a political consciousness, long dormant because of the ferociously repressive nature of the old regime. This was as true, we found, in the Trás-os-Montes as in Lisbon or Porto or the Alentejo, once the repressive machinery was dismantled.

For a glimpse of another side of life in the Trás-os-Montes, it was interesting to spend a day on a landowner's estate, the Quinta do Atayde (Atayde Estate). A white cube of a manor house, dating back to the sixteenth century, built like a fortress, its outer walls a good three feet thick, it belonged to the Tenreiro family, which had been in the region since the thirteenth century. The present tenant is Dr António Maria Tenreiro, Portugal's only cardio-vascular surgeon, who operates in a hospital at Porto five days a week, spending his weekends on the family estate. We arrived on a Sunday morning and other guests were expected. Simmering in a blackened cauldron were half a dozen dismembered fowls. Hanging alongside the huge fireplace was a small mace, complete with spikes and chain. Among various portrayals of Christ on a cross on the smoke-darkened walls of the dining room were two portraits of 'Che' Guevara, also with a very Christ-like expression – a reminder that Dr Tenreiro was known for his progressive ideas.

Flanking the steps of the main entrance were stone-age tools found in the area: oval-shaped pieces for pounding grain and sharpened scrapers for softening up animal pelts, according to our host's interpretations, along with remnants of Celtic times, and decorative bits from the ruins of a nearby Roman villa – evidence of the continuity of human activity in the region.

With retainers dozing in the sun outside, and hounds yawning under the massive oak dining table inside; the swimming pool and well-clipped lawns, and a sprinkler system watering fields of vegetables; orchards of peaches, apricots and almonds leading to olive groves and vineyards in the distance, it was a different world to that in which we had been living the previous week.

Dr Tenreiro, a lively personality with a massive head and the traditional stubby, sensitive fingers of a surgeon, introduced us to his underground 'armoury', where he selected a few bottles of wine for lunch from a formidable arsenal of bottles, the estate's choicest vintages from several decades. One of the first questions I posed, with the image of the diminutive women cannery workers of Cachão in mind, was why there was such a difference in size between rural and city people.

'Because, for centuries and generations, the peasantry has never enjoyed a decent diet,' he replied. 'There are some anthropological factors, but essentially it is a lack of decent food and medical care. Children that survive the terribly high infant mortality rate in the rural areas get a poor start in life from babyhood onwards. Under the fascist regime, health conditions that were bad enough to start with got steadily worse.' He handed me some statistics on comparative consumption of key foods in terms of grammes per day:

	Milk	Meat	Cereals
West Germany	671	159	180
France	601	227	225
Spain	322	115	242
Italy	387	129	351
Greece	448	111	331
Portugal	166	74	379

'Is it any wonder that we are breeding midgets in the most backward areas of the countryside?' he asked.

A nobleman and his noble lady from a neighbouring estate were among those who came to sample the wines and poultry – and everything that went before and after – including a very smooth fifty-year-old *aguardente*. Their estate covered 300 hectares, five times the size of the Quinta do Atayde, which was already very large for that part of the country. Asked what they thought of the changes since 25 April, it was the noblewoman who primly replied:

'Perhaps the tendency has been to move too quickly.' (How often were we to hear this theme phrase and its variations?) Asked whether the increased wages for the labourers made any difference to their affairs, she said: 'We always pay our labourers well. Their living conditions are good – even bathrooms in the cottages. But they are too stupid to know what is good for them. They stored potatoes in the baths. And, for instance, I gave them good cooking oil – the same that we use. But they asked for another of inferior quality and accused us of keeping the "good" oil from them. You give them bathrooms, showers, but they remain dirty – like animals, really.' Her husband nodded in agreement. With her piled-up hair, jewels and delicate hands, she looked like one of Velázquez's savage portraits of the Spanish aristocracy of his day. Dr Tenreiro spoke cheerfully of the inevitability of land reform, at which the couple shuddered and said, in effect: 'At least, not in our times!'

After the aristocratic guests had left, we drove through arid mountain ranges to Moncorvo, where Dr Tenreiro wanted to show us the local twenty-one-bed hospital. It was beautifully equipped – like the Cachão agro-industrial complex. There was an excellent operating theatre: 'A surgeon comes once every three months to do tonsil operations,' explained Dr Tenreiro. 'There are "Potemkin" hospitals like this in every township in this area.'[5]

Only six of the twenty-one beds were occupied, one by an elderly woman in a private room with a telephone and TV set. She had no specific illness but had languished for three years, seemingly dumped there by one of the landowning families, who did not know what else to do with her. The weekly fee for such a room was more than the annual income of a small landholder. There was also a well-equipped dental clinic – a dentist came twice a week, but there were rarely any patients,

---

5 [EN] 'Potemkin hospitals' is an allusion to the 'Potemkin villages' created by Stalin's regime in the Soviet Union in the early 1930s. Such villages were fake communities where ostensibly happy, prosperous peasants gave Western visitors the false impression that living conditions in rural areas were exemplary, when in fact famine was rife. An equivalent Portuguese expression is *só para o inglês ver* ('just for the Englishman to see'), meaning a façade, or 'merely for show'.

explained the pleasant nursing sister who showed us around. Two doctors took it in turns, month by month, to make afternoon visits.

'No ordinary peasant or labourer could ever afford to come here for treatment,' said Dr Tenreiro, 'but it looks good in tourist guidebooks to talk about hospitals or clinics in every township. Somebody earned fat commissions on the purchase of the equipment, paid for by the people through taxation.' He went on to speak of the backward state of hospital care in general.

'We need at least twenty times as many surgeons in my specialty alone,' he said. 'If I examine a patient tomorrow, it will be four or five months before I can see him or her again, the waiting list is so long. The operating theatre at my hospital is available for me only two mornings a week. This means – as heart operations are always long and complicated – that I can only operate twice a week. No matter in what field you look, you will find the same heritage of decades of fascism. Inefficiency, inadequacy, neglect – a total disregard for anything to do with the human condition.' But he was optimistic for the future.

'The 25 April coup has released new energies and talents. It has given young people fresh hopes, and they are determined to catch up for half a century lost to fascism. Show-case installations like the Cachão complex and the Moncorvo hospital can be put to good use once there is a regime truly determined to serve the people. The young officers have paved the way for this. Many people like myself, who felt completely hopeless about the future – even though we personally had no material problems – are now optimistic. We have an ancient civilisation behind us. Our people have done great things in the past; they are capable of great things in the future. Half a century of fascism was enough to keep us centuries behind in many fields. But, with a democratic regime, we can make up for lost time and perhaps surprise the world again.'

This was a typical opinion of many people at the top of their professions, even though, because of their economic and social positions, they had enjoyed a privileged status under fascism. Intellectually, however, they had felt humiliated by intolerance and obscurantism; and, as patriots, they suffered at the contempt with which Portugal was regarded by the liberal and progressive world outside.

15
Sardines

Among the twenty-odd fishermen grouped around a table in the back room of a fishermen's pub in Peniche, there was a heated argument as to what year should be the starting point for the story of the Portuguese sardine – which is what I had asked about. Eventually, as there were only three generations of their leaders present, it was decided to start in the mid-1930s, and not 1926, as some wanted. It turned out that no one there had personal recollections of events in 1926! So, it was Joaquim Farrapilha, with a brick-red face dominated by an enormous slanting nose, who was chosen to speak first. Well into his sixties, he was as tough as a gnarled old oak.

'Fishing in the early thirties was different from that of today,' he said. 'When we spotted visually the sardine shoals, we threw bran on the water and, when the fish surfaced, we threw hand grenades and netted all we could of those that were stunned. We put out to sea like soldiers into battle, our belts stuffed with hand grenades. I was a boat master in those days. It was a dangerous business – very often someone lost a finger or an eye or got a fragment in his body. Occasionally someone was killed. The father of Manuel Francisco here was killed by a grenade going off too soon. The nets were also primitive, home-made jobs, and we always lost a lot of fish just hauling them into the boats. After Manuel's father was killed in 1934, the government forbade the use of grenades. But, as we had no other way of catching the fish, we defied the ban.

'One day the police came to search our houses. One fisherman ran ahead to warn the others. We got rid of as many grenades as we could – just pitching them into the sea – but some of us had no time. The grenades were discovered, and we were arrested.

'I was among fifty-six masters and seventeen ordinary fishermen arrested. That was on 13 November 1935 – we had defied the ban for over a year. Somebody ran to the church and started ringing the bells – the traditional warning of disaster. People flocked to the centre to find out what had happened. When they were told that the boat masters had been arrested, they considered this a real calamity. Without the masters, no boats would put to sea, with or without grenades.

'People swarmed to the city exit to block us from being taken off to the police headquarters at Caldas da Rainha. Others cut the telephone wires. Fishermen went out with their boats to prevent us being taken away by sea. Peniche was completely cut off. The Republican Guards were furious. At one point, they opened fire, and a fisherman was killed. When word of this got around, a truckload of peasants with hunting guns arrived from a village in the outskirts. It looked as if the Republican Guards would have to back down, but they managed to get a liaison officer away on a motor-bike along a beach track to warn the garrison at Caldas da Rainha.

'Troops were sent, and then we knew we were beaten. Our people were used to standing up to the police and fighting back. But not against troops. In those days – as again today – soldiers were considered "sons of the people". So, the crowd broke up and went home, and the fifty-six masters were taken away. But the fishermen went on strike. As long as the masters were under arrest, not one boat would put out to sea. One fisherman, employed by one of the biggest companies, broke solidarity and went out, but when he returned the others poured petrol over his catch. He never tried again.

'There were big demonstrations against the police – the women joined in, too – hurling stones and bottles. Some of the younger people were arrested and taken to the fortress, where they were tortured. A democratic doctor took up the battle in the courts. What with the demonstrations and street battles, the fact that no boats were going out and the efforts of the doctor, the authorities caved in, and we were all released after a few weeks. We consider that struggle ended in victory.' And that was the end of Joaquim Farrapilha's story, brought out with lots of reminders of points overlooked – the important role of the women, for instance – as the jugs of wine went round. One of the issues which caused heated discussion was the relative value of the efforts of the democratic doctor and the street battles in securing the release of the masters.

It was the turn of Manuel Maria Francisco of the next generation, equally tough, with a ruddy, weather-beaten face, to take up the tale.

'I was born in 1926 – so I'm as old as the fascist regime,' he said by way of introduction. 'In my childhood I knew nothing but suffering, misery, starvation. I was eight when my father was killed at sea by a hand grenade. I started going to sea at thirteen – no wages – as a sort of cabin boy. Fishing methods had changed. The boats were bigger, and the master had become very much the owner's man. Not like before, when people like Joaquim was a master – he was someone in whom the fishermen had confidence, because he was the best seaman and looked after their interests. The role of the master had definitely changed.' (There were interjections of approval at this. No *raconteur* could have had a more attentive and critical audience. It was the story of their lives that was being unfolded, and the fishermen listened with tense, taut faces to every word.) 'In my time, the masters had privileged positions. Even if they owned nothing before but agreed to side with the owners, they were given shares in the company to identify them completely with the bosses.

'When I started, I was told: "If you want a job, be prepared to starve; listen to what you're told, and never answer back." I was everybody's slave – and ate the other fishermen's leftovers. Out of this was born a spirit of revolt, and I decided to devote my life to fighting with other fishermen against those who exploited us.

'In 1958, some of us started organising a Fishermen's Association. The Navy officer who headed the port authority at that time was a liberal – Silvano Ribeiro – and he went against the government line in authorising us to form this association. The government suspected him of being a communist, and PIDE agents were sent to search his house and dig up the proof. There was no evidence, and the Navy stuck by him. Ribeiro encouraged us to go after better conditions.[1]

---

1 [AN] It was the Peniche fishermen who, after 25 April, brought the name of Silvano Ribeiro to the attention of the Armed Forces Movement. When one of the Navy representatives on the Military Junta, the 'Red' Admiral Rosa Coutinho, was sent as high commissioner to Angola, it was Silvano Ribeiro – by now an admiral – who replaced him.

Figure 15.1. Fishermen manoeuvre their boats to unload the day's catch – baskets of sardines – on the quay at Portimão, 1972. Labour disputes about working conditions in the fishing industry, a major employer and primary source of food for most Portuguese people, were frequent during the dictatorship. (Photo by Fernando Ricardo)

'In those days, the man at the top of the whole fishing industry was a leading fascist, "Admiral" Tenreiro, who was also head of the Portuguese Legion.[2] He had never been on a warship, or even been to sea in his life, yet he held the official rank of admiral.[3] Typical! He was the national head of the Casa dos Pescadores, the corporative body of which owners and fishermen were members – theoretically with equal rights – but in which all decisions were taken exclusively in the owners' interests. The port commander was automatically head of the local Casa dos Pescadores and normally automatically sided with the owners. Silvano Ribeiro was an exception. He invited one of the fishermen in whom *he* had confidence to suggest that he line up nine others in whom the *fishermen* had confidence, to set up a ten-member committee. Once that was done, they should draw up a list of demands to improve their conditions.'

I interrupted to ask how the sardine fishing was organised at Peniche, and whether it was typical of the other sardine fishing centres.

'The boats are owned by capitalists who may just specialise in fishing alone, or they may be linked with the canning industry, or fishing may be just one of several enterprises. The fishermen do not get fixed wages, but instead a percentage of the value, which increases according to the weight of the catch. This system is roughly the same all over. At the time we started to organise the association, conditions were intolerable. We worked every day of the week. When we were not at sea, we were repairing nets or doing boat maintenance work. The owners always took over half the value of the catch on the pretext of the high "costs" of fuel, replacing nets, boat repairs, and all sorts of things over which we had no control. Many of our fights were over the percentage points in sharing the value of the catch. There were many other reasons for discontent, and Silvano Ribeiro made it clear that he thought our grievances were justified. There were no provisions for medical care, for instance, and once a fisherman was considered too old to put to sea, he received a pension of fifty escudos a month from the state, plus another fifty from

---

2 [EN] Henrique Ernesto Serra dos Santos Tenreiro (1901–1994), Portuguese Navy officer and highly controversial figure of the Estado Novo regime, served as the government delegate to oversee fisheries organisations. Investigated for financial irregularities after the Carnation Revolution, he died in exile in Brazil..

3 [AN] I learned later that this was not quite correct. Admiral Tenreiro occasionally boarded a warship at Lisbon, with pomp and ceremony, but disembarked at Estoril in Cascais Bay before it reached the open sea.

a fund established generations ago by one of our queens, who seems to have had a soft spot for fishermen.[4]

'No one could possibly live on 100 escudos a month, so, in practice, no one ever got "too old" to put to sea. His mates would see to it that he remained aboard as long as he wanted, and the masters simply had to look the other way regarding the work he did.

'I was one of the nine approached to join the committee,' continued Manuel Francisco. 'At first, the fishermen were suspicious of the idea; so was the PIDE. Although we had the support of the port commander, we had to meet secretly. We drew up a list of claims that Silvano Ribeiro found reasonable. 1959 was an election year, and we all supported Delgado. Through election meetings, we were able to propagate our claims. Ribeiro backed us up. Every year fishermen and owners have to be registered with the port authority. Ribeiro registered all the fishermen, but only those owners who accepted our demands. The owners then held separate meetings with the fishermen: "If you don't withdraw your claims and accept *our* conditions," they said, "no boats will put to sea." Some threatened to transfer their operations to other ports – and a few actually did. Only two out of nearly fifty owners accepted our claims. We were not strong; the committee was new, there was a lack of unity, and the owners could exploit the divisions. Also, there was no possibility of outside support. Not to go to sea for any length of time meant that our families starved, whereas the owners – most of them, anyway – had various other interests to keep them going, so we did not have much leverage on them.

'At that time, each fisherman got 1.5 per cent, or 1,500 escudos, for a catch worth 100,000 escudos, and there were twenty to twenty-five men per boat. Our reply to the lock-out threat was to say that it was we who would not let the boats leave shore unless our claims were met. Strike action, in fact, began. But the police came with machine-guns and arrested five of the suspected "ringleaders". Members of our committee of ten were harassed, our houses continually searched by PIDE agents, and there were all sorts of other threats. Finally we had to settle for less than

---

4   [EN] Manuel Francisco most likely referred here to the Instituto de Socorros a Náufragos (ISN), founded in 1892 by Queen Dona Amélia de Orleães (1865–1951) as a royal initiative to create a benevolence society for the assistance of shipwrecked mariners. The ISN was overseen by the state and its mission broadened to include financial assistance to injured or aged fishermen.

the 1.5 per cent of the catch per man, so we were worse off than before. Later, Ribeiro was replaced by another port commander, who simply nominated a committee – a bosses' committee dominated by the masters.

'I was named a member, together with the master of the boat on which I worked. That was the end, as far as I was concerned. I fled to France and got a job as a construction worker. About 200 other fishermen quit at the same time. We had suffered a defeat.' He concluded by saying that he had settled in France, and had returned to Peniche for his summer holidays to see relatives and his old comrades. 'I'm a socialist,' he said, 'and that means I'm an internationalist, and carry on the fight for socialism wherever I am.'

It fell to Carlos Cordeiro, athletic, thirty-one years of age, with a shrewd, intelligent face, to bring the saga of the sardine fishermen right up to date.

'I'll start with the first of April 1970, which was the date to start registering boats and crews for the following twelve months. The crews of the first four boats were called in by the port commander, who read out the terms of the contracts. To everyone's surprise, a fisherman stood up and said: "I don't accept." Although nothing had been discussed or organised, all the other crewmen took the same position. On the following days, other crews were called in. They all refused the conditions. It was quite extraordinary – spontaneous support for one spontaneous action. The port commander tried new tactics, calling in three men from each boat to accept on behalf of the others. Nothing doing. They all said "No," and when they reported back to their crews, they were all supported. "No" meant that no boats put to sea. There was a total strike for twenty-eight days.

' "Admiral" Tenreiro ordered the port commander to send three delegates to Lisbon to discuss matters with him. I was one of the three. There was no discussion. "Either you accept the owners' conditions," said Tenreiro, "or you continue the strike. If you continue to strike, you will starve and your families will starve." We returned and reported to the crewmen. We had no political organisation at that time, so it was decided to accept the contracts. Again, we had to accept less than the 1.5 per cent of the catch per man – but we had won an important concession. We got time off from 5:00 p.m. on Saturday until midnight on Sunday, to spend a bit of time with our families.

'Things went on like that for a few years, until September 1973, when the fishermen asked me to approach the port commander and ask for the right to sleep at home on Sunday nights, and put out on Monday morning. The port commander would not give me, as an individual, a direct answer, so the fishermen appointed a committee to put their case to him. We were demanding to put to sea at 10:00 a.m. on Mondays. After four meetings, which got us nowhere, the port commander sent for the PIDE to sit in on the discussions. But as long as the PIDE were there, no one would open his mouth. Eventually, they were withdrawn. A compromise was reached, by which we would put to sea at 3:00 a.m. on Mondays instead of midnight. September 1973, it must be remembered, was while the election campaign was going on – always a favourable moment for action. We held many meetings to discuss fishermen's rights. As a prominent member of the local CDE, I was under especially close PIDE supervision.

'The committee had agreed to the 3:00 a.m. solution, but it had to be ratified by the fishermen as a whole. We held a mass meeting at which the new contracts were accepted, with some minor amendments. These were approved by the owners, but when we took them to the port commander, he said: "Absolutely impossible." He had two more meetings with the committee, and a third with the fishermen alone, without the committee, trying to force them to modify the contract. They remained unanimous in their support of the committee. The port commander then called in the owners and ordered them to cease fishing operations altogether.

'It was thus that the great lockout was started by the owners, which was still going on by April 25th.' Carlos Cordeiro then related the events described above in Chapter 2, regarding the street celebrations on 25 April, when it was discovered that the armed forces had come in to liberate the political prisoners in the Peniche fortress – and not to repress the fishermen. He continued:

'On 1 May, there was a large demonstration in front of the town hall. I headed a delegation to see the port commander – Maxfredo Ventura Dias – to tell him that he was no longer president of the Casa dos Pescadores, and that he should surrender the key. The next day, there was a big meeting of all the fishermen – not only the sardine crews – to elect a five-member committee to run the Casa dos Pescadores in the interests of the fishermen, not of the owners, from now on, and empowered to negotiate contracts. We of the committee went to Lisbon to visit the National Fishing Organisation, where we received immediate recognition of the committee. With that, we went for a showdown with Tenreiro, and told him: "You no longer have any competence in our affairs." Then, on to the Military Junta of National Salvation, where we had a three-and-a-half-hour meeting with the two real admirals, who confirmed us as the official representatives of the Peniche fishermen. Not only that, but Admiral Rosa Coutinho issued instructions that the method of taking over at Peniche should be regarded as a model for the rest of the fishing industry. He advised us to start new negotiations with the owners.

'The port commander was kicked out, while Tenreiro lost all authority when the Portuguese Legion was dissolved; but we still could not reach an agreement with the owners. The Junta of National Salvation sent a delegation to reason with them, and extracted an agreement that was nevertheless unacceptable to our committee. The owners and masters then tried to divide us by urging the crews to put to sea over the heads of the committee. But they refused. We then drew up a list of claims and said that only those owners who signed contracts on these conditions would have crews. A couple of owners signed immediately; others followed, and by 17 May they had all accepted, and all boats were putting to sea again.

'By this time, the old Casa dos Pescadores had been transformed into a real fishermen's association, which is why the crewmen dared stand up to the owners. Before, many of them had been afraid to say a word, for fear of being sacked – especially those who had wives and kids to support.'

I asked, 'What were the main gains won through that complicated struggle?' – and the reply illustrates what tough battles had to be fought for what seemed a miniscule improvement in conditions. Formerly, there had been three categories of haul: up to 50,000 escudos' worth of fish, between 50,000 and 120,000, and over 120,000. For the first category, the fishermen received 36.9 per cent of the market value to divide between them; for the second, 39.2 per cent, and for the third, 49 per cent. Every fraction of a percentage point in each of the three categories was the result of bitter struggles. The outcome of the most recent one was that the lowest category, of 36.9 per cent, was dropped. The other gain also seemed marginal.

'In the old days, each fisherman had the right to take two fish home for family consumption. They were searched when coming off the wharves, to make sure they had no more than two. Later, that system was changed so that each crewman got twenty escudos' "*caldeirada* money" after each outing.[5] But we were still searched for concealed fish when leaving the wharves, and this was very humiliating. In any case, you couldn't have much of a *caldeirada* for twenty escudos. Under the new contracts, the searching was stopped – that was the main thing – and the "*caldeirada* money" increased to forty escudos.'

The Peniche Fishermen's Association, of which Carlos Cordeiro is now the president, has 4,500 members, of whom over 3,000 are seagoing. Conditions in the other fishing ports, I was assured, were even worse than at Peniche, but an all-round improvement of conditions was expected when the various fishermen's associations merged into one big federation on a national basis.[6]

After listening to all that, it was going to be difficult to look a Portuguese sardine in the eye again, without thinking of the incredibly tortuous battles waged by the men who catch them, just to get a few hours' sleep on a Sunday night and the right not to be searched for a sardine or two in their pockets. Those who claim nothing has changed in Portugal might ponder over the rise and fall, respectively, of fisherman Carlos Cordeiro and 'Admiral' Tenreiro!

---

5 [AN] *Caldeirada* is the equivalent of the famous French *bouillabaisse*, but much more highly spiced.

6 [AN] Since our meeting, Carlos Cordeiro was put in charge of organising fishermen's associations all over the country and meets every week in Lisbon with the undersecretary of state for the fishing industry. He is typical of young activists whose energies and talents were recognised after 25 April.

16
Decolonisation

The eight months between the start of the London talks on Guinea-Bissau and the signature of the historic documents on Angola's independence on 15 January 1975, represent Portugal's 'short march' in winding up half a millennium of empire in Africa. Certainly, this had been preceded by the 'long march' of the peoples of Guinea-Bissau, Mozambique and Angola in many years of bitter and heroic armed independence struggles. And the eight months' period was twice interrupted – while Portugal first rid itself of a prime minister, before agreements on Guinea-Bissau and Mozambique could be concluded, then of a president, before agreement on Angolan independence could be reached. (President Spínola was not prepared to put up much of a fight for Guinea-Bissau, which has little in the way of natural resources, but he was prepared for even an armed showdown with the Armed Forces Movement over Angola, with its riches of petroleum, minerals, diamonds, timber and other materials, the extent of which have not even been properly prospected.)

If the London negotiations, starting 25 May 1974, were surrounded by an air of complete unreality, those officially known as the Algarve summit on Angola, conducted on Portugal's southern coast, were marked by realism, cooperation and generosity. The final act there was a moving if solemn ceremony, reflecting not only its truly historic significance, but probably also the thoughts of Portuguese and national liberation movement leaders alike: that there were stormy waters to be navigated before the excellent agreement reached became reality. The three Angolan leaders affixed their signatures alongside those of three Portuguese ministers.

Figure 16.1. Negotiating Angola Independence (the Alvor Agreement), 15 January 1975; Algarve, Portugal. Standing left to right: Admiral António Rosa Coutinho; Agostinho Neto, leader of the MPLA; Portuguese President Francisco da Costa Gomes; Holden Roberto, leader of the FNLA; Jonas Savimbi, the UNITA leader; Foreign Relations Minister Mário Soares; Minister of Interterritorial Coordination António de Almeida Santos. (Photo by Fernando Ricardo)

Agostinho Neto, MPLA leader in a discreet western suit; Jonas Savimbi, the UNITA leader, curly black beard and flashing eyes in open-necked jungle greens. Holden Roberto, leader of the FNLA, glum behind his dark glasses, wearing a Mao-type jacket.[1]

With the Atlantic rollers crashing on the beach outside, Agostinho Neto – one of the best contemporary poets in the Portuguese language – speaking on behalf of the three national liberation movements, referred to the nearby Ponta de Sagres, from where fleets of Portuguese caravels

---

1 [AN] MPLA (Popular Movement for the Liberation of Angola); UNITA (National Union for the Total Independence of Angola); FNLA (National Front for the Liberation of Angola).

set out on their hazardous voyages of discovery from the fifteenth century onwards. These voyages, he said, 'contributed positively by contact with other peoples and continents in marking a new phase in human society. Here, relatively close to Ponta de Sagres,' he continued, 'we have put an end to the unjust relations which much later were to besmirch the brilliant feats of the Portuguese navigators. Here,' and he pointed to the documents that had just been signed, 'the ambitions of the colonialists have been buried for ever.'[2] The faces of some of the Portuguese present – especially Melo Antunes, alongside President Costa Gomes, who presided over the ceremony, Prime Minister Gonçalves, and Admiral Rosa Coutinho – lit up when Neto referred to the 'fourth national liberation movement – that is, the Armed Forces Movement, which catalysed popular aspirations here by overthrowing fascism in Portugal, thus establishing a solid basis on which to end colonial exploitation'.

These were words to warm the hearts of Melo Antunes and Rosa Coutinho, who had worked the hardest, first to get the rival liberation movements to agree on a common negotiating position, and then to negotiate an agreement acceptable to all four parties. Indeed, these two had worked behind the scenes to improve – from the Angolans' viewpoint – the draft they had hammered out as a common negotiating position at Mombasa (Kenya) prior to coming to the Algarve.

It was this that made the atmosphere at the Algarve different to that at London or, indeed, at any other decolonialisation conference I have attended. There was sincerity and goodwill on the part of the colonial power towards the former colony – no feeling of a corporation lawyer's approach, trying to 'trick the natives' with built-in breakdown clauses. The traditional 'divide and rule' formula had become instead 'unite and be free', with the Portuguese negotiators playing a major role in the unity process. It is noteworthy that, in both the Mozambique and the Angola negotiations, it was senior officers of the Armed Forces Movement who played the decisive role.

The London negotiations, on the other hand, started off within the outmoded Spínola concept of a 'confederation', with long-drawn-out procedures to decide on 'self-determination' – which had been decided

---

2 [EN] Ponta de Sagres: Sagres Point, a dramatic headland that towers above the Atlantic Ocean near the southwest tip of continental Portugal; the site of an historic fortress and court associated with Prince Henry the Navigator.

long since by the people of Guinea-Bissau. I reported from the London Conference at the time:

> This is a conference of apparent goodwill, and the atmosphere seems good. But the Guinea-Bissau delegation is far more conscious of the historic nature of the talks here than the Portuguese delegation. (Foreign Minister) Soares is mandated to negotiate a military cease-fire and to discuss a form of 'self-determination' to be decided by referendum. The mandate of Major (Pedro) Pires of the African Party for the Independence of Guinea-Bissau and the Cape Verde Islands (PAIGC) is to get an agreement which will be a model for those later to be concluded between Portugal and its southern African colonies of Mozambique and Angola. Also, to get Portugal's new government to see that talk of 'self-determination' and 'referendum' in this context are old-fashioned terms that have lost their meaning.
>
> It is a replay of the old record that has been heard from Panmunjom in 1951, to Jerusalem and Damascus in May 1974 – of the side in the wrong wanting a purely military disengagement to get its troops out of an untenable situation, while the other side wants an overall, lasting political-military agreement.
>
> It can be taken for granted that it is because Soares realised this that he returned to Lisbon to demand a widening of his mandate.[3]
>
> I have been assured that the three (leading) resistance movements, the PAIGC in Guinea-Bissau, FRELIMO in Mozambique, and the MPLA in Angola, are prepared – like the Vietnamese in their dealings with the French in 1954 and the Americans in 1973 – to be generous; to give guarantees regarding the protection and rights of Portuguese nationals in their territories, and also for Portugal's legitimate economic interests in the area.
>
> But the crucial term they want to hear is 'total independence' – not the vague notion of 'self-determination'. As one of the members of the Guinea-Bissau delegation told me:
>
> 'Self-determination would have sounded wonderful in 1945. But

---

3   [AN] On the eve of his departure for London, Mário Soares had told a group of us in Lisbon that he expected to sign an agreement within two days. He returned to Lisbon on the fourth day and, after two more days in London, the negotiations were adjourned!

not in 1974. We have been recognised as an independent state by nearly ninety countries. We have observer status – just like West Germany got a year ago – at the UN. We have been accepted by overwhelming majorities into the World Health, and the Food and Agriculture Organisations of the UN. Last year the UN approved, by ninety votes to six, a resolution condemning Portugal's illegal occupation of the territory of our sovereign state of Guinea-Bissau. So how can one talk of the need for our self-determination?'[4]

But that was part of the unreality within which Spínola had dictated that 'decolonialisation' should be negotiated. It took the second political crisis in mid-July 1974 to release a few powerful whiffs of reality into the situation. Just one week after Vasco Gonçalves took over as prime minister, a small item appeared in the government gazette. It was a small 'rectification' to the Constitution recognising 'the right to self-determination of peoples *with all its consequences*'.[5] A few days later, President Spínola, on behalf of the new government, made the historic declaration that these 'consequences' included the 'right to political independence, to be proclaimed in terms and on dates to be agreed upon'.[6]

Things moved quickly after that. Further negotiations in Algiers between Major Pires and Mário Soares in mid-June had got nowhere. They met again in Algiers on 8 August, and Soares's original prediction of an agreement within forty-eight hours was fulfilled – but it was a very different agreement to the one he was proposing in London.

Agreed texts were submitted to their respective governments; there was a final meeting on 22 August to tidy up some details, and on 26 August complete agreement was announced. On 10 September, Portugal recognised *de jure* the independence of Guinea-Bissau, and, a little later, that of the Cape Verde Islands, where the population could decide via elections to a national assembly whether they wanted union with Guinea-Bissau or not.

The process by which Mozambique gained its independence was similar to that of Guinea-Bissau. Despite the public and well-photographed heartiness when Mário Soares first met with the FRELIMO leader Samora

---

4 [AN] *Guardian* (New York), 5 June 1974.
5 [AN] My italics.
6 [AN] See page 109.

Machel at the opening session on 5 June, the talks were broken off the following day, because there was no common negotiating position.[7] A communiqué noted that both sides 'recognised that the establishment of a ceasefire depends on prior global agreement related to fundamental political principles'. As Samora Machel had declared three days before talks started that 'peace in Mozambique is inseparable from independence', it is evident that all Soares had been able to offer was the old formula of an immediate ceasefire and some vague principles of 'self-determination'. But, as Samora Machel had made clear in his 2 June statement: 'It is not independence that we are going to negotiate with the Portuguese. Independence is our inalienable right. We intend to discuss the transfer of powers.' And he stressed that this transfer should be to FRELIMO as the sole legitimate representative of the Mozambique people – a right acquired by having led the armed independence struggle. But Spínola was still dictating how decolonialisation was to be approached. In another commentary from Lisbon at that time, I noted that:

> Some of the younger officers, meanwhile, are already muttering doubts as to their choice of Spínola as a leader, and wondering whether they might not have to do it all over again!
>
> Spínola's speech on 11 June, in which he set forth his impossible neo-colonialist plans for the African territories, only confirms that Foreign Minister Mário Soares's handshakes and embraces with the heads of the PAIGC and FRELIMO delegations in London and Lusaka, respectively, had nothing to do with negotiating positions. The terms for settlement were the cold, neo-colonialist pattern chosen by Spínola. As revealed in the latter's 11 June speech, they are almost a replica of the absurd terms Washington offered at the beginning of the Paris talks on Vietnam. It took four and a half years of negotiations, and some of the bloodiest fighting of the war, to bring them to reason.
>
> This is what Spínola is 'offering' the liberation movements of Guinea-Bissau, Angola, and Mozambique:

---

7   [AN] FRELIMO (Mozambique Liberation Front) is the country's only national liberation movement. The talks were at Lusaka, Zambia. [EN] Lusaka is the capital city of the landlocked nation of Zambia, which borders Mozambique to the northwest.

- A ceasefire, equivalent to asking the resistance forces to lay down their arms and disclose their whereabouts.
- Accelerated economic reconstruction. The same was offered by the US government to Vietnam. But where is it?
- Political settlement after the ceasefire. What happened in Vietnam? Exactly as with the French in 1954, the US in 1973 fulfilled only that part of the military terms that suited it. The US got its POWs back and its demoralised army safely home – and then repudiated the political clauses. Is anyone foolish enough to think that African freedom fighters are not aware of the way imperialists and colonialists honour their pledges?
- Broad democratic organisations, political freedoms, *et cetera*. Where have we heard this song before? The Vietnamese people have been waiting eighteen years for these freedoms and elections, promised them in the 1954 agreements with the French and the 1973 agreements with the Americans. Did the CIA agents bring this revamped draft of the Paris Agreement (on Vietnam) with them to Lisbon when they arrived in force a month after the coup?[8]

After Vasco Gonçalves became prime minister, there were further talks between Mário Soares and Samora Machel – and also private talks between the latter and Major Melo Antunes, by this time minister without portfolio, but charged with decolonialisation, among other tasks. Finally, agreement was reached in Lusaka on 7 September between Mário Soares, Melo Antunes and Dr Almeida Santos, minister for interterritorial coordination on the Portuguese side, and a FRELIMO delegation headed by Samora Machel, for a gradual transfer of powers to FRELIMO. Complete independence was to be achieved on 25 June 1975, the thirteenth anniversary of the founding of FRELIMO.

In my first discussion with Melo Antunes, he had insisted that Portugal must be 'original' in its approach to building up a new society in Portugal, as also in its approach to decolonialisation. The process of separation as embodied in the Mozambique agreement was in keeping with this. A transitional government was to be set up to run things until independence day, under a prime minister appointed by FRELIMO. Six of the nine ministers would be nominated by FRELIMO, the other three by the high

---

8   [AN] From the *Guardian* (New York), 26 June 1974.

commissioner, to be appointed by the Portuguese president. To ensure observance of a ceasefire – which had, in fact, been in effect long before the negotiations were completed – a joint military commission would be set up with an equal number of members from Portugal and FRELIMO.

'The independent state of Mozambique,' states the agreement in a passage which must have made Spínola grind his teeth with rage, 'will exercise complete sovereignty in the internal and external domain, establishing political institutions and choosing the social system which it considers in the best interests of the people.'

Immediately after the agreement was signed, there were riots provoked initially by white racist groups, whose outlook could be judged from the names of the two main participants: 'The Dragoons of Death' and the 'Independent Front for the Continuance of Western Civilisation'. These riots provoked counter-riots by Africans a few days later. What was absolutely decisive in preventing a generalisation of racial violence was another original solution – the setting up of joint Portuguese–FRELIMO military patrols which, according to eyewitness accounts, were quite impartial in dealing with those fomenting the riots. The entry of FRELIMO units into Lourenço Marques on 14 September was a matter for great rejoicing by the African community by all accounts, but the presence of Portuguese and FRELIMO soldiers, locked in a fight to the death such a short time previously, now sitting side by side in patrolling jeeps, had a sobering effect all round.[9] The ordinary man in the street, white and black, felt he was protected.

Spínola's reaction to the Lusaka agreement was his speech three days after it was signed, calling for the 'silent majority' to assert itself!

Brigadier Otelo de Carvalho, after attending one of the earlier negotiating sessions in Lusaka with Mário Soares, relates how he accompanied Soares to the Belém palace to report to the president. After Mário Soares had presented an account in customary diplomatic language, Otelo de Carvalho with soldierly bluntness, 'the only language I know', said there was only one thing to do and that was to accept the FRELIMO proposals, which 'appear to me to be the only correct and possible ones'

---

9 [EN] Lourenço Marques: the colonial capital city of Mozambique from 1898 to 1975, named for a Portuguese explorer. A principal port located on Delagoa Bay in the southern part of the country, the capital's name was changed to Maputo when Mozambique became an independent nation.

if Portugal wanted to extricate itself with its 'head high'. Spínola exploded and refused to listen to reason. He threatened that 'at his level' he would ask President Nixon to send US troops to Mozambique. When the brigadier objected that Nixon himself would not be interested in fomenting a Vietnamisation of the war in Mozambique, Spínola retorted that if Nixon refused, South Africa would oblige.[10]

Spínola later sent a communiqué to all Lisbon newspapers denying he had said any such thing, and claiming this was part of a campaign by Otelo de Carvalho to discredit him. However, at a press conference of the coordinating committee of the MFA on 31 December, the military spokesman, replying to a question, said:

'We have no doubts whatsoever as to the veracity of the statement made by Brigadier Otelo Saraiva de Carvalho, as the matter was known to the coordinating committee at the time it occurred. Besides, this was not the only time that General Spínola has made certain incriminating statements – similar to the one that has been mentioned. However, no one in the coordinating committee attaches any importance to these, as such things are always considered in the light of Generals Spínola's personality. He is a highly controversial military figure, endowed with great virtues and great defects, who has carried out the historic mission allotted to him. This mission was fulfilled, although it was shorter and not up to the standard that the Armed Forces Movement had hoped for from the beginning. The coordinating committee regards the matter as closed.'

From sources in Lourenço Marques at the time of the race riots, it was learned that Spínola did ask South African forces to intervene. There are considerable suspicions in the Mozambique capital that the riots were, in fact, started to provide the pretext for such intervention. South Africa by that time had realised, however, that it was militarily 'over-extended'. Prime Minister Vorster was indeed putting pressure on the Smith regime in Rhodesia to come to terms with its own nationalist movements, so that he could withdraw his own militarised 'police units' from Rhodesia, concentrate on defending his own frontiers, and take care of his own internal security problems.[11] Vorster showed enough

---

10 [AN] As related by Otelo de Carvalho in the Lisbon monthly *Portugalia*, in its issue of 23 December 1974.

11 [EN] John Vorster, born Balthazar Johannes Vorster (1915–1983), a conservative Afrikaner politician and strong adherent of the Apartheid policy who served as prime minister of South Africa from 1966 to 1978.

realism not to take on a war with FRELIMO but, on the contrary, to try to find a modus vivendi with the new emerging force in neighbouring Mozambique – even to the extent of denying refuge to untold numbers of white racists fleeing across the frontier.

The methodology used by the captains in implementing their programme, in decolonialisation as with other problems, was a step-by-step approach, summing up after each step before tackling the next one. In a way, it was a military approach: attack and secure an objective. Consolidate, and push on to the next and the next. On the overall field it was the same. Smash the fascist superstructure, for a start. Then, press on with decolonialisation. After that, the monopolies and absentee landlords.

In decolonialisation, Guinea-Bissau was tackled first because it was relatively simple. No Portuguese settler population; one national liberation movement, firmly in control of most of the country. The main issue was the modality of transfer of powers and the safe withdrawal of Portuguese troops. But the experience was useful in the approach to Mozambique – more complicated because of the 200,000 Portuguese settlers, or residents, but, again, with only one national liberation movement. The agreement there, especially the sharing of military and police powers on a bilateral basis, helped pave the way towards what everyone had predicted would be insoluble – the problem of Angola, with great wealth, half a million Portuguese, three national liberation movements and, in oil-rich Cabinda Province, a potential Katanga or Biafra, with a secessionist movement already established.[12]

Hardly was the ink dry on the Mozambique agreement, however, than the captains decided to press on to Angola, on the sound military principle of giving the enemy no respite. Rush his strongholds before he has time to reinforce! By this time, it was clear to a majority of the captains as to who was the real enemy. Not the national liberation movements, but Spínola and the forces he had chosen to champion – the monopolies, the banks, the multinationals and the foreign interests

---

12 [EN] In post-colonial Africa, Katanga and Biafra were territories within, respectively, the Republic of the Congo and Nigeria, which attempted to gain independent statehood because of regional demographic differences and ethnic tensions, combined with their abundance of valuable natural resources (Katanga's uranium, diamond, cobalt and copper mines), or geographic advantages (coastal Biafra controlled sea access). These areas thus became hotly contested militarily during domestic conflicts of the 1960s–1970s.

– strategic as well as economic. It had become clear by then (if not in his book, *Portugal and the Future*) that Spínola's concept of decolonialisation was in fact neo-colonialisation. His reaction to the Lusaka talks made plain that, if Portugal was too weak to impose neo-colonialisation, then he was prepared to have 'multinationalised neo-colonialism' – at least in Angola. That is why speed was of the essence.

In his resignation speech, General Spínola referred to the 'climate of anarchy' that had been created. He warned that 'under the flag of liberty, new forms of slavery are being prepared', and that the decolonialisation process 'was being corrupted with the deliberate intention of substituting undemocratic measures that do not correspond to the real interests of the African population'.

No one quite knew what Spínola had discussed in his tête-à-tête with President Nixon in the Azores Islands on 19 June, or with President Mobutu of Zaire, at Sal in the Cape Verde Islands, on 15 September – a few days after his appeal to the 'silent majority'. Fears were expressed in Lisbon that some sort of US–South Africa–Zaire axis was contemplated, to ensure that the riches of Angola did not fall into the wrong hands – that is, the hands of the Angolan people!

With these developments as a spur, in just six days of negotiations at the Algarve summit, a sixty-paragraph agreement was signed, under which Portugal recognised the three national liberation movements as the 'sole legitimate representatives of the people of Angola'. This pulled the carpet out from under the various groups which had been set up as future comprador-type props for neo-colonialism, including the Cabinda secessionist movement (FLEC: Liberation Front for the Cabinda Enclave) and the PCDA (Angolan Christian Democratic Party), accused of plotting with some of the white racists to set up a provisional government and declare 'independence' on the Rhodesian model.[13]

Angola is recognised as a single, indivisible entity, with Cabinda an 'integral and inalienable' part. During an interim period, starting with the establishment of a transitional government on 31 January 1975 and

---

13   [EN] Burchett's phrase, 'comprador-type props for neo-colonialism', refers to a long colonial-era tradition of foreign trade companies or governments employing indigenous agents to engage in commerce, or in economic/political manipulation and exploitation. Literally, *comprador* means 'buyer' in Portuguese, but the term has entered general use in Macau, in Hong Kong and across Asia, to signify an influential intermediary engaged to further Western colonial interests.

ending with complete independence on 11 November 1975, the country is governed by a three-member presidential college, composed of a representative of each of the three independence movements. Decisions within the presidential college are taken by a two-thirds majority, and the chairmanship rotates month by month in alphabetical order – FNLA, MPLA, UNITA. Of thirteen ministers in the transitional government, four are named by Portugal – economy, public works, housing and urbanism, and transport and communications. In addition, Portugal will be responsible for foreign affairs and defence during the transitional period. The three movements nominate three each of the remaining ministries. For each ministry headed by a minister of one movement, there are two secretaries of state representing the other two.

Everything possible has been done to ensure non-interference by the Portuguese in matters which do not concern them during the transitional phase. There is strict parity between Portugal on the one side and the three movements on the other in matters of joint concern, and strict equality between the movements in all spheres. The armed forces are integrated into a single army of 48,000 during the transition, of which Portugal contributes 24,000 and the three movements 8,000 each. Portuguese troops in excess of the 24,000 will withdraw from Angola by 30 April 1975, while the 24,000 in the integrated army are to be gradually withdrawn after Angola's independence day, the process to be completed by February 1976. A police force is established on the same principle; armed forces and police are under the jurisdiction of a national defence council, comprised of the Portuguese high commissioner, the three members of the presidential collegium, the commanders of the three branches of the Portuguese armed forces in Angola, and the military commanders of the three national liberation movements.

Whether the transition is smooth or not, and whether Angola then becomes a harmonious, multi-racial state, depends more on the extent to which the three movements can shelve their considerable differences and work together than on their mutual relations with Portugal. It is not within the scope of this study to deal with the dangers of outside intervention, but with the attitudes and techniques adopted by the captains in the dismantling of the African empire.[14]

---

14 [AN] In the north, Angola has a long common frontier with Zaire, where there are up to one million Angolan nationals. From these the FNLA leader, Holden Roberto,

The question of nationality and status for Angolans of Portuguese origin, or for Portuguese residents, is settled in a typically flexible way. Anyone born or domiciled in Angola has the right to Angolan nationality – but it is not obligatory. Portuguese, for instance, can opt for Portuguese nationality, and a mixed Portuguese–Angolan commission is set up to work out the status and rights of Portuguese in Angola and Angolans in Portugal who prefer to retain their respective nationalities. It will be an interesting plebiscite of confidence in the agreement to see how many Portuguese settlers opt for Angolan nationality.

That Portugal is to have a special status within an independent Angola is clear from Article 55 of the agreement, which states that the Portuguese government and the three movements 'have agreed to establish lasting and constructive links in all fields, notably in the cultural, technical, scientific, economic, commercial, monetary, financial, and military fields, on the basis of independence, equality, freedom, mutual respect, and reciprocity of interests'. Five joint commissions are set up to study various aspects of economic, scientific and cultural cooperation.

One of the first tasks of the transitional government was to set up an electoral commission to draft an electoral law, prepare electoral lists, and register the candidates proposed by the three movements, respectively, for elections to a constituent assembly to be held by 31 October 1975. The only candidates would be those of the three movements. At all levels of administration, the principle of a triumvirate of authority, with the chairmanship of the various departments and committees rotating month by month, is preserved. It is hoped that this day-to-day cooperation at all levels will help to create unity at the base of the three movements – a consensus which will gradually work its way up to the top, and eliminate either the rivalries, or those who stand in the way of them being eliminated. There are few illusions that this will be easy.

A question in many people's minds is, how was it possible for a professional army, steeped in centuries of protecting a colonial empire, trained

---

is said to have recruited his 15,000-strong army, trained by American 'green berets'. Holden Roberto is the brother-in-law of President Mobutu Seso Seko of Zaire. There is uneasiness within the ranks of the other two movements, and among progressive Portuguese, as to the real intentions of President Mobutu and Holden Roberto. The author, not having been as yet in the former African colonies, is not competent to judge the validity of these fears.

ideologically and militarily for colonial war, to suddenly turn around and become the vanguard in ending the wars, and dismantling the empire, even at the risk of provoking civil war at home? Was this not too good to be true?

On each occasion when I have asked activists of the Armed Forces Movement, what was the decisive factor that led them to risk their lives and careers in plotting, and finally in overthrowing, the regime, the replies always centred on their disgust with the colonial wars, and the way they were being waged; disgust with the attitude of the white racists whose interests they were defending. When I put that question to Brigadier Otelo de Carvalho, he spoke of his three tours of duty in Africa, two of them in Angola, one in Guinea-Bissau.

'For me and many of my comrades,' he replied, 'an anti-colonial-war consciousness was formed during those tours of duty. Why were we fighting? Why were our comrades dying? Why were the Africans being killed? For the sake of big monopolies and capitalists – so they could get their hands on raw materials and exploit the cheap labour of the Africans. We were fighting and dying so that the privileges of the rich could be maintained. We gradually came to see things in this light.

'During my first service in Angola, we worked off some of our frustrations by trying to help the population. We did plenty of good things, building roads, schools, hospitals, sanitation works ... But, by my second tour of duty, I understood that this was useless. To really bring happiness to the Angolan people, their country had to be returned to them. We were involved in an unjust war.'

'I first went to Angola in 1961,' he recalled. 'We officers, and the sergeants, used to whip up morale with slogans such as "Angola Is Ours", "Save the Fatherland", and other types of patriotic appeal. When I returned in 1965, the atmosphere was quite different. There were still not many desertions at that time, but you couldn't stimulate any enthusiasm with the old slogans. Things were already bad, and went from bad to worse, because everyone understood that it was a futile as well as an unjust war.

'By 1973, at the end of my last tour of duty, the only hope of the officers' corps was that we could create conditions for the government to find a political solution. We would hold the situation while Caetano found the solution. But the inefficiency and immobilism of the government was terrifying – that's why we decided that the only way to end the wars was to end the regime.'

Obviously, it was the hopelessness of the situation – the fact that there was no chance of defeating the national liberation movements militarily – that pushed the officers to question the nature of the wars, and finally the nature of the regime that insisted on carrying on the wars. But there had always been examples of individual moral revulsion by military officers at the wars and the regime, to inspire the generations of captains that overthrew it. Otelo de Carvalho related that his hatred towards the dictatorship started when, as a cadet, he saw mounted Republican National Guards break up an election meeting of Air Force General Humberto Delgado in 1958.

'I and some fellow cadets wanted to listen to what he had to say. But the Republican Guards swept down, striking out brutally at everyone, including us. Of course, Delgado lost the election, but we were furious when the generals called him a "clown" and hurled all sorts of other insults at him. For us, he was a brave and distinguished officer – a hero.' This was well before the wars in Africa began, and General Delgado was campaigning against the repressive nature of the regime and the total lack of democratic freedoms. But one of the most spectacular protest actions during the whole half century of fascism was directly linked to another officer's moral revolt at what he found in Africa – the preconditions of the armed liberation struggles.

This was the extraordinary case of an individualist predecessor of today's captains – namely, Captain Henrique Carlos Galvão, originally a staunch Salazar supporter, who helped bring him to power. He became a provincial governor in Angola, representing an Angolan constituency in the Lisbon national assembly, and was later appointed senior inspector of overseas territories. A more solid and devoted supporter of Salazar and his fascist regime would be difficult to find. But, in 1947, he was sent on a mission to report on economic conditions in the African territories. What he found there converted him into one of Salazar's bitterest enemies. He managed to read a report on his findings to the national assembly, but from that point on it was suppressed. From accounts which leaked out years later, he condemned the inhuman conditions in which Africans were exploited as 'beasts of burden' under all sorts of forced labour impositions; the virtual non-existence of public health or educational facilities in any of the three territories; the terribly high infant mortality rate, and the short life expectancy of the African population.

As a result, his official career ended abruptly but, since he continued to make his voice heard, he was arrested and jailed in 1951. Sentenced to three years' imprisonment when he came up for trial in 1953, he was kept behind bars through the usual formula of 'state security measure' until 1958, when he was tried again under thirteen charges, including 'subversion' and 'incitement to revolt', and sentenced to a further sixteen years. 1958 was an election year, and even from prison Captain Galvão made no secret of his support for General Delgado. Salazar could reasonably expect that nothing further would be heard from his erstwhile friend and supporter!

But on 23 January 1961, the name of Henrique Galvão suddenly burst into the headlines like a bombshell in an unprecedented – at least in the twentieth century – act of 'piracy on the high seas'. A 20,000-ton Portuguese ocean liner, the *Santa Maria*, had been seized by a certain Captain Henrique Galvão. The first news the world had of the incident was a message from the ship's radio in the name of the 'Independent Junta of National Salvation, led by General Humberto Delgado, the legally elected president of the Portuguese Republic, who was fraudulently deprived of his rights by the Salazar administration'.

At that time sixty-five years of age, Captain Galvão had escaped from the prison hospital in 1959, sought asylum in the Argentine Embassy in Lisbon, and from there went into exile. The *Santa Maria*, on a holiday cruise with some 600 tourists aboard, had put into Curaçao, in the Dutch West Indies, as its last port of call before the seizure. Galvão and his men came aboard there, disguised as tourists and crew members – which suggests some collaboration with the *Santa Maria* sailors. After a brief gunfight, in which the third officer was killed and eight others wounded, Captain Galvão and his well-armed supporters took command. For the next ten days he played a game of hide-and-seek with ships and aircraft of several nations, including US, British, Dutch and – belatedly – Portuguese warships. The story made daily headlines all over the world, quoting Captain Galvão's messages denouncing the Salazar dictatorship.

Finally, after an exchange of messages with the US Navy, on the eleventh day the *Santa Maria*, with all flags flying and decorated from stem to stern, put in to a triumphant welcome at Recife in Brazil, where the passengers were landed unharmed, full of praise for Captain Galvão's gallant behaviour. He and his men were accorded political asylum in Brazil.

One would have thought that might suffice in the way of a brilliantly successful propaganda achievement for one year. But, ten months later, Galvão was in the headlines again, when he was expelled from Morocco for having organised the hijacking of a Portuguese airliner, which showered Lisbon with anti-Salazar leaflets two days before the national assembly elections on 12 November 1961. Two years after that, he turned up at the trusteeship council of the United Nations – seriously risking extradition back to Portugal, where another twenty-two years had been added to his original sentence, for the seizure of the *Santa Maria* – to demand that the Portuguese people be encouraged and helped to exercise 'self-determination' by overthrowing the Salazar regime, and installing a government which would immediately negotiate the independence of Angola and other overseas territories.

That Captain Galvão and Admiral Delgado were individualists without any chance of success, everyone agrees. But they were also heroic figures, prepared to risk all for their ideals; capable of inspiring another generation to emulate their courage and idealism, but also to avoid the weaknesses of individual action by banding together in a collective effort with mass support – which is what the captains did. Delgado and Galvão – and other officers who carried out extraordinary feats to dramatise their hatred of the fascist regime – are legendary heroes among the Portuguese people, but especially within the armed forces.

On the question of decolonialisation, as in other matters, the officers of 25 April, by sailing into the uncharted waters of original solutions in dismantling an empire, have shown the vision and spirit of their forefathers, who bequeathed to history such names as Henry the Navigator, Vasco da Gama, Magellan, and others of the golden days of Portuguese maritime exploration. The successful implementation of the independence agreements implies the emergence and consolidation of progressive regimes in the three African territories, and in Portugal itself. One can only wish them all: *Boa viagem* ('Bon voyage')!

17
Happy Birthday

The defeat – but only partial elimination – of the right-wing forces involved in the 28 September coup attempt sowed the seeds of another attempted counter-revolution. Spínola, as noted in an earlier chapter, had made a 'tough, defiant speech, aimed at further encouragement of the "silent majority"' when he abdicated. The deepening cleavages between the parties inside the coalition government, especially over the question of facing up to the monopolies, was bound to encourage plotters intent on putting the revolutionary process into reverse gear. The fourth governmental crisis in mid-January, when Socialists and Popular Democrats threatened to resign unless their concept of 'pluralistic' trade union leadership was accepted, instead of the single trade union federation supported by the Communists, was only a smokescreen behind which the much more serious issue of 'to nationalise or not to nationalise' key sectors of the economy was fought out inside the government. This had been a major factor, ever-present on the sidelines, in each of the preceding crises.

Passions were aroused in Portugal itself and abroad over such issues as whether 'democracy' was at stake over choosing the type of trade union organisation, whereas the question in the behind-the-scenes debates concerned the extent to which the teeth were to be extracted from the main monopolies, starting with the banks. Mário Soares was hailed elsewhere in Western Europe as the champion of 'democracy and freedom' on the trade union issue, but his speeches at home and abroad seemed to have little effect on the leadership of the Armed Forces Movement, which appeared less impressed of the need for a 'pluralistic' trade union leadership than for a strong, monolithic organisation to be called upon in emergencies. They came down on the side of a single trade union federation.

The controversial law to this effect was passed, and the Socialists and Popular Democrats grumbled, but remained within the government. What was really at stake was revealed when warnings were issued that, if the banks were nationalised, foreign investments and trade with West Europe would dry up, as would the remittances back home of Portuguese abroad, which represented such precious contributions to the country's foreign trade reserves. The behind-the-scenes battle over the long-awaited emergency economic law continued, with almost weekly announcements that it was 'about to be promulgated'. It was an open secret that the MFA leadership, supported by the Communists, wanted a 'tough' law, capable of halting the widespread sabotage of the economy, particularly the closing down or bankruptcy of small and medium enterprises because the banks were denying them ordinary commercial credits, and the monopolies were refusing to deliver essential materials.

On 18 February 1975, the Socialists and the leader of the Popular Democrats, Sá Carneiro, were given sharp reprimands by Captain Pinto Soares, on behalf of the MFA's coordinating committee, for having started 'typical reactionary rumours about the threat of civil war'.[1] Carneiro had said in a TV interview that the country was in a 'pre-civil war period'; the Socialist party leadership claimed that it was 'saving the country from civil war'. The comments of Captain Soares appeared in the form of an interview with a correspondent of the Barcelona paper, *El Noticiero Universal*. With soldierly bluntness, the captain said:

> There are grave periods in the life of a nation when certain rumours can be considered bordering on criminal activities ... The pattern being followed is very clear. By giving to understand that the Armed

---

1 [EN] Duarte Nuno Pinto Soares (1943–), military officer who served two tours of duty in Angola before joining the clandestine Armed Forces Movement in 1973. He took part in the Coordinating Commission of the MFA, the Council of State in June 1974, and the Revolutionary Council in March 1975, but resigned due to internal dissension in August 1975. Later the same year he served as Comandante of the Portuguese Military Academy.

Forces are divided, it is easy to affirm that internal opposition can only be resolved by armed struggle between two or more parties. This is pure slander, which the MFA is beginning to consider as criminal, and which may require proceedings against those responsible.

The captain went on to say that, if there were any tendency towards civil war in the country, 'which is not the case', it could only have its origins in 'reactionary provocations, which are neither the work of those within the military movement, who believe in democracy, nor of any within those parties which are truly on the left'. As for rumours of dissensions within the MFA, Captain Soares commented: 'These rumours are always launched by those whom it would suit to really have such dissension within the MFA. Or, they are rumours which form part of the political intrigues characteristic of certain pluralistic regimes, and which are always stepped up at the approach of an election campaign.' He went on to say that the factors which united the Armed Forces Movement were always far more important than any which divided them, and that decisions taken were 'always unanimous even though some divergencies of opinion might exist'.

The tone of these very sharp observations reflected growing irritation within the MFA at what the leaders considered the obstructive role of the Socialists and Popular Democrats; impatience that key legislation was being held up because of partisan party politics and, above all, considerable anger that an attempt was being made by the Socialists and Popular Democrats to reproduce partisan party wrangles within the Armed Forces Movement, where unity was considered sacred. Part of the acerbity of Captain Soares's remarks was also due to rumours of a growing rapprochement between Mário Soares and ex-president Spínola, on the basis of the latter coming out for 'democratic socialism' (as he had done in an interview with the weekly *Expresso* on 11 January), and Soares being prepared to support Spínola for president at elections later in the year, in exchange for himself getting the post of prime minister. The warnings of the Social Democrat and Popular Democrat leadership about chaos, anarchy, impending civil war, *et cetera*, echoed those of Spínola in his abdication speech and contributed to what the MFA leaders considered as wholly unnecessary tension. As the date for the constituent assembly drew closer, it became evident that Mário Soares, by his strong attacks on the Communists, was angling for the votes of

Spínola's 'silent majority'. In his speech at Faro, opening the election campaign, Soares claimed that only the Socialists had saved the MFA from becoming 'prisoners of the Communists', and Portugal from becoming 'a second Cuba'.

Supporting the 'chaos and anarchy' predictions were the activities of some extreme left-wing groups, whose positions leaned so far to the left that they effected a junction with those of the extreme right. The violent attack by ultra 'leftists' against the congress of the Democratic Centre and Social (CDS) Party in Porto in mid-January, and against an electoral rally of the PPD at Setúbal a month later, helped prepare public opinion at home and abroad for strong measures to preserve 'law and order'.

Around 11:30 on the morning of 11 March, Lisbon residents were surprised to hear and see helicopter gunships and transports, and a couple of T-6 trainer bombers, flying low over the city. Shortly afterwards, the sound of exploding rockets and machine-gun fire could be heard from the direction of the airport. The fifth and most dangerous crisis, and the second attempted coup since 25 April, had been triggered by a treacherous air attack against the 1st Light Artillery Regiment, stationed alongside Lisbon's international airport. Fifteen soldiers were wounded in that first attack, one of whom died some hours later. Blood had been shed within the armed forces – a demarcation line had been crossed. It seemed that civil war had started. Almost simultaneously, a couple of hundred paratroopers were flown in by NordAtlas transport aircraft, some to occupy the airport, the major part to assault the 1st Light Artillery Regiment, well known for the left-wing views of both officers and troops and considered a 'red bastion' within the armed forces. Meanwhile, in the heart of Lisbon, officers of the still unpurged National Republican Guards had arrested their commander (freshly appointed to offset the notoriously reactionary characters of most of the officers) and thrown in their lot with the *putschists*.

An hour after the first attack, two groups of armed civilians, each commanded by uniformed officers, arrived in helicopters at the Rádio Clube Português (the country's only medium-wave radio station) at Porto Alto, thirty kilometres northeast of Lisbon.[2] By firing a few machine-gun rounds into the generator and removing a vital part from

---

2 [EN] Here Burchett made an error of geography; his original text stated that Porto Alto is southwest of Lisbon.

the transmitter, the station was put out of action. It was significant that each group included a member of the Champalimaud family: Miguel and José Carlos, nephews of António Champalimaud, who heads the economic empire bearing the family's name. Shortly after this piece of sabotage, teams of the National Republican Guards set out in armoured cars to destroy the antennae of the RTP station (Portuguese Radio and Television) at Monsanto in the western outskirts of Lisbon. But COPCON forces had moved faster and already occupied the station; the armoured cars made a fast about-turn and headed back to Lisbon, unsuccessfully radioing for air strikes against the antennae.

Western press reports and comments tried to belittle the scale of the coup attempt, stating that a couple of T-6 planes were entirely inadequate to support such a coup, and even suggesting that the whole thing was a fake to justify the drastic measures announced by the MFA immediately afterwards. In fact, according to officers who accompanied Spínola into exile, confirmed by the preliminary report of a commission of enquiry, it was – on paper at least – a competently organised affair, the full ramifications of which could not immediately be known. Phase one succeeded by the establishment of a coup headquarters at the Tancos air base, some 100 kilometres north of Lisbon, and by the takeover of the National Republican Guards headquarters in Lisbon. Phase two only partially succeeded, with the seizure of Lisbon airport, the positioning of paratroopers for an assault on the 1st Light Artillery Regiment, and the sabotage of Rádio Clube Português, the main voice of the Armed Forces Movement. Phase three never got started, because of the partial failure of phase two, so the elements involved were not exposed. Spínola was in the thick of it all – and, as on 27–28 September, he proved to be a victim of his own delusions of grandeur. He issued orders right and left, without first making sure that they would be obeyed. Typical of his caste, he thought that once the action was launched, he could count on the personal loyalty of unit commanders who had unquestioningly obeyed his orders on various battlefields in the colonies, and that those unit commanders, by Gad, would be obeyed unquestioningly by their troops. His monocle once again symbolised his one-eyed view of things. And, if he overlooked the changed relationships and attitudes within the armed forces, he also totally overlooked the role of the people. The slogan 'MFA-POVO' (MFA-People) was a concept, in his view, worthy only of contempt.

How could he imagine that mothers with babies in their arms were to play a decisive role in preventing the assault on the artillery barracks? At the moment of almost eyeball-to-eyeball confrontation, when one shot could have unleashed a massacre, it was the people who moved in, placing their bodies between the opposing guns, asking the paratroopers what on earth they were up to. It turned out that the latter had been told they were there to quell a revolt in the 'red regiment'! Eventually, there was a fantastic dialogue between the paratrooper officers and those of the regiment – all recorded by TV crews, who had arrived in the meantime – the former saying they were there to disarm the artillerymen, the latter saying they would resist. The outcome was decided by the rank-and-file paratroopers, throwing down their weapons in disgust when they realised they had been duped.

The people also went into action in Lisbon, completely surrounding the Republican Guards headquarters in Carmo Square, limiting and finally preventing the exit and entry of the GNR's armoured units. Such a spontaneous popular mobilisation could not have entered into the calculations of Spínola and his military aides.

What in fact had taken place? The account of the co-plotters who fled with Spínola and that of the preliminary report agree on a number of points. Reports from Spain, where former PIDE agents and other renegades had set up a 'Portuguese Liberation Army' with the support of international mercenaries – including the former Nazi SS officer, Otto Skorzeny – were passed on to Spínolists within the armed forces, to the effect that the 'communists' had drawn up a list of 1,500 military and civilian personalities to be the victims of an 'Easter Massacre'.[3] A latter-day St Bartholomew's Eve![4] When this was brought to the attention of Spínola, who was high on the list of intended 'victims', by the Spanish secret police, he claimed he had also been warned of this by French

---

3   [EN] The Exército de Libertação de Portugal, or ELP, a far-right counter-revolutionary force organised by Agostinho Barbieri Cardoso, former sub-director general of the PIDE, on 6 January 1975 and directed from Madrid. Scores of ELP arson and vandalism attacks targeted mainly the PCP, as well as other party offices of the political left, in northern Portugal. The ELP ceased operations in April 1976. Austrian-born Otto Skorzeny (1908–1975) escaped to Spain after World War II and became a mercenary military adviser, helping reactionary governments plan covert operations.

4   [EN] A reference to the Saint Bartholomew's Day Massacre, that began in Paris on 24 August 1572, in which Roman Catholics killed thousands of Huguenot Protestants across France over a two-month period.

intelligence sources. His first reaction was to reinforce the considerable defences at his residence at Massamá, just outside Lisbon. Mines on the footpaths leading to the house, booby traps in the trees, a formidable collection of weapons at his side – like an early American settler threatened by 'Injuns'! His second reaction was to associate himself with a plot to overthrow the regime.

Following a series of secret meetings among the main plotters, starting from 8 March, in which members of the Champalimaud family – including António's son Manuel – played a leading role, Spínola left Massamá to set up his headquarters at the Tancos air base late on the night of 10 March. At 9:00 the following morning, he personally briefed the pilots of the helicopters and eight T-6 trainer-bombers which were to spearhead the action, explaining that it was necessary to maintain the 'continuity' and the 'purity' of the process started on 25 April. Officers were dispatched to the Monte Real air base, 150 kilometres north of Lisbon, where F-86 jet fighter-bombers were stationed. In the name of General Spínola, orders were given for pairs of F-86s to fly low-level intimidation passes over the Avenida da Liberdade, in the very heart of Lisbon, over the COPCON headquarters and over the 1st Light Artillery Regiment headquarters. The first pair took off, while Spínola's emissaries briefed other pilots for follow-up actions. Some pilots, according to the official report, began objecting to being drawn into what they suspected was a right-wing plot. But before the objectors won out, a second pair of F-86s had taken off on the same mission, including low passes over the Santarém–Lisbon road, along which Spínola was confident that tank units were advancing on the capital. Three Aviocar transport planes laden with paratroops from Tancos had landed, in the meantime, to secure the Monte Real air base. Ground personnel by this time had been tipped off from Lisbon as to what was going on. They tried to arrest Lieutenant Colonel Quintanilha, Spínola's chief emissary, and showed every intention of resisting the paratroopers. Quintanilha managed to get away in his helicopter, and the three Aviocar transports headed back, together with the paratroops, to Tancos.

Within about four hours of the start of the coup, it was clear that it had failed. It seems that the final blow for Spínola was when the commander of the Cavalry (tanks/armour) School at Santarém, seventy kilometres north of Lisbon, Captain Salgueiro Maia – considered a 'Spínolist' – having received a mysterious order to march on Lisbon, flew up to Tancos to assess what was going on.[5] 'What on earth are you doing making a coup?' he was reported to have asked Spínola. To which the latter retorted: 'What on earth are you doing, not advancing on Lisbon with your tanks?' Indeed, too many 'old comrades-in-arms' of former days had failed to respond to appeals and orders, or had been prevented from doing so by their subordinates and rank-and-file troops. By 3:30 p.m., the game was up. Spínola, Quintanilha, and fourteen other officers took off in three helicopters for Spain, as the first stop to exile in Brazil.

With regard to the real forces behind the coup attempt, the commission of enquiry, in its introduction to the preliminary report, notes that:

> The counter-revolutionary events of 11 March represent the culmination of the most gigantic campaign that the forces of international and national capital, the big financial and industrial bourgeoisie, and their allies, had mounted against the young and growing Portuguese democracy. In this campaign, large military, economic and political resources were employed, adapted to the specific circumstances of our country, but inspired by models already tried out in other countries where progressive regimes have been overthrown.
>
> The speech of ex-general Spínola [he had been stripped of his military rank immediately after 11 March] on 30 September 1974, when he resigned as a result of the 28 September crisis, can be considered the beginning of a preparatory campaign for the counter-revolutionary coup. From that date, the reactionary forces started mobilising all their resources for recapturing political power. To attain this goal, which simultaneously implied the establishment of a state of emergency, the dismantling of the Armed Forces Movement and the restoration of 'order' by repressive means, the basic strategy deployed was that of the 'destabilisation' of the political-social situation.

In other words, the commission of enquiry concluded that what had been attempted was a carbon copy of the anti-Allende coup in Chile!

---

5 [EN] Fernando José Salgueiro Maia (1944–1992), a captain who played a crucial role in the 25 April MFA coup d'état. Troops under his command were tasked with occupying the key government ministries quarter in central Lisbon. Maia's parlay during a standoff near Praça do Comércio, Lisbon's historic waterfront square, convinced loyalist forces to stand down and join the revolution; he later negotiated the peaceful surrender of Marcelo Caetano at the GNR barracks in Largo do Carmo.

The report listed the names of 163 persons involved in the plot – eight civilians, the rest military. The latter included five rank-and-file soldiers, twenty-five non-commissioned officers, forty-two lieutenants, thirty-three captains, twenty-seven majors, eighteen colonels, and five generals. It was clearly an officers' plot, with no grass-roots support. The preliminary report underlined the key role played by the people.

'The coup failed,' it states, 'because, in the decisive trial of strength, the people and the armed forces won.' The account by the commander of the 1st Light Artillery Regiment mentions that 'arms were distributed to the people ... The aid of the civilian population was the decisive factor during the attack.' Thus, just as during the 28 September coup attempt, the organisational reality of the People–Armed Forces Movement alliance emerges as the vital factor in blocking the road to counter-revolution. (That the MFA have taken good note of this was evident at a press conference given in Lisbon by Brigadier Otelo de Carvalho on 29 April, when he was asked what would happen in case of outside military intervention: 'We will mobilise the masses,' he replied, 'we will arm the people and go over to guerrilla warfare.')

The report recommended that the government 'continue to take firm and decisive measures, which will lead irreversibly and without any vacillation to a Socialist society.' It also advocated a 'democratic purge' within the state administration and armed forces, and stepping up the work of information and political explanations at all levels. In fact, the reaction of the MFA leadership to the aborted coup had been swift and devastating. The main banks and insurance companies were taken over, together with their assets, which included newspapers, hotels, and other 'booty' which is gradually being discovered. A twenty-eight-member 'Revolutionary Council' was set up as the supreme body of the Armed Forces Movement, supplanting the former Junta of National Salvation, state council, and other overlapping bodies. After the president, the Revolutionary Council is the country's supreme organ of power. The Armed Forces Assembly was expanded from 200 to 240 members, to include rank-and-file soldiers and NCOs. The long-debated question as to whether the MFA was to play the role of 'motor' or 'arbiter' was thus settled in favour of 'motor'. This became clearer than ever with the signature of a political pact, in the first days of April 1975, between the Revolutionary Council and half of the twelve political parties set to participate in the 25 April elections to a constituent assembly. They included the four parties represented in the coalition government.[6] It was the guarantee that, whatever the electoral results, the MFA would remain the dominant force in the country, and that nothing, including the drafting of the constitution, could be done without their approval. This would also be the case after the elections to a legislative assembly, due to be held within about six months of the constituent assembly elections. Among the provisions of the pact are the following:

- Changes in the composition of the provisional government up to the time of the legislative assembly elections can be made only by the president of the republic, with the approval of the prime minister and the revolutionary council.
- The MFA sets up a special commission to work with those elected to the Constituent Assembly in drafting a constitution 'within the framework of the MFA programme and the present platform'.
- The new constitution must be approved by the revolutionary council.
- The pact remains in force for a transitional period of from three to five years.
- The sovereign organs of the republic, listed in order of importance, are:
    - President of the Republic
    - Revolutionary Council
    - Assembly of the Armed Forces Movement
    - Legislative Assembly (when elected)
    - Government
    - Courts

The president is elected by a joint electoral college, comprising the members of the Legislative Assembly and that of the armed forces assembly, this ensuring that he has the approval of the MFA, regardless of the political complexion of the legislative assembly. The president is head of the Armed Forces. It is he who appoints the prime minister and, with the concordance of the latter, appoints ministers of the

---

6 [AN] Representatives of the MDP (Portuguese Democratic Movement) were brought into the government in a reshuffle after 11 March, in which, also, Melo Antunes replaced Mário Soares as foreign minister.

government. The president, in agreement with the prime minister, may also dismiss government ministers.

The functions of the Revolutionary Council include 'defining, within the framework of the constitution, the necessary programmatic orientations for internal and external policies, and watching over their application'. Within this general mandate, the Revolutionary Council will 'evaluate and approve' legislation initiated by the government and legislative assembly in virtually every field of activity. It may propose amendments to the constitution.

The National Assembly will be composed of 250 members; the 240 members of the MFA Assembly will include 120 from the Army, 60 each from the Navy and Air Force. Legislation not approved by the Revolutionary Council can be resubmitted and passed if it obtains a two-thirds vote in the National Assembly. If two motions of censure against the government are passed within thirty days by the National Assembly, the government will fall, but not the prime minister. He will be charged by the president to form a new one. In any case, the ministries of Defence, Internal Affairs, and Economic Planning will be reserved for nominees of the MFA.

A vital paragraph in the pact is one that states: 'Apart from the articles which constitute the basis of this agreement, the constitution must represent the consecration of the programme of the Armed Forces Movement; of the conquests legitimately obtained during the process of the implementation of the programme, and imposed by the revolutionary dynamic which opened, and irreversibly committed, the country to Portugal's own road to socialism.' The leadership of the MFA was obviously determined to ensure that, as Prime Minister Vasco Gonçalves expressed it on the eve of the Constituent Assembly elections: 'We are not going to risk losing in one day of elections what has taken so many years and so much suffering to obtain.' The pact was the guarantee that any future governments could only go forward, not backward; the gains of the revolution would be maintained.

Shortly after the pact was signed, the government announced the nationalisation of some thirty large enterprises, including fourteen engaged in the production and distribution of electric power; five big petrol-distributing networks; four transport companies, including TAP, the country's only airline; and Portugal's only steel-making plant. The nationalisation of other key sectors of the economy, including cement, mining, petrochemicals, cellulose, tobacco processing, breweries, shipbuilding yards, and metal-working enterprises, was under study, and would certainly be undertaken before the legislative assembly elections.

The formation of the Revolutionary Council cut through the endless debates over the measures to be taken to curb the monopolies. The economic basis of groups like CUF, Champalimaud, Espírito Santo and others in Portugal, as well as in the African territories, had been dealt crippling blows, with more to come.

If it seems strange to see a group of officers of diverse social and class backgrounds, such as comprised the MFA leadership, showing such enthusiasm for dismantling the monopolies and committing Portugal to socialism, one must understand that – more than any other section of the population, except the very politically conscious – the eyes of the military were gradually opened to the nefarious roles of the monopolies, because they touched their own lives and activities. They gradually realised – as Otelo de Carvalho was to tell me – that they were being sent to Africa to kill and be killed in a cause which had nothing to do with the national interest, or their own personal interests, but everything to do with protecting the ill-gotten gains of the monopolies. They staked their lives and careers on a very risky venture to end this. In overthrowing the fascist regime, most of them probably felt that their historic role was over. They gladly relinquished power to a civilian administration, which they expected would implement their programme. It did not, and within a few months Spínola – who had managed the Champalimaud steel mill at one period in his life and was known for his close links with the family – told the officers to go back to their barracks. Instead, some of them moved into the administration. But whatever difficulties they encountered – from economic sabotage to the 28 September and 11 March plots, and especially over decolonisation – they found that the main source of the troubles were the monopolies.

Gradually, an inescapable conclusion became widespread. Fascism was a triple-headed monster. It was no good lopping off the heads of repression and political power, as the captains had done, without going after that third head of economic power. As long as one head was left, the fascist body would continue to make trouble. Government, the repressive machinery of the state and economic power were so inextricably integrated that all three had to be dealt with. Economic power had, in fact, been the base of the other two heads. Those within the leadership of the MFA who were also in the administration became ever more convinced of this, through the practical business of handling day-to-day problems.

Many well-meaning – and some not so well-meaning – dogmatic theoreticians in Portugal, reinforced by their friends from abroad, wring their hands and say: 'No good can come of it. What is the class basis of the MFA? How can they pretend to want socialism?' Only a few months previously, the same individuals had been asking, 'How can they pretend to be sincere about decolonialisation?' When agreement was reached on Guinea-Bissau, they said, 'Ah, yes, but what about Mozambique?' After that question was settled: 'But they will never give up Angola!' Well-versed in theory, which they have never had an opportunity to test out in their own countries, because they have never reached the point of seizing power, the dogmatists and sectarians from abroad have totally failed to grasp the significance of the MFA–People alliance. They cannot see that there has been a conscious choice made by enough MFA leaders to persuade a majority within their ranks that, unless they identify themselves with the aspirations of the people, the working class, the peasantry, the progressive intellectuals, the petty bourgeoisie – badly oppressed by the fascist regime – and all those who fall within the category of the 'under-privileged', as it is spelt out in their programme, they will fail. The politically conscious section of the people, the majority within the active part of the population, understood immediately that, without maintaining the alliance with the MFA, they cannot consolidate the gains from overthrowing fascism, far less move on to build a socialist society.

The great merit of the MFA is that its members were able to draw the correct conclusions from the defeats in the colonial wars and carry out a revolution. It is only by evaluating the developments in the first year, since April 1974, that one recognises the need to upgrade what happened from 'coup d'état' to 'revolution'.

In a speech at the ceremonial signing of the pact between the MFA and the main political parties, President General Costa Gomes said: 'Considering the representativity of the parties here present, we are sure that the parameters of the platform signed here today will be ratified by the overwhelming majority of the Portuguese people.' This prophesy was dramatically justified in the elections which followed three weeks later, when the six of the twelve parties that refused to ratify the pact received a total of 3.37 per cent of the vote! (Which is not, by any means, to claim that only 3.37 per cent of Portuguese voters oppose socialism.) But the elections themselves – the way they were conducted, the almost 92 per cent of voter turnout, and the results obtained – represented the greatest endorsement of the MFA leadership, and support for those parties which at least officially backed the MFA–People alliance. Held on the first anniversary of the overthrow of fascism, the elections were the finest birthday present the MFA could have wished for. The four parties represented in the government coalition received just over 80 per cent of the vote, the Socialist Party clearly leading with 37.82 per cent. If one classes the Popular Democrats (PPD) with the right (officially they claim to be Social Democrats), and add their percentage of the vote to the frankly rightist 'Democratic and Social Centre Party' (CDS), the rightists collected 34 per cent of the votes cast. Blank or spoiled votes were less than 7 per cent of the total, although voters had been told that, even if they had not made up their minds which party to vote for, it was better to take part in the election as a civic gesture, and that they could always vote 'blank'.

When one considers that to have participated previously in a reasonably free election in Portugal, one had to be at least twenty-one, male, and literate, and that four million of those who voted on 25 April 1975 had never voted before in their lives, the results were spectacular. A triumph for the People–MFA alliance and for the mutual respect between the people and the armed forces – which was certainly enhanced by the political 'dynamisation' campaigns carried out by the MFA in the most politically and culturally backward areas of the country, to break down reactionary concepts fostered by forty-eight years of fascism before 25 April and, in many areas, by the village priests ever since.

In the days immediately following the overthrow of fascism, people often expressed their political options through the red, pink or white carnations in their buttonholes. Later, the reds, pinks and whites blossomed forth into a dozen different emblems of supporters of the parties involved in the Constituent Assembly elections. Two days before voting day, I watched a grey-clad policeman guarding the Spanish embassy hasten from his post to grab a leaflet from a long-haired, bearded young man handing them out on the corner of Avenida da Liberdade, in the last few hours before campaigning closed at midnight on the 23rd. It happened to be one exhorting passers-by to 'VOTE PCP ... FOR A DEMOCRATIC PORTUGAL ON THE ROAD TO SOCIALISM'. He returned to his post, intently reading the contents. It was impossible not to reflect on how, just one year earlier, that same policeman would have dashed to arrest, beat up, or even shoot down – if he ran – anyone daring to distribute such a tract! As noted earlier, the periods before elections and before May Day were marked by heightened repression and arrests.

Elvira Nereu, mentioned earlier as having been jailed for trying to organise some modest action to celebrate May Day 1974, was standing as a candidate on the MDP list for Lisbon on 25 April 1975. The Lisbon buildings were covered with brightly coloured posters inviting citizens to vote for any one of a dozen parties, from the 'Popular Monarchists' to the Trotskyist 'International Communist League', with the Communist, Socialist, Popular Democrat and three rival 'Marxist–Leninist' parties among those in between. It would have meant long jail sentences and 'no sleep' torture for even putting up a Popular Monarchist poster a year earlier. Now that times had changed, it meant an automatic thirty days in jail for being caught tearing them down!

Polling day was a nationwide fête. Touring villages within a fifty-kilometre radius of Lisbon was a very moving experience. A stocky peasant woman at Quintal hamlet – set in beautiful, rolling pasture lands – shyly asked the officials at the voting table how she should vote and for whom. Patient explanations were given. 'I can only vote for one party?' she asked. She took the ballot paper, held it upside-down and sideways, comparing the emblems with one pinned inside her scarf, stolidly marking a cross and folding the paper in the approved manner, and handing it over to be dropped in the ballot box. I watched similar procedures scores of times in different centres. At another hamlet – Odrinhas – 80 per cent of the registered voters had already performed their duty by midday. Many were sitting on stone benches, enjoying the spring sunshine and waiting for the results to be announced. At fashionable Sintra, where early risers were rarer than in the farming villages, the proportion of voters by lunchtime was fewer. We asked the owner of a posh restaurant what the voter turnout would be. 'One hundred per cent – except for anyone really ill. Anybody who doesn't vote will never set foot in my bar again!'

In the picturesque fishing village of Ericeira, a carnival atmosphere prevailed. Alongside Christ on a cross behind the ballot box was the slogan: 'The Vote! A People's Weapon!' At Mafra, the site of an enormous convent – Portugal's biggest building, we were told – long since turned into an army barracks, soldiers and civilians in endless lines shuffled patiently towards the voting tables. We were told of someone seriously ill being carried in to vote, who said: 'I'd rather die voting than not vote.' To judge by the almost 92 per cent turnout, this seemed to be a typical attitude. In a sense, it was a way of saying 'thank you' to the captains; it was also the feeling that, for the first time in the lives of most of them, their opinions were being sought. There was no sense of the passions aroused by partisan political conflicts – except in Lisbon and some other big cities during the main electoral rallies – but one had the rather moving impression of the humblest of Portugal's citizens feeling they were taking part in an historic act, in which each of them was regarded as the equal of his neighbour. Certainly, the results showed that, in the most politically and culturally backward areas, the smallholders mainly voted as the priest instructed them. But they voted; and, for the overwhelming majority, took the first step in an apprenticeship for democratic decision-making.

The results were an overwhelming vote against the *recognisable* right. People showed clearly what they did *not* want: a return to fascism. They rejected the ultra-right (the Popular Monarchists received only 0.56 per cent) and the ultra-left. The Trotskyists received 0.19 per cent; the three 'Marxist–Leninist' parties grouped together in the Popular Democratic Unity party (UDP) received 0.79 per cent (sufficient under the proportional representation system to elect one deputy); the other two 'Marxist–Leninist' parties received 0.57 and 0.23 per cent, respectively. Apart from the UDP, the only other party outside those in the government coalition to elect deputies was the CDS, with 7.6 per cent of the vote.

The next highest vote after the Socialists was 26.38 per cent for the Popular Democrats, followed by the Communists with 12.53 per cent, giving them eighty and thirty seats, respectively. The Democratic Movement received 4.12 per cent for five seats, much fewer than had been expected – the results of their pioneering work in the more backward areas were reaped mainly by the Popular Democrats and the Socialist Party.

As the industrial working class in Portugal is roughly estimated at one million, the Communist Party considered that a vote of over 700,000 indicated that the majority of these had voted for the PCP. It was felt that

Figure 17.1. Demonstrators from the PCP (Portuguese Communist Party) take to the streets in Lisbon to celebrate the 25 April military coup d'état, the overthrow of the oppressive Estado Novo regime, and the implementation of comprehensive voting enfranchisement in Portugal. (Photo by Eduardo Gageiro)

the space of one year was very small to offset the forty-eight years of fascism, in which communists were equated with the anti-Christ. The very clear option for the socialist road taken by the Revolutionary Council certainly won hundreds of thousands of votes for the Socialist Party – a large proportion of the voters being conditioned to express themselves for the ruling ideology.

The elections represented a fitting and crowning triumph for the officers who executed the 25 April revolution. In bringing them to a successful conclusion, they could be justifiably proud of having fulfilled all the essential targets set for the first year of their programme. 'Happy Birthday' was the least one could wish the officers of the MFA as 25 April 1975 ushered in election day, and one looked back to all that had been accomplished in a single year. For me, it was fascinating to step into the same bank where I had made my first contacts with enthusiasts for the revolution, exactly one year previously. I had to pass under a large banner strung across the entrance, on which was inscribed, in big red letters on white cloth: 'BANCO DO POVO' (People's Bank). Similar signs adorned every major bank in Lisbon!

Wilfred Burchett
Lisbon, May Day, 1975

BOOK II (1976)
Portugal Before and After the 25th of November

18

Turning the Wheel Back

The Portuguese Revolution has proceeded from crisis to crisis, each marking the end of one definitive stage and the beginning of another. The most critical of all was that at the end of November 1975, when the country was brought to the brink of a Spanish-type civil war. Ironically enough, this was at the moment when, on the other side of the frontier, General Francisco Franco, the winner of that conflict, was being buried. Many of the elements which sparked off the bitter and bloody Spanish Civil War forty years earlier were present in Portugal on 25 November 1975, when a leftist Regiment of Parachutists seized the five main Air Force installations in the Lisbon area, including the Air Force headquarters in Lisbon's Avenida da Liberdade, and capturing General Pinho Freire, Air Force commander of the Lisbon region. In solidarity-supporting actions, some other units friendly to the Parachutists – the Military Police Regiment, the RALIS (1st Light Artillery) Regiment guarding Lisbon's international airport and the highway leading to the capital from the north, and a few other elements – made half-hearted gestures. But, without any centralised leadership, advance planning, coordination between units or agreement with political parties, these isolated insurrectionary actions were quickly crushed.

The only deaths occurred when a tank-supported commando unit assaulted the military police headquarters, a few hundred yards from the Belém presidential palace, in which two commandos and one military policeman were killed. Other left-wing units were 'neutralised' by negotiations. Within forty-eight hours, more than a hundred progressive officers, sergeants and soldiers had been arrested, and 'wanted' lists had been published of over twenty others. The COPCON internal security force had been disbanded, and all senior officers – with the exception of its commander, Brigadier Otelo de Carvalho – had been arrested. The progressive chief of staff of the armed forces, General Carlos Fabião, had 'resigned'.[1] Within the days that followed, five left-wing members of the nineteen-member Revolutionary Council – including the popular Admiral Rosa Coutinho – had been dismissed, two of them arrested. Veterans who had played key roles in the 25 April coup were under arrest, purged, disgraced or demoted. Civil war had been averted, at the cost of a virtually bloodless takeover of the military hierarchy by rightist officers. How did things reach such a point?

One has to go back to the Constituent Assembly elections, held seven months previous to the flashpoint on 25 November. The results of these elections, as noted in the previous chapter, were not supposed to find any reflection in the composition of the government or its policies. As election time approached, the more far-seeing members of the Armed Forces leadership realised that holding any type of elections, within only one year of the overthrow of half a century of fascism, was a mistake. But, since they had been provided for in the political programme of the Armed Forces Movement (MFA), it was a matter of military honour – so the majority within the MFA leadership argued – that they be carried out on time. The device of a political pact, signed between the main political parties and the MFA, was designed to neutralise the dangers of a political power struggle stemming from the election results. According to the pact, the task of elected deputies was to be strictly limited to the drafting of a constitution in line with the MFA programme. In reality, the election results were exploited immediately by the Socialist and Popular Democrat parties to demand a share in government proportionate to their electoral percentages. They

---

1 [EN] Carlos Alberto Idães Soares Fabião (1930–2006), a military officer and member of the Armed Forces Movement. In December 1973 he denounced and foiled a right-wing coup attempt planned by General Kaúlza de Arriaga. He took part in the MFA 25 April coup and afterwards served as military governor of colonial Guiné in 1974, prior to independence. He was a member of the Junta of National Salvation and the Council of State; beginning in March 1975 he served on the Revolutionary Council. In 1974–75 he was commander in chief of the Army.

'forgot' about the pact by interpreting their electoral successes as a mandate to govern.

Thus started a whole phase of partisan political in-fighting, with intimations from the Socialists and Popular Democrats that it was time for the Armed Forces Movement to return to the barracks and leave the running of the country to the politicians. Gradually, the political pact was buried under the banner of 'Freedom, Democracy and Pluralism'. A vigorous anti-communist campaign was whipped up, especially in the north, where offices of the Communist and MDP parties were burned, and physical violence was used against party cadres. The pretext was communist intentions of establishing an 'atheistic, totalitarian dictatorship' and similar allegations. What was really at stake, but neither Socialists nor Popular Democrats wanted to come out and say it, was the tempo and direction of the Portuguese Revolution. The nationalising of the big monopolies and the banks, and the expropriation of the big estates, was not to the liking of the Socialists and Popular Democrats – and even less so to their backers in Western Europe and the United States. But they could not openly campaign against such measures and retain their socialist and social-democrat followers. Defence of 'democracy' and opposition to 'communist dictatorship' were more acceptable slogans under which to slow down and divert the revolutionary processes.

It was left to a group of influential military officers to state, in very guarded language, the real issues. The declaration of the 'Group of Nine', all members of the ruling Supreme Revolutionary Council and headed by the prestigious Major Melo Antunes, exploded like a bombshell, shattering the image of monolithic unity which the Revolutionary Council had always presented until then.[2] The document specifically accused the Gonçalves government of going too far and too fast, demanding a slowdown and a change of government. Presented in the form of 'it is not so much what is being done as the way in which it is being done', in discussing the nationalisations, the document states that, in a departure from the spirit of the MFA programme:

---

2   [AN] The other signatories were Captain Vasco Lourenço, Major Canto e Castro, Commander Vitor Crespo, Major Vítor Alves, Brigadier Franco Charais, Brigadier Pezarat Correia and Captain Sousa Castro. Sixteen other officers, not members of the Revolutionary Council, were named as supporting the document, first published on 8 August 1975.

Parallel to the dismantling of half a dozen of the great financial and monopoly groups, other nationalisations went on (at a rhythm impossible to absorb without a grave risk of rupturing the existing social and cultural fabric) accompanied by a very rapid disintegration of forms of social and economic organisation which served to support large sectors of the small and medium bourgeoisie, without the creation of new structures capable of ensuring the management of the production units and distribution networks, or to maintain the indispensable minimum of social relations between the Portuguese people as a whole.

Obviously referring critically to the takeover of factories in Lisbon and farms in the Alentejo, the document continues:

The gap grows ever wider between a very small minority group – part of the proletariat from the Lisbon and Alentejo areas – who have definite revolutionary aims, and practically the whole of the rest of the country, which reacts violently to the changes that a certain 'revolutionary vanguard' wants to impose without taking into account the complex historical, social and cultural reality of the Portuguese people.

The document

rejected the model of an Eastern European style of socialist society, to which we would inevitably be led by a political leadership which obstinately believes that a 'vanguard' with a very narrow social base would carry out the revolution in the name of the whole people, and which, in practice, tolerated the infiltration of this 'vanguard' into the centres of political power and military structures. The bureaucratic leadership associated with totalitarian regimes is absolutely rejected by those who in the past fought against fascism and, logically, now take up positions to combat new forms of totalitarianism.

Here, the Melo Antunes group was coming out against a new concept of 'people's power', launched in the name of the MFA on 8 July in an attempt to short-circuit the inter-party political strife by advocating a proliferation of committees of workers, peasants, neighbourhood residents and rank-and-file soldiers, to build up into people's assemblies. From the local and village levels, these would build up to a sovereign national people's assembly. All this must have seemed strongly reminiscent of the workers and peasants' soviets of the Bolshevik Revolution, accompanied by the slogan: 'All Power to the Soviets'. This was a particularly horrifying concept to the Popular Democrats and all to the right of them. The 'Nine' also rejected the West European Social Democratic concept:

> We reject the model of social democracy as practised in many countries of Western Europe, because we believe that the big problems of Portuguese society cannot be overcome by reproducing in our country the classical formulas of advanced capitalist states. It would be a tragic mistake, at a moment when everything points to a general and global crisis of capitalism, to be tempted to repeat the experiments of social democracy – even with their seemingly immediate and real, but obviously illusory, benefits. We fight for a policy of the left through which we can build a socialist society.

The doctrine of a 'revolutionary vanguard' was rejected in favour of a 'broad and solid social bloc of support and a national plan for a transition to socialism'. On foreign policy, the 'Nine' called for the development of relations with all countries and 'the maintenance of our ties with Europe, reinforcing and deepening our relations with certain economic entities, the European Economic Community and the European Free Trade Association'. Emphasis was laid on the need for a 'gradual transition, peaceful and without convulsions', to a socialist society. Finally, the 'Nine' concluded that the programme they had outlined 'cannot be carried out by the present leadership, even if it is partially renewed, given its lack of credibility and manifest incapability to govern'.

This was the powerful first salvo of what developed into a violent campaign to oust Vasco Gonçalves as prime minister. It was the beginning of a split within the Armed Forces Movement, which led, step by step, to the events of 25 November, with their disastrous consequences for many veterans of the 25 April coup.

That there was room for criticism of the Communist Party and the methods used to speed up the revolutionary process is clear from the speech by Álvaro Cunhal on 7 December, aimed at putting together some of the pieces shattered by the explosion on 25 November. Appealing for a united front of all anti-fascist forces, he warned of the dangers if 'communists failed to understand the new situation, or insisted on pursuing previous policies and methods . . . The working masses must understand the new realities; they must understand that our system of alliances and our forms of struggle must be revised.' What is obvious is that many Communist Party veterans, who had spent up to twenty years in prison, still had their noses deep in the literature of the Bolshevik Revolution. It was symptomatic that, at the height of the November crisis, John Reed's *Ten Days That Shook the World* was very popular among CP militants!

The various political parties had found their partisans within the Armed Forces Movement, which had aimed to be above party politics. A few days after the 'document of the Nine' appeared, there was a rival 'document of COPCON' – published on 12 August – the authorship of which is generally attributed to Otelo de Carvalho. If so, nothing could have been more symbolic of the division within the MFA, with Melo Antunes and Otelo de Carvalho, two of the chief architects of 25 April, taking diametrically opposite sides. Whether he wrote the 'document of COPCON' or not, Otelo obviously approved every word of it. It recognises that the elections were an error:

> The holding of elections in the conditions in which they were held, contributed to the people's confusion of the instruments available to them for controlling the state and power structure.
>
> Within a bourgeois structure, a poll can result in only one thing – a victory of the bourgeoisie.
>
> The MFA must bear a great measure of responsibility for having made the elections a point of honour, an aspect which was well exploited by those who have an interest in such elections.

Touching on the reasons why the Socialists and Popular Democrats were able to find good ammunition to attack the MFA, and insist that the military should 'return to the barracks', the document continues:

> The breakdown and impotence of four provisional governments is not just the result of the leadership which the Communist Party tried to impose by infiltrating the state apparatus and the organs of social

communication;³ the PS, PPD, and MPD-CED, which were also in the governments, shared the blame, though now they are trying to shrug it off. As far as the parties to the right of the PS and the PS leadership are concerned, all that could be expected were attempts to hinder and reverse the revolutionary process as a means of guaranteeing the privileges of the big bourgeoisie, and the unbridled exploitation of the workers.

Implicitly, these two documents reflected the fact that divergent class interests had now emerged and found their reflection inside the Armed Forces Movement.

'The solution of the present situation, for which the MFA bears a large measure of responsibility,' states the COPCON document, in direct criticism of that of the 'Nine',

> will not be found in palliatives for the right ... Progress in the construction of socialism will certainly not be made by the maintenance of political alliances within the government ... The proposal as it stands will lead to the recovery of the right, giving it room to manoeuvre for the destruction of the revolution, despite the patriotic and democratic intentions of the document's signatories.

The COPCON document was severe on the 'Nine' for their economic policies.

> The economic perspectives of strengthening links with the EEC and EFTA will reinforce the subjection of the country to a shameful economic, financial and political dependence.⁴ Those who retained any illusions about the designs of these organisations should have lost them completely with the publication of the recent conditions for

---

3   [AN] One of the charges in the Melo Antunes document.
4   [EN] EEC: the European Economic Community, founded in March 1957 under the Treaty of Rome. The EEC's initial purpose was to bring about economic integration, including a common market and customs union, among its six member states: Belgium, France, Italy, Luxembourg, the Netherlands and West Germany. EFTA refers to the European Free Trade Association, a regional trade organisation established in May 1960. Portugal was one of its seven founding member states, along with Austria, Denmark, Norway, Sweden, Switzerland and the United Kingdom.

> 'financial aid to Portugal'. The revitalisation of private enterprise by the massive investment of foreign capital means, purely and simply, the loss of NATIONAL INDEPENDENCE.
>
> How can a project be called 'left' when it completely bypasses the role of the masses and denies the right of action to its vanguard? How can one criticise the pace of the nationalisation programme?
>
> Portugal ... must also terminate its subjection to the EEC and EFTA, which have practised a policy of blackmail in their relations with Portugal.

It was on the question of political and administrative power, however, that the COPCON document sent thrills of horror down the backs of those who favoured a bourgeois-type Western capitalist democracy – one reason why right-wing elements marked COPCON down on the list of organisations to be dissolved.

> Any revolutionary programme for resolving the situation must, above all, achieve the realisation of the MFA–People alliance, which guarantees that the workers take the lead in the solution of their own problems. Without such participation, socialism is impossible. The next task is to get *an organisational structure of the popular masses on its feet*, forming and achieving the recognition of councils in the villages, factories and neighbourhoods, which will be the organs through which the workers can take decisions conducive to the solution of their problems ... *They will have to be real organs of political power*, the sole barrier capable of victoriously withstanding fascist and imperialist aggression.[5]

Again, on the question of who is really to run the country, COPCON states: 'Power will be constituted by the MFA and by all the truly revolutionary organisations which call for and defend the principle of power for the workers.'

The position of the 'Nine' was essentially that of the Socialist Party; that of COPCON – although often critical of the Communist Party for its 'assertive methods' – was much closer to that of the Communists. As the 'Nine' had demanded the ouster of the prime minister, who was also

---

5   [AN] My italics, W. B.

Turning the Wheel Back

chairman of the Revolutionary Council, and they represented a minority within the Council, they were summarily expelled. But they had important allies, within and outside the Armed Forces Movement, which, it must never be overlooked, was a progressive oasis within the reactionary officer corps of the armed forces as a whole. The 'Nine', although, at that time, to the right of the MFA, were well to the left of the permanent officers' corps, which is probably why they became known as the 'moderates'.

Such a parting of the ways as the 'Nine' and 'COPCON' documents represented was almost inevitable. Only a tiny minority within the MFA grasped the full implications of what they had started on 25 April 1974. What united them was their hatred of the fascist regime in perpetuating hopeless colonial wars. Later, they were united also to resist right-wing coups aimed at restoring fascism or a similar right-wing dictatorship. Few understood that, to dismantle the fascist regime and ensure it would never be restored, it was also necessary to destroy its power base, or that this meant nationalising the monopolies and banks and expropriating the big estate owners. The industrial magnates, bankers and absentee landlords were also the leading fascists. In doing this, it was inevitable that personal or family interests of some of the officers were also affected. In any case, the MFA was involved in something of which the majority of its members never dreamed. Under these circumstances, it is remarkable that unity was maintained for so long, while progressive and often controversial measures were implemented. They stood firm, for instance, over the question of a single instead of a pluralist trade union organisation, despite the great campaign against this by the Socialist Party and all parties to the right of it, plus the Catholic hierarchy, supported by the entire Western press and news media.

Until the 'Nine' published their document, decisions of the Revolutionary Council were always announced as 'unanimous', despite whatever opposition might have emerged in discussion. Now it was openly divided. The two documents crystallised two opposing concepts and brought the divisions and hesitations out into the open. The 'Nine' document was welcomed by the career officers, and pressure mounted for the removal of Gonçalves. Bowing to this, President Costa Gomes replaced him with Admiral Pinheiro de Azevedo, named prime minister on 29 August, while Gonçalves was appointed chief of staff of the Armed Forces. But this posting was also contested by the 'Nine' the following day, backed up immediately – and significantly, in the light of later events – by the chief of staff of the Air Force, General Morais e Silva.[6] On 2, 3 and 4 September, the Army, Navy and Air Force assemblies met, prior to a full meeting of the 240-member AMFA (General Assembly of the Armed Forces Movement). The Army met first and rejected the Gonçalves nomination, demanding a restructuration of the General Assembly before the next meeting. The Navy was next, supporting the Gonçalves nomination. The Air Force, with an assembly hand-picked by General Morais e Silva, rejected Gonçalves, and it was announced that the Air Force delegation to the General Assembly would likewise consist exclusively of officers designated by General Morais e Silva, instead of elected delegates, including men drawn from the rank and file. On 5 September, Vasco Gonçalves refused the chief of staff position on grounds of insufficient support. Since then, the General Assembly of the Armed Forces has ceased to function, as the Air Force decision on appointing delegates robbed it of any significance.

On 19 September, the sixth provisional government was formed under Admiral Pinheiro de Azevedo, with the Socialists and members of the 'Nine' holding four seats, the PPD two, and the Communist Party one unimportant portfolio, Public Works and Environment. Thus, the Socialists and Popular Democrats succeeded in obtaining a government which reflected the results of the Constituent Assembly elections – and the stage was set for a turn to the right. The Communist Party made it clear that participation in the government did not mean that it would not oppose anti-working-class measures within the government, and outside of it.

---

6   [EN] José Alberto Morais e Silva (1941–2014), a pilot and officer of the Portuguese Air Force who participated in the MFA coup. After 25 April, he took command of the pilot training programme at Air Base 1 near Lisbon. On 12 March 1975, following the failed right-wing countercoup attempt, he was made commander in chief of the Air Force, a position he held until January 1977. He was a supporter of the Group of Nine and played an important role in the events of 25 November 1975.

19
Balance Sheet

One thing for which the 'militants' reproached the 'moderates' was that the latter evaded the question as to whether there was a revolution underway or not, and if so, was it desirable? A revolution had its own dynamic and momentum, they argued, and could not stand still. Either it went on, or it went down the slippery slope of counter-revolution. Any 'gradual and peaceful' transition to socialism through parliamentary democracy was an illusion, they maintained. Violent reactions to nationalising the monopolies and expropriating the big landowners was inevitable, and the response to such reactions would also be violent. Not that anyone had visions of the bankers and absentee landlords out in the street, doing battle with their class enemies. But there were plenty of elements in the officer corps ready to do battle for them – not to mention the fascist Spain-based ELP (Exército de Libertação de Portugal, or Portuguese Liberation Army), whose activities were becoming more and more apparent.

It was not realistic, argued the COPCON militants, to expect unemployed agricultural labourers to see their families starve in the traditionally revolutionary Alentejo while rich land went uncultivated, and wait for the Trás-os-Montes smallholders – who at least produced food for their own consumption – to make up their minds about land reform. This had become an urgent question in the Alentejo, which produced most of the country's wheat, not only for solving unemployment, but for solving the country's food problem.

In mid-November 1975, I visited the Herdade de Outeiro, a farm of some 700 hectares in the Beja district. It was the first to have been expropriated. I spoke with António dos Larnos Morêncio, a tall, lean young man with a scrubby beard, and a member of the management committee of what was now part of a farming cooperative. He had been one of twenty-four workers on the farm, the owner of which was one José Gomes Palma, who lived in Lisbon and rarely visited his property.

'After Vasco Gonçalves became prime minister,' said Morêncio, 'we got a ninety-day labour contract, negotiated by our Agricultural Labourers Union through the Ministry of Labour. Half of us were immediately sacked – including a man who had worked on the farm for fifty-four years – because the contract provided for higher wages. In any case, it ran out on 26 September [1974] and the owner refused to renew it, because, we think, he was counting on the 28 September coup to put the fascists back in power. No wages were paid after that, and we got no instructions to cultivate the wheat fields for the next year's crop. We worked the land ourselves without wages but protested to our union – we had neither food nor money. After a while, we told the manager that, if his boss was not going to plough and sow wheat, we would. There were also the olive trees to be pruned. When the union representative saw the property was abandoned, he suggested that twenty of us go back and put it in order. The manager refused to let us work. That was on 9 December. We reported this back to the union. "It's up to you to decide," we were told.

'We went back and started to prune the olive trees. The owner got a feeling of where things were headed, so the agent was ordered to move 70,000 kilos of wheat from the storehouse. We refused to let it be moved away. The owner then took us to court, claiming we were ruining his olive trees and stealing his wheat. A technician was sent, and he reported back that the trees had been competently pruned. The trade union rep argued that the owner had no right to move the wheat until our back wages had been paid. Then the manager started selling off the livestock, so we demanded a meeting with the owner. He was too busy in Lisbon, the manager said, so all of us labourers held a meeting and decided to take over. That was on 27 January, and we have been working the farm ever since.'

This was an example of what the Socialists and Popular Democrats charged were 'wildcat takeovers' of the landed estates. (Later, post-facto approval of these actions was conveyed in a decree of 15 April 1975, providing for three main categories of expropriation. If the owners had fled to Spain or Brazil, or had been moving their herds and flocks across to Spain, the farms could be taken over by the workers. This was permitted also in cases when their wages had not been paid for one month. If an estate was not cultivated, or under-exploited, the Agricultural Workers' Union could intervene, and settle the necessary numbers of labourers there to bring it into full production.)

The action at Herdade do Outeiro was the prelude to similar actions throughout the Beja district where, at the time of my visit in November 1975, virtually all big estates had been taken over. By then the Outeiro farm had been incorporated into a 'collective unit of agricultural production' of the 'Alentejo Vanguard' cooperative farm in the Santa Vitória parish of Beja district, formed on 17 October 1975, with 218 members, of whom ninety-eight were women. Members' ages ranged from fourteen to seventy-two, and they had elected a management committee of ten. The cooperative covered 5,574 hectares, of which all but fifty were exploitable. On the day the cooperative was formed – in a legal ceremony with the civil governor of Beja present, as well as representatives from the land reform committee and the Armed Forces Movement – a work plan was presented to the general meeting of members: 3,500 hectares to be planted with wheat and other grains, 770 to remain as they were – groves of olive, cork and eucalyptus. By the time I visited the co-op five weeks later, fences around the *coutadas* or hunting lodges had been taken down and the land ploughed and sown with wheat; olive groves and cork forests had been cleared of undergrowth, and everything looked spick and span. The cooperative had been formed after takeover actions, similar to those at the Herdade de Outeiro, on nine neighbouring estates.

I spoke with Francisco de Assunção Baptista, an organiser of the Beja district agricultural workers' union. A slow-spoken man with a rugged, peasant's face, he had spent eighteen months in prison under the fascist regime for organising agricultural workers, during which he learned French – so we were able to converse directly. What did the changes mean? He gave a short laugh.

'When you were last around here,' he said, 'unemployment was a serious problem.[1] There were estates of over a thousand hectares that

---

1 [AN] See Chapter 12.

employed only three or four men. Now we are short of workers. And our wheat harvest this year was 24 per cent above that of last year. Next year it will be bigger again, because we are sowing 10 per cent more land. If the labourers hadn't taken the initiative to plough and sow last year, even without pay, the wheat harvest in this area would have been a disaster. The estate owners wanted to sabotage the new regime by not gathering the olives or cork and not sowing wheat. Now, 270,000 hectares in this whole area are under workers' control. The big estates are finished, and we don't intend to touch the medium and small farmers.'

In the Portalegre district, very close to the Spanish frontier, it was the same picture. A neat, smiling countryside, with cultivated fields right up to the white-washed walls of the beautiful Alentejo villages and towns. Over 200,000 hectares had been taken over, leaving only four big estates still to be 'expropriated'. Grain production in the region was 35 per cent above the previous year. Estates which previously employed thirty to forty workers now provided work for 200–300, and there was a shortage of labour – especially for seasonal work. (It happened to be the start of the olive-picking season.)

For an overall view of the situation, I visited Évora and spoke with António Gervásio,[2] member of the Central Committee of the Communist Party, and one of the leading strategists of land reform. A brisk, efficient man, one could easily picture him as a bank manager. 'Over 700,000 hectares – 70 per cent of the total area of farming land in the Alentejo, is now under control of the agricultural workers,' he said.

'The absentee landlords have been expropriated. The few who are left have estates which are of no economic interest. This rapid advance is due above all to the agricultural workers themselves, supported by their trade union and the Communist Party. While in Lisbon they were arguing over what sort of land reform to carry out, here the agricultural workers acted. As a result, instead of chronic unemployment in the

---

2 [EN] António Joaquim Gervásio (1927–2020), agricultural worker, politician and member of the Central Committee of the Portuguese Communist Party (1963–2004). Jailed as a political prisoner multiple times; held at the fortress in Peniche from 1971 until the 25 April 1974 coup. Served as a deputy of the PCP during the Constituent Assembly (June 1975–June 1976). He became a key leader of the agrarian reform movement in Portugal, that sought to redistribute land ownership and to promote agricultural workers' cooperative organisations.

south, there is a shortage of labour, and there are many cases of emigrant workers returning to join the cooperatives.'

I asked, 'What is the difference between the Socialist and Communist Party policies on land reform, now that Lopes Cardoso is minister for agriculture?'[3] Cardoso had been a fervent advocate of land reform. 'The Socialists wanted the sort of reform that took place in France after the French Revolution,' replied António Gervásio. 'Cut the big estates up into strips and hand them out to individual farmers. But the agricultural labourers did not want this. They do not have the property-owning complex of small peasants. They have always been labourers, working collectively on big estates, and they wanted to keep working that way – but for their own benefit and that of the country. Besides, the type of machinery available was intended for large-scale cultivation. Another argument used was that, if the agricultural workers formed their own cooperatives, there would be no seasonal labour available for the small and medium farmers. The opposite has proved true. Thanks to good organisation and the mechanisation already available, the labourers are in a position to help the small and medium farmers more effectively than ever. Relations between them are excellent.'

'Who now owns the land taken over from the *latifundia*?' Gervásio laughed and said: 'The Good Lord. There are no owners. The agricultural workers are a true rural proletariat and have no yearning to be property-owners. What they have formed are neither true cooperatives – although that is what they usually call them – nor state farms. They are "collective agricultural production units". They cultivate the land, sell their produce, take their wages and running costs out of the revenue, and invest what is left over in improving the farm. The results for the first year, despite great difficulties and sabotage, have been excellent. For the first time in many years, Portugal has not needed to import wheat for bread. Some specialised wheat for noodles was imported, but this will not be necessary next year, because there will be a big increase in the cultivated area; in some areas, twice or even three times as much land will be sown with grain.'

In a speech on 24 October 1975, to the Constituent Assembly in Lisbon, the communist deputy for Évora, Dinis Miranda, put the wheat harvest that year at 650,000 tons, compared to an average of 400,000 to

---

3 [AN] See Chapter 8.

500,000 tons under the estate-owners.[4] An average of 250,000 tons had to be imported each year – about the extra amount produced in 1975.

There is no doubt that the taking over of the big estates is the greatest economic achievement of the Portuguese Revolution. Instead of some 800 big estate owners, most of them living in Lisbon, each employing a dozen or so permanent farm hands – with a huge reserve of unemployed labourers to draw on for seasonal work – there are now some 130,000 agricultural labourers, permanently employed, and putting into production hundreds of thousands of hectares of extremely fertile land which had been fenced off as hunting reserves for occasional use by the absentee landlords and their city cronies.

'The landlords themselves speeded up the process of their expropriation,' remarked António Gervásio. 'When contracts were signed to give the labourers a living wage, they either fired half their workers, or refused to pay at all. To sabotage the country after the 25 April coup, they stopped cultivating the land. When they began to see that some sort of land reform was inevitable, they started selling off their cattle and machinery. It was then that the agricultural workers said "Enough!" and moved quickly to cultivate the land and stop the removal of cattle and equipment. In many cases, it was too late, and the owners had completely emptied the estates of everything but the land and trees.'

Among half a dozen big units I visited was the 'Red Carnation', an agricultural and stock-raising cooperative in the same Montemor sub-district, which I had visited in the summer of 1974.[5] It covered 6,800 hectares, and had been formed by pooling the lands of seven big adjoining estates. Typically, all the proprietors lived in Lisbon, coming to their magnificent homes – with fireplaces literally big enough to roast an ox – for an occasional holiday. The seven together had previously employed about eighty labourers; now there were over 300, 60 per cent of them women. Here, 2,400 head of beef cattle and 300 milch cows had been 'expropriated' without loss. I talked with a member of the elected management committee, thirty-four-year-old Albino Manuel Reis, who had worked on one of these estates from the age of five.

---

4 [EN] Dinis Fernandes Miranda (1929–1991), agricultural worker, militant member of the Portuguese Communist Party and politician. He spent twelve years incarcerated by the Estado Novo for his political activities; he was released after the 25 April coup. He served on the political commission of the PCP from 1976 to 1988.

5 [AN] See Chapter 12.

'We rarely saw the owner,' he said. 'He owned several other estates and a bank. When we took this one over, he pretended he could not even recall the various other properties he owned. But he probably remembered when they were taken over.' I asked if there were contacts with neighbouring co-ops, and what sort of relations they had with the small and medium farmers.

'There are twenty-five co-ops in the Montemor sub-district,' he replied, 'of which this is the biggest. Most of them are organised on the size of the *freguesia* [the smallest administrative unit in Portugal]. Together, they cover the whole Montemor *conselho* [sub-district, or next biggest administrative unit]. Linking the twenty-five together is a secretariat, which meets weekly in Montemor. The League of Small and Medium Landholders also sends delegates to these meetings. Problems of organisation are discussed, experiences are exchanged, common policies on salaries are worked out, shortages of seed or equipment on one co-op are made up from neighbouring ones; the small and medium farmers can submit requests for manpower, or help in ploughing or harvesting. They were very suspicious at first, but now we have very close relations, based on doing everything possible to increase production for the good of everyone. The small owners, for instance, have access to our three olive presses.'

I asked about eucalyptus trees, as there were rumours in Lisbon that the labourers were cutting them all down, losing valuable revenue from export sales for paper pulp. 'Not true,' he replied. 'What is true is that, to avoid employing labourers in cultivation, the landowners planted eucalyptus trees, which need practically no labour, letting them grow into money after nine years. We have 150 hectares of eucalyptus trees planted five years ago. They reach exploitable age after nine years. We will leave them till then, but where the land is suitable for grain cultivation, it will be ploughed up. The estate-owners looked at everything from the viewpoint of easy profits, never re-investing to serve agriculture. We look at everything from the viewpoint of solving the problems of useful employment and growing enough food for the country to become independent of imports from abroad. The estate owners drained the countryside of its wealth and never put anything back. They hated us agricultural labourers, and did everything to make us disappear as a class. We were permanent thorns in their side.' (According to figures cited by Dinis Miranda in the speech quoted above, 77,000 agricultural labourers emigrated from the countryside between 1971 and 1974; and during the twenty years between 1950 and 1970, the holdings of 6,180 small and medium landowners were swallowed up annually by the absentee landlords. Most of those holdings were taken out of production, added to the hunting reserves, or planted with eucalyptus – the profits of which went into city bank accounts, not ploughed back into the land.)

What becomes clear in talking with the labourers who took over the big estates is that this was not a move dictated by ideological considerations, but by the most basic of practical considerations: unemployed labourers and land left untilled; food shortages in the cities, with agricultural products forming the largest item of Portugal's imports. These were problems crying out to be solved on an individual, human level, and on a national level.

Similarly, in industry, the question of keeping factories in production – especially, at first, those abandoned by their multinational owners – could not await the outcome of interminable bickering among the political parties, or the setting up of 'adequate managerial structures', such as the 'Nine' had demanded. Workers were idle, staring at machines they were competent to handle. In many cases, they started to produce, and market the results of their labour.

These were spontaneous reactions to specific situations, and it was found that the workers were quite capable of maintaining production and managing industrial units through elected committees. Gradually, the principle of workers' participation in management was extended to small and medium industries, which were in financial difficulties but of sufficient interest to the economy for the state to invest capital to keep them going. In such cases, there was mixed private–state–workers' management. In cases where owners had abandoned their enterprises – usually having fled to Brazil – and these were of economic interest, the state provided finance and raw materials, and they continued to function under state–workers' management. By the time the government expropriated the big monopolies – whose owners and directors were deeply involved in the 11 March coup attempt – the responsible ministries had accumulated a lot of experience in state–workers' management. Thus, the changeover from monopoly capitalism to state capitalism – as an important step along the road to socialism – was comparatively smooth. (Enterprises of the multinationals – even those which had been abandoned – were exempted from the nationalisation decrees.) I was assured that there had been no decrease in industrial production due to worker participation in management. During the short lifespans of the fourth and fifth governments, I was informed that industrial production had increased in numerous heavy industry enterprises under workers' or state–workers' management.[6]

Land reform and the nationalisation of the industrial and financial oligarchies had been done, and these were the two most important achievements of the revolution – as well as the most contested behind the scenes. When I asked a veteran socialist journalist, 'What was the real reason for the savagery of the attacks against Vasco Gonçalves?' he replied: 'The concrete reason was that land reform had been started by the agricultural labourers and peasants themselves. Gonçalves approved and encouraged this; he fought hard for it to be institutionalised. The same with the nationalisation of the enterprises. Although foreign interests were not touched, it is clear that, once land reform and nationalisation have been consolidated and we have a viable economy, we can discuss the question of foreign investments. Even though their interests were not touched, Western governments and some of the big multinational firms put terrific pressure on the Socialist Party to stop the nationalisations, or there would be no more foreign investment and Portugal's exports would be boycotted. The nationalisations were the real reason for the attacks on Vasco Gonçalves – but they were camouflaged under accusations of his being "dictatorial", "a tool of the communists", and other such emotion-provoking terms.' He, and others with whom I spoke, however, did not think that these most important gains of the Portuguese Revolution could be taken away without armed resistance.

---

6 [AN] At the time of the November 1975 crisis, there had been six provisional governments since 25 April 1974. From 12 July 1974, until 29 August 1975, the second, third, fourth and fifth governments had been presided over by Vasco Gonçalves, the formation of each born out of some serious crisis. The fourth government, formed on 25 March 1975, following the abortive coup, comprised eight MFA ministers, two each from the Socialists, Communists, and Popular Democrats, one from the pro-Communist MDP, and five independents, of whom two were left-wingers. It ceased to function on 11 July when the Socialists withdrew, followed by the Popular Democrats three days later. The fifth government, formed on 31 July, excluded all political parties but contained a number of left-wing MFA officers and left-wing independents, especially in the economic field.

20
The Future

Probably one of the elements which induced Melo Antunes and the 'Nine' to issue their document was the 'Political Action Plan of the Armed Forces Movement', approved by the Revolutionary Council on 21 June. This in effect endorsed 100 per cent the expropriation of farms and factories, workers' management, and every concrete measure which would advance the cause of a socialist revolution. The first point states:

> The MFA is the liberation movement of the Portuguese people; it stands above party, and its essential aim is that of national independence. The MFA recognises that this national independence involves a process of domestic decolonialisation, which can only be achieved by means of the construction of a socialist society. By 'socialist society', as the final aim to be attained, we understand a classless society, obtained through the collectivisation of the means of production, eliminating all forms of exploitation of man by man, in which all individuals will be given equal opportunities of education, work and promotion, without distinction of birth, sex, religious belief or ideology.

Points six and seven must have horrified the Socialist and Popular Democrat parties, and all forces to the right of them, who hoped that a turn of the political wheel would undo the wholesale expropriations before it was too late.

The MFA restates its determination to carry out, and ensure that others carry out, in their entirety, the terms of the constitutional agreement platform freely laid down with Portuguese political parties, and solemnly states that it will denounce, and will take action against, all attitudes which, openly or covertly, seek to question and undermine that pact.[1]

In accordance with the principles laid down, the MFA considers that it is its duty to make it publicly explicit that the sole power of the Constituent Assembly is to perform the patriotic mission of drawing up the political constitution of the Portuguese nation, and *it is forbidden to indulge in any other form of official interference in national, political, or administrative life.*[2]

This implied very serious differences between the MFA and the political parties, especially the Socialists and Popular Democrats, who made no bones about their sympathy with Spínola's view that the MFA's place was 'back in the barracks'.

The sixth provisional government started a quiet purge of leftists within the administration, especially in those ministries dealing with economic affairs, replacing many provincial prefects and other officials who had been appointed in the purge of fascist officials immediately after 25 April.[3] The slowing-down process demanded by the 'Nine' took many forms. The newly formed agricultural cooperatives found their credits blocked, that seed grain and fertilisers were unobtainable, and when they made direct arrangements with workers committees at CUF, one of the plants of which had mountains of unsold fertilisers, to buy direct, there was suddenly a shortage of transport. (In my visits to the Alentejo co-ops, I found COPCON trucks delivering seed grains and fertilisers.) The 'slowdown' operated in all fields, including foreign policy, with the refusal – despite massive popular pressure – to recognise the MPLA government in Angola, and even with the recall in midair of a plane carrying Portuguese and foreign delegates to the

---

1   [AN] The political Pact, W. B.
2   [AN] My italics, W. B.
3   [AN] See Chapter 8.

independence ceremonies.[4] By means of wage freezes and other economic measures, the sixth government quickly alienated large sections of the working class; and this time, when they took strike action or came out in big demonstrations – as was the case with the building workers who besieged the government – they had the support of the Communist Party.

Based on decisions taken at the last meeting of any importance of the General Assembly of the Armed Forces on 9 July 1975 – and stimulated by the swing to the right of the sixth government – there was a great proliferation of revolutionary organisations within the armed forces, with intense activities in the weeks that preceded 25 November. The setting up of such organisations was encouraged by progressive officers within the Revolutionary Council, such as Admiral Rosa Coutinho, chief of staff General Carlos Fabião, General Otelo de Carvalho, and others. Rosa Coutinho, as executive president of the Revolutionary Council and the Armed Forces Movement, played a vitally important role in shaping MFA policies. Fabião, de Carvalho, and Rosa Coutinho headed what was clearly the left within the armed forces; Melo Antunes and the others of the 'Nine' headed the centre. Among the best-known rightists were General Morais e Silva, commanding the Air Force, General Pires Veloso[5] – whom the sixth government appointed to replace a known leftist, Eurico Corvacho,[6] as commander of the North

---

4 [EN] The Popular Movement for the Liberation of Angola (MPLA: Movimento Popular de Libertação de Angola) was a militant Marxist pro-independence organisation led by Agostinho Neto, founded in 1956 to fight against Portuguese colonialism.

5 [EN] António Elísio Capelo Pires Veloso (1926–2014), a career officer who served in Angola (1961–64) and Mozambique (1965–74). Following the 25 April coup, as the final Portuguese governor and high commissioner for São Tomé and Príncipe, he negotiated the transition to independence (July 1975). As a military commandant in northern Portugal on 25 November 1975, he played a key role in thwarting the left-wing coup attempt focused on Lisbon.

6 [EN] Eurico de Deus Corvacho (1937–2011), artillery officer and core member of the MFA who played a fundamental role in the 25 April coup by monitoring potential military opposition around Porto. Subsequently, he became a member of the Revolutionary Council and was named commandant of Portugal's northern region; between March and September 1975 he guarded against civil disturbances and counter-revolutionary activity throughout the north, including threats and arms entering Portugal from Spain. On 5 September 1975, he and other far-left officers were relieved of their command and removed from the Revolutionary Council.

military region – and Colonel Jaime Neves,[7] head of the Commando regiment in the Lisbon region. Of the three services, the Navy was traditionally the most 'left', the Air Force the furthest to the 'right'. But cutting across all this was the growing radicalisation of the lower ranks, greatly accelerated by the rightist policies of the sixth government, and its obvious attempt to a bring the armed forces to heel as an obedient tool of a bourgeois state.

The most dramatic development among the lower ranks was the appearance of SUV (Soldiers United for Victory) at a press conference in Porto on September 8 – ten days after Pinheiro de Azevedo replaced Gonçalves as prime minister – one soldier, one officer and one new recruit, hooded to avoid reprisals, announced the formation of SUV, as a non-party organisation of the rank and file 'to guarantee unity in the class struggle' and to fight reaction within the armed services.[8] Two days later, some 1,500 soldiers and sailors demonstrated in Porto, together with several thousands of people from workers' and residents' associations. SUV organisations began to spring up in all four military regions (North, Centre, South and Lisbon). Shortly afterwards they were joined by ORS (Sergeants Revolutionary Organisation),[9] and many more associations of demobbed[10] soldiers, disabled soldiers and others. On 25 September, there was a SUV demonstration in Lisbon attended by 5,000 soldiers and sailors among a marching crowd of 15,000. By November, inter-committees had been established to link the various servicemen's associations with each other, and also with various workers' and residents' assemblies. Obviously, such moves were anathema to the military conservatives and to the political parties, except the Communists, who favoured these developments.

To counter these developments and also the refusal of COPCON to take any action against popular organisations – Otelo de Carvalho steadfastly maintained that COPCON's job was to prevent

---

7   [EN] Jaime Alberto Gonçalves das Neves (1936–2013), a career Army officer who served four tours of duty in Angola and Mozambique. A member of the MFA, he supported the 25 April coup. As a politically centre-right commander of special forces commandos in 1975, he played a decisive role in the events of 25 November 1975, which placed centrist MFA officers in control of the provisional government.
8   [EN] In Portuguese: 'Soldados Unidos Vencerão'.
9   [EN] In Portuguese: 'Organização dos Sargentos Revolucionários'.
10 [EN] That is, 'demobilised'.

counter-revolutionary coups – the sixth government founded a rival to COPCON in the form of AMI (Military Intervention Force),[11] commanded by a centrist, Brigadier Melo Egídio.[12] It was to be composed of a regiment each of Commandos, Marines and Parachutists, and mercenaries recruited from commandos demobilised after service in Angola. With higher pay and special privileges, the AMI was to constitute an élite force to maintain 'law and order'. The first AMI operation was on 7 November, when a unit of sixty Parachutists was ordered to occupy Rádio Renascença (owned by the Catholic Church but taken over by its left-wing Catholic workers in May and run as an independent, left-wing and very popular radio station). Its news and commentaries were highly critical of the sixth government. While the Parachutists occupied the station, two AMI personnel, one military, one civilian, blew up both its transmitters. The first reaction was a plenary meeting of the Marines, with an overwhelming demand that their unit be removed from AMI. Then came a meeting of furious Parachutists, which also resulted in a unanimous decision to quit AMI and place their units under COPCON command. An offer by General Morais e Silva to come and explain matters to the Parachutists at their Tancos base, some 120 kilometres north of Lisbon, was refused. One hundred twenty-three of the regiment's 130 officers then left the unit and placed themselves at the disposal of General Morais e Silva for 'reassignment'. The Parachutists were in a mutinous mood, which approached explosion point when they were officially 'disbanded' – supplies and pay suspended.

COPCON assured their pay until the end of the year; the SUV, ORS and other servicemen's associations, and the powerful Workers' Commission for the Lisbon Industrial Belt, pledged support. Western military attachés started totting up the units in the four military regions on which the government could count in the event of a showdown. Reports poured in from soldiers' vigilance committees all over the country of preparations for a right-wing coup.

---

11   [EN] In Portuguese: 'Agrupamento Militar Independente', an independent military intervention force.

12   [EN] Nuno Viriato Tavares de Melo Egídio (1922–2011), a senior military officer, colonial administrator and politician who served in Angola and Mozambique; respected within the MFA by political moderates and centrists. He would later serve as governor of Macau, 1979–81.

Figure 20.1. Political demonstrators from various parties fill the main throughfares in Lisbon and celebrate one year of progress towards a fully realised democratic government in Portugal; Avenida da Liberdade ('Liberty Avenue') on May Day, 1975. (Photo by Fernando Ricardo)

It was at about this time that building workers in the Lisbon area, supported by an estimated 80 per cent of all workers in the building trade, went on strike for higher wages – culminating in their action of surrounding the parliament, where the Constituent Assembly deputies were meeting, and besieging Prime Minister Azevedo and other government members for thirty-six hours, until they finally gave in to the pay demands. At one point, the construction workers were supported by thousands of factory workers and peasants from the surrounding area. The 'victory' culminated in a monster demonstration on 16 November, of between 200,000 and 300,000 workers, peasants, and a fair sprinkling of soldiers and sailors in uniform, escorted into the city's biggest square – the Praça do Comércio – by tractors, bulldozers, mobile concrete-mixers and truckloads of cooperative farmers from the Alentejo.[13] It was by far the biggest demonstration since that of 1 May 1974, but this time it was a specifically working-class display of the clenched fist.

The reply came a few days later, when the prime minister announced – on 20 November – that the government was suspending its activities until the Revolutionary Council could guarantee its security. This was accompanied by calls from Mário Soares and Sá Carneiro for the dismissal of Otelo de Carvalho and Carlos Fabião, and attacks on the president for his 'hesitancy', 'weakness' and 'lack of decision'. The Socialist and Popular Democrat leaders threatened to move the government and Constituent Assembly to Porto, in the conservative north, and the advisability of dividing the country roughly along the thirty-ninth parallel was discussed in the pro-socialist press.

Things were obviously moving rapidly towards a climax. In a very curious boast to the press on 21 November, Colonel Jaime Neves said that his Commandos were 'ready immediately to launch operations to replace all those officers and men who have shown by their actions that they are incapable of serving, in a supra-party manner, the Army and the Portuguese people'. That same night, the Revolutionary Council met and decided: (a) to replace Otelo de Carvalho as head of the Lisbon

---

13 [EN] Commerce Square (Praça do Comércio), also known as the Palace Terrace (Terreiro do Paço), a grand waterfront public space of great historic and cultural significance, rebuilt following the 1755 earthquake, surrounded on three sides by government ministry buildings, facing the main harbour anchorage on the River Tagus.

Military Command by Captain Vasco Lourenço,[14] a member of the 'Nine', (b) that Otelo remain head of COPCON, (c) that he also be placed in charge of the People's Power Project[15] and (d) that the AMI strike force would be disbanded.

Meetings were held the next day in all twenty-one main military units in the Lisbon military region, and eighteen of them refused to serve under Vasco Lourenço. The three that accepted were the Commandos, the Cavalry (tanks/armour) School, and an anti-aircraft unit at Cascais. Captain Lourenço announced next day that he refused the assignment for 'lack of support'. Otelo de Carvalho, in the meantime, had accused the sixth government of 'from the beginning being more concerned with eliminating the left than with governing'. There were more left-wing demonstrations, demanding the government 'to call off its "lock-out" or resign', according to the mildest slogans; demanding the return of Vasco Gonçalves in the more militant ones. The Revolutionary Council scheduled a meeting on the night of the 24th to make a decision on who was to be military commander in Lisbon. Tensions continued to build.

At a ceremony of swearing allegiance to the flag, on the 22nd, with General Fabião presiding, the 1st Light Artillery Regiment (RALIS) lined up with clenched-fist salutes – instead of the traditional fingertips-to-cap – and had amended the usual oath of loyalty to:

> We soldiers swear to be faithful to the Motherland and fight for its independence.[16] We swear to be always on the side of the people; in the service of the working class, the peasants, and other labouring people. We swear to fight with all our might, with voluntary acceptance of revolutionary discipline, against fascism, against imperialism, for democracy and people's power, for the victory of the socialist revolution.

---

14   [EN] Vasco Correia Lourenço (1942–), Army infantry officer and member of the MFA who served one tour of duty in Guinea; during the 25 April coup was stationed in the Azores Islands. He was named to the Council of State on 24 July 1974. On 14 March 1975 he was nominated a member of the Revolutionary Council, serving until its dissolution in 1982.

15   [EN] In Portuguese: 'Projecto de Poder Popular'.

16   [EN] In the Portuguese edition, the original pledge was made to the *Pátria*, from the Latin masculine word for nation.

At a big Socialist Party rally in Lisbon on the 23rd, clearly aimed at putting pressure on the Revolutionary Council for the following day's meeting, Mário Soares launched a fierce attack on the Communists and the MFA. He threatened to 'paralyse the country' in case of a 'Communist left-wing military' solution to the crisis, taunting the Communists with: 'We have beaten you in the elections; we will beat you with weapons in the streets.' The previous day he had rejected a suggestion that he sit down with Álvaro Cunhal to try to find some way out of the crisis. While the Revolutionary Council was in session on the night of the 24th, small landholders and landlords, manipulated by rightist forces, cut all roads and the railway line – by felling trees across them – linking Lisbon with the north. There were also attacks by armed bands on some of the cooperatives in the Alentejo. In the small hours of the morning, the Revolutionary Council announced its decision – Vasco Lourenço was reconfirmed as commander of the Lisbon military region.

At 4:00 a.m. on the 25th, the Parachutists took over their own headquarters at Tancos and two other air bases which they were supposed to guard (Air Base Number 5 at Monte Real and Air Base Number 6 at Montijo), the Air Force regional headquarters at Monsanto (where they locked up the regional commander, General Pinho Freire), and the Air Force headquarters, almost opposite the Tivoli Hotel in the heart of Lisbon.[17] It was only *after* they had carried out this very professionally executed action, that they contacted other friendly units asking for supporting action. The Marines promptly turned them down, denouncing the action as 'adventurist'; the military police, the 1st Light Artillery Regiment, and the military administration school took some very indecisive measures, mainly taking up positions to defend their own bases.

The rest is history. The military situation was speedily brought under control, mainly by Colonel Jaime Neves and his regiment of Commandos, supported by tanks from the Cavalry School. There was no resistance except, as mentioned earlier, at the military police headquarters; there was no mobilisation of the masses in support of the Parachutists. 'There

---

17 [EN] Aníbal José Coentro de Pinho Freire (1935–1999), politically moderate general officer and Deputy Chief of Staff of the Portuguese Air Force who resigned his post when accused by the MFA leadership of having been 'command deficient' during the 25 April coup. Reinstated, he served on the Revolutionary Council and the Junta of National Salvation. Arrested by perpetrators of the 25 November coup attempt, he was freed the following day.

was neither a plan for military action, nor a centralised command, nor political objectives. How can one talk of coups or an insurrection?' said Álvaro Cunhal, addressing Communist supporters on 7 December, refuting charges that the Communist Party was behind an attempted 'left-wing coup'. He blamed 'insurrectionist policies' of the extreme left for the crisis, attempting to 'settle scores' and struggling for control of various units, as well as trying to halt the drive to the right. The Parachutists, after a plenary session of their assembly on 27 November, a few hours before they surrendered their Tancos headquarters, claimed they were not involved in any coup attempt, but had made the gesture to draw attention to the injustices done to their regiment, and to reinforce their demands for the dismissal of the Air Force commander, General Morais e Silva. Cunhal admitted that some individual communists might have been involved, saying: 'The Communist Party was not implicated directly or indirectly in this adventure. It is possible that individual communists showed their solidarity with the troops who revolted – we have a party of over 100,000 now, of which the vast majority entered politics only a few months ago.'

One of the first results of the elimination of the left from the Revolutionary Council, and the dissolution or decapitation of left-wing units, was a demand for the abolition of the political pact by the Popular Democrats, for its renegotiation by the Socialists, and a united demand from these two parties for a 'return to the barracks' of the Armed Forces Movement. This latter demand was certainly shared by the hard-liners among the military officers, who had crushed the half-hearted rebellion. The Popular Democrats also called for the expulsion of the Communists from the government, a demand which provoked a serious inter-party crisis, the former secretary-general Emídio Guerreiro heading a revolt against Sá Carneiro's anti-Communist leadership. This led to one of the two PPD ministers, five state secretaries in the government, and twenty-one of the PPD's eighty deputies in the Constituent Assembly, declaring themselves 'independents'.[18]

---

18 [EN] Emídio Guerreiro (1899–2005), mathematician, political activist, soldier and politician, once described as 'a cross between Don Quixote and Che Guevara'. A World War I veteran and early opponent of the Estado Novo, he lived as a political exile and fought against fascism in Spain and France, 1932–74, returning to Portugal after the 25 April coup. Politically aligned with the PPD/PSD, 1974–76, he was elected interim party secretary-general in 1975.

The vigour with which the rightists acted, on the pretext of putting down a 'left-wing coup' – a sort of 11 March in reverse – alarmed officers like Melo Antunes and those of the 'Nine' who were genuine anti-fascists and believed in the vanguard role of the MFA. They saw themselves being overrun from the right. No matter what their criticisms of the Communists, one thing was clear – the Communists had unswervingly supported the vanguard role of the MFA from the beginning. The Communist Party was the only one with any mass following to have done so. This provided the basis for what must have seemed to many people a curious *rapprochement* between Melo Antunes and the Communists after the 25 November crisis. On the question of how to block the road to fascism, Cunhal had been explicit in his 7 December speech. He appealed for the formation of the 'broadest possible anti-fascist front, grouping together civilians and military personnel, regardless of their political or religious affiliations, and whatever opinions different groups have of each other. One single criterion is demanded – that of defending democratic rights and freedoms. The Communist Party,' said Cunhal, 'stands for a vast social, political, military, democratic and progressive anti-fascist front.'

Melo Antunes was not slow to respond.

Replying to journalists' questions on 10 December, Melo Antunes said the essential thing to bar the way to a return to fascism was the maintenance of the alliance between the armed forces and peoples' organisations. While asserting that 'elements close to the Communist Party had directly participated in the uprisings,' he added that 'they were not, however, obeying directives from the Communist Party leadership', and blamed 'leftist groups' in and outside the armed forces for 25 November. Rejecting any idea that the MFA should withdraw from politics, he said that the MFA 'must continue to play a fundamental role in Portuguese political life. If it disappeared, the revolution would be ended with it'; furthermore, 'the participation of the Communists is indispensable for building up a democratic and socialist Portugal'.

One of the questions that has puzzled many people is, how was it possible that units like the Military Police, Parachutists, and Marines could be labelled 'left wing' and 'vanguard' units of the revolution? And why, for instance, did both Cunhal and Melo Antunes blame 'ultra-leftists' for the events of 25 November? It has been the policy of left-wing parties – including the Communists – to gain as much influence as possible within the armed forces. The most active among the non-Communist left were the PRP/BR (Party of the Revolutionary Proletariat – Revolutionary Brigades), the UDP (Popular Democratic Union), the LUAR (League of Revolutionary Unity and Action), and the MRPP (Movement for the Reconstruction of the Party of the Proletariat). Each of these competed for preponderant influence in one or another of the military units. The PRP/BR and UDP, for instance, were believed to be particularly strong in the Military Police. The Communist Party was particularly strong in the Marines, because they were under the Navy. The left was very much reinforced in a number of units – such as the Military Police – by progressives who returned from exile, having left the country to avoid being conscripted for the colonial wars. No action was taken against them as 'deserters' when they returned, so long as they reported for military service. They were allowed to choose the branches and – where feasible – the units in which to serve. Most had affiliations with one or another of the left-wing parties and were directed by their parties to the units in which they had most influence. But the parties distrusted each other and were united only by their hostility towards the

Figure 20.2. Brigadier General Vasco Lourenço, left, and Lieutenant Colonel António Ramalho Eanes during operations to suppress and disband COPCON, followed by a purge of far-left MFA officers from the transitional Portuguese government, on 25 November 1975. (Photo by Fernando Ricardo)

Communist Party. This fragmentation and – with the notable exception of LUAR, which for ten years prior to the 25 April coup had carried out armed resistance to the fascists – political inexperience of the non-Communist left, explains both the 25 November action and its lack of coordination or purpose. Lack of political experience – most of the ultra-left parties had mushroomed into existence after 25 April – meant that they were wide open to infiltration, and to manipulation at the top.

Whether the Parachutists were manipulated, to give rightist officers the pretext to stage what was a meticulously prepared countercoup, was hard to establish. Also uncertain is to what extent the CIA had a hand in the affair; it was known that the deputy head of the CIA station in Lisbon was a Chile expert, who had funded the operations of the opponents of President Allende just prior to his overthrow. There was also something sinister in the way COPCON was liquidated, without anyone firing a shot in its defence. Early on the afternoon of 25 November, according to a report published in the pro-Socialist *Jornal Novo* of 2 December, there was a meeting of top COPCON officers at their Fort Alto do Duque headquarters. The report continues:

> At about 3:00 p.m., forces from the Amadora Commando Regiment arrived. It was forbidden for anyone to leave. After a few telephone calls, the situation seemed to have been normalised with the appearance of Brigadier Vasco Lourenço.[19] In the meantime, Lieutenant Colonel Ramalho Eanes arrived in disguise and without rank badges.[20] He read out a list of officers who had to be escorted to the Commando headquarters. Included in the list were Colonel Artur Fernandes Baptista, COPCON's chief of staff; Major Barão da Cunha, head of the COPCON public relations department; and Air Force Major Arlindo Dias Ferreira,[21] . . . Lieutenant Colonel Arnão Metelo,

---

19 [AN] Promoted to brigadier a few hours earlier, with the confirmation of his post as Lisbon area commander.

20 [EN] António dos Santos Ramalho Eanes (1935–), a long-serving military officer, politician and administrator. Stationed in Angola when the 25 April coup occurred, he aligned with the Armed Forces Movement. Upon his return to Portugal, he became president of RTP (Rádio e Televisão de Portugal) and led military opposition to the coup attempt by far-left MFA officers on 25 November 1975. He served as president of Portugal from 1976 to 1986.

21 [AN] Five other staff captains were then listed.

COPCON's deputy chief of staff, and Major Eurico Corvacho,[22] who turned up in the meantime, were ordered to present themselves to the presidency (where they were also arrested).

Otelo de Carvalho had also been convoked to the presidency, where he was held incommunicado until he was informed that COPCON had been disbanded. The arrest of the top COPCON officers took place, according to the *Jornal Novo* account, ninety minutes before a state of emergency was declared. Later in the day, Colonel Ramalho Eanes – promoted to brigadier – replaced Carlos Fabião as chief of the Army staff.

Whether sufficient unity among anti-fascist forces can be mustered to bar a restoration of fascism was the focus of discussion among progressives in the weeks that followed the 25 November events. The strength is there; the will is there – but the essential ingredient of unity was the big question mark. With the political complexion of the Revolutionary Council drastically changed by the purge of its most progressive officers, the question as to whether progressive officers within the Armed Forces Movement can continue to impose their views within the armed forces, and within the country as a whole, is one which only time will answer.

---

22 [AN] A former chief of staff.

Afterword

The Portuguese Laboratory

Tariq Ali

The following text was published in 1978. It marked the beginning of the end of the period of radicalisation that gripped much of Europe from 1968 to 1975. The Portuguese events were the closest that a European country came to a socialist revolution. The uniformed uprising that seized Lisbon and overthrew the Caetano government on 25 April 1974 toppled in a morning the most long-lived fascist state in history and one of the most stable capitalist regimes anywhere this century. By the same stroke it set the stage for the end of the oldest colonial empire in the world. Thirteen years of guerrilla war in Africa had sapped the whole economy and society of metropolitan Portugal, and destroyed the allegiance of most of the younger officers in the army and navy to its political system. The coup itself encountered minimal resistance, yet for the same reason it initially left intact an important part of the state apparatus of Salazarism. But the tutelage exercised by the corporate state over the whole of civil society was immediately suspended, and the fascist secret police rounded up. For the first time in three decades a communist party entered the government of a western European country. Immediate and massive popular acclaim met the takeover from above of 25 April.

Wilfred Burchett, an old friend, provides a fascinating and gripping account of the struggles that took place. A generalised social assault from below was unleashed upon the structures of the old order. A wave of workers' struggles challenged the economic pattern of Portuguese capitalism while, under pressure from the African liberation movements, decisive steps were taken towards independence for the colonies. By November 1975 it was obvious that the revolutionary wing had been defeated by social democracy, a verdict confirmed by the elections that followed. My essay was an attempted self-criticism of the strategic and political mistakes that our side had made. We live in very different times now, but history remains unpredictable, and the past has many lessons, positive and negative, to offer.

Tariq Ali
London, January 2025

What, generally speaking, are the symptoms of a revolutionary situation? We shall certainly not be mistaken if we indicate the following three major symptoms: (1) when it is impossible for the ruling classes to maintain their rule without any change; when there is a crisis, in one form or another, among the 'upper classes', a crisis in the policy of the ruling class, leading to a fissure through which the discontent and indignation of the oppressed classes burst forth. For a revolution to take place, it is usually insufficient for 'the lower classes not to want' to live in the old way; it is also necessary that 'the upper classes should be unable' to live in the old way; (2) when the suffering and want of the oppressed classes have grown more acute than usual; (3) when, as a consequence of the above causes, there is a considerable increase in the activity of the masses who uncomplainingly allow themselves to be robbed in 'peacetime', but, in turbulent times are drawn both by all the circumstances of the crisis *and by the 'upper classes' themselves* into independent historical action.

Without these objective changes, which are independent of the will, not only of individual groups and parties but even of individual classes, a revolution, as a general rule, is impossible. The totality of all these objective changes is called a revolutionary situation.

V. I. Lenin: *The Collapse of the Second International*, 1915

On 25 April 1974, a military revolt overthrew the decaying fascist regime of the Portuguese dictator Caetano.[1] The rapidity of the overthrow shocked the entire world. The originality of the historical process took everyone by surprise. Was it really the case that the oldest and most tenacious of fascist regimes had been displaced or were we merely witnessing a 'palace *coup*', a change of personnel which would preserve intact all the institutions and structures of Salazarism? The events which shook Portugal in 1974–75 were remarkable on many counts. Italian fascism (1923–44), German fascism (1933–45) and Japanese fascism (1934–45) had all been overthrown by the intervention of outside armies. Portuguese fascism (1926–74) was overthrown by an internal revolt, itself precipitated by a set of costly colonial wars in Africa and a deteriorating economic situation at home.

The colonial wars had been going on for over thirteen years. Portugal, the weakest of all the old colonial powers, was also the most tenacious. Marcelo Caetano had proclaimed in the 1930s that 'Africa is more than a land to be exploited ... Africa is for us a moral justification and a *raison d'être* as a power. Without it we would be a small nation; with it we are a great power.'

The African colonies began their revolt with an urban insurrection in Angola in 1961 and with guerrilla warfare in Guinea-Bissau in 1963 and Mozambique in the following year. Unable and unwilling to follow the British model of decolonisation (political independence to the local ruling elite and intimate economic links), the Portuguese rulers now paid the price for their short-sightedness. Between 1964 and 1974 they sustained 60,000 casualties. By 1969 the expenditure on defence was 42 per cent of the entire state budget and, by 1971, the amount increased to 58 per cent of the total. Add to this the fact that Portugal's population is 9 million. Sustaining a colonial army of 200,000 with such a small population cannot but be a crippling exercise. The 'civilisers' of Africa had an adult illiteracy rate of 40 per cent at home. Furthermore, Portugal had the highest rate of infant mortality in Europe.

The size of the army led to an increase in the length of conscription. Many of the conscripted junior officers were university students. The impact of the war (i.e., the fact that they were losing it) coupled with the fact that the Portuguese secret police, the PIDE, had no authority within

---

1   Originally published in Tariq Ali, *1968 and After* (London: Blond & Briggs, 1978).

the army, meant that the flow of radical literature was smoother inside the army than in the rest of society. While some of the works of John F. Kennedy were banned in bookshops, the *Communist Manifesto* and various other Marxist texts circulated inside the army. Furthermore, soldiers and officers on their way to Africa were officially supplied with handbooks on guerrilla war by authors such as Mao Zedong, Vo Nguyen Giap and Che Guevara, in order that they might understand the mind of the enemy. In many cases, the handbooks instead succeeded in radicalising their Portuguese readers. One such reader was a young officer named Otelo Saraiva de Carvalho.

On the home front, the Salazar regime had been compelled to accept the internationalist logic of capital and abandon their protectionist economic policies. Restrictions on foreign capital were removed in the early 1960s. These restraints had enabled indigenous capitalism to accumulate its strength, and a number of consortiums dominated the economy. The largest of these was the CUF (Companhia União Fabril), which owned over a tenth of the country's industry including the chemical and textile industries. The weakness of Portuguese capitalism prevented the state from helping the further development of these companies. The turn to foreign investment was thus not an optional extra, but a necessity.

Familiar names were soon to be seen on billboards in Portugal: ITT, Timex, Ford, Grundig, Renault, British Leyland and Plessey. These companies found Portugal a paradise: colonies, low wages and a corporate state. From 1.5 per cent in 1960, the scale of foreign investments rose to 27 per cent in 1970. The impact of this foreign-financed industrialisation process increased the size of the urban working class from 25 per cent of the total adult population in 1950 to 35.8 per cent in 1970. The proportion of the population employed on the land fell from 47 per cent in 1950 to 30 per cent in 1970. Those who could not be absorbed into the internal labour market went to Western Europe: by 1973 there were nearly 2 million Portuguese workers outside the country, an important transmission belt for new and, in certain cases, radical ideas. The population increased in the predominantly urban provinces of Lisbon, Setúbal and Porto.

In the countryside, there was a division between the large landed estates in the south and the *minifundia* in the north. The former were mechanised and employed agricultural labourers. The small farmers in the north were racked by debts and dominated by the Church. The north–south division was to be consistently reflected in the country's politics after the overthrow of Caetano and the dismantling of fascism.

The increase in the size of the urban working class after the entry of foreign capital brought its own 'diseases'. Inflation hit Portugal with a surprising intensity, reaching a rate of 21 per cent in 1973. At the same time, a strike by transportation workers in July 1968 signalled the emergence of strength within a working class exploited and repressed by fascism for over three decades. As the recession developed in the rest of Western Europe, many migrant workers began going home, swelling the ranks of the unemployed, but bringing with them a whiff of what it was like in the rest of the continent in terms of politics and trade unionism. In 1973, strikes broke out in the engineering and car industries: Ford, General Motors and the Lisnave shipyards (the largest in the world, owned by the CUF in partnership with Dutch and Swedish companies), ITT, and finally in the air transport services. This pattern was continued in the following year. The strikes were by no means generalised. Their character was fragmentary, but they nonetheless reflected an important and growing class consciousness in the urban centres of Portugal.

The external and internal problems confronting the Salazarist state produced growing divisions within the ruling class. Internally, some favoured political relaxation and integration within the European Community. As far as the guerrilla wars in Portugal were concerned, the divisions were even more pronounced and, because of the importance of what was at stake, more serious. On 28 February 1974 a book was published in Lisbon, entitled *The Future of Portugal*, by the former military commander of the expeditionary force in Guinea-Bissau, General Spínola. The theme of the book was to propose a Gaullist-type solution, granting autonomy to the former colonies within a federation including Portugal. Spínola argued that: 'If we do not achieve this solution, we will inevitably drift towards disintegration, losing our African territories one after the other.'

These relatively moderate proposals produced a furious backlash from the diehard colonialists ensconced in the upper reaches of the governmental and state apparatus. They discussed the replacement of Caetano for permitting the publication of the book, and the political police seized large numbers of copies from bookshops throughout the country. The Spínola book exposed the simmering discontent within the government and the army: junior officers and NCOs demanded a set of reforms; the infantry company of Caldas da Rainha, fifty-five miles away from Lisbon, threatened a march on Lisbon. The hardliners struck on 13 March 1974. They removed Generals Spínola and Costa Gomes from their posts, instituted repressive measures against dissident soldiers and attempted to stabilise the situation. But they were too late, for within the army there already existed an organisation of officers who were not prepared to wait any longer for the reforms which they felt were necessary to put Portugal on the right track. This was the Armed Forces Movement (MFA). It had been organised in 1973 to oppose a Caetano decree granting equal rights to conscript officers, but soon transcended this narrow professional issue. Indeed, given that conscript officers joined the MFA several months later, it would appear that the initial point of dispute could well have been a pretext to organise meetings within the army.

In January 1974, the MFA circulated a document among its supporters entitled: 'The Movement, the Armed Forces and the Nation'. It was the first real sign that a major reformist opposition to Salazarism existed within the army. The document spoke of the colonial wars as 'the gravest question which underlies the general crisis of the regime' even though it called for a 'political solution which safeguards national honour and dignity' – a clear sign that the more radical officers were anxious to prevent any premature break with the supporters of the monocled General Spínola. However, the document contested the 'myth that our armed forces are politically neutral' and accused the army of sustaining a regime of repression in Portugal itself. This was a remarkable development foreseen by no political analyst. It was a direct reflection of the tensions which existed in society as a whole inside a conscript army. The fact that all opposition parties and currents were underground, that the student movement had suffered heavy repression and that there was no freedom of the media resulted in the desire of the majority of the masses for democratic rights being channelled through an unlikely source: a section of the officer caste of the Portuguese army. The character of this caste had somewhat altered over the preceding decade. The progeny of traditional 'martial families' were finding increasingly unattractive their careers in an army fighting three wars and sustaining heavy casualties. Furthermore, the opening of Portugal to foreign capital provided alternative employment on the managerial level for the children of the wealthy. The result was dramatic. In 1961–62 there had been 257 admissions to the elite military academy; in 1971–72, when the army needed more officers than ever before, the figure was down to seventy-two. The vacuum was filled by conscript and non-commissioned officers drawn largely from university graduates. At the same time the conscription period was increased from two to four years. The influx of new ex-student officers, many of whom had been radicalised by the post-1962 wave of student agitation in Portugal, was to have an important impact inside the army: many of the students were sympathetic to the politics of the Socialist and Communist parties, while others were more in tune with the aspirations of the far left.

The MFA leadership followed the discussions on its initial document and formulated a draft programme, the task of which was to codify the aims and demands of the movement. Thus, the programme contained demands for overthrowing the Caetano regime, organising a large-scale *saneamento* (purge) to cleanse the army and the police of fascist influences, the immediate dissolution of the hated political police and the convocation within twelve months of an elected constituent assembly. As far as the economy was concerned, the draft programme sketched out a schematic 'anti-monopoly strategy' and called for measures which would have 'the essential objective of defending the interests of the working classes'. As far as Africa was concerned, the programme was extremely muted, restricting itself to calling for a 'political' rather than a military solution and pledging 'an overseas policy which leads to peace'. There was no mention of a withdrawal from Africa. The programme as a whole was left-reformist in tone. The fact that it could only be implemented by a forcible overthrow of the corporatist regime gave it a potency which was beyond the control of its initiators.

On 25 April 1974, Caetano was deposed by a well-executed military coup: the officer who played a leading role in coordinating the work necessary was Carvalho. The takeover in Lisbon proceeded smoothly, enabling the MFA to consolidate its national position. Later, Carvalho admitted in an interview that they were all surprised by the extent of popular support inside the army itself for the overthrow of the Caetano regime. There were some units, commanded by right-wing officers, who were prepared to resist. In order to prevent an outbreak of violence the MFA leaders concluded an agreement with Spínola. This haughty figure refused to talk to any officer of the MFA below the rank of colonel.

Caetano formally handed over power to Spínola. A Portuguese civil servant described the Spínola–Caetano encounter as 'a meeting of two gentlemen, of two friends who respect each other and who share a great sense of honour and responsibility'. Caetano was provided with a military plane to leave for Brazil, where he was welcomed by the military dictatorship and appointed Professor of Comparative Law at the country's leading university. It was a fitting appointment for a fascist in a country where the only law that prevailed was despotic and barbaric.

Spínola appeared on television on 26 April and promised free elections and democratic rights. The statement he read out was clearly a compromise and the Junta of National Salvation over which he presided was composed exclusively of generals and admirals, who had served long tours of duty in Africa. The masses demonstrated their joy at the overthrow of the regime without inhibition or restraint. They secured the release of all political prisoners within a week. Almost overnight, they transformed a society marked by fifty years of fascist rule and decay into one where everyone could speak their mind. The fascist-regulated press found itself taken over by its employees. A campaign was immediately launched in the liberated press for the abolition of reactionary religious edicts which prohibited divorce for those unfortunate enough to have been married in a Portuguese church! Education began to be reorganised. The night of ignorance, of repression, of a clerico-fascist morality, had come to an end. Many wondered whether it was all a dream. The reactionary members of the ruling junta, including Spínola, regarded these events as a nightmare. Their military minds found the breakdown of traditional law and order repugnant. While Spínola's position as head of state protected the reactionary officers in the army from the wrath of the *saneamento*, the navy was not immune to anti-fascist measures. Several hundred officers proclaimed their support for the MFA and demanded the removal of eighty-two admirals and vice-admirals because of their intimacy with the Salazar regime. Their demands were met.

The first Provisional Government sworn in by Spínola reflected the political crisis confronting a collapsing state. Apart from reactionary military men, there were two ministers each from the Communist and Socialist parties. This attempt to contain the working-class movement by tying the two workers' parties to the state was, however, unable to limit the mass upsurge. If anything, it discredited the Communist Party in the eyes of the workers. A Communist, Avelino Pacheco Gonçalves, was named minister of labour, and the Communist Party waged a ferocious ideological campaign against strikes. It was a display of extremely short-sighted opportunism in a country which had, only a few weeks previously, been under a fascist government whose official ideology had likewise disapproved of any form of strike action. May Day 1974 was an historic event in the calendar of the Portuguese working class: it was the first occasion in half a century that they had been able freely to commemorate this day. A massive wave of strikes shook Portugal after 1 May 1974. They were a novel combination of everyday economic demands fused with struggles against the fascist apparatus and its representatives. In addition, strikes which had been repressed in 1973 were now resumed, with an additional demand: that all workers dismissed for leading the strikes in the preceding year be immediately rehabilitated. In the construction industry, workers of most of the major companies went on strike and organised flying pickets to defend their struggle. On 13 May the workers in the Panasqueira iron mines unleashed a strike which lasted a week until their demands – which included a guaranteed minimum monthly wage of 6,000 escudos, an extra month's pay every year, one month's paid holiday and free medical care – were granted. The following week saw the chemical, automobile and related industries paralysed by a series of strikes. Although the official trades unions had been state-controlled, democratic forms of organisation emerged in many factories, jealously guarding their autonomy against all encroachments.

In many cases, the workers won major demands, but the mobilisations receded towards the end of May. The movement had not been consciously unified: the two mass parties of the workers were in government, though it is unlikely that they would have attempted a general strike had they been out of office. The Portuguese Communist Party in the first phase after the overthrow of Caetano acted not unlike the French Communist Party in May 1968. It was desperate to preserve 'order' at all costs. It attacked those on its left, who were supporting and helping to organise the strikes, as 'consciously or unconsciously acting in favour of reaction'. They were described as ultra-leftists taking undue advantage 'of an inexperienced, politically very young, working class that could be plunged into adventure'. The Communist-organised demonstration on 30 May 1974 to pledge support for the party's anti-strike crusade was a miserable flop: 6,000 people marched behind the

Communist minister for labour, singing the old national anthem and carrying portraits of General Spínola! 'Social peace' was the main slogan of Mr Cunhal's party in the period after 25 April 1974. The 'politically very young working class', however, continued to ignore the advice of the leaders of the Communist Party, mature though they were in the ancient art of class collaboration. The postal workers' strike which erupted in June 1974 became an important test for the workers' parties. It was the first national strike after 25 April. The ideological offensive against the postal workers was orchestrated and led by the Portuguese Communist Party. José Vitoriano, a member of the Central Committee, was reported in the French Communist Party's daily paper, *L'Humanité* of 21 June, as saying: 'Today it is the fascists and reactionaries of every stripe who want more strikes. Yesterday they repressed them with blood and iron. Today they are their principal promoters.' It was hardly surprising that the *Financial Times* of 18 June saw fit to note that: 'The Minister of Labour, Avelino Gonçalves, nevertheless works hard at settling conflicts that seriously affect production, and it is extremely important to note that it is nearly only the Communists who are counselling caution in the use of the strike weapon at this time.' The notion that it was the fascists and reactionaries who were promoting the strikes, was, of course, ludicrous. It was a slander that bore all the hallmarks of the Stalinist school of falsification. It should be stressed that throughout this period of the First Provisional Government the policies and tactics of the Portuguese Communist Party were to the right of the Socialist Party; in fact, many Socialist Party cadres were more sympathetic to the strikers and their demands at this time. The postal workers' strike, supported incidentally by 97 per cent of the workers, was defeated by a military occupation of the post offices and repression against sections of the media which backed the strike. Military officers who refused to occupy the post offices were suspended, and newspapers reporting the suspension were penalised. None of this met with opposition from the Portuguese Communist Party. It is vital to remember the role played by the PCP in this phase in order to evaluate its electoral standing and its inability to resist the ideological offensive of social democracy in the following year.

The Junta had been able to inflict a defeat on the postal workers, but it soon discovered that it was impossible to repeat the process in the African arena. The Junta was now confronted with a pincer movement.

On the one hand, it confronted the African liberation movements, while at its right flank were the reactionary, colonialist Portuguese settlers, opposed to any concessions. The federal solution envisaged by Spínola, Costa Gomes and the military High Command was a non-starter. The African guerrillas refused to agree to a ceasefire if all they were offered in return was a pan-Portuguese fantasy. In Portugal itself, virtually the entire far left was beginning to agitate for immediate and complete independence. A Maoist newspaper, *Luta Popular*, was suppressed and its editor imprisoned for inciting troops to refuse to fight in Africa. Under growing pressure, both the Socialist and the Communist parties demanded that negotiations with the liberation movements commence without a prior ceasefire. The Portuguese right wing attempted to boost Spínola's reputation in the country, comparing him to de Gaulle. But there was no analogy between post-Caetano Portugal and the French Fourth Republic. Spínola's primitive anti-communism was not enough to guarantee his victory against the left and the masses. The Portuguese had just got rid of fascism. They were not keen on embarking on a course which turned out to be a modified version of the Estado Novo, with a monocled Bonaparte at its head.

The failure of the Communist and Socialist Parties to contain the working-class upsurge in the summer of 1974 had clearly alarmed sections of the ruling class, and they were now prepared to consider a strong state led by a strong president, ruling by decrees confirmed by occasional plebiscites. But proposals to put some of these ideas into practice were firmly rejected by the Council of State, a body not known for its radicalism. The Council was obviously more aware of the deep divisions inside the army than a number of left-wing commentators writing for the revolutionary press in Western Europe and North America. The impasse in which the supporters of Spínola now found themselves led to the fall of the government. Spínola tried to reconstitute it by appointing Colonel Firmino Miguel, one of his trusted aides, as the new prime minister, but the MFA leadership blocked this and insisted that Vasco Gonçalves, a member of the MFA Coordinating Committee, become the next head of government. Four important leaders of the MFA were brought into the Second Provisional Government, including Costa Martins, Melo Antunes and Vítor Alves. At the same time, Vítor Crespo and Vice-Admiral Coutinho, two officers trusted by the MFA leaders, were despatched post-haste to Mozambique and

Angola respectively. It was now obvious that the MFA had decided to disregard Spínola's supporters in the army, ditch the federalist dream and begin negotiations to end the war and organise a Portuguese withdrawal. Melo Antunes and Mário Soares were authorised to carry out such a plan. The decolonisation proposals of the MFA and its governmental strength represented a serious setback for General Spínola's political project. The right wing within the army decided to accept defeat for the moment, but there is considerable evidence to suggest that it began plotting a coup to defeat the MFA and impose a strong, presidential form of government.

For its part, the MFA utilised the advent of the Second Provisional Government to put into practice a number of the proposals contained in its draft programme. A *saneamento* was carried out in the fields of education and local administration. With regard to the latter, it should be mentioned that the eagerness of the PCP to fill the places of the sacked fascists without any recourse to mass opinion was to have damaging effects at a later stage. As censorship was now almost totally abandoned, the hunger of the masses for socialist ideas and texts could be fully assuaged. A hundred flowers bloomed in the real sense of the phrase. Marxist literature could be found everywhere; pamphlets by Lenin were displayed in the smallest shops; revolutionary and socialist ideas were discussed regularly in the mass media; Eisenstein's classic film, *Battleship Potemkin*, was seen by huge audiences in Lisbon. The ideological mechanisms of the old order were in a state of virtual collapse. The Portuguese ruling class had still not found effective new channels for reasserting its hegemony. Some of the demonstrations which took place in Portugal in 1974, and even more in 1975, reflected the dramatic changes which had taken place. Who could have predicted that the spectre of Petrograd would appear for the first time in post-war Europe in the streets of Lisbon, rather than Milan or Paris or Barcelona? The demonstrations of soldiers, sailors, workers and students marching with linked arms on the streets of Portugal sent a tremor of fear through the capitalists in the West.

The summer of 1974 saw further developments in the country, which led to the further isolation of reaction and, ultimately, to a confrontation from which the latter rapidly retreated. In Africa, the two emissaries of the Second Provisional Government, Mário Soares and Melo Antunes, negotiated the independence of Guinea-Bissau and Mozambique in

September. A white settler revolt in the Mozambique capital was suppressed by a joint expedition of Portuguese troops and African guerrillas. This came as a serious blow to Spínola and the right wing, as it effectively ended their dream of a Greater Portugal. At the same time, the MFA leaders postponed a purge of fascist army officers but organised a military unit known as COPCON (Continental Operations Command) with responsibility for defending the authority of the government. COPCON's commander was Otelo Saraiva de Carvalho, who was promoted to the rank of brigadier and also given charge of the military district of Lisbon. This was clearly a move by the MFA radicals to institutionalise the semi-dual power structure which existed in the army. COPCON was used to 'solve' industrial disputes and persuade workers to end occupations, but it did not open fire on any banned demonstration. Meanwhile, the workers of the giant Lisnave shipyards demanded a more thoroughgoing *saneamento* and issued a communiqué. This declaration symbolised the new mood of the Portuguese working class. It indicated that the advanced workers, at any rate, had understood that what was taking place in the country was not simply a process of democratisation, but posed more fundamental questions. For that reason, the short communiqué is reproduced in full:

> In struggling to rid the Lisnave management of its fascists, the workers have become aware they are not only fighting for the downfall of the fascist structure inside Lisnave, but also against the whole of the exploiting ruling class.
>
> In this way the workers of Lisnave are joining with the brave fight of TAP, of *Jornal do Comércio,* of Siderurgia, of Texmalhas, backing all the struggles from North to South, and leaving the constricting walls of the factory to come onto the streets and show:
>
> That our fight to rid ourselves of fascists is not a secondary fight, it is a principal struggle because it is part of the permanent fight against all the forms of fascism being constantly generated by monopoly capitalism.
>
> That where there is initiative and organised struggle by the oppressed classes, the forces of reaction retreat. Where there is lack of vigilance on the part of the people, the counter-revolutionary forces advance and wipe out the freedoms already achieved.
>
> That we support all the laws and measures of the Provisional

Government which help to increase the freedom of the workers, and of the peoples exploited and oppressed by Portuguese Colonialism.

That we do not back the Government when it comes out with anti-working-class laws which undermine the struggles of workers against capitalist exploitation.

That we shall actively fight the 'strike law' because it is a big blow to the freedom of the workers.

That we reject the 'lock-out law' as a law against the workers and for the protection of the capitalists, granting the bosses the freedom to starve thousands of workers.

Because we know that the 120 million escudos are not, as the Melos, Champalimauds, Quinas & Company claim, to create 120,000 jobs, but to create better conditions for exploiting the workers.

That we reject all attempts, no matter where they come from, to sabotage and divide the working masses in their fight against fascism and capitalism.

That we support the Armed Forces so long as they support the struggles of the oppressed and exploited classes against the oppressing and exploiting classes.

LISNAVE WORKERS PURGE FASCISTS
DEATH TO PIDE – DEATH TO FASCISM
RIGHT TO STRIKE – YES!
LOCK OUT – NO!
SOLIDARITY WITH THE COMRADES ON STRIKE

The Lisnave workers organised a one-day strike on 12 September 1974 and called a demonstration outside the Ministry of Labour. Despite the fact that the march was banned, it did take place. The COPCON units moved aside to let the workers march to their destination where they handed in their communiqué. It was an extremely important indication of the mood inside sections of the army. It was also regarded as a provocation by Portuguese reaction, which had been viewing the deteriorating situation inside the army with growing unease. The twin processes of decolonisation abroad and democratisation at home (especially the energy of the latter) were seen by Spínola and the right wing as developments which had to be stopped. In the northern part of the country, the old members of the fascist organisations had been regrouping under new names, intended to deceive, but which fooled no one. A COPCON raid on the offices of the so-called Progressive Party in Porto revealed an armoury and fascist personnel. On 10 September, Spínola broadcast a speech appealing against 'anarchy' and calling on the 'silent majority' to oppose 'extremism'. This was clearly not a spontaneous decision by the would-be Bonaparte. It had been taken in consultation with the right wing in the army and sections of the ruling class. Spínola's speech was welcomed by all the forces opposed to the 'hasty' decolonisation and democratisation which were underway. A demonstration by the 'silent majority' was called for on 28 September, setting the stage for some form of confrontation.

The workers' parties and the trades unions were alarmed by this move. They saw in it an attempt by the displaced forces of Salazarism to try and reverse, or at least modify, the relationship of forces which had developed in Portuguese society. On 26 September, the Communist and Socialist parties and Intersindical, the CP-dominated trade union federation, issued a joint communiqué describing the proposed 'March on Lisbon' as a fascist attempt to strangle democracy; they organised the formation of militias to resist all attempts at a presidential putsch. The transport workers decided that they would not man the specially booked trains and coaches. On the morning of 27 September, the liberated Rádio Renascença called on workers to organise 'picnics in the evening' on all the main roads which led to Lisbon. The workers' militias set up armed roadblocks throughout the city. These militias consisted of members of the SP, the PCP and a whole range of far-left groups. It was a united front par excellence. It created extreme tension inside the Presidential Palace. Spínola was alarmed by these developments much more than by the open fascist intrigues leading to the demonstration. Once again, there were moves by armed forces to break the roadblocks and barricades of the workers' movement. Vasco Gonçalves and Carvalho were summoned to the Presidential Palace and, in effect, placed under arrest. The COPCON units were contacted by Spínola's aides, but refused to take orders from anyone but Carvalho. Once again, it was the divisions in the army which foiled the attempts of reaction to carry out a coup. On the morning of the proposed demonstration, no newspapers were published, on Spínola's orders. The general and his aides were fearful lest the availability of information further inflame the masses. They also ordered a radio silence except for official broadcasts. This was broken at 8:30 on the morning of 28 September by an MFA communiqué stressing its determination to carry out the measures outlined in its programme and asking the masses to remain on guard against the intrigues and movements of reaction. COPCON commandos joined the workers on the barricades. At midday, a mass demonstration assembled in the centre of Lisbon to block the 'silent majority'. In its vanguard were the workers of Lisnave and TAP, the Portuguese airline. Within the next two hours, Spínola banned the reactionary march. His capitulation swelled the size of the workers' demonstration which transformed itself into a celebration of a victory.

Two days later, on 30 September, the inevitable happened: Spínola resigned after delivering a speech attacking decolonisation in Africa and 'the inversion of authority' at home. The MFA leaders believed this victory was sufficient. They did not address a reply to Spínola detailing the manoeuvres of reaction in the preceding months. It was a grave political error, reflecting the lack of a determination to be able to go on the offensive. In an interview with *Diário de Lisboa* after the overthrow of Spínola, the best-known radical inside the MFA leadership said: 'I knew I was not fighting against Spínola. That was never my intention and it never occurred to me to go against him or to make some sort of *coup d'état* to remove him from power. It was he who was convinced of this.'

If Carvalho was not speaking in such a fashion to maintain the unity of the army (in itself a utopian desire), then all one can say is that it reflected the utter political confusion that dominated the High Command of the MFA, a confusion which compelled it to be permanently on the defensive. If you have no clear conception as to how your own programme is to be implemented, you tend to *react* to events instead of shaping them. Thus, the fall of Spínola was treated by the MFA as a routine event. In Cuba, Fidel Castro, by contrast, had used the counter-revolution to his advantage: he had patiently explained what reaction was plotting and had educated the masses in such a way that the final stage of the Cuban Revolution was an enormously popular occasion with mass participation. The failure of the MFA to teach the masses was not a surprise. The MFA was itself a hybrid and heterogeneous movement which contained within it most of the colours of the rainbow. Nonetheless, the left did exercise considerable influence and could have deflected the movement, provided it had understood what was at stake.

But if one cannot expect a worked-out strategy from an organisation which inhabits a vital section of the state apparatus and acts under its constraint, the role of the Communist and Socialist parties in helping the masses assimilate the lessons of what was going on was virtually nil. Both parties tended to support the MFA and tended to treat the MFA as a uniform and cohesive political bloc; they did not put forward any alternative line of action for the masses for fear of weakening it. The one occasion on which they carried out an independent political act of significance was the setting-up of barricades in September 1974. But, here too, their aim was to provide mass backing for the MFA against Spínola and his right-wing supporters. The independent *political* capacity of the Portuguese working class was circumscribed by its inexperience and the straitjacket imposed on it by decades of fascist rule. Once Spínola was ejected the two parties went back to business as usual. The working class was learning fast, but it was conscious of its limitations. The barricades of September showed the strength of the masses and its parties. They also revealed that the mobilisation had a sufficiently strong impact on the MFA to pressure it to remove Spínola. The mistake was that it regarded this as a victory.

Spínola was replaced by Costa Gomes, a veteran from the same milieu, but more able and prepared to compromise, when necessary, with the MFA. The Lisbon daily, *Diário de Notícias*, remarked on the changeover that 'between Generals Spínola and Costa Gomes there is all the difference between an emotive and an intellectual. Two men, two styles but the objectives remain the same . . . This excludes any alarmist hypothesis.' The removal of Spínola ensured that the country's first general elections in fifty years would be held on schedule as promised. The ruling class was not pleased by the imminence of the elections; they had not been able to create a political instrument which could win a mass base and ensure stable bourgeois rule. Post-war Italy had seen the formation of the Christian Democratic Party. Backed by the United States, Italian capitalists and the Vatican, this party still rules Italy. In ideal circumstances the Portuguese ruling class would have attempted the post-war Italian solution, but they were confronted by a world which had considerably changed. The United States had suffered a severe defeat in Indochina, while its internal credibility was dented by Nixon and the growing Watergate crisis. In Western Europe, the post-war euphoria fed by the economic boom had given way to recession and unemployment. In addition, there had appeared a new group of militants, to the left of the traditional workers' parties, which was sympathetic to revolutionary ideas and strategies. The Portuguese ruling class was uneasy about the outcome of the elections promised for 1975 because it feared that the Socialist and Communist parties would gain an overall majority, which could increase rather than end political instability. It was this anxiety which prompted sections of the army in league with the deposed General Spínola to attempt a right-wing coup on 11 March 1975. The attempt proved to be abortive. The plotters found little support and the ranks of the army remained loyal to the central leadership of the MFA. Spínola and his aides fled, after a short stay in Spain, to Brazil. This defeat did mark a serious setback for the whole bourgeois order in Portugal, but the mass mobilisations which greeted the failure of the coup saw the spectre of Petrograd raise its head in Lisbon once again. Soldiers and sailors fraternised with the workers. Red flags were flown on a number of tanks. The mass movement lurched forward and demanded in its slogans and chants more radical measures to deal with the growing economic crisis.

Once again, the PCP played an important part in the anti-Spínolist agitation. But it preferred to act in liaison with its faction inside the MFA. For the truth is that the PCP, while talking at great length about the 'unity of the MFA', had built its support around Gonçalves and the Fifth Division. It now exercised control over a section of the MFA apparatus which was far from democratic. They systematically weeded out from central commands those unsympathetic to them; not only right-wingers and reactionaries, but also social-democrats and socialists. The formation of the 'Group of Nine' at a later stage was partially in response to the attempted 'colonisation' of the state apparatus by the Gonçalves/PCP faction.

The 11 March coup was, in many respects, a pathetic affair. Within a matter of hours, the Gonçalves faction had used it to consolidate their grip on the MFA council and to marginalise Melo Antunes and his supporters. At the same time, the PCP-dominated bank workers' unions took over the main banks. Official nationalisation was announced a few days later.

Over the preceding year, the rate of inflation in the country had risen to 35 per cent. A quarter of a million workers were unemployed. At the same time, there was economic sabotage, investment strikes by Portuguese monopolists and by multinationals, restriction and suppression of credit to small and medium-size enterprises and the flight of capital. The left alleged that the United States was intervening through its favourite 'destabilising' apparatus, the Central Intelligence Agency. Memories of Chile were still strong throughout Western Europe. It was alleged that the American ambassador to Portugal was a high-powered officer of the Agency. This was denied at the time, but it is worth recalling that Frank Carlucci, appointed ambassador to Portugal by Henry Kissinger in January 1975, was made deputy director of the Central Intelligence Agency in December 1977. Jonathan Steele, reporting from Washington in the *Guardian* on 23 December 1977, wrote in relation to US involvement in Portugal in 1975:

> American officials have conceded that large sums of money were being channelled to anti-Communist parties and trade unions at that time through the CIA, West European intelligence services, and political parties, particularly the West German SPD. After the abortive right-wing putsch within the army in March 1975, which led to General Spínola's exile from Lisbon, some officers accused Mr Carlucci of involvement. The US State Department denied the charges.

The economic sabotage and the response of the mass movement prompted the government to embark on a project of large-scale nationalisations. The Military Revolutionary Council assumed open control of the government and passed a decree nationalising the banks, insurance companies and a number of other industrial concerns. Sixty per cent of the country's economy was soon nationalised. The only major monopoly to escape was the CUF enterprise, but even its workers were agitating for it to be taken over. Several dozen factories were occupied by the workers and a form of workers' control existed. In the large estates in the Alentejo, in the southern tip of the country, agricultural workers seized estates and established collectives, while empty buildings, luxury homes and hotels were taken over by homeless people.

It was in this atmosphere and these conditions that the country's first elections for half a century took place. Members were elected to a Constituent Assembly on 25 April 1975. The result was a victory for the workers' parties. The combined vote of the Socialist Party (38 per cent), the Communist Party (13 per cent) and the MDP/CDE (a CP front – 5 per cent) was 56 per cent. António de Figueiredo, a social-democratic observer, commented that 'a new Portugal may be able to achieve, if not a revolution, at least a process of accelerated evolution capable of achieving socialism in the context of a freer society.' In other words, the Portuguese political situation was ripening into a pre-revolutionary crisis. The election results were a striking proof that the workers wanted their own government, a workers' government which would bring about some form of socialist democracy. They were to find themselves disillusioned extremely rapidly.

The combined impact of the elections and the deteriorating political and economic situation brought about further splits in the army, which were reflected within the MFA. On one side, a rapid process of radicalisation was taking place at the level of rank-and-file soldiers, and this had played a decisive part in defeating the coup of 11 March. Soldiers of several key regiments had refused to obey orders. In addition, specially convoked soldiers' assemblies were removing reactionary officers from the army. The imposition of a *saneamento* from below clearly worried the moderate sections of the MFA High Command. Some of them obviously wondered whether the whole process would end with the election of officers! There were even instances of soldiers and revolutionary officers providing military training for workers in a number of proletarian districts in Lisbon.

In these conditions, the elections to the Constituent Assembly were utilised by Portuguese capitalists and their backers to try and disrupt the process of radicalisation. Having failed to bring about a stabilisation of the system through the extra-parliamentary channels of a rightist military coup, they now attempted to create a polarisation between the extra-parliamentary mass mobilisations and the Constituent Assembly. The problems which allowed the ruling class to go on the offensive were not unrelated to the fact that the MFA left wing, the Portuguese Communist Party and the overwhelming majority of the far left made their own counterposition from the other side. An understanding of what happened in the summer of 1975 is impossible unless one studies closely the strategy and aims of both the ruling-class formations and the working-class parties.

The outcome of the elections to the Constituent Assembly were not regarded by the masses as irrelevant. Given that they were the first elections based on universal adult franchise in fifty years, it is hardly surprising that they had an overall national impact. Following the elections, the Socialist Party leaders were triumphant and on the offensive. Their organisation had emerged as the largest single party in the Assembly. If they chose to form a government with Communist participation, they could do so with an overall majority. Soares did not want an SP–CP government, but mass pressure from below could well have forced him to create one. Instead, the Communist Party, nursing its wounded pride at being defeated by the Socialist Party, refused, on its part, to countenance any such compromise. They chose to strengthen their links with their supporters within the MFA and, in effect, preferred an MFA government under the prime ministership of Vasco Gonçalves to a government representing the will of the people. This 'will' was the result of a bourgeois democratic election. The point was that there was at that time no other way in which the *masses* could determine who should represent them and who should form the government. Thus Soares, aided and abetted by the German SPD and financed from diverse sources, embarked on a campaign against the Fifth Provisional Government of Vasco Gonçalves. He was also aided objectively by the bureaucratic and manipulative strategy of the Communist Party and by the infantile leftism of the most important groups of the revolutionary left. In a developing pre-revolutionary state, there was no organisation which attempted to come to grips with the central strategic problem which confronted all Portuguese revolutionaries: how the masses could be won over to revolution. The vanguard, the workers, students and soldiers in Lisbon and Porto were clearly ready for a socialist revolution. How could their views and new consciousness be utilised to win over the masses? This remained the unsolved dilemma of the Portuguese Revolution. In Portugal, as in Chile (albeit in very different circumstances) the revolutionary left failed to find the road to the masses, whereas the Communist Party demonstrated once again its refusal to trust the masses.

The summer of 1975 inaugurated a decisive new period for the Portuguese revolutionary process. Up till then, the revolution had advanced. Every date since 25 April 1974 had taken the mass movement forward. 28 September 1974 and 11 March 1975 had seen serious setbacks for the ruling class and its projects. In a despondent state, the main political party of the ruling class, the Popular Democratic Party (PPD) had accepted after 28 September the role of the MFA as the central arbiter in Portuguese political and economic life. It clearly hoped that the Spinolist remnants within the MFA would be able to maintain control until the elections rocketed them (the PPD) into a governmental coalition. The elections to the Constituent Assembly, however, provided an overall majority to the SP and the CP. The failure of the CP and the far left to intervene in the crisis of the Socialist Party by implementing the tactic of the united front allowed Soares to mount an offensive against socialism in the name of democracy.

Given the chorus of black propaganda throughout the Western European press in the summer of 1975, a campaign orchestrated, incidentally, by the Central Intelligence Agency, and directed against the 'breakdown of law and order', 'anarchy', etc., it is important to get the facts straight. While the MFA were not pleased with the idea of holding elections at that stage (for a mixture of confused and ultra-left reasons) they had no option but to authorise them. At the same time, they appealed to the people to cast blank votes in order to show their approval for the MFA which was, in the words of Admiral Coutinho, attempting to construct a 'third political force' in the middle of the CP and the SP. It was an unrealistic and inane attempt to solve the dispute between the SP and the CP, for the simple reason that it stressed the irrelevance of politics. But it was politics for which the masses were thirsting. Ninety-two per cent of those eligible to vote went to the polls and only 7 per cent cast blank votes. Before the elections, the MFA had signed a pact with all the political parties whereby the latter agreed that the task of the Constituent Assembly was to frame a constitution and that the results would not be binding on the selection of a new coalition government, but would merely provide some form of guidance for restructuring the same. Soares was a signatory to this pact which accepted the dominant role of the MFA after the elections.

Vasco Gonçalves proclaimed after the election that he was not dissatisfied with the results, as 'the election will not decisively influence the revolutionary process'. What Gonçalves did not realise was that, without mass support, the revolutionary process cannot be completed. It is possible that he harboured illusions that socialism could be brought about behind the backs of the majority of the population and with the support of an active and dynamic minority of workers. If he was suffering from such delusions, it was because his military training had not alerted him to appreciate the uneven development of mass consciousness. Furthermore, he was being backed to the hilt by the Portuguese Communist Party: some of its activities in this period created the impression that Cunhal and his Central Committee actually harboured hopes that an alliance with Gonçalves and a section of the army could catapult it into power, thus neatly avoiding the dilemma of the election result. In other words, the Communist Party hoped that, through its alliance with Gonçalves, it could leap over the masses and then manipulate them into line. It was a bureaucratic conception, and it was doomed to fail. However, for the immediate post-election period, it suited both the Gonçalves faction within the MFA and the Communist Party.

The May Day rally organised in 1975 was held under the auspices of Intersindical. The chief guest was the prime minister, Vasco Gonçalves, and he was joined on the platform of the May First Stadium by leaders of the Communist Party. This was the first major rally since the elections. Its ostensible purpose was to celebrate international workers' day. In reality, it was a manipulated occasion designed to exclude the Socialist Party and indicate that the elections were irrelevant. It was yet another attempt by the Communist Party to somehow circumvent the tricky problem of devising a strategy to win over the masses. The Party throughout underestimated the independent political capacity of the Portuguese working class. This resulted in a bureaucratic and manipulative approach to politics. It was, in its own way, an admission that the masses would not respond to the politics of the PCP. When Mário Soares and thousands of Socialist Party workers entered the stadium to join the rally, they were chanting: 'The People have voted. The Socialists have won.' The reply which a revolutionary Marxist would have made to such a slogan would have been along the following lines: 'What you say is true. Let us now discuss how to set up a workers' government consisting of all workers' organisations. In our opinion, such a government should be based on working-class institutions. In order to carry through socialist measures, we must mobilise the enormous potential of the working people themselves. Let us therefore extend and institutionalise the already existing organs of popular power so that the voice of the entire working class can be heard through them. Are Soares and the Socialist Party leaders prepared to work towards such a government? We certainly are, because it best reflects at the present time the interests and desires of the Portuguese working class.'

An appeal of this sort would have opened up a dialogue and put Soares on the defensive, in a position where he would be forced to explain to his own working-class supporters why he was opposed to forming a workers' government. The reply of Cunhal and Vasco Gonçalves to the chant of the SP workers was to prevent Soares from addressing the rally and finally to instruct soldiers to escort him from the stadium. Actions of this sort merely fuelled the forces of reaction. The question was not that they would have remained inactive or passive had the PCP and the Fifth Provisional government *not* made these mistakes. The point is that they could have been marginalised and defeated by a workers' and soldiers' united front.

On the heels of the short-sighted, sectarian exclusion of the Socialist Party from the May Day rally came the episode centred on the newspaper *República*. Under the Salazarist regime, *República* had been kept alive by money from various liberals and social democrats and so it had reflected their views. Its proprietor, Paulo Rego, was a leading member of the Socialist Party who, after the events of 25 April, served for a period in the coalition government which actually penalised *República* for defying censorship laws. Rego, at that time, made no protests against censorship, nor did Soares wage a campaign for unfettered democracy. In the period following the Constituent Assembly elections, and after a growing split between the CP and the SP, *República* emerged as a strong supporter of Soares and was widely regarded as an SP paper. Rego decided to dismiss two printing workers and replace them with two SP supporters. The printworkers went on strike, occupied the plant and demanded Rego's dismissal. The paper was closed down and COPCON troops were stationed outside its offices. When it reopened after five weeks, the workers remained adamant and produced the paper themselves, forming it into a weapon of the class struggle. The Socialist Party left the coalition government in protest and Soares spoke at meetings throughout the country to defend 'democracy'. The incident was presented in the entire Western press as an attempt by the Communist Party and its supporters in the MFA to deny the Socialist Party the right to publish its own newspaper. The hue and cry over *República* was used by forces well to the right of Soares to unleash a counter-revolutionary offensive in the north of the country. In reality, the Communist Party had little to do with the takeover of *República*. It was a decision of the printworkers, many of whom were sympathisers and supporters of a semi-Maoist far-left group which was extremely hostile to the Portuguese Communist Party. That the group in question was ultra-left is beyond dispute. It should have certainly opposed the sacking of two printers, but it was politically incorrect to deny Rego, and indirectly the

SP, the right to publish *República*. For, whatever the motives, it created the impression that the country's largest political party (in terms of electoral representation) was being denied the right to produce a newspaper. Despite the CP's manipulation of the media, Soares was *not* prevented from appearing on television to air his views. So, the campaign of the SP leaders was quite calculated: it was intended to polarise the working class against the revolution by waving the banner of democracy. It was a tragic and unnecessary polarisation. And the far left paid the price in the months that followed for not understanding that the question of socialist *democracy* was not an irrelevant abstraction which could be ignored.

Soares now went on the offensive. A massive campaign against the radical officers, the CP, the far left and workers occupying factories was unleashed in the name of 'democracy'. It is now known that the CIA alerted its agents and friends throughout Western Europe for the occasion. The problem lay in the fact that the CP and the far left (with the partial exception of the Trotskyist International Communist League – LCI) found themselves still unable to respond to the SP on the question of 'democracy'. Now was the time to work out the tactics necessary to isolate the SP leaders from their base. A concerted attempt to unite the working class was desperately needed. Instead, the CP and some far-left groups attempted physically to prevent the SP from marching in Porto and Lisbon. The attempt to set up barricades to prevent the Socialist Party organising mass demonstrations was easily defeated by the presence of large numbers of pro-SP workers, but it made it increasingly difficult for any united front to counter the threat of a bourgeois offensive. Furthermore, it enabled Soares to move the party to the right without meeting any massive opposition from within his ranks.

In fact, many of the old fascist notables were finding themselves a new home in the CDS and the PPD (the self-proclaimed Centre-Democrats and Social Democrats respectively). Thus, an anti-working-class offensive, led by Carneiro for the right-wing parties, would have been more logical, and would have met a united working-class resistance. Soares had succeeded in building a party from a handful of individuals. True, he had been helped directly, and indirectly, by the Communist Party. But he had proved to be a skilful demagogue and a leader capable of understanding the importance of timing in politics. In its early days, after the overthrow of Caetano, the Socialist Party had engaged in a display of leftist rhetoric. Its original statement of aims was well to the left of the Spanish, Italian and British Communist Parties. It spoke a language which drew it closer to the mood of a growing number of workers:

> The Socialist Party fights the capitalist system and bourgeois domination ... The Socialist Party is implementing a new conception of life that can only be brought about through the construction of workers' power ...
>
> The struggle against fascism and colonialism will only be achieved by the destruction of capitalist society and the construction of socialism ... The Socialist Party refutes those who say they are social democrats but continue to preserve the status quo, the structures of capitalism and the interests of imperialism.

The fact that a social-democratic party had to construct a working-class base speaking a militant language is, in itself, a reflection of the overall political situation which developed after the overthrow of fascism in Portugal. Language such as this was precisely the petard on which the revolutionary workers and soldiers could have hoisted Soares and his friends. That they failed to do so was to become a tragedy for the Portuguese Revolution. Having carved out a base for the Socialist Party inside the working class, Soares then participated in the April 1975 elections as the leader of a party which offered both socialism and democracy. His victory gave him the necessary confidence to act as a national leader and he began increasingly to posture as the 'saviour of the nation' – he was the leader who offered the ruling class an end to 'anarchy' in the factories and the countryside and a stabilisation of the status quo. The leader he resembled was not so much the German social-democrat Noske, who drowned the workers' vanguard in blood, but Mitterrand, the suave spokesman of French social democracy.

What cannot be doubted is that those who wanted a bloody counter-revolution – groups like the fascist ELP based in neighbouring Spain – made full use of Soares's campaign and, in the name of 'democracy', in July and August started a campaign of terror and violence in the northern part of the country. The Archbishop of Braga, an ardent supporter of Portuguese fascist dictators, used democracy as an excuse to parade out on to the streets and bless those about to perpetrate acts of violence against the left. While trade unions and far-left groups were attacked as well, the main brunt of this wave of counter-revolutionary violence was borne by the Portuguese Communist Party. Its headquarters were devastated by bomb attacks in twenty-five centres, while another twelve were severely damaged. In northern towns, Communist militants were confronted by large lynch mobs who had been blessed by the Catholic Church and egged on by the right-wing parties. In the face of this assault, the Party found itself virtually paralysed. Its Central Committee meeting held on 10 August to discuss the danger in the north came up with no specific proposals to meet the threat. The most concrete measure the party decided on was to set up a fund to rebuild the headquarters which had been destroyed.

The Portuguese Communist Party was the strongest working-class party after the fall of Caetano and it had a record of struggle against the dictatorship. Its leaders and militants had suffered torture, harassment, long prison sentences and often death. Its prestige was extremely high, as was demonstrated by the reception awarded to Cunhal on his return to Lisbon from exile. Party membership when Caetano was overthrown was 5,000; within a year, it had jumped to 50,000. The majority were the more politically conscious workers in the urban centres. Many of them joined the party not to break strikes or support censorship, but to move towards socialism. More to the point, these workers had not been subjected to decades of Stalinist propaganda vilifying the far left. As a result, many of them remained responsive to the initiatives of the far-left groups.

The failure of the Communist Party to use its strong working-class base to unite the working class against its enemies was not accidental: it was the direct product of the PCP's basic ideas on the character of the struggle taking place in Portugal. It did not believe that socialism was on the agenda. In that sense, it was truer to its real beliefs than Soares. Furthermore, its actions throughout the first phase after the overthrow of fascism were designed to establish a capitalist democracy. It opposed strikes, defended press censorship, and tried to contain the mass upsurges which were shaking the country. In 1931, Trotsky had described the strike movement which followed the overthrow of the Spanish monarchy in terms apposite to the Portuguese working class in 1974:

> The overwhelming majority of the Spanish proletariat does not know what organisation means. During the time the dictatorship lasted, a

> new generation of workers grew up, lacking in independent political experience. The revolution awakens – and in this lies its force – the most backward, downtrodden, the most oppressed toiling masses. The strike is the form of their awakening. By means of the strike, various strata and groups of the proletariat announce themselves, signal to one another, verify their own strength and the strength of their foe. One layer awakens and infects another. All this together makes the present strike wave absolutely inevitable. Least of all do the communists have to be afraid of it, for this is the very expression of the creative force of the revolution. Only through these strikes, with all their mistakes, with all their 'excesses' and 'exaggerations', does the proletariat rise to its feet, assemble itself as a unit, begin to feel and to conceive itself as a living historical force.[2]

But the Portuguese communist leaders were afraid of the strike movement and attempted to put an end to it, without much success. It was at this time that the leftist demagogy of the Socialist Party enabled it to outdistance Cunhal's party. The Communist Party believed in a 'national and democratic revolution' in alliance with small and medium-size capitalists and farmers. However, the tempo of the situation was such that these formulas and tactics designed to implement them were soon outpaced by events. After the victory of 28 September 1974 – the Night of the Barricades – the PCP realised that strike-breaking was a recipe for political suicide. It stopped concentrating on its alliance with the Socialist Party and with the Popular Democrats within the government, and pushed hard instead to establish an alliance with the MFA. The latter was now in control of the state, it had overthrown Caetano, and it enjoyed a certain prestige in the country as a whole. The PCP put forward the notion of the 'People–MFA alliance'. In this alliance, the PCP was to be the main representative of the mass of working people. Together, they could prevent Portugal from making a deal with imperialists and attempt to carve out a 'third way' forward. The PCP thus shifted its positions and started a frenetic, sectarian and manipulative campaign to ensure that its members held important posts in the unions, the local councils, the state machinery and the mass media. The result

---

2 Leon Trotsky, 'The Role of Strikes in a Revolution', in *The Spanish Revolution* (New York: Pathfinder Press, 1974).

was growing friction with the Socialist Party, which was able to portray the PCP as a power-mad, Stalinist party which manipulated the masses.

The reactionary offensive in the north found the PCP paralysed. It had, by now, thrown most of its eggs into the MFA basket, but the MFA as such could not help defend it against reaction. Furthermore, the polarisations in society were being reflected more and more within the MFA and there were growing calls for the dismissal of Vasco Gonçalves because of his close links with the PCP. Certainly, the fact that the newspapers dominated by the PCP, including the *Diário de Notícias* (the Portuguese equivalent of *The Times*), insisted on presenting Gonçalves as if he were the leader of an Eastern European state while at the same time publishing articles on the joys of Bulgarian collectivisation, did not advance the cause of either Gonçalves or the PCP. If anything, it turned sections of the masses *away* from the PCP. The best way to defeat the manoeuvres of reaction was to try and establish democratic organs of popular power. But the PCP was frightened by the prospect of giving real power to the masses. At the same time, it failed completely to immobilise the peasant base of the Catholic Church in the north by a wide-ranging decree of reforms. In an area of abject poverty and mass illiteracy (60 per cent of people could neither read nor write) the Catholic Church was strong, playing on the superstitions of the peasants. The government did not write off their debts to landlords or banks. No serious attempt was made to provide subsidies and interest-free loans, though in some areas a start was made on improving education and social facilities. So far as the northern peasants were concerned, the 'People–MFA' alliance had not particularly benefited *their* people.

The failure to mobilise the masses and encourage their initiatives went hand-in-glove with another weakness: in their eagerness to cement an alliance with the MFA, the PCP failed during the early stages to appreciate that there was a growing crisis in the army. This provided an unexpected turn to Portuguese events after the July–August days, which were described in the *Daily Telegraph* of 14 August as 'the most heartening thing to have happened in Europe for years'. Communists were being physically assaulted, their headquarters were being subjected to terrorist attacks and the *Daily Telegraph* and most of the British press were standing by and applauding, not to mention misreporting these events. The only European bourgeois paper which managed to preserve a certain balance was the French daily, *Le Monde*. The July–August days came to an end with the resignation of Gonçalves, brought about by moderate forces within the MFA who were in league with Soares. The new prime minister was Admiral Pinheiro de Azevedo, who took over on 29 August 1975 and on 19 September organised the Sixth Provisional Government. Within eighteen months, Portugal had witnessed the rise and fall of six governments. No one could deny that there was a severe political crisis in the country.

However, any hopes on the part of the ruling class that the fall of Gonçalves would mean stability were soon shown to be completely illusory. The objective force of the workers' struggles was leading more and more towards dual power in the factories. The strikes-occupation-workers' control pattern had spread beyond the massive industrial combines in Lisbon and was extending to middle-sized firms, and the distribution sector. Similar actions had already led to the nationalisations of the banks and the insurance companies – the first capitalist country in Western Europe where these crucially important sectors had been taken over by the state. The rapid development of workers' and tenants' committees linked the factories to the neighbourhoods and the communities. However, the fact that, in some of these commissions, the influence of the far left was so strong led some groups to imagine that it represented an indication of the overall relationship of forces. This was a serious error, as it led to underestimating the strength of the Socialist Party and overestimating the implantation of the far left. Nonetheless, the continued activity of the working class, while uneven and suffering from a lack of centralisation and political focus, was seriously hampering the efficient operation of the Portuguese economy. To the political and economic crisis was now to be added another dimension, far more serious in character as it threatened the cohesion of the state apparatus itself.

The army constitutes the spinal cord of every state apparatus. If damaged, it adversely affects every other organ and induces a state of paralysis. Even in the bourgeois parliamentary states of Western Europe, North America, Japan and India, it is, in the last analysis, the coercive force on which the state rests, to be used only in cases of emergency. Engels's definition of the state as 'armed bodies of men' retains its essential validity. The army and its structures are thus of vital importance for both the oppressor and the oppressed. No revolution can be successful unless these structures are weakened, pierced and ultimately destroyed.

Every successful revolution, starting from the Russian, has had to confront this problem. For revolutionaries in the West today, it poses a very real problem, for, clearly, the idea that the armies of capital in the West will be weakened by inter-imperialist wars as in 1914 or even in 1945 is ludicrous. The Portuguese experience was, therefore, of tremendous importance as it was the first post-war occasion where a growing political awareness was taking place in the army. The causes of this can only be explained by seeing world politics as an interrelated process. The liberation struggle of oppressed African peasants, city-dwellers and workers had played an important part in the overthrow of fascism in Portugal, almost inverting the process which followed the liberation struggle in Algeria. There, a war pursued by a Socialist Party government and not opposed by the Communist Party had been lost as well, but this had resulted in the overthrow of the Fourth Republic and the emergence of a right-wing, Bonapartist military saviour. His seizure of power had taken place without being challenged by any political strikes by the French working class. In Portugal, the situation was completely the opposite.

The polarisation of the Portuguese working class as a result of the 1975 elections was reflected within the upper reaches of the MFA. The two positions were polarised around documents prepared by different factions within the MFA. The first document was drafted by Melo Antunes and Vítor Alves. It was signed by seven other MFA officers, including the two regional commanders, Charais in Coimbra and Correia in Évora. The growing breakdown of discipline in the army had led to soldiers refusing to obey orders and beginning a *saneamento* within the most hallowed institution of the Portuguese state. A number of reactionary officers had been dismissed. In early August, Jaime Neves, the colonel at the head of the Amadora commandos, near Lisbon, was removed, but managed to get himself reinstated with the help of COPCON; Carvalho, Antunes and Alves decided that things had gone too far. Their document reflected their social-democratic preoccupations. The 'Group of Nine', as they came to be known, were aligned politically with Soares, though some of them probably felt that he had carried his anti-leftist offensive too far. The 'Group of Nine' were the Girondins of the Portuguese revolutionary process. They considered that the revolution had achieved a great deal and should now be subordinated to the electoral results. Antunes and his comrades believed in bourgeois, not socialist democracy. Their document was fairly explicit:

> Things have moved too fast to avoid tearing the existing social and cultural fabric. The social and economic organisation of the small and medium bourgeoisie quickly disintegrated, without new structures being created to guarantee the management of production and distribution units and to maintain a minimum of morality in the relationships among all Portuguese.
>
> Hand in hand with this, we have witnessed a progressive deterioration of the state machinery. Wild and anarchistic forms of management have appeared everywhere, even within the MFA itself. Well-organised partisan organisations eager to seize the various power centres have tried to profit from the disorder ...
>
> The country is profoundly shaken.

The document went on to demand the removal of the Gonçalves government and attacked the crude manipulations of the Fifth Division, which was in charge of propaganda. Interestingly enough, while attacking the 'bureaucratic and totalitarian model' of Eastern Europe, the Nine also stated that Western-style social democracy was not sufficient: what was needed was a peaceful, national transition to 'socialism'. In other words, the authors of the document wanted to stop the revolutionary process, but not through a counter-revolution. Rather, they wanted to institutionalise or freeze the *existing* relationship of class forces through creating and strengthening bourgeois democratic institutions.

Four days later, on 13 August, another document appeared, published by a group of COPCON officers and entitled 'A Working Proposal for a Political Programme'. It was a populist text, but it called for strengthening the organs of popular power and the creation of a Popular Assembly. It attacked Gonçalves and the PCP from the left, thus objectively isolating the Fifth Provisional Government by constituting the second half of the pincer. However, the COPCON document attacked all political parties, while laying stress on the 'MFA–People Alliance' and calling for ending all dependence on imperialism. The COPCON document also called for the election of officers and argued that this was the only way in which discipline could be maintained. Many of the individual demands of the COPCON document were correct, but its utopian and populist character meant that it could not be seen as a realistic strategic alternative to the Antunes manifesto. The Girondins of the Portuguese Revolution had a more coherent approach than its Jacobins. The key weakness of the COPCON programme was its conception of organs of popular power moving forward on the one hand and the MFA guaranteeing their success on the other. What this left out of account was *politics*. Political parties do not exist as abstract entities hanging in mid-air. They reflect the divisions between and within different social classes. They cannot be wished away. If the embryonic organisms of dual power had developed and been extended, it would have been utterly bureaucratic to prevent different political currents or parties from speaking or arguing for their political positions. Similarly, the whole notion of the 'MFA–People Alliance' was both populist and apolitical. Real political differences existed inside the MFA. The COPCON document itself was an oblique response to the Group of Nine. The question it raised was simple: what section of the people should align with which section of the MFA? And, it might be added, on what political basis?

However, the fact that two politically counterposed documents were produced by military officers and circulated within the MFA was in itself a unique historic occasion. Here was the officer caste of a bourgeois army debating its differences on paper. Of course, both sides were aware that the only other method of conducting debates within the military was with tanks and heavy artillery and neither wanted that for obvious reasons. The two documents were soon circulating throughout the Portuguese Army and being discussed in a fairly democratic fashion. More important, soldiers' assemblies were putting them to a vote after discussions. A clear political polarisation was taking place within the army and around written documents. The result was a sharp acceleration in the political maturity within the army. This created a further differentiation and led in early September to the announcement of a new organisation. This was the Soldados Unidos Vencerão (SUV – Soldiers United Will Win). It was the first organisation of rank-and-file uniformed soldiers and represented the extreme left wing of the radicalisation in the army. It was the answer from below to the MFA, which was throughout restricted to the officers.

SUV made its first appearance in the northern city of Porto. Its first statement, issued on 8 September, explained that it was organising soldiers to fight against reactionary officers in the barracks:

> For more than six weeks it has been clear that reaction is raising its head in the barracks. Many facts show this: the purge of left-wing soldiers... the attacks on comrades who struggled for popular power in the barracks, the fact that the ADUs (Assemblies of Unit Delegates) are being turned into disciplinary instruments which condemn comrades instead of being what they should be: organs which discuss and struggle for the interests of the workers in uniform, for pay increases, free transport, purging of reactionary elements in the barracks, links with the base organisations...

The formation of SUV presented the state with a serious challenge to its authority. It soon spread from the north to the centre and the south of Portugal. Its manifesto and appeal (printed as an Appendix at the end of this section) was a conscious break with all past ambiguities, and a mass expression of the class struggle inside the army. It organised its own demonstrations. Soldiers regularly defied their officers to attend these occasions, which turned out to be large affairs, swelled as they were by workers and the left groups. 'Portugal will not be the Chile of Europe' was the most popular chant of the soldiers. Coming from their mouths, it had a somewhat different impact than when it was shouted by the far left.

The Sixth Provisional Government was confronted with increasing opposition. Within the army, the SUV was growing, and naval ratings were also beginning to join its ranks. The government responded by disbanding regiments, transferring leftist officers and limiting repression. On a number of occasions, these measures backfired. The government had set itself a primary task, namely, 'to re-establish order, authority and discipline' in the army, the factories and the media. It was a government dominated by supporters of the Group of Nine. Its aim was to contain the working-class upsurge, and its main backer inside the working-class movement was the Socialist Party. In fact, as the early attempts of the Sixth Provisional Government to take over the workers' radio stations collapsed because soldiers who had been sent to clear out occupying workers instead *sided* with them, it was obvious that tensions were increasing inside the

Socialist Party. During the summer, it had been in opposition to the government. Now, in the autumn, it was backing the Azevedo government, and Soares's speeches were concentrating on preaching 'order' and attacking 'anarchy'. The Socialist Party had drifted rapidly to the right. A non-Marxist commentator, Tony Banks, wrote in the official organ of the British Labour Party, *Labour Weekly*, on 12 September 1975:

> Since the April election, when the SP won thirty-eight per cent of the votes, Dr Soares has led his party towards the right. There is mounting dissent within the SP about the party programme and the personal leadership of Soares.
>
> There have been many expulsions of those expressing their discontent, and although the SP campaigned on a Socialist programme, its growing denunciations of nationalisation measures carried out by the MFA seem to indicate a readiness on the part of the SP to stand aside from attempts to construct a popular front and to indulge in the sort of inflammatory anti communism that has given rise to violence in the North . . .
>
> My own feeling is that the SP is now being used by the old ruling class to give it respectability and to thwart any real progress towards socialism.

The autumn of 1975 provided yet another opportunity to unite the Portuguese workers' movement against the reactionary offensive in the north and those who wished to extend it to the south. In the first few weeks of October, the crisis had deepened and the decomposition of the army appeared to be gathering speed. Sixteen out of twenty military units in Lisbon now had elected representatives who met regularly to discuss a common policy. Supplies of arms to reactionary troops from the Beirolas arsenal were blocked by left-wing soldiers. Strikes by steelworkers and agricultural workers supported the soldiers. If a civil war had been unleashed by the right at this stage, it is obvious that Lisbon and the south would have fought with the left, and the Socialist Party would have experienced a rift in its ranks if it had attempted to do otherwise. But the right did not launch a civil war, for just that reason. They were aware that, if there was a straight left–right split, there would be massive pressure on the moderates in the MFA either to remain aloof or to back the workers. As the Azevedo government re-enlisted and re-armed the demobilised 'elite troops' it also passed decrees calling on the workers' militias to disarm. An innocent observer in Lisbon in October could well have imagined that this was a country on the verge of a semi-spontaneous seizure of power by a working class led by the far left and a rank-and-file soldiers' movement. The observer could be forgiven for dreaming, but far-left groups aspiring to lead the Portuguese masses could not be taken too seriously for believing the same. Since the events which unfolded in November saw the far left at the centre of the stage in Lisbon, it is useful to discuss the various groups to the left of the Communist Party.

A dominant feature of left-wing politics since May 1968 has been the emergence of a vanguard of workers and students who have either outgrown the political tutelage of the traditional social-democratic and Stalinist apparatuses within the European workers' movement or have never been attracted to them. It is this group on which the far left is based in Europe and North America. Portugal was no exception, but, here, the rapid pace at which the political crisis developed saw also the growth of the far-left groups. The traditions to which they aligned themselves were Maoism, Trotskyism, syndicalism or, in some cases, a mixture of all three. The dominant characteristic of MES (Left Socialist Movement), the largest far-left group, was its centrism: a constant vacillation between reformist and revolutionary positions. The MES was composed essentially of three different layers. Its origins were in radical Catholicism and its leadership came predominantly from this milieu. It had an important base among the textile and engineering workers, and it had a fair sprinkling of Marxist intellectuals. While it participated in most local far-left demonstrations, there was a strong tendency on the part of the national leadership to adapt to the Communist Party, particularly during the period of the Fifth Provisional Government of Vasco Gonçalves. The two far-left groups which emerged from 'armed struggle' against the Caetano regime were the LUAR, led by the legendary 'bandit' Palma Inácio, and the Revolutionary Party of the Proletariat (Revolutionary Brigades) – PRP-BR. The latter produced a regular weekly paper, *Revolução*. Its politics were a combination of populism and syndicalism, and its strategic thrust was largely ultra-left. It had some working-class support in the south and inside COPCON. It also had illusions about the MFA and idolised Otelo Carvalho. For a while it believed in building revolutionary unions, thus isolating itself from the mass of workers.

The Maoists were divided into four groups, the most influential among them being the Popular Democratic Union (UDP). It did not raise the slogan of workers' power but, like the PCP (which it denounced as 'socialist-fascist') it raised 'national-democratic' demands. It had an important following within the working class. The other dominant group was the MRPP, which consisted largely of university students and the children of old Salazarist functionaries. Its demented political line led it to identify the Portuguese Communist Party as the main internal enemy and the 'Soviet social-imperialists' as the dominant external threat. As a result, it participated in the anti-communist mobilisations of reaction in the north.

The smallest of the far-left groups was the Trotskyist International Communist League (LCI). Its political line, especially in relation to the masses, was the most refined and it was not, except for a limited period, afflicted with the disease which characterised the entire far left in Portugal: anti-parliamentary cretinism. But the LCI was small, with a weak foothold in the working class and therefore somewhat susceptible to being overwhelmed by the rest of the non-Maoist far left. It was, in addition, hampered by the lack of a regular weekly newspaper. As the Portuguese section of the Fourth International, it received support from its comrades elsewhere in the continent, but the failure of the latter to insist on the *political* necessity of a weekly revolutionary Marxist paper adversely affected the enormous potential which the LCI possessed. The LCI understood the importance of elections to the Constituent Assembly, while the rest of the major groups tended to underestimate the importance of national politics. In 1931, Trotsky had sharply criticised the Soviet Communist Party newspaper *Pravda* for a similar blindness in the context of Spain:

> By speaking *only* of the seven-hour day, of factory committees and arming the workers, by ignoring 'politics' and by not having a single word to say in all its articles about elections to the Cortes, *Pravda* goes all the way to meet anarcho-syndicalism, fosters it, covers up for it . . . To counterpose the slogan of *arming the workers* to the reality of the political processes that grip the masses at their vitals means to isolate oneself from the masses – and the masses from arms.[3]

---

3 Leon Trotsky, 'The Spanish Revolution and the Dangers Threatening It', in *The Spanish Revolution*.

A similar error was made by the MES and the PRP-BR in the important period opened up by the fall of the Gonçalves government. The non-Maoist far-left groups had certainly understood the need for unity, but they sought to unite the proletarian vanguard based in the south, not the masses. On 25 August 1975, the Revolutionary United Front (FUR) was introduced at a press conference. The significant feature of this Front was that it included the Portuguese Communist Party and a leftist branch of the Socialist Party, the FSP, in addition to the PRP, MES, LUAR and the LCI. The main reason why the CP entered the Front was to use it to drum up some last-minute support for the faltering government of Vasco Gonçalves. Indeed, the weak political basis of the FUR was strongly criticised by the Secretariat of the Fourth International. It made five cogent points of criticism, which effectively summed up the weaknesses of the FUR:

> (a) The accord in effect sanctioned the CP's policy of supporting the Government and maintaining the unity of the MFA, precisely at the moment that the MFA was being ripped apart by the pressure of antagonistic class forces.
> (b) The accord mentioned no concrete objective that would permit the unification of the working class and the actual stimulation of workers' self-defence and self-organisation.
> (c) Because of this absence, and because of the lack of proposals to the SP (a party that currently groups together nearly half of the proletariat), the accord sanctioned the present division of the workers' movement and did not contribute to surmounting this major obstacle to the development of the revolutionary process.
> (d) Furthermore, the 'unitary accord' envisaged the formation of a 'front' in which the MFA is included on the same footing as the autonomous organs, parties, and revolutionary organisations of the workers' movement. This not only appeared as a stamp of approval of the CP's project of creating a 'democratic and socialist popular front', but also fell within the framework of the perspective of integrating the autonomous organs in opposition to their real independence of the institutions of the bourgeois state.
> (e) Thus, the accord could easily serve the objective of the CP (as it did during the 27 August demonstration), which is to utilise the weight of the workers' vanguard to negotiate compromises on the

level of the state apparatus, the government, the army, and the MFA under the best possible conditions.

Now, the relationship of forces permitted revolutionaries to seize this opportunity to lead the CP to take a position on the implementation of the essential tasks necessary for the progress of the revolution. Here, again, the lack of concrete objectives and the concessions made to the CP's political orientation prevented the lessons of the policy of the CP leadership and the rupture of the 'front' from being clearly drawn before the masses. Once again, the Portuguese far left, hypnotised by the situation in the army, ignored the crucial question of winning the masses. Lisbon and its enclaves were, naturally, of key importance, but they were not the whole of Portugal. The FUR was an organisation which reflected the chauvinism of the vanguard (the Portuguese Communist Party withdrew from it after a week of 'unity') and an inability to construct a real united front, which was urgently needed. In the face of an offensive by capital, revolutionaries propose a united front of *all* workers' organisations, including the most moderate and those with right-wing, class-collaborationist leaders. The FUR's failure even to appreciate this problem was shown at one of its demonstrations where the main chant was: 'Down with the Constituent Assembly'.

October and November saw a growing opposition to the Sixth Government within the working class. Land occupations increased rapidly, and 600,000 hectares were occupied in a month alone. Workers occupied the Ministry of Social Security to protest the presence of a former PIDE official. On 16 November, there was a demonstration of 100,000 workers. Coming on the heels of the victory of the construction workers, the most popular slogans were those directed against Azevedo and his government. The bakers were threatening to follow the construction workers if the Ministry of Labour did not meet their demands.

At the same time, talk of coups and countercoups dominated the press. Soares alleged that a left-wing coup was being prepared. The left-wing soldiers and SUV countered with similar charges of a right-wing coup. The PRP and the MES, excited by these developments, spoke of seizing power. There were still no proper representative organs of dual power. On 8 November, the PRP made a public declaration on the question which was clearly preoccupying the minds of its leaders:

> The PRP defends armed insurrection ... The objective conditions for a victorious armed uprising exist today in Portugal. Knowing the devotion to the revolutionary process of a great many officers of the army and navy, and knowing also the positions which they hold at the level of unit commands, it is easy to think of a scheme based on a sortie by these troops, in an operation of the type of 25 April.

This was, presumably, an elaboration of their statement of 30 September where they had announced that: 'It is now time for the revolutionary forces and the workers to pose the question of an insurrection.' The sentiments were repeated on 10 November. Not only was this a fantasy, but it was supposed to be carried out by army and navy officers. The friends of the PRP in Britain, with whom the latter was in close touch, were the Socialist Workers' Party (then the International Socialists). Tony Cliff, the SWP's central theoretician, attempted to give some fraternal, though belated, advice to the PRP and warn them against premature insurrection. The advice was ignored. The internal regime of the PRP was, like its politics, commandist, and differences were not tolerated or encouraged.

Carvalho had refused to use COPCON against the construction workers. He had accepted, and, on occasions, even urged, the fraternisation of soldiers and workers. He had made a number of pronouncements, some of them thoroughly confused, but nonetheless in favour of socialism. He was, and this is the important factor, seen by tens of thousands of workers and soldiers as the only coherent alternative to the Group of Nine. In reality, his alternative, in so far that it existed, was extremely sentimental and subjectivist and his view of the revolutionary process was tinged with romanticism. Sometimes he sided with the far left (especially the PRP, which, in its turn, referred to him in glowing terms: 'We underline the courage of this soldier, who is always ready to advance without fear', wrote *Revolução* on 8 May 1975); on other occasions, he flirted with the PCP; then again, there were the constant attempts to reach an accommodation with Melo Antunes and the Group of Nine. It is possible that all this reflected a sincere desire to unite these differing forces against reaction, but it was a confused sincerity as it ignored the primacy of *politics*. Carvalho had been one of the central organisers of 25 April 1974. He had operated with Jacobin skill and succeeded, but he had not been able to move politically beyond that experience in any clearcut and cohesive fashion.

The Portuguese Revolution was, in many ways, a combination of old, very old and new. The French Revolution was mingled with the Russian, though while there were Girondins and Jacobins and Mensheviks in plenty, the number of Bolsheviks (real, not imitation models) was small and not limited to a single organisation. But there were also problems which the Bolsheviks had not faced: the stranglehold of bourgeois democracy in Western Europe and the contrast this offered to Stalinism in the East. This division had been emphasised by the right-Menshevik Soares:

> What divides us is not Marx or the construction of a classless society... what divides us is Stalin, the totalitarian concept of the state, the all-powerful single party, the rights of man, and the problems of freedom. What divides us is not 'nationalisations' or 'agrarian reform' but how these are to be controlled – by a bureaucracy dependent on centralised power, or by the democratic control of the workers wherever it spontaneously emerges. What divides us is not the neighbourhood committee or other forms of direct democracy (these are included in our programme) but the question of their democratic representation...

This is what the Portuguese Kerensky said, but he received no adequate response from the Stalinist Cunhal nor, it should be added, from the main far-left groups.

Carvalho's reply was to declare that direct democracy and the MFA were 'good' and political parties were 'bad'. Throughout the upsurge, Carvalho's actions were determined by the relationship of forces. If the workers' strikes were strong, he would side with them. If Gonçalves was weakening, then he would help to topple him. If the Group of Nine was gaining ground in the upper echelons of the MFA, he would submit to their pressures. A good man? Yes. A well-meaning and brave man? Certainly! But a revolutionary leader of the masses? No, alas not. But none of this detracted from his popularity within the vanguard of the Portuguese working class and the army. 'Otelo is with us' was a common sentiment and within limits it was true, for, although Carvalho was unable to provide any real leadership for taking the mass struggle forward, he was uncompromisingly against any repression of the workers or the soldiers. In that sense, his presence in the apparatus was of some importance and for that reason the basis of his popularity was not irrational.

While the PRP was the far-left group most in favour of armed insurrection, the other major grouping, MES, was not far behind them. In its weekly paper, *Poder Popular*, of 5–11 November the MES leaders gave their considered views of the political situation:

> The military, political and economic conditions exist for the development of a popular offensive. From the military point of view, the right does not possess the soldiers to carry out a coup; from the economic point of view, the rising cost of living, unemployment and the satisfaction of the most immediate needs are problems that cannot be resolved without a revolutionary regime; from the political point of view, illusions about bourgeois democracy, illusions about the reformists, are beginning to be clearly overcome and the workers finally understand that it will not be the politicians who will make the revolution in their name; only the masses through their organisation and their struggle will be able to make the socialist revolution triumph.

The same issue of the newspaper which contained this simplistic nonsense contained an even worse theoretical atrocity. After linking the Socialist Party of Soares to fascism, the MES weekly went on to declare that

> consequently, we cannot separate our slogan 'Death to the ELP [the fascist "Portuguese Liberation Army"] and those who support it' from the slogan 'Down with Social Democracy'. That, comrades, is why the MES says – and this is ever more correct and appears ever more clearly – that Social Democracy is a phase in the transition to fascism.

This delirious ultra-leftism showed the far left at its weakest and most vulnerable; but it was only the strongest expression of a political line that had been in operation from the spring of 1975.

It was Carvalho's removal as the military commander of Lisbon by the military High Command, now in the grip of the Group of Nine, that precipitated the crisis of 25 November. This date marked the end of the most dynamic phase of the unfinished Portuguese revolution. Lourenço, the officer who replaced Carvalho, was reluctant to play the role. He changed his mind at least once but was persuaded by his political mentors. The Army High Command, under the control of the moderates and the right, was determined to start a purge of leftist officers and soldiers from the army and navy. On 23 November, Lourenço's appointment was confirmed. It was obvious that those opposed to the left were expecting some sort of a reaction. Many leftist officers were convinced that a right-wing coup was being prepared. In any case, given the general rhetoric of the far left and the provocations of the right, the paratroopers at Tancos (the latest converts to a radical solution in the country), revolted and occupied their base in solidarity with Carvalho. The right-wing officers had been gathering at the military base at Amadora, from where they were preparing to quell any insurrections in favour of Carvalho. According to a statement from the latter on the November events, Eanes and Neves were expecting the Artillery Regiment (RALIS) and the COPCON units to protest on the streets, but were surprised by the Tancos reaction. The COPCON and RALIS remained disciplined and while they took some important positions in the city, they were not instructed to go on the offensive. The Amadora commandos led by Jaime Neves, numbering 800, moved into Lisbon and reoccupied the positions held by RALIS. A number of left-wing officers and activists were arrested, and the media under the control of the far left was retaken. It was a *political* rather than a military defeat. And it was a defeat for infantile and ultra-left political predictions and analysis. Many left-wing soldiers clearly believed the far-left propaganda which proclaimed that most workers were ready for a seizure of power. The soldiers, acting alone, responded in the only way they knew: militarily. They were easily contained, and a State of Emergency was declared. This premature action by the Tancos paratroopers provided the pretext for activating a plan which Soares and the Group of Nine had long been preparing, which involved stabilising the army and the economy. Within twenty-four hours, the moderates were in complete control. There was no general strike, no mass demonstration. No Lisbon Commune either, and just as well. It would have been a short-lived and messy affair.

The quotation from Lenin at the head of this essay retains all its validity. *Without the independent activity of the masses, there can be no revolution.* That there was a developing pre-revolutionary mood in Portugal is undeniable, but for that to be transformed into a revolutionary situation needed the masses. Their radicalisation would have been decisive in aiding the decomposition within the army. The correct response to Carvalho's dismissal would have been to organise assemblies of his soldiers to discuss the issue. If they opposed it, as he maintains they would have, and the army still insisted on replacing him, then a call for solidarity from the workers should have been made and a general strike organised. But, even here, the only force capable of calling a proper strike was the PCP and not the far left, despite illusions to the contrary. And for the PCP to call a general strike which would have involved a show of independent mass actions was almost inconceivable.

The Portuguese laboratory finally exploded on 25 November 1974. The wrong combination of ingredients was responsible for its sudden end. The only way in which the legitimacy of the Constituent Assembly – and of the Soares leadership, plus the Group of Nine – could have been challenged was through the emergence of centralised organs of dual power which organised the *masses*. These did not exist. What did exist were popular committees, which organised the most advanced sectors of the masses, but which were manipulated by the PCP and the far left.

The legitimacy of the Soares project would have been challenged immediately after the Constituent Assembly elections. Given the scope of the PSP's official programme, the correct strategy would have been to take it at face value and demand its *implementation*. The PCP should have proposed that Soares become prime minister of a provisional government and Gonçalves the chief of staff, after the April 1975 elections. The formation of a workers' government, committed to socialist policies, would have accelerated mass radicalisation and enabled the formation of factory committees and popular committees to implement these policies. The character of these committees would have been strengthened when Soares reneged on his pledges, or if reaction had unleashed an armed counter-revolutionary offensive. In that sense, 1917 is not irrelevant when discussing Portugal in 1975. Kerensky was, for a period, defended by the Bolsheviks, who demanded the dismissal of the bourgeois ministers. The Constituent Assembly in Russia could only have been dispersed once the fully fledged soviets had conquered power!

It is an interesting paradox that, while the French Communist Party derailed the general strike of May 1968 by subordinating it to elections, the Portuguese Communist Party showed its contempt for the masses by attempting to bypass the much *more* democratic procedures for a Constituent Assembly in favour of bureaucratic manipulation of sections of a weakened state apparatus. In Portugal, the Constituent Assembly was, for a period, a more accurate reflection of the overall relationship of forces than in Russia in 1917. It focused the hopes of the majority of Portuguese after decades of fascism. It produced a constitution that claimed to be both democratic and socialist. A development like this could not be bypassed. The development of soviets would have to be geared to the contradictions present in the Constituent Assembly and the 'unfinished' character of the upheaval that overthrew Caetano. The PCP was remarkably blind to this fact. Most of the far left was intoxicated with the scent of insurrection. A Marxist political strategy was only to be developed with the benefit of hindsight.

25 November marked the beginning of a new phase, but the governments which followed did not engage in large-scale denationalisations *à la* Pinochet, nor could they dismantle workers' control bodies in a number of industries. In the first four months of the next year, nearly 400 factories went on strike against the austere new policies. What was ended was the situation in the army and on the estates, where a new law was passed prohibiting any further seizures. Bourgeois democracy was partially stabilised, despite the disappointment of many on the extreme right and the far left, and elections were organised in April 1976 for a legislative assembly. These produced a clear majority for all the workers' organisations: the SP, CP and far left received a combined vote of 53 per cent, thus expressing the overall relationship of social forces which 25 November was unable to destroy. The SP and the CP captured the south with large majorities (60 per cent in Lisbon, 76 per cent in Setúbal, 75 per cent in Beja, 73 per cent in Évora) and the PPD and CDS captured the northern provinces (61 per cent in Bragança, 53 per cent in Braga, 63 per cent in Viseu, 57 per cent in Vila Real), thus demonstrating the inability of the SP and CP to win over the peasants. However, Soares formed a minority government and refused to ally himself with either the PCP or the PPD. In December 1977, he was brought down by a bloc of the PCP and the right on the question of his readiness to accept all the conditions of the International Monetary Fund for bailing out the ailing capitalist economy. 25 November represented a severe setback, but not a defeat for the masses. To recover all the lost ground, it will be necessary to assimilate all the lessons of the Portuguese experience and

incorporate them in a revolutionary strategy which can win over the masses. The revolutionary left failed the test in Portugal. Whether it can meet the challenge likely to be thrown up in France and Spain will depend on its willingness to learn from its errors in Portugal.

Appendix 1: The SUV Manifesto

1. The SUV (Soldiers United Will Win) is a united anti-capitalist and anti-imperialist front that arises at a time when fascist reaction is organising again, making use of the hesitations and divisions introduced among the workers as well as the policies of governments that are neither willing nor able to defend the just demands raised in the struggles of the workers and peasants, of whom we, soldiers, are a part.

2. Already, on several occasions, we have made concessions to the bourgeoisie, particularly by subordinating our struggle to the alliance with the MFA (Armed Forces Movement), a movement of officers which, because of its contradictions and hesitations in the past, serves a counter-revolutionary policy today. This has cost us not only the abandonment and hostility of important layers of the population (notably among our peasant brothers) but also the demoralisation of many fighters in our own ranks, and has resulted in sluggishness in face of the reactionary offensive inside and outside the barracks.

The SUV sets itself the task of unleashing an independent offensive on a class basis:

– To struggle for a democratic life in the barracks by imposing the election and democratic functioning of the ADUs (Assemblies of Unit Delegates), the free circulation of the workers' and people's press and propaganda, and the holding of general assemblies of soldiers each time that we call for them;

– To struggle for the formation of soldiers' commissions: organs of power of the workers in uniform in the barracks, elected and recallable at any time by general assemblies of soldiers;

– To stimulate and deepen the liaison with the organs of popular power (workers' commissions, village councils, tenants' commissions) strengthening the power of the exploited through Popular Assemblies.

– For the expulsion of reactionary officers;

- Against all attempts to purge progressive military men;
- For the improvement of the living conditions of the soldiers (against the poor pay, for free transport, for common quarters and mess halls, against militarist discipline).

3. The SUV struggles alongside all the workers for the preparation of conditions that will permit the destruction of the bourgeois army and the creation of the armed forces of workers' power: the revolutionary people's army.

> ALWAYS, ALWAYS BY THE SIDE OF THE PEOPLE –
> THAT IS OUR WATCHWORD!
> WORKERS, PEASANTS, SOLDIERS,
> AND SAILORS, UNITED WE WILL WIN!

Appendix 2: SUV Appeal to the Workers and Soldiers of Europe

We Portuguese proletarians are now going through some particularly difficult moments in our revolutionary struggle against the bourgeoisie, capitalism and imperialism.

A year and a half after the fall of the fascist dictatorship, capitalist reaction is redoubling its attacks in the factories, the fields, the neighbourhoods, and the barracks, utilising either insidious demagogy or open terrorist violence, but always with the same goal: to stop the progress of the alliance of workers, peasants, soldiers and sailors, an alliance leading to the establishment of workers' power; to prevent at any price the abolition of the class privileges it has won through exploitation and oppression; to prevent its disappearance as a ruling class.

The bourgeoisie and the capitalists still have powerful weapons; two of these are especially threatening, unless we are able to fight back in time. The first is our disunity, our inability to push our independent offensive through to the end on a real class basis. On many occasions, we have made this concession to the class enemy, notably by subordinating our struggle to the alliance with the MFA, a movement of officers whose contradictions and hesitations have cost us the abandonment and hostility of important layers of the population (especially the rural population), the demoralisation of many fighters in our own ranks, and sluggishness in face of the reactionary offensive inside and outside the barracks.

We must counter this danger with our own class organisation, by breaking down the militarist hierarchy and raising an overall challenge to the power of the state apparatus of the bourgeoisie, of which the army is an integral part. The creation of the SUV and the demonstration the SUV organised on 10 September represent important steps in this direction, especially when it is recalled that this formidable response of 50,000 workers (among them 1,500 soldiers and sailors who marched in uniform despite the escalation of militarist manoeuvres and repression) took place in a region that has been the centre of the terrorist offensive and of reactionary demagogy.

The second powerful weapon in the hands of our class enemies is undoubtedly the broad international support from which it benefits. That is the result of the common interests that link the exploiters throughout the world. Recent history shows us how powerful and terrible this weapon is, this counter-revolutionary potential of imperialism. It is up to us, proletarians of Europe, to determine the forms of battle, which can be waged only through our class solidarity, through the organisation of our national struggles into a single international battle to make sure that any attack by imperialism receives the response it deserves: the indestructible force of the entire international workers' and people's movement.

Today it is Portugal. Tomorrow it will be Spain, France, Italy, and others. Difficult battles are approaching. Against the common enemy our common solidarity is urgent and necessary; it is for this reason that we address you.

LONG LIVE MILITANT AND COMBATIVE
PROLETARIAN INTERNATIONALISM!
PORTUGAL SHALL NOT BE THE CHILE OF EUROPE!
WORKERS, PEASANTS, SOLDIERS, AND SAILORS,
UNITED WE WILL WIN!

Soldados Unidos Vencerão, 12 September 1975.

Index

Page numbers in bold denote figures.

A questã o agrá ria em Portugal (Cunhal) 79
Abreu, Manuel 101
absentee landlords 100, 102, 107, 128, 146, 151–2, 157, 159–60, 242–6
Acção Nacional Popular (Popular National Action) 38–9, 81, 82, 83
administrative districts 151
administrative power 236
African colonies xxv, 5, 28, 29
African wars 5, 32–3, 43, 44, 46–8, 49, 58, 66, 109, 203–5, 220, 265, 267, 273
The Age (journal) xxiii–xxiv
agricultural labourers 145–57, **148**, **156**, 239
   association 155–6
   barracks 154
   cultural backwardness 150
   education 148–50
   emigration 153–4, 160–2, 165–6, 245–6
   general conditions 146
   great strike movement, 1962 152–3
   labour contract 240
   malnutrition 146
   numbers 153, 244
   social conditions 148–51
   unemployment 146
   wages 155, 240, 244
   working hours 155
Agricultural Labourers Union 240, 241

Águas de Moura 153
Air Force 65, 238, 252
airports, closure xvii
Alentejo, the 103, 145–57, 146, **148**, **156**, 176, 239, 240–1
   absentee landlords 102, 151–2, 157
   barracks 154
   cultural backwardness 150
   districts 145n1, 151
   education in 148–50
   emigration 146, 153–4
   general conditions 146
   grain production 242, 243–4
   great strike movement, 1962 152–3
   hunting preserves 147
   malnutrition 146
   small owners 151–2
   social conditions 148–51
   unemployment 146
   wildcat takeovers 242–6
Alfonso de Albuquerque (frigate) 48
Algeria 293
Alice (Trás-os-Montes resident) 164–6
Aljube prison 78, 79
Alves, José 77–8
Alves, Vítor 92, 293
Amélia de Orleães, Queen 186n4
AMI (Military Intervention Force) 253, 256
amnesty, 1941 69
Anarchists 60

Index

Angola 5, 8, 28, 42, 47, 109, 140, 166, 204, 205, 250–1, 265, 273–4
   Alvor Agreement 191–3, **192**, 200–2
   transition to independence 200–3
anti-fascist forces, unity of 57
anti-working class offensive 287
Antunes, Ernesto Augusto de Melo, Jr xviii, 8–9, 31, 41–4, 46, 92, 121, 193, 197, 218n6, 231, 232–3, 234, 251, 259, 273–4, 293–4
Applied Magnetics, crisis 137–9
Araújo, José de Almeida 122
Argozelo mine 172
armed forces xxix
   Communist Party cells within 65–6
   decomposition 297
   demoralisation 46–9
   political awareness 293
   proliferation of revolutionary organisations within 251–2
   radicalisation 252, 282, 295
   role of 53
   strength 265–6
Armed Forces Assembly 217
Armed Forces Movement (MFA) xvii, xviii, xxvi, 19n7, 237
   5th Infantry Regiment mutiny 34
   aims 36
   and Cabinet decisions 90
   call for return to barracks 231, 234–5, 258
   class base 66
   communications 31
   and Communist Party's 1965 programme 55–7
   coordinating committee 41, 273
   Costa Gomes's links to 33–4
   CP support 66, 259, 278–9, 283
   and decolonisation 203–7
   democracy faction xxvii
   dissension rumours 211
   divergent class interests 235
   first open act of defiance 28
   fracture xxvii, xxix, 282, 292–3
   growing irritation with 211
   as independent political movement 46
   leadership 44, 46, 66, 219, 220–1
   manifesto 33
   Marines (Portuguese navy) 16, 17–18, 19, **20**, 21
   merit of 221
   military sub-committee 31
   motivations 41–9, 51–3, 203–7
   'The Movement, the Armed Forces and the Nation' 268
   as national liberation movement 193
   outpouring of gratitude towards 13, 14
   overseas postings 28
   pact with main political parties 217–20, 221–2, 230–1, 258, 284
   PIDE activities against 32
   'Political Action Plan of the Armed Forces Movement' 249–50
   political consciousness 43, 45
   political inexperience 89
   political subcommittee 31
   popular support **50**, 51, 52–3
   primary original goals xxix
   professional discontent 27–8
   programme 4–5, 39–40, 52, 66, 93–4, 219, 230, 269, 274
   provisional government cabinet members 92–3
   readers of Indochina books 7, 8–9
   release of political prisoners 26
   retreat from public life xxix
   role 90, 103–4, 259, 283–4
   September crisis 111, 112, 118, 123, 124, 276–7
   sincerity 43
   Spínola's links to 33–4
   state council representation 90
   strength 28
   and trade unions 209–10
   triumph 226
   unity 51
   WB's fascination with xxix
armoured car escape 74–5
Arriaga, Kaúlza de 15, 30, 112, 119
artillery captain interview 27–32, 33–4, 46–7, 58
Assembly of the Armed Forces Movement 238
At the Barricades (Burchett) xxi–xxii
austerity 45
Australia xx–xxi, xxiv
Avante (journal) 22, 59
Azambuja 98–101
Azevedo, José Pinheiro de **39**, 237, 238, 292, 297

backwardness 135–6
balance of payments 161
banking sector 128–9, 131, 210, 292
Banks, Tony 297
Baptista, Francisco de Assunção 241–2
Beja 240–2
Belém presidential palace, September crisis 112–17, **116**
Belgium 143

Index

Belo, Alfredo Estêves 173, 174
Bento, Captain 173-4
Bermeo, Nancy xxvi
black propaganda 284
Bolshevik Revolution, 1917 45, 303
book censorship 7-8
borders, closure xvii
Bradbury, David xxii-xxiii
Braz, Manuel da Costa 92
bread strikes 88
Burchett, Wilfred
   activist point of view xxi
   arrival in Lisbon xvii-xviii, xix, 3-5
   bibliographies xx
   book censorship 7-8
   Cold War journalistic output xviii-xix, xx-xxv
   door opening effect of Indochina books 7-9
   enthusiasm for the captains xviii
   Hiroshima bombing report xx
   as independent radical xxi, xxii
   interviews xix, xxv-xxvi
   journalistic career xviii, 5
   journalistic mission xx
   journalistic moral compass xxii-xxiii
   motives xxii-xxiii
   point of view xix
   political preferences xix
   Portuguese Revolution coverage xviii-xix
   Portuguese Revolution contextualization xxv-xxx
   positioning xix
   purported Communist membership xviii-xix
   style xviii, xxx
   visit with Kissinger xxiii-xxiv
Burchett, Winston xx

Cachão 173-5, 178-9
Caetano, Marcelo 27, 30, 30n5, 31, 32, 33, 34, 36-7, **37**, 38, 49, 136-7, 147, 265, 267-9, 287
Caldas da Rainha 182
caldeirada 189-90
Cândida (Trás-os-Montes residents) 162-4
Cape Verde Islands 195, 201
Captains' Coup xvii
   5th Infantry Regiment mutiny 34
   12 September meeting 27-8
   aims 29
   arrest of the five officers 32, 34
   Caetano surrenders 36-7
   casualties 38
   catalyst 32
   contact missions 28
   convergence of currents 29-30
   'Coup d'état! Courage' 15-19
   crises following 26
   discussion groups 28
   Junta of National Salvation 37, 38-9
   Lisbon airport seized 36
   march on Lisbon 34-6, 268
   Military Academy meeting, 15 March 34-5
   motivations 5
   National Republican Guard called out 35
   new committee set up 31-2
   news of released 3-5
   PIDE centre surrounded 36
   planning and preparation 27-34
   potential repercussions 5
   Praça do Comércio **35**, 36
   programme 8, 39-40
   and publication of Spínola's book 32-3, 267
   rapidity 265
   success 269
   timing 30
   uncharacteristic aspect xviii
Cardoso, Agostinho Barbieri 214n3
Cardoso, António Lopes 98, 99, 243
Cardoso, Fernanda Lopes 99
Carlos, Adelino da Palma 90, 92, 95, 97, 103
Carlos, José 71, 77-8
Carlucci, Frank xxiv-xxv, 281
carnations 6, 11, 17, 222
Carneiro, Francisco Manuel Lumbrales de Sá xxvii, 90, 210, 255, 287
Carrero Blanco, Luis, assassination 30
Carvalhas, Carlos Alberto do Vale Gomes 132-4, 137, 138
Carvalho, Otelo Saraiva de xviii, xxv, 28, 31, **39**, 47, 93, 93-4, **94**, 112-17, 118, 120n8, 198-9, 204-5, 220, 230, 234, 251, 252-3, 255-6, 262, 266, 269, 275, 277, 293, 302-3, 304-5
Carvalho, Rogério de 24
Casa de Povo 100
Casa dos Pescadores 100n2, 185, 188, 189
Castro, Fidel 278
Catholic Church 95, 105-6, 237, 253, 288-9
Cavalry (tanks/armour) School, Santarém 215-16
Caxias prison 15-16, 71, 74
   liberation 16-19, 20-3, **20**, 26

CDE (Democratic Electoral Commission) 22n10, 42, 81–3, 102, 103, 188
censorship 7–8, 9–10, 39, 274, 286
CEUD (Comissão Eleitoral de Unidade Democrática) 81–2
Champalimaud (company) 85, 129, 220
Champalimaud, António 213
Champalimaud, José Carlos 213
Champalimaud, Manuel 215
Champalimaud, Miguel 213
chaos and anarchy predictions 210–12
Chaves 105
Chega xxix–xxx
child labour 149
Chile 51, 84, 95–6, 124, 261, 280
China xxiii, xxiv, 85
CIA xxiv–xxv, xxix, 84, 120, 261, 281, 284, 287
civil war tendency 211
clandestine work 69–70, 73, 75
class interests 235
client states 5
Cliff, Tony 302
Clotilde (Trás-os-Montes residents) 162–4
Coimbra University, student troubles 31
Cold War xviii–xix, xx–xxv
colonial question, the 42, 43
colonialism 42, 45
COMETNA 133
Comintern 70
common lands, enclosure 147, 171
company directors, sacked 127
Confederação Geral dos Trabalhadores Portugueses (General Confederation of Portuguese Workers) 85n6
conscription 265
constituent assembly, election promise 39–40, 57
Constituent Assembly elections xxvi–xxvii, 107, 211–12, 219, 221–4, 226, 230–1, 238, 284, 286, 306
 outcome 281–4
 polling day 223–4
 results 222, 224, 281
 unease about 280
 voter turnout 224
constitution 219
cooperative farming 166
COPCON (Continental Operational Command) 93–4, 112, 114, 115, 117, 118, 122, 124, 213, 230, 234–7, 239, 252–3, 261–2, 275–7, 286, 293–5, 305

Cordeiro, Carlos 23–4, 187–90
Corvacho, Eurico de Deus 251–2
Council of State 273
countercoup risk 51
counter-revolution xxvii, 239, 286, 288
'Coup d'état! Courage' 15
coup of 1926 129
coutadas de caça (hunting preserves) 147
Coutinho, António Alva Rosa 69, **94**, 123, 189, 193, 230, 251, 284
Cova da Lua 164–6
Covas, Maria Teresa 101
Cruz, Dr 105–7
CUF (Companhia União Fabril – United Manufacturing Company) 83–5, 129, 220, 250, 266, 281
Cunha, Joaquim Moreira da Silva 29
Cunhal, Álvaro 44n3, 71, 78–9, **79**, 92, 257, 259
 arrest 62
 criticism of the Communist Party 233–4
 imprisonment 79–80
 May Day, 1974 13, **14**
 November 25 action 258
 Peniche Fortress escape 77–8
 provisional government appointment 90
 A questã o agrá ria em Portugal 79
 return from exile 11
 Rumo à Vitória 159–60
 torture 62

Daily Telegraph (newspaper) 291
death penalty 61, 70, 70n4
decolonialisation 43
decolonisation 5, 41, 66, 90, 109, 191–207, 220, 265, 273–4, 276
 Armed Forces Movement (MFA) and 203–7
 methodology 200–3
 Spínola and 191, 193–4, 195, 196–7, 198, 199, 201
 transition to independence 200–3
 See also Angola; Guinea-Bissau; Mozambique
Delgado, Humberto da Silva 30n5, 165, 186, 205, 206, 207
Democratic and Social Centre Party (CDS) 212, 222
Democratic Movement 111–12, 118–19, 121, 124, 155, 161, 224
democratic purge 217
democratisation 10n10, 43, 44, 275
denunciations 24

Index

DGS (Directorate General of Security) 16n4, 30
Diário de Lisboa (newspaper) 138–40, 278
Diário de Notícias (newspaper) 279, 291
Dias, Maxfredo Ventura 188
Diogo Neto, Manuel 123
document of COPCON 234–7, 293–4
document of the Nine 231–9, 234, 237–8, 249, 293–4
dual power xxvii
Duarte, Joaquim Fernando 71

Eanes, António dos Santos Ramalho **260**, 262, 305
economic counter-offensive 127–34
economic disruption, monopolies 83–9
Economic Law 125, 210
economic policy 40, 90
economic power 220–1
economic problems 45–6
economic restructuring 43–4
economic sabotage 127, 156, 280–1
education 148–50, 175
Egídio, Nuno Viriato Tavares de Melo 253
El Noticiero Universal (newspaper) 210–11
elections, local councils 97–105
electricity supplies 166, 167
ELP (Exército de Libertação de Portugal, Portuguese Liberation Army) 239
emigration 153–4, 167, 168, 169–70
  agricultural labourers 153–4, 160–1, 165–6
  returnees 168–9, 266
Emissora Nacional 113, 118
'End Dictatorship' manifesto 60
England 142
Ericeira 223–4
escudo, value of 16n5
Espírito Santo group 129–30, 220
Estado da Índia 49n8
Estado Novo, the xix, xxix, 10n11
European Economic Community 226, 233, 235
European Free Trade Association 233, 235
Évora 27, 151, 155, 242–6
Exército de Libertação de Portugal 214n3
exports 128
Expresso (journal) 95–7

Fabião, Carlos Alberto Idães Soares 230, 251, 255, 256, 262

farming cooperatives 240–1, 245
Farrapilha, Joaquim 181–3
Fascism and fascist state infrastructure 38–9, 45, 56–7, 83–5, 97–101, 127–34
Federalist Movement/Progress Party, headquarters raided 122
Feminist Movement 74
Fernandes, António Dionísio 166–8
5th Infantry Regiment mutiny 34
Figueiredo, António de 281
Figueiredo, Lieutenant Colonel António 122
first open act of defiance 28
fishermen 181–3, 185–90
  anti-police demonstrations, 1935 182–3
  arrests 181–2
  conditions 185
  gains 189–90
  great lockout 188–9
  grievances 185, 186
  hand grenades 181–2
  labour disputes **184**, 186–7
  organisation 183, 185, 186–90
  role of the master 183
  wages 185–6, 186–7
Fishermen's Association 183
five officers, arrest of 32, 34
food problem 239
Ford, Gerald xxiv
foreign capital 132, 135, 140, 268–9
  average investment 142
  investors 142–3
  penetration 140–2
  restrictions on removed 266
  scale of investment 266
foreign currency 128, 161
foreign policy 233
France 161, 308
Francisco, Manuel Maria 181, 183, 185–7
Franco, Francisco 68, 69, 229
Fraser, Cecil 138
Freedom, Democracy and Pluralism campaign 231
Freire, Aníbal José Coentro de Pinho 229, 257
Freire, Paulo 104
FRELIMO (Mozambique Liberation Front) 47, 195–9
French Revolution 303

Galvão, Captain Henrique Carlos 205–7
General Assembly of the Armed Forces 251

General Data Electronics 138
general elections
    1969 22n10, 42, 81–2
    1973 22n10, 81, 82, 188
German fascism 265
Gervásio, António Joaquim 242–6
Giniger, Henry 101–2
Goa 47, 48–9
Gomes, General Francisco da Costa 33–4, **39**, 52, 93, 115, 117, 121, **192**, 193, 237–8, 268, 279
Gonçalves, Avelino Pacheco 88, 271, 272
Gonçalves, Vasco dos Santos xviii, xxv, 7, 44–6, 51–2, 88, 92, 219, 233, 240, 283–5
    CP support 284
    and decolonisation 193, 195
    dismissal calls 291
    May Day, 1975 285
    named prime minister 93
    replaced 237–8, 291–2
    savagery of the attacks against 247
    September crisis 110, 113, 121
government coalition 222
Grant, Bruce xxiii–xxiv
Great Britain 142
great strike movement, 1962 152–3
Greece 5
Group of Nine 231, 234, 235–7, 246, 249, 250, 259, 280, 293–5, 296, 302, 305, 306
Guardian (newspaper) 281
Guedes, Manuel 67, 77–8
    arrests 61, 63, 70–1
    clandestine work 69–70
    'End Dictatorship' manifesto 60
    escape 65
    imprisonment 64, 70–1
    interrogation and torture 61–3, 63–4
    military tribunal 64–5
    naval career 58–9
    naval trial 63
    organises naval Communist organisation 59–61
    Spanish exile 68–9
Guerreiro, Emídio 258
Guinea-Bissau 5, 8, 28, 43, 44–5, 47, 49, 109, 140, 204, 265, 274–5
    London negotiations 191, 193–5
    transition to independence 200

Hanoi, Vietnam People's Army advance into 13–14
Harriman, Averell xxii
Heenan, Tom xx, xxii

Herdade de Outeiro **156**, 240–1
hospitals 178–9
hunting preserves 147, 167, 168

illiteracy rate 105, 162
Imperial Chemical Industries 132
Inácio, Hermínio da Palma 18n6, 298
India 48–9
industrial nationalisation 246–7
industrial working class 224
industrialisation 127–9, 131
inflation 40, 267, 280
informers 24
Iniciativa Liberal xxix
Instituto de Socorros a Náufragos 186n4
International Communist League 223, 287, 299
International Labour Organisation 144
International Monetary Fund 307
international situation 45
investment strikes 280
Italy 265, 279
ITT Corporation 84, 122, 144

Japanese fascism 265
Jornal Novo (newspaper) 261–2
July crisis 95
Junta of National Salvation 89, 189, 217, 270–1, 272
    and Cabinet decisions 90
    first press conference **39**
    power handed over to 38–9
    programme 39–40
    purge 113, 123, 124
    September crisis 69n2, 113
    set up 37
    Spínola appointed head 38, 269–70

Kissinger, Henry xxiii–xxiv, 33, 281
Korean War xxi

labour costs 138, 143–4
labour movement, PIDE spies 87–8
labour relations 132–4
Labour Weekly (newspaper) 297
land occupations xxvi, 301
land reform 157, 240–6, 247
landed estates, wildcat takeovers 240–6
landowner's estate visit 176–8
Largo do Carmo, Lisbon 36–7, 36n11, 37
latifundia, the 128–9, 146
Le Monde (newspaper) 291
League of Small and Medium Landholders 245

Lebução 162–4
legislative assembly elections, 1976 218, 307
Leipzig trial, the 163
L'Humanité (newspaper) 272
Liberal Party 122
Lisbon 59, 161, 167, 176, **225**, 297–8, 305
   25 November action 255–62, **260**
   airport seized 36
   atmosphere 4, 6
   Avenida da Liberdade 6, 11, **12**, 13, 229, **254**
   building workers strike 255
   Constituent Assembly elections 223, 224
   Estádio da FNAT (Fundação Nacional para a Alegria no Trabalho) **14**
   influence of the Communist Party 102
   Largo do Carmo 36–7, 36n11, **37**
   March 11 countercoup attempt 213–14
   march on 34–6, 268
   May Day, 1974 11, **12**, 14, **14**
   military garrison 36
   Praça do Comércio **35**, 36, 255
   Praça dos Restauradores **12**
   São Bento palace 41
   September crisis bullring rally 110–12
   Tivoli Hotel 4, 6, 10, 58, 119–20, 257
   WB's arrival in xvii–xviii, xix, 3–5
Lisbon Aljube central prison 64
Lisnave shipyards 139, 267, 275–8
literacy campaign 104–5
living standards 40, 135–6, 178
local council elections 97–105
local councils, expectations of 105–7
logic of struggle 72–3
Loureiro, Carlos Maia **35**
Lourenço, António Dias 21–3, 55, 67
Lourenço, Vasco Correia 256, 257, **260**, 304–5
LUAR (League of Revolutionary Unity and Action) 259, 261, 298
Luta Popular (newspaper) 273

Macedo (Trás-os-Montes residents) 162–4
Machel, Samora 47, 195–6, 197
Madeira 38, 59
Magro, Aida 20–3, 73, 74
Magro, José Alves Tavares 20–1, 67
   armoured car escape 74–5, 152
   arrest 72, 73
   clandestine work 73, 75
   great strike movement, 1962 152
   imprisonment 72–4
   interrogation 73
   joins Communist Party 74
   Peniche Fortress escape tunnel attempt 75–6
   personality 71–2
   torture 72
   worst moment 73
Maia, Fernando José Salgueiro **35**, **37**, 216
Maia, Joaquim 155–6
malnutrition 146
March 11 countercoup attempt 280
   attack 212–15
   buildup 209–12
   cause of failure 217
   commission of enquiry 216–17
   final blow for Spínola 215–16, 279–80
   forces behind 216–17
   press reports 213
Marques, Jaime Silvério **39**, 93, 117, 123
Martins, José da Costa 92
Martins, Vasco dos Santos xix, 7–8, 9
Marxism–Leninism, role of xxvi
Mascata, Jerónimo Nunes 99–100
Matos, Luís Salgado de 143
May Day, 1935 63
May Day, 1974 9–10, 11, **12**, 14, **14**, 22–3, 58, 83, 271
May Day, 1975 285
MDP (Portuguese Democratic Movement) 22, 82, 101–2, 103–4, 218n6, 223
measures of state security formula 70
medical treatment 178–9
Melo, Carlos Galvão de **39**, 123
Mendonça, Camilo de 173, 175
MES (Left Socialist Movement) 298, 300, 301, 303
Metallurgical Workers' Union 133
Metro strike 88
MFP (Portuguese Federalist Movement) 96
mid-January crisis, 1975 209
Miguel, Mário Firmino 92, 116, 123
Mihaylov, Georgi Dimitrov 163
Military Academy 27
minimum wage 86, 137
Ministry of Corporations and Social Assistance 132–3
Ministry of Defence 28, 29, 34
Ministry of Finance 137, 138
Ministry of Information and Tourism 6

Ministry of Labour 85, 86, 87, 88, 132–4, 138, 240, 276
Ministry of the Interior 137
Miranda, Dinis Fernandes 243–4
Mirandela 161, 162, 171
Mocidade Portuguesa 83
Moncorvo hospital 178–9
Mondlane, Eduardo 47n6
monopolies 83–5, 239, 246, 265
  the Big Four 129–31
  capital 130
  countercoup 83–9
  dismantling 127–34
  economic basis crippled 220
  economic disruption 83–9
  exemption from taxation 131
  foreign capital 132
  foundation 127–30
  groups 130
  labour relations 132–4
  state protection 130–1
Montalegre 105–7
Montemor-o-Novo 145, 151, 153, 244–6
Morêncio, António dos Larnos 240
Mota, Joaquim Magalhães 101–2, 105
Moura, Francisco José da Cruz Pereira de 81, 90, 103
'The Movement, the Armed Forces and the Nation' 268
Movimento Democrático Português (MDP) 81n1
Mozambique 5, 8, 28, 30, 43, 47, 69n2, 109, 120n8, 140, 191, 265, 273–5
  decolonisation negotiations 193
  Lusaka agreement 195–9
  transition to independence 200
MPLA (Popular Movement for the Liberation of Angola) 132
MRPP (Movement for the Reconstruction of the Party of the Proletariat) 260, 299
multinational enterprises 86
  Applied Magnetics crisis 137–9
  attractions for 136, 142, 143–4
  closures 137–9
  foreign capital penetration 140–2
  role of 135–44
  state protection 137
  vested interests 144
  working conditions 136

National Assembly 38–9, 219
National Fishing Organisation 188
national liberation movements 5, 43, 49, 273, 293

National Republican Guard (GNR) 16, 17, 34, 35, 83, 113, 115, 118, 205, 212, 213
national unity 46
nationalisations 219–20, 246–7, 280, 292
Navy 58–61, 63, 238, 252, 270
Nazi Germany 69
Nehru, Jawaharlal 48
Nereu, Elvira, Constituent Assembly elections 223
Nereu, José Francisco 48–9, 162, 163, 167, 169, 174
Nereu, Maria Elvira Barreira Ferreira 15–19
Neto, Agostinho **192**, 192–3
Neves, Jaime Alberto Gonçalves das 252, 255, 257, 305
New York Times (newspaper) 101–2, 104–5
Nixon, Richard xxiii, xxiv, 198–9, 201, 279
Northern Trade Union Federation 85n7
north–south division 266–7
no-sleep torture 16, 61, 62, 63, 71, 72
November 25 crisis (1975) xxix, 229–30, 255–62, **260**, 304–7
  causes 230–8
  deaths 229
  document of COPCON 234–7
  document of the Nine 231–9
  flashpoint 230
  memory politicised xxix–xxx
  replacement of Gonçalves 237–8

O Marinheiro Vermelho [The Red Sailor] (journal) 60–1, 64
optimism 42–3
ORS (Sergeants Revolutionary Organisation) 252
Orwell, George xviii
Osório, José Sanches 92, 123
Ossikovska, Vessa 162n3

Paris 3n1, 161
Partido Popular Democrático (Popular Democratic Party) 90n11
Passão, Manuel João 145–57
  education 148–50
  great strike movement, 1962 152–3
  travel 150
Pathet Lao 77n5
PDC [Christian Democratic Party] 96–7
Pearson, Michael xxv
peasants xxv–xxvi, 105, 106, 173, 177. *See also* agricultural workers

Index

Peniche 23, 181–3, 185–90
Peniche Fishermen's Association 190
Peniche Fortress 22, 23–4, 64, 71, 75–8
People–MFA alliance 58, 66, 87, 217, 221–2, 236, 290–1, 294–5
People's National Action Party 30
people's power 232–3
People's Power Project 256
Pereira, Costa 85
petrochemical industry 132
Pham Van Dong 72, 79
PIDE (political police) 16, 28, 58, 69, 83, 186, 188, 265–6
  abolition 39
  activities against the Armed Forces Movement 32
  agents educational level 63
  all-pervasive presence 24
  files 24
  imprisonment 78, 79
  informers 24
  labour relations investigations 133
  name change 30
  shadow of 26
  and trade unions 134
  use of torture 61–4, 68
PIDE (political police) headquarters 7, 24, **25**
  storming of 18, 26, 36, 38
Pilger, John xviii–xix, xxi, xviin1
Pinochet, Augusto 85n5, 144, 307
Poder Popular (newspaper) 304
'Political Action Plan of the Armed Forces Movement' 249–50
political countercoup 89–94
political dynamisation campaigns 222
political execution 62
political experience, lack of 261
political power 236
political prisoners 9
  amnesty 39
  liberation 16–24, **20**, 26, 270
  Magro 20–1
  Nereu 15–19
  number 26
  quality 26
political stability 136
Ponta de Sagres 192–3
Popular Democratic Union (UDP) 224, 260, 299
Popular Democrats (PPD) 222, 224, 230–1, 258, 283
Popular Monarchists 223, 224
Porta 102
Porto 36, 59, 104, 161, 176, 252, 255
Porto Alto 212

Portugal and the Future (Spínola) 32–4, 267
Portuguese Action Movement (MAP) 119
Portuguese Communist Party (PCP) xix, xxvi, xxvii, 10n11, 11, **225**, 226, 238, 269, 270–3, 280
  1965 programme 53, 55–7
  alliance with Gonçalves 284–5
  armed forces cells 65–6
  clandestine work 69–70
  Constituent Assembly elections 224, 281–2, 284
  contempt for the masses 306–7
  continuous struggle 80
  counter-revolutionary violence against 286
  criticism 233–4
  disillusionment xxix
  expulsion from Comintern 70
  failure to unite the working class 287–91
  and FUR 300
  influence 67–8, 102
  interpretation of the coup 52–3
  isolation 70
  land reform policy 243
  leadership 70
  legislative assembly elections, 1976 307
  local council elections 101–2
  May Day, 1974 58
  May Day, 1975 285
  multiple warhead offensives 87
  November 25 crisis (1975) 258, 259–61, 306
  organisations within the armed forces 58–61
  reorganisation, 1941 69
  role of xxvi
  September crisis 110–11, 111–12, 279
  Soares's attacks on 211–12
  Spínola's attack on 118
  strategy 66
  strength 67
  support for Armed Forces Movement (MFA) 66, 259, 279, 283
  switch of strategy and tactics 87
  and takeover of *República* 286
  vitality 67
  wages resolution 84
  youth section 59, 60
Portuguese fascism, internal overthrow 265
Portuguese First Republic 60n8

Portuguese General Confederation of Labour (Confederação Geral do Trabalho) 60n9
Portuguese Legion 83, 133, 189
  abolition 39
Portuguese Liberation Army 214
Portuguese Military Academy 8
Portuguese Republican Party 60
Potemkin hospitals 178
Poulo Condor 72
power structures xxvi
president, the 218–19
presidential elections 92
priests 107, 163
private–state–workers' management 246
pro-fascist notables, authority of 107
Programme of the Armed Forces Movement 4–5
Progress Party 110
Progressive Party 276
provisional government 39–40, 57, 109, 247
  cabinet 92–3
  cabinet decisions 90
  economic policies 90
  international support xxvii
  programme 52
  second 273–80
  set up 90
  sworn in 270
psycho-political action 121
psycho-political support 58
public opinion, armed forces sensitivity to 59

Quinta do Atayde (Atayde Estate) 176–8

radical literature, flow in army 265–6
Rádio Clube Português 36, 113, 212–13
Rádio Renascença 36, 113, 253, 277
Rana, Álvaro 85, 86
Rebelo, General Horácio Viana 28–9
Reed, John 234
Reforma Agrária xxx
Rego, Paulo 286
Reis, Albino Manuel 244–6
remittances 161
República (newspaper), takeover of 286
restructuration process 84–5
Returned Soldiers Association 110
revolution 239
Revolutionary Council xxix, 217–20, 226, 230, 231–9, 237, 251–2, 255–6, 257, 258, 262, 281

Revolutionary legitimacy xxvii
Revolutionary Navy Organisation 63
Revolutionary Party of the Proletariat (Revolutionary Brigades) 259, 298, 300, 301–2, 304
revolutionary process, citizen engagement xxvi
Revolutionary United Front (FUR) 300
Rhodesia 5, 43, 199
Ribeira tin mines 172
Ribeiro, Silvano 183, 185, 186
Rio de Onor 166–8
Roberto, Holden 202n14
Rocha, Francisco Canais 85–6, 88
Romão, General António Amaro 35
Rosa, Eugénio Óscar Garcia da 139–40, 144
ruling class, divisions within 267
Rumo à Vitória (Cunhal) 159–60
rural areas
  dismantling the fascist infrastructure 97–101
  north–south division 266–7
rural neglect 171–3
  remedying 173–6
  See also Alentejo, the; Trás-os-Montes
rural proletariat 243
Russian Revolution 45, 302

Salazar, António **25**, 31, 48, 49, 60, 69, 70n4, 127–8, 131, 136, 140, 206
Salisbury, Harrison xxi–xxii
Santa Maria (ocean liner) seizure 206, 207
Santarém, Cavalry (tanks/armour) School 215–16
Santos, António de Almeida **192**, 197
São Bento palace, Lisbon 41
sardine fishermen 181–3, 185–90
  anti-police demonstrations, 1935 182–3
  arrests 181–2
  boat ownership 185
  conditions 185
  fishing methods 183
  gains 189–90
  great lockout 188–9
  grievances 185, 186
  hand grenades 181–2
  labour disputes **184**, 186–7
  organisation 183, 185, 186–90
  role of the master 183
  wages 185–6, 186–7
scholarship xxv–xxvi
Seara Nova (journal) 9

Seara Nova publishing house xix, 6–10
Sebastião (Trás-os-Montes resident) 162–4
September 12 meeting 27–8
September crisis 69n2, 109–25, 276–8, 279
  arrests 119, 122
  Belém presidential palace 112–17, **116**
  CIA involvement 120
  consequences of 122–5
  Costa Gomes appointed interim president 121
  Federalist Movement/Progress Party headquarters raid 122
  flash point averted 117
  Lisbon bullring rally 110–12
  Otelo de Carvalho's account 112–17
  raid on MAP 119
  seriousness of 122–3
  Spínola's 10 September speech 109–10, 209, 277
  Spínola's resignation speech 120–1, 216, 278
  Tivoli Hotel 119–20
Signetics Corporation 138
silent majority, the 97, 109, 110, 111, 118, 120, 209, 277
Silva, General Alberto de Andrade e 29, 30, 32
Silva, General Manuel António Vassalo e 48–9
Silva, José Alberto Morais e 238, 251, 253, 258
Sixth Provisional Government 238, 247, 250–1, 253, 256, 292, 296, 301
Skorzeny, Otto 214
small and medium enterprises 131
smallholdings 159–60
Soares, Duarte Nuno Pinto, chaos and anarchy predictions 210–12
Soares, Mário Alberto Nobre Lopes xxvii, 10, 11, 67, **91**, 107, 209–10, 218n6, 255, 257, 274, 283–4, 301, 305, 306, 307
  attacks on the Communists 211–12
  and decolonisation 194, 195–7
  general election, 1969 81–2
  May Day, 1974 13, **14**
  move to the right 287
  provisional government appointment 90
  rapprochement with Spínola 211
Soares, Pedro 52–3, 77–8, 88–9
social democracy xxvii
  rejection of 233
Social Democratic Party (PPD-PSD) xxvi–xxvii, xxvii, 238
social justice 44
socialism, commitment to 220
Socialist International 82
Socialist Party (PS) xxvi–xxvii, xxvii, 222, 224, 226, 230–1, 237, 238, 243, 246–7, 257, 270–1, 278–9, 282–3, 285, 286–8, 290–1, 292, 296–7, 307
Socialist Workers' Party 302
social-movement theory xxvi
Soldados Unidos Vencerão (SUV) 252, 295–6, 301
  Appeal to the Workers and Soldiers of Europe 309–10
  Manifesto 308–9
soldiers' vigilance committees 253
Souphanouvong, Prince 77n5
South Africa 5, 43, 199
Spain 5, 44, 65, 68–9, 166, 214
Spanish border 166
Spanish Civil War 229
Spínola, General António Sebastião Ribeiro de 11, 26, 32–4, 37, **37**, **39**, 97, 220, 267–8, 270
  10 September speech 109–10, 209, 277
  appointed head of Junta of National Salvation 38, 269
  attack on the Communist Party 118
  confirmation as provisional president 38
  and decolonisation 191, 193–4, 195, 196–7, 198, 199, 201
  exile 213, 280
  links to Armed Forces Movement (MFA) 33–4
  March 11 countercoup attempt 213–14, 214–16, 280
  rapprochement with Soares 211
  replacement by Gonçalves 51–2
  reputation 273
  resignation 123
  resignation speech 120–1, 201, 216, 278
  September crisis 109, 110, 111, 112, 113–15, 117, 118–19, 276–8
  speech, 7 June 90–1
state apparatus, threat to cohesion 292
state capitalism, changeover to 246–7
State Council 38–9, 90, 92, 97
State of Emergency, November 1975 305
statue treatment (torture) 61
Steele, Jonathan 281
strikes 84, 86–7, 152–3, 255, 267, 271–2, 286–7

strikes-occupation-workers' control pattern 292

Tancos air base 213, 215, 257, 258
TAP, nationalisation 219–20
Tengarrinha, José Manuel Marques do Carmo Mendes **20,** 103–4
Tenreiro, António Maria 176–9, 185, 187, 189
Terrill, Ross xxiii
three Ds, the (decolonisation, democratisation and development) 8n8
Timex 136, 137
tin mines 172–3
Tivoli Hotel, Lisbon 4, 6, 10, 58, 119–20, 257
tobacco interests 128–9
Tomás, Américo 30, 36, 38
torture 61–4, 68, 71, 72
Totta and Azores Bank 83
trade unions xxvii, 134, 267
 demonstration, 1 June 1974 88
 leadership 209–10
 May Day, 1974 22–3
 purges 13, 84
 September crisis 111
Trás-os-Montes 102, 103, 105–7, 159–70, 175–6, 239
 conditions 162–70
 Cova da Lua 164–6
 economic-social situation 159–61
 electricity supplies 166, 167
 emigration 160–2, 165–6, 167, 168–9, 169–70
 hospitality 162–4, 169, 176
 illiteracy rate 162
 landowner's estate visit 176–8
 Lebução 162–4
 Quinta do Atayde (Atayde Estate) 176–8
 Rio de Onor 166–8
 smallholdings 159–60
 stature 174
Trotsky, Leon 289–90, 299

ultra-racists 47

unemployment 146, 239, 241–2, 242–3, 267, 279, 280
União Nacional (National Union) 38n13, 42, 81, 83
Unilever Limited 15
United Nations 207
United States of America
 investments in Portugal 142–3
 involvement in Portugal 281
 Nixon administration xxiii, 279
 Portuguese Revolution role xxiv–xxv
 Watergate scandal xxiv, 279
 and WB xx, xxiii–xxv
uprising, 1931 59
urban working class 266
US Navy 206

Vasco da Gama fort, Goa 49
Vasco da Gama (ship) 59, 60
Velasco, Fernando Bélico 37
Veloso, António Elísio Capelo Pires 251
Verão Quente ('Hot Summer') xxviii
Vicente, João 161–2, 171–2
Vietnam and the Vietnam War xxii, xxiii, 8–9, 13–14, 29, 30, 32–3, 72, 98
Vila Real 105
Vitoriano, José 272
Voice of America 118
Vorster, John 199
voting strength 107

wages 84, 85–6, 137, 143–4, 155, 175, 185–6, 240, 244
West Germany 142, 143, 144
Why the Vietcong Wins / Vietnam Will Win! (Burchett) 8–9
wildcat takeovers 240–6
Wilfred Burchett: Public Enemy Number One (film) xxii–xxiii
Workers' Commission for the Lisbon Industrial Belt 253
Workers' Day 10, 11, **12**, 14, **14**
world economic depression 135
World War II 69, 127–8

Zaire 202n14